All-Age Lectionary Services
Year B

All-Age Lectionary Services

Year B

Resources for all-age worship

These service outlines were originally published by Scripture Union as *Light for the Lectionary 2008/2009*. They have been fully revised with new material added or available online.

Copyright © Scripture Union 2011

ISBN 978 1 84427 545 8

Scripture Union England and Wales

207–209 Queensway, Bletchley, Milton Keynes, MK2 2EB, England

Email: info@scriptureunion.org.uk

Website: www.scriptureunion.org.uk

Scripture Union Australia

Locked Bag 2, Central Coast Business Centre, NSW 2252

Website: www.scriptureunion.org.au

Scripture Union USA

PO Box 987, Valley Forge, PA 19482

Website: www.scriptureunion.org

British Library Cataloguing-in-Publication Data: a catalogue record of this book is available from the British Library

Printed and bound in China by Imago Publishing Limited

Cover design: Grax Design

Internal design: Helen Jones

Typesetting: Richard Jefferson, Author and Publisher Services

Scripture Union is an international Christian charity working with churches in more than 130 countries, providing resources to bring the good news about Jesus Christ to children, young people and families and to encourage them to develop spiritually through the Bible and prayer.

As well as our network of volunteers, staff and associates who run holidays, church-based events and school Christian groups, we produce a wide range of publications and support those who use our resources through training programmes.

Foreword from the
Bishop of Southwell and Nottingham

Worshipping together as the whole people of God has to be a wonderful thing. The vision we are given of heaven in Revelation includes this – 'there was a great multitude that no-one could count, from every nation, tribe, people and language, standing before the throne and in front of the Lamb …' (Revelation 7:9). No homogeneous group in terms of culture, language, or age in this great future vision. Our worship today is intended to be both a foretaste of heaven, and being caught up in the worship of heaven now.

Worshipping as all ages together reflects the reality of the future, and the present; the whole people of God proclaiming God's praise.

Far too many people 'give up' on all-age worship because it is demanding. We do have to think about all the ages that will be present; all the levels of knowledge, skill, experience and so on that will be engaging in this worship together. This demands the highest level of expertise, not the lowest common denominator. It raises the level of our worship rather than making it childish. It enables us all to be child-like and mature in Christ.

Those who have produced this material are serving the church well. Use it to the full; use it creatively and enter into the joy of the future; have a foretaste, and a current experience, of the worship of heaven.

+ Paul Butler

Contents

Leading all-age worship

Leading all-age worship that is focused around the Lectionary is a privilege, as leaders introduce God to people of all ages, of various abilities, learning styles, spiritual maturity and backgrounds.

In Scripture Union, we believe that the ministry of all-age services is vitally important for the following reasons:

- Children and young people benefit because they experience what it means to be part of God's new community, as everyone contributes, learns and worships together. (Children build relationships with a much wider range of people than would normally be possible in contemporary society. It is easier for them to have a go, make a mistake and try again. Their gifts and skills also help adults grow in their faith. Their opinion and wisdom matter, since God cares for us all as unique individuals. We can all know him and experience his love.)

- Adults benefit as they learn from children and young people, often with a greater variety of approaches than are usually on offer. (All-age services are not an opportunity for Sunday group leaders or people with no responsibility for children to have a Sunday off. Relationships can be developed in additional ways and on different levels.)

- Visitors or people on the fringe often feel more comfortable because fewer assumptions are made of them. (It should be OK to just sit and watch. Often churches offer an all-age service at festival times, welcoming to all, free from jargon and appropriate.)

- People with a variety of learning styles and abilities benefit because the interactivity and creativity in evidence in all-age worship require a variety of approaches and responses.

- The team that leads all-age services benefits because the components to a service call for a variety of gifts, encouraging people to take risks, grow in maturity and enjoy being part of a team.

- The church is making a statement about the nature of 'church' – everyone matters, all can know and belong to God, all can be included and all can contribute, whatever their age, ability or spiritual maturity. (All-age services, however messy they may be, are one of the most exciting opportunities for church leaders to nurture faith, from any starting point.)

All-age services could be one of three different styles of a meal. All have value but which do you find the most satisfying? Which of these styles best suits your church?

Type of meal	What motivates this choice?	How it is consumed	What's good	What's not so good	How to describe
Soup only	the cook – wants a quick, easy meal	easily digestible	satisfying on a cold day	everyone eats the same whatever their needs or preferences	everything together and comfortable
Buffet meal	the diner – eats whatever takes their fancy	at least one dish for everyone	tasty with variety	not necessarily well-balanced	join in when you want to
Three-course meal	the cook – promotes healthy eating, adventurous new dishes	eat in order: starter main course dessert	variety, guarantees nurture	hard work for the cook	balanced and nourishing long-term

- How do you make decisions about what happens in your all-age services?
    - ☐ Whatever is easiest
    - ☐ What you have always done
    - ☐ What church members want
    - ☐ What visiting parents and carers want
    - ☐ What the leadership perceives people need spiritually
    - ☐ Who is available at any one time
    - ☐ Other

- What are the good things about your all-age services?
    - ☐ They make the majority of people happy
    - ☐ Children and young people enjoy them
    - ☐ Provide choice
    - ☐ A Sunday off for Sunday group leaders
    - ☐ Encourage spiritual growth
    - ☐ Reach out to those on the fringe
    - ☐ Enable people to grow their gifts
    - ☐ Other

The service outlines in this book assume that the leaders of all-age services are committed to the spiritual growth of everyone present and that ideally every activity should be relevant to some degree for everyone. We have to be honest – this is not always possible, but that at least is the aim.

The congregation may include people with disabilities or poor eyesight, those who find reading a challenge, those with strong views on music, the very young or the outsider. In trying to include one group of people, you may connect with several others. For example, using a variety of approaches to learning, those with reading difficulties may feel catered for. As very young children worship with adults who are welcoming, trustworthy and joyful, they will be experiencing something of who God is. The Scripture Union website provides an especially wide range of options for younger children. The *Big Bible Storybook* and the *Tiddlywinks* material, both from SU, are also invaluable resources for this age group.

May God continue to bless you in this vital ministry!

'Tricia Williams
All-age editor

What's in All-Age Lectionary Services Year B?

ACTIVITIES

Bible foundations: a guide to the issues involved in at least two of the set passages for the day plus background information.

Bible reading: suggestions for preparing and presenting the reading of the Bible to the congregation.

Bible retelling: ideas for drama, storytelling and other suggestions for alternative ways of presenting the Bible passage.

Bible talk: engaging ways to share the Bible and discover the message for today in a mixed-age congregation.

Beginning the service and **Ending the service:** a recognition of how important these are in holding a service together.

Prayer activity: creative ideas for praying in response to the message of the Bible.

Prayers of intercession: suggestions for talking with God on behalf of our world in need.

Prayer of confession: a guide not only to recognising our need of God's forgiveness, but also asking for forgiveness and cleansing.

Helpful extras: a number of additional features including **Music and song ideas, Game, Statement of faith** and download suggestions.

Notes and comments: further advice or background information on adapting the material for your purposes.

WRITERS

Janet Berkovic, Sarah Bingham, Vanessa Cato, Matt Campbell, Andrew Chuter, Andrew Clark, Andrew Evans, Lizzie Evans, Marjory Francis, Andy Gray, Darren Hill, Gill Hollis, Lisa Holmes, Piers Lane, Mike Law, Eric Leese, Joel Lewis, Jane Maycock, Tim Norwood, Rona Orme, Amy Robinson, Sera Rumble, Hil Sewell, Paul Wallis, Ali Walton, Joanna Wilks, John Wilks, Pam Williams, 'Tricia Williams, Ro Willoughby, Robert Willoughby, Ruth Wills

WEBSITE

Free downloadable additional resources are available from www.scriptureunion.org. uk/light. Other resources are also available on www.lightlive.org.

There is the opportunity to link the services throughout the Advent season with some of the following suggestions.

1. Begin each service with a **trumpet call** as a symbol of individual awakening and also the royal arrival of a king. See note below.
2. Choose a **common theme hymn** such as 'Longing for light' by Bernadette Farrell. On occasions use this as a hymn, or it can be used to frame intercessions as on Third Sunday of Advent. It is in the Spring Harvest Songbook 2004/5 and *Hymns Old and New*. The verses begin as follows: Longing for light, Longing for peace, Longing for food, Longing for shelter. An alternative would be Brian Doerksen's song based on Psalm 13, 'How long, O Lord?'.
3. Create a **colour** theme for each service. The colour embodies the message. The congregation is encouraged to wear at least one article that carries the theme colour each Sunday.

Advent Sunday	Gold/Yellow
	(waiting for a king)
Advent Two	Green (hope)
Advent Three	Red (for a herald) or
	White (for purity)
Advent Four	Blue (for Mary)
Christmas Day	Party colours

The congregation needs to be alerted to this colour scheme in advance. It makes Advent special and celebratory and it involves everyone. (When this idea was tried in 2007, it was extremely successful and meaningful. Many unexpected people entered into the fun of it.)
4. If an **Advent wreath** is used, the candles for each Sunday could reflect these same colours. Lighting the candles is a recognised ritual in many churches during Advent.

Note

In some churches, instead of a trumpet, a shofar horn could be blown, if available. This horn was used in biblical times to proclaim the arrival of a king. Later Judaism associated it with the message 'Awake you sleepers and consider your deeds'.

ADVENT SUNDAY

READINGS: **1 Corinthians 1:3–9; Mark 13:24–37**
Isaiah 64:1–9; Psalm 80:1–7,17–19

Bible foundations

Aim: to celebrate God's blessings as we wait for Jesus to return

As we move into the season of Advent, the theme which has been running through the readings towards the end of Year A comes into renewed focus. Paul's letter to the Christians in Corinth shows again just how central the expectation of Jesus' return was in his thinking. In Mark 13, Mark records much the same material as Matthew 24 presenting the same problems for interpreters, but the idea of watching and waiting remains at the centre. During Advent we see the age-long hopes of Israel coming to expression in Jesus. Isaiah 64 and Psalm 80 contain pleas that God will come to act on behalf of his people, a prayer and a hope which occurs increasingly frequently as the Old Testament era draws to a close. Injustice, oppression and a general sense of unease led to the conviction that, unless God were to come in a new way, there was no hope. Throughout, there was a confident trust in the faithful God who keeps his promises given to the patriarchs and the prophets.

We celebrate the fulfilment of those promises in Jesus' coming but we also identify with the longings for justice expressed in Psalm 80 and Isaiah 64. There is still a lot wrong with the world. We want Jesus to come back to put everything right but just as many were surprised when he came for the first time, so many will be surprised when he comes again. The difference is that many did not recognise him then; next time everyone will, but not everyone will be ready. We can enjoy friendship with God, but there is much more to look forward to.

Beginning the service

Advent is a time when we are called to be alert and awake. It is also a time when we look for the return of Christ our King. This service could begin with a trumpet fanfare on a trumpet/cornet or on an organ.

Explain that the meaning of Advent is 'coming'. We celebrate the first coming of Jesus and we look forward to his second coming and return. If you have used the Advent ideas on page 14 comment on the gold/yellow in evidence in the clothing of the congregation. Thank them for joining in. They can be invited to process round the worship space. Ask someone why they are wearing gold and recap on the Advent expectation of Christ's return.

Bible reading

The reading from 1 Corinthians 1:3–9 is read with the emphasis on the 'you'. Eye contact with the congregation and hand gestures (beckoning out to the congregation) will make people feel that this reading affects them personally. Preface the reading with an introduction: 'Paul writes to the Christians at Corinth and to us. He reminds us of the range of benefits we enjoy in Christ.'

The reading from Mark 13:24–37 is prefaced with the introduction: 'Jesus tells his disciples that we do not know when he will return but that we should be on standby and at action stations.'

Bible talk

With: Eight boxes each wrapped as a present and labelled with a word containing a

key letter highlighted in some way – perhaps in a different colour – as follows: 1.**P**eace, 2.g**R**ace, 3.everywh**E**re, 4.**S**peaking, 5.knowl**E**dge, 6.cha**N**ge(d lives), 7.gif**T**s, 8.fellow**S**hip. Alternatively these words can be displayed on a board, OHP or PowerPoint. The highlighted letters spell 'presents'.

When people have to spend time apart they sometimes leave a message or present for the person they love. The film *PS, I Love You* illustrates this rather dramatically (a young widow discovers that her late husband has left her ten messages intended to help ease her pain and start a new life.) Jesus left us many presents. The early Christians had memories to help them look back to when Jesus walked in Galilee and in Jerusalem. Many had seen his miracles and heard his teachings. They could also look forward to his promised return. But while they waited, some felt a sense of anticlimax. They were living between two great events (his first coming and his return/second coming). They must have sometimes felt deflated and directionless.

But Jesus had left them various presents that were to fire up the church. In this time in between his first and second coming they had many causes for celebration.

Present 1 – Peace

Ask a person to bring you Present 1. Remind people of the reading from 1 Corinthians, written to a group of Christians whom Paul cared for which instructed them how they were to live as followers of Jesus. Ask people to follow in their own Bibles what you say from Paul's letter.

Paul reminds the Corinthians they now have **peace** (v 3). Ask for definitions of 'peace' – stillness and absence of conflict. God is justly angry at our failings but Jesus took on his shoulders the anger we deserve. He dealt with the conflict between God and humanity on the cross. So we can have peace with God and with one another.

Present 2 – Grace

Ask another person to bring Present 2. Paul frequently reminds the Christians of God's **grace** (vs 3,4). Through Jesus, God has poured on us his favour and love. It is grace because we have done nothing to deserve it. Grace means receiving something you haven't deserved.

Present 3 – Everywhere

For 33 years Jesus did not travel far. After his resurrection, ascension and the coming of the Holy Spirit, he was available to Christians **everywhere** – in Galilee, in Corinth and throughout the world. This is another bonus.

Present 4 – Speaking

To people living in what had been the Greek empire, the powers of persuasive **speaking** and knowing the truth were all important. They loved to talk and debate. Paul reminds them that God's power enables us to speak his truth, his message (v 5).

Present 5 – Knowledge

Because of Jesus we have **knowledge** (v 5). We grasp the truth about God, about life, about how to live.

Present 6 – Changed

One great cause of joy in church life is the evidence of **changed** lives (v 6).

The Corinthian Christians once lived for themselves and did not believe Paul's message. Then they came to realise that what he said about Jesus was true. Their lives were turned around and transformed. Paul could bear testimony or witness to that!

Present 7 – Gifts

After Jesus' death and resurrection he sent his Holy Spirit as a gift to the church and the Spirit gave **gifts** to enable people to preach, encourage, prophesy and speak in tongues (v 7).

Present 8 – Fellowship

People who followed Jesus and belonged to him had been drawn into the **fellowship** of God the Father, God the Son and God the Holy Spirit (although he is not mentioned in v 9). This then draws people to belong to one another, in fellowship together.

We all live in this in-between time, a time between Jesus' first coming and his second. Yet he has left us with great gifts to celebrate. We can experience his peace, his grace and his presence everywhere, we are given the ability to speak for Jesus and have knowledge of the truth, we can see changed lives around us, and we are given special gifts and fellowship in the church. Let some children arrange the boxes in a tower so that the highlighted letters in top to bottom order spell the word 'presents'. For these reasons, Paul begins his message to the Corinthians with 'thanks' (v 4). Whatever else he has to tell them later in his epistle, he begins by highlighting eight reasons for rejoicing.

The present boxes could be left under the Christmas tree once it has been put up, to act as a reminder.

Prayer activity

This passage lends itself to two styles of prayer.

Option 1:

Ask a group of people to prepare prayers on these topics:

Lord, you have given us **peace**. Help us to extend that peace in our lives, in our neighbourhood and in the world. We remember especially...
Lord, you have shown your **grace** to us. Help us to show love and favour to others. We pray for...
Lord, you are **everywhere**. Help those who feel cut off from your presence. Be with those in...
Lord, you have given us language and the ability to **speak**. We think of those with the special responsibility of using words... We pray for ourselves as we tell others the good news.
Lord, you have given us **knowledge** and you are truth. We remember those who handle truth in their daily life...
Lord, you **change** lives and give us new life. Strengthen those who turn to you. We pray that our changed life can be obvious to others. Help us to obey you in each area of life, especially...
Lord, you have given your people spiritual **gifts**. Especially we pray for the use of...
Lord, you have placed us in the **fellowship** of the church. Help us as a church to show togetherness by... Help us to make this church an outpost of heaven.
We ask this in Jesus' name. Amen.

Option 2:

Make sure that the presents are on clear view. Put people into small groups to suggest how they might thank God for these gifts. Each group will need a leader to lead a discussion. Groups can either express spontaneous thanks, such as thanks that God is with us everywhere, that we have a sense of belonging within the church fellowship, for the gifts that the Spirit has given us and thanks for specific people. Younger children can easily identify with this.

Or the leader can pray as follows:

Lord, we thank you for Jesus. We thank you for the **peace** he gives us, which so many people long for. Jesus has reconciled us with God.
Lord, we thank you for Jesus' life and teaching. Above all we praise you for his message of **grace**. Despite our own failings you shower your love and kindness on us.
Lord, we thank you that you are **everywhere**. Wherever we are, under the sea, in the air, on the land or in space; whichever continent we walk on, we have access to you.
Lord, we thank you that you give us the ability and responsibility to **speak** for you. Thank you for the privilege of telling others about you.
Lord, we thank you that in Jesus you have shown us true **knowledge**. We rejoice that we now know that you are the truth.
Lord, thank you that you bring us to our senses. We see that life without you is meaningless. Thank you for putting us back on track and transforming and **changing** our lives so we are more like Christ.

Lord, thank you that you have equipped your church with gifts. We thank you for those among us who preach, and teach; those who prophetically relate God's Word to today, those who encourage us.

Lord, thank you for our church's **fellowship**. Thank you for everyone who gives and shares and shows their love in practical ways. For so many good things, Lord, make us grateful and appreciative.

Amen.

Prayer of confession

A Prayer of confession, based on the set reading from Psalm 80, is available as a download (YearB.Advent1_1).

Ending the service

Jesus says, 'Be on guard! Be alert!... you do not know when the owner of the house will come back'. Mark 13:33,35. Use this as a *Learn and remember* verse to draw the service to a close.

Helpful extras

Music and song ideas

The theme hymn 'Longing for light'; 'Make way, make way'; 'Lo he comes with clouds descending'; To celebrate **peace** – 'Peace is flowing'; **grace** – 'Only by grace'; 'Amazing grace'; **everywhere** – 'All over the world'; **speaking** – 'Tell out my soul'; **knowledge** – 'Thou art the way'; 'All my days'; **changed life** – 'There is a hope so sure'; 'Light of the world'; **gifts** – 'O God beyond all praising'; **fellowship** – 'Brother, sister, let me serve you'.

Personal testimony

A person could speak or be interviewed, focusing on one of the eight presents highlighted in the **Bible talk**. In particular 'transformed life' or 'a sharing church fellowship' would lend themselves to celebration and encouragement.

Notes and comments

The **Bible talk** is based on the TNIV. Check that the Bible version you regularly use works with this talk.

The congregation needs to be reminded of the theme colour for next week, which is green.

Online resources

All suggested downloads are available at www.scriptureunion.org.uk/light. Visit www.lightlive.org for additional activities for children, young people and adults.

SECOND SUNDAY OF ADVENT

READINGS: **Isaiah 40:1–11; Mark 1:1–8**
Psalm 85:1,2,8–13; 2 Peter 3:8–15a

Bible foundations

Aim: to explore how the Lord God promises hope

The period from 587–538 BC was a dark one in Jewish history with the larger part of the nation in exile in Babylon. In a world where TV screens so often show displaced people we have some idea of what 'being in exile' meant. In such misery and isolation the words we read in Isaiah 40 brought hope with the promise of the one who will come to lead the people home. God's people did return home in 538 BC, but this could not be seen as the complete fulfilment of the promise. The people were never really free, they never managed to worship God as he intended and in many ways were still in 'exile'. So when John arrived, with a message which echoed Isaiah's, there was a sense of hope in the air. Some at least saw him as the messenger who would prepare the way for the coming of the deliverer. But, as the psalmist notes in Psalm 85:13, the preparation for the coming of the Saviour involves righteousness. Hence John's call for repentance, so that the people might be ready.

As we look forward to Christmas, as we sing 'O come, O come, Immanuel', remembering that Jesus has set us free, and as we prepare to discover his presence with us in new ways, we too need to clear the rubbish out of the way. Our 'way' may be blocked with all manner of things that need to go if we are to meet with Jesus. Each of us, whatever our age or experience, can understand to some extent that the things we do can please Jesus and open the way for him. Alternatively, we can distress him and close the way. The challenge is to identify and turn from the things that get in the way.

Beginning the service

If you have chosen to begin each Advent service with a trumpet call (see page 14) then once again the organ with a trumpet stop or a trumpet or cornet player can sound a fanfare to herald in the Advent message.

Introduce the subject of hope by commenting on the themed colour of green that many in the congregation are wearing.

Bible reading

The reading from Isaiah 40:1–11 is crying out to be proclaimed. If possible, find someone with a loud voice (which could be enhanced by PA) to learn these 11 verses and proclaim them, with suitable arm gestures, as they walk around the church building.

The Gospel reading using the TNIV or CEV lends itself to a dramatic delivery. The narrator reads most of the passage but there is a voice for Isaiah in verses 2b,3 and a voice for John in verses 7b,8. If a trumpet is being used at the start of the service (see page 14) then a trumpet can also sound after verse 2a to suggest the idea of the prophet/messenger as a royal herald.

Bible talk

You could present the **Bible talk** in two parts, following each **Bible reading**.

Part 1
With: 2 x 50 pence pieces; a ball and chain; certificate of pardon; clearway/motorway road sign; a globe – pictures would serve as an alternative – images available as a download (YearB.Advent2_1)

God gives more than he promises
Hide a couple of 50 pence pieces around the worship area. Invite children to search for a 50 pence piece. In fact you have hidden £1 (or 2 x 50p together). Your claim was true. There was 50p. But there was more. God's promises are like this. He is gracious and kind. He keeps his promise but gives us far more.

In the Old Testament reading from Isaiah 40 the Jews had been in exile in Babylon. Explain the background to this. God speaks words of comfort through his prophet.

God promises to remove the things that drag us down
Arrange for someone to bring to you a ball and chain or a picture of one. Isaiah said that his people's hard service/slavery has been completed. There is the hope of freedom. In the United States a ball and chain was used to restrict slaves. One ball and chain has been found with a very short chain so the slave could never pick up the heavy ball. He always had to drag it behind him. God promises to remove the things that drag us down. Invite the children to walk round the worship space pretending to drag a heavy ball that is chained to their foot that they cannot pick up.

God promises to forgive
Next someone brings to you a certificate of pardon or a picture of one. Isaiah said, 'her sin has been paid for'. There is hope of forgiveness. It is hard for some people to accept pardon from anyone, least of all God. But God is a forgiving God. How does that make us feel? Everyone is invited to applaud our forgiving God.

God promises a new direction

Ask next for the copy of a clearway or motorway sign. Isaiah said that God promises a time when a highway through the desert will be constructed and be made straight to welcome a king, God the King, as he leads his people home. There is the hope of return and the hope of that journey taking place on a road without potholes and roadworks and dangerous bends. Ask people to put a coat or shoe or book in the aisle, then invite the children to clear the obstacles and make it straight again.

God promises that all the world will recognise him

Arrange for someone to bring you a globe. Isaiah said that when God leads his people back from Babylon to Jerusalem all people will see the event. There is the hope of worldwide recognition for God. Invite everyone to say, 'The Lord reigns. Let the earth be glad' twice.

These promises were kept. The hopes were realised and fulfilled. The Jews were released from Babylon, no longer slaves but free. They were no longer suffering for their past sins but were pardoned. They were no longer downcast in exile but now God led them home to Jerusalem through the desert. They were no longer hidden in Babylon but the nations were aware of what God had done for his people.

We looked for 50p and found much more. During Isaiah's time God's promises and the people's hopes were fulfilled. Later they were to be fulfilled in even greater ways.

Part 2

With: the props from Part I

John the Baptist picks up these promises proclaimed by Isaiah. Remind everyone who John the Baptist was.

Pick up the ball and chain of slavery. John the Baptist was speaking to a people who were virtually slaves to the power of Rome. They were living under a Roman army of occupation which could demand their service. John hints at the fact that, through Jesus, God will give us a greater freedom – not just from Rome but from sin (v 4).

Remind people of the certificate of pardon. John preached 'forgiveness of sins'. It was a pardon – not just a pardon for one occasion but a pardon constantly available through repentance (v 4) and trust in Jesus.

Show the motorway sign again. Isaiah spoke of a way being laid down in the wilderness. John is in the wilderness, the area on the east bank of the Jordan. He is not organising people into work gangs to make a literal path or road but his 'earthmoving' is teaching them a path of behaviour, a lifestyle which is God's way of life.

Look together at the globe. John's ministry was to the Jews of Judea and Jerusalem. But soon non-Jews would be attracted to his teaching. (Luke writes in 3:14 that Roman soldiers, who were not Jews, wanted to know what John's message meant to them too.) The nations would not merely observe the new way, the straight path of life, but join it and share in it for themselves. It would not just be a few foreigners worshipping with the

Jews, for in Christ the non-Jews would be in the majority.

The Lord promises hope through the word of his prophets. He makes true promises and, in sending Jesus, those promises were both fulfilled and surpassed. Not just freedom from physical slavery but freedom from slavery to sin; not just a one-off pardon but forgiveness always available to those who repent; not just a literal path/roadway but a way/path of life and living; not just a life that others would observe but a life that everyone can share.

Prayer activity

Either collect suggestions from people all together or split the congregation into groups with each group taking a section to create their ideas, which are then gathered by the leader to turn into prayer. A third alternative is for individuals to be given a piece of paper with two columns divided into four sections. In one column are the following words or images: 'ball and chain', 'certificate of pardon', 'clearway' and 'globe'. In the other column, people write their own suggestion for a modern-day slave, a situation needing forgiveness, areas of life where God is needed to set things right and an international concern. Even if not used in the service, this is a summary of the Bible talk and its application, a prayer reminder for this week.

If leading from the front, hold up the ball and chain and invite people to suggest examples of slavery today, eg migrants exploited for financial gain, or migrants used as sex slaves. Organisations like Tearfund, Stop the Traffik and those involved with fair trade seek to correct slavery of this sort. Ask for examples of people who are chained and held back by mental burdens, eg guilt, loneliness and fear. Hold up the certificate of pardon and ask for examples of situations where pardon is needed, eg family insults, careless words. Use the motorway/clearway sign to think how Jesus came to straighten out our lives, eg in our words, our emotions, our thoughts. Activities like prayer and Bible study groups can be mentioned.

Finally, use the globe to invite concerns from around the world. In the context of the Isaiah passage, it is particularly appropriate to name mission partners working to spread the light of God's knowledge.

(Holding up the ball and chain.) Lord, you hear the cries of those who are oppressed, chained and burdened. We remember especially those exploited for money... those burdened in their minds...

(Holding up the certificate of pardon.) Lord, you promise forgiveness. As you are so ready to forgive, help us also to forgive. We remember especially...

(Holding up the motorway/clearway sign.) Lord, you want us to have direct access to you. Help us to clear away the obstacles in our own lives. Especially help us to... Renew us, remould us and recreate us, we pray.

(Holding up the globe.) Lord, you are creator of the world. We bring before you the troubled areas of the world. Especially we pray for those in... trying to teach others of your truth. Protect them; guide them; give them courage.

Guide us in your truth and teach us, for you are God our Saviour, and our hope is in you all day long.* We thank you for sending Jesus

to fulfil our hopes. Amen.
(*Psalm 25:5)

Prayer of confession

In using the idea of God causing his people to breathe again, breathing prayers can be used. (See page 7 of *Multi-Sensory Prayer* by Sue Wallace, Scripture Union, 2000.)

This prayer uses similar ideas:
(Breathe in slowly.)
Lord, we breathe out our hatred. *(Breathe out.)*
Fill us with love. *(Breathe in.)*
We breathe out our quarrelsome nature. *(Breathe out.)*
Fill us with peace. *(Breathe in etc.)*
We breathe out our meanness.
Help us to celebrate goodness and encourage others.
We breathe out our indifference.
Fill us with enthusiasm for you.
We breathe out our selfishness.
Help us to reach out to help others.
We breathe out our greed.
Help us to share.
We breathe out our fear.
Fill us with trust and confidence in you.
(Invite people to rest in God's presence.)
Cause us to come back to life.
Bring us back to the life you want us to live.
Make us breathe again.
Make us breathe in the power of your Holy Spirit.
We claim Christ's promise to send the Holy Spirit,
and we ask this prayer in Jesus' name. Amen.

Ending the service

Last year a company called the 'Diabolical Gift People' sold a box with the promise of an imaginary friend inside it. The box was empty. It was a joke. The box was full only of air and imagination. Today we've heard how God gives us not a diabolical gift but a heavenly one – Jesus. God's promise box is full, not empty. He is not an imaginary friend on offer but a real one. In fact God's promises are fulfilled beyond expectation. It is in this God that our hope is founded.

Helpful extras

Music and song ideas

'Longing for light' is the suggested theme hymn for Advent (see page 14). It talks in verse two of 'longing for hope'. Other relevant songs include: 'In Christ alone'; 'Lord of all hopefulness'; 'All my hope on God is founded'; 'Lord of our life and God of our salvation'; 'In heavenly love abiding'; 'There is a hope so sure'. 'All my hope on God is founded' or 'There is a hope so sure' could be the final hymn.

Notes and comments

It is important to alert the congregation to next week's colour. (It will be white or red.) Thank those who came in this week's colour.

A ball and chain can be made, or cheap ones are available from fancy dress shops.

Online resources

All suggested downloads are available at www.scriptureunion.org.uk/light. Visit www.lightlive.org for additional activities for children, young people and adults.

THIRD SUNDAY OF ADVENT

READINGS: **Isaiah 61:1–4,8–11; John 1:6–8,19–28**
Psalm 126; 1 Thessalonians 5:16–24

Bible foundations

Aim: to investigate the way John the Baptist pointed to Jesus

The season of Advent, traditionally associated with the coming of the King, is also seen as a season of penitence in preparation. But into that time of penitence shines the shaft of light that promised that the darkness was ending and the light coming. That naturally gives rise to a sense of joy, and today is often known as Gaudete Sunday, from the Latin word meaning 'to rejoice'. The source of that joy is evident. Darkness depresses and in winter (at least in some latitudes) we long for the longer, brighter, warmer days. The exiles described in Psalm 126 rejoiced because the night of their exile was over. Isaiah 61 looks forward to a day when sadness will be replaced by joy and praise because God has come. Paul encourages the Thessalonians to live in a way that is marked by joy.

The message of John, therefore, as he points to the light, is a source of joy to all those who will listen. We know the end of the story, which ought to make us even more joyful. But it is worth trying to capture the sense of anticipation which the Jewish nation felt and which, for some at least, rose to fever pitch when John arrived. Jesus is coming, the light is shining, and the darkness with all that it brings by way of fear and doubt is about to be dispelled. Each age group will see this in its own way, but all will be able to enter into the sense of joy at what God is about to do in Jesus. John offered the hope of light; Jesus was the light.

Beginning the service

Again an Advent trumpet fanfare can be sounded as explained for previous Advent services – see page 14.

Comment on the number of people wearing white (or red – see **Notes and comments**) to represent the cleansing of baptism. Ask if anyone can remember a trailer they have seen on television for a programme that is going to be on over Christmas. Explain that John the Baptist was a bit like a trailer for Jesus.

Bible reading

The reading from Isaiah 61:1–4,8–11 is read closely coordinated with the appearance of images projected on a screen as follows: verse 1, prison bars; verse 2, tears, or a picture of a grieving person; verse 3, a crown; verse 4, blocks of stone; verse 8, Old Bailey statue of justice; verse 9, a globe/world map; verse 10, jewel(s); verse 11, growing seed. These are available as a download (YearB. Advent3_1). This could also be read to quiet background music that has a feeling of hope. The reading from John 1:6–8,19–28 is delivered in a dramatic way. There needs to be a narrator, a voice for John the Baptist, a voice for the crowds and a voice for the Pharisees.

Bible talk

With: a signpost with space for four destinations; an 'arrivals board' with space for these four, to function as concrete visual aids. The destinations are: 'A reformed people'; 'A baptised people'; 'A new people' and 'A humble people'. Alternatively pictures can be drawn. Prepare cards with the four

destinations and the four arrivals. (The same four phrases are repeated.) You could simplify the phrases such as: 'Turned round people', 'Cleaned people', 'New people' and 'Humble people'. Instead of an 'arrivals board', four volunteers could be labelled with one of the phrases. They keep walking around the church until the time comes to arrive!

Four key aspects of John's ministry are highlighted.
1. In John 1:23 it is made clear that John's role was to make straight the way for the Lord. He taught people how to behave, how to sort out their lives and how to straighten their crooked paths. Ask for examples. What this involves is explicit in Luke 3:10–14. This gives us our first signpost destination, **A reformed people**. You may need to explain this in terms of people who have turned round and gone in the opposite direction from where they were heading. *(Attach the first destination to the signpost.)*
2. John's role was to baptise people as a symbol of clean lives, the washing away of sin, and of becoming members of a new Israel, John 1:26. Just as God's first people (Israel) had passed through the waters of the Red Sea, this symbolic action of baptism in the Jordan implies that God's new people (a new Israel) pass through water again. This is our second destination, **A baptised people**. *(Attach the second destination.)*
3. In John's Gospel we read that John the Baptist baptised on the other side of the Jordan, on the east bank in Gentile territory (1:28). Most Jews travelling from Judea to Galilee would avoid Samaria. In order to do this they went to the Jordan valley and walked up the eastern bank opposite the

Samaritan western bank. Here travellers would be plentiful and John would meet many people. This means a third destination is to have **A new people** including non-Jews. *(Attach the third destination.)*

4.   John makes clear his own humility. John says in verse 27 that he is not worthy to untie the thongs of Jesus' sandals. This is a great statement of humility because loosing sandal thongs was a slave's task. John does not consider himself worthy even for this. The fourth destination is **A humble people**. *(Attach the fourth destination.)*

John's signpost was pointing towards a reformed, a baptised, a new and a humble people.

With the arrival of Jesus it is clear who John had been pointing to.

1.   Jesus teaches that people need to be reformed. The Sermon on the Mount talks of a radical reformation – not just actions but thoughts are to be examined. *(Move A reformed people to put it on the arrivals board.)*

2.   Jesus teaches the importance of baptism (Matthew 28:19. There is no evidence Jesus actually baptised anyone. (See John 4:1,2.) Baptism is an act of cleansing and of membership. If a baptism is taking place during the service, make reference to that. (A baptised people can now go on the arrivals board.)*

3.   John had indicated that God's plan would include non-Jewish people and ministry in non-Jewish lands. Jesus' ministry did the same. He visited non-Jewish places and met and healed non-Jews. *(The idea of A new people belongs on the arrivals board.)*

4.   Just as John taught humility so did Jesus. Jesus' birth and his coming in human form are part of that message, and also his washing of the disciples' feet. *(The arrivals board needs to include A humble people.)*

So John was the signpost pointing to Jesus. He is the royal herald preparing the way for his King. He is the messenger and Jesus is the message. He talks of Christ: Jesus is the Christ.

Prayer activity

There are two options.

Option I
With: Post-it notes; pens/pencils; a board divided into a cross, each 'quarter' labelled with one of the prayer categories below

Four categories are taken from the reading from Isaiah 61: the poor, the broken-hearted, the prisoners and those suffering injustice. On Post-it notes individuals or groups are invited to write a name or place associated with one of these groups. With younger people present, you may need to suggest items for consideration or show suitable images on the screen or board. You could invite people to come to the front to talk about relevant topics, locally, nationally or internationally. This might include prayer for the recently bereaved.

At the front there is a board divided into a cross with a category in each quarter. During a time of meditative music such as 'I cannot tell' people bring their note to the front and place it in the relevant compartment. A soloist could sing the hymn, especially the second verse. Verse four is a fitting climax when all the notes have been placed.

Option 2
The theme hymn for Advent 'Longing for light' is used. The chorus is sung as an introduction.

Lord, we ask for transformed lives. We ask that you will help us to lead holy lives so others can see we are your people. As Christ showed us how to live, help us to show others.
(The first verse and chorus are sung.)
Lord, you are a God of peace. We pray for those parts of our world where there is war and suffering and fear.
We pray for those who are heralds of the gospel. We remember those who teach and preach Christ, in difficult and dangerous and hostile lands.
(The second verse and chorus are sung.)
God our Father, we thank you for the plenty we enjoy. We think of the starving and poorly nourished. We think with sorrow of those without food. We think of those with little water or only polluted water to drink. Move our hearts to sympathise, to give and to act.
(The third verse and chorus are sung.)
Father, we have houses and homes. We have roofs above our heads and walls around us. We have heating to keep us warm. We pray for those who have none of these. We pray that we can waken up to our responsibility to share and to equip the needy with basic necessities.
(The fourth verse and chorus are sung.)
Lord, you gave us examples of humility and service in John and in Jesus. Help us to serve one another, to minister to each other's needs.
(The fifth verse and chorus are sung.)
Lord God, hear our prayers. Listen to our

pleadings. Christ is the light. He is our light. He is the world's light. We ask our prayers in his name. Amen.

Prayer of confession

With: a knotted string or rope that can be unravelled

This is prefaced by inviting some young people to unravel a knotted string or rope. It is an image of making the crooked straight. This is a symbol of the role of John. Alternatively, eight to ten people could hold hands and then get into a tangle by stepping over each other's joined hands. As the prayer is said, they unknot themselves.

Lord, so often our lives get twisted, so often our lives become tied up in knots. They can grow entangled and snared with wrongdoing. We know that we need to be sorted out. Straighten out our thinking, so we can focus on you and on our neighbours.
Unravel our twisted emotions so we can love you.
Disentangle us from everything that snags us, makes us forget you or takes us away from you.
We confess these errors in our lives.
Lord, sort us out and purify us through and through. Keep us on the straight and narrow path, walking in your ways.
Help us to live life as you intended so we may honour your name, for Jesus' sake. Amen.

Ending the service

The service ends with a reading of 1 Thessalonians 5:16–24, the epistle for today. Alternatively the service ends on a note of joy with Psalm 126.

Helpful extras

Music and song ideas
'Longing for light' as explained in **Prayer activity**; 'Make way, make way'; 'On Jordan's bank the Baptist's cry'; 'Hark a herald voice is calling'; 'These are the days of Elijah'.

Game
Create two groups (which could include everyone, divided into two) and place the two groups either side of the church. Give one side a series of messages written on pieces of paper. Only one message will contain a message about God which is 'Get ready for Jesus.' All the other messages will be along the lines of 'Eat eggs and bacon'; 'Go to bed at ten o'clock'; 'Don't be late for school'. The group with the messages shout out their message as many times as possible and as loud as possible for half a minute. The other group listens out for the one message about Jesus. Can they hear it above the noise? What is it?

After 30 seconds everyone sits down. What messages did people hear? What was the one message about Jesus? What might that mean? Explain that John's message was simple and he proclaimed it so that people could hear. But there were distractions in that some did not want to hear but there were some surprising people who did hear, including Roman soldiers. Advent is all about getting ready for Jesus.

Notes and comments

White has been selected as the theme colour for this week. It is the colour of purity.

However, red is an alternative because it is a colour associated with heraldic dress, announcing the arrival of a king. Furthermore, it might lead to a more celebratory mood. Whichever colour is chosen, at the start of the service the young people can march round the worship space to fanfare music.

The congregation should be alerted to the theme colour for next Sunday, which is blue.

As a variation to singing during the offertory, let the congregation listen to a relevant hymn or song like 'I will offer up my life'. In this way the congregation can focus on the offering itself.

If there is a baptism during the service, make appropriate connections with the theme of this service.

For further development of the **Bible talk**, you could go beyond the Gospel reading. Isaiah 61:2 shows that the new era was associated with judgement – 'the day of vengeance of our God'. John the Baptist's teaching in the other Gospels, especially in Matthew 3:7–10, is a threatening ministry scaring people into repentance. **A judging God** could be a fifth destination on the signpost. Jesus' ministry focuses far more on God's love. In this case the arrivals board would more aptly refer to **A loving God**. To this extent John's message has a slightly different emphasis.

Online resources
All suggested downloads are available at www.scriptureunion.org.uk/light. Visit www.lightlive.org for additional activities for children, young people and adults.

FOURTH SUNDAY OF ADVENT

READINGS: **Romans 16:25–27; Luke 1:26–38**
2 Samuel 7:1–11,16; Psalm 89:1–4,19–26

Bible foundations

Aim: to celebrate and declare the good news about Jesus given to Mary and the prophets

Throughout the ages, God had been working like an artist in the studio. He had given glimpses into what he was doing, as though giving people the opportunity to look into the studio and see the picture taking shape. There are hints throughout the Old Testament, going back as far as Genesis 3:15, which include the promises to David in 2 Samuel 7 and Psalm 89. For the most part the full glory of what God was doing had been hidden. But the curtain was about to be pulled back so that the full picture could be seen in all its glory. This is what Paul means when he writes to the Romans about the mystery – not something strange but something yet to be fully revealed.

When Gabriel comes to Mary we see more of what the picture will finally look like, but still do not see the whole. We can be grateful to God not only for what he has been preparing his people for, but also for the fact that he has given us the hints. The prophets have seen the good news but not fully understood it. Mary is not only the recipient but the bearer – in more senses than one – of that good news. Throughout the history of the promise there has been a series of unlikely and in some cases miraculous births – Sarah (Genesis 18:11), Rebekah (Genesis 25:21), Ruth – and Elizabeth and Mary stand in that line. Mary's cooperation is essential. Gabriel's news must have been extremely disturbing and confusing as Mary's response shows. But she is prepared to listen and do what God asks. Her obedience is good news. So while we celebrate God's amazing plan, let's also celebrate all the people who had a part in that, and face up to the challenge to do what we can to be and to bring good news to others.

Beginning the service

An Advent fanfare can begin the service once more (see page 14). If you are following the suggested colour theme, the church will be a sea of blue. Blue is the traditional colour of Mary. It is a colour associated with heaven and faithfulness. Blue paint was also a very expensive colour and so in early works of art, Mary was painted in what was a precious colour to demonstrate her worth.

Today we will be thinking about the good news that Mary received; good news for us all. *(Invite everyone to stand up if they are wearing something blue.)* As this is the last Sunday of Advent, it would be appropriate to recap the colours to see what people have remembered about the Advent theme.

Alternatively, talk about the way people are going to celebrate this Christmas, to lead on to your celebration in this service.

Bible reading

The reading in Luke 1:26–38 lends itself to dramatisation. There is a narrator, the angel's voice and a voice for Mary. A solo or recording of Graham Kendrick's song, 'Let it be to me according to your word' could follow the reading.

Bible talk

Part I
With: six black boxes labelled and numbered as follows: 1. Worthlessness; 2. Loneliness; 3. Fear; 4. Lostness; 5. Meanness and 6. Powerlessness

The first part of this talk is optional but

prepares the celebratory tone of Part 2 and provides a focus for the **Prayers of intercession**.

There are six labelled black boxes at the back of the worship area. People bring a box forward when invited and they start to build a wall or barrier.

Box 1: Some people don't feel valued. They lack self-esteem and need to be appreciated.
Box 2: Some people are alone. They lack company and friendship.
Box 3: Others are afraid. They need encouragement and reassurance.
Box 4: Others are lost. They need to feel they belong to a family and to friends.
Box 5: Some are sad because of meanness. They feel there is a lack of giving and caring.
Box 6: Some feel powerless. They feel they are small individuals who have little or no influence.

We need to show that although individuals may feel tiny this is no cause to be depressed. God is involved in the smallest details of life. The wall shows us six problems of modern life that may crowd in upon us and exclude the light. The walls make life seem dark.

Part 2
With: copies of Luke 1:26–38 (TNIV) printed out for people to read and mark as appropriate (or Bibles available); Bible quiz answers either displayed on lengths of paper or using the PowerPoint download (YearB. Advent4_1).

The good news is that God has acted to deal with problems like those suggested in Part 1. The following questions are now used to bring out the key messages from the Gospel reading. Ask the congregation the following questions, one at a time. Suggest that they check in their Bibles for the answers or on the copies of the reading from Luke 2:26–38, as suggested in **Notes and comments**. After they have given each answer, show your answers on the display board or as PowerPoint slides. Make sure that the letters in bold are aligned to spell GOOD NEWS at the end of the question time.

1.   What was the first thing the angel said to Mary? (She was 'hi**G**hly favoured'. This message is repeated in v 30. She 'f**O**und favour'.)
2.   How did the angel comfort Mary in the same verse? ('The L**O**rd is with you.' Mary was worried at the appearance of an angel.)
3.   What did the angel go on to say (in v 30)? ('**D**o not be afraid.')
4.   What does the angel announce (in v 31)? (Mary will have a 'so**N**' who will be God's Son, called 'J**E**sus'. The name means 'Saviour'.)
5.   What is God going to do for his son (in v 32)? (He '**W**ill give him the throne'.)
6.   How will all this happen (see v 35)? (By the 'Holy **S**pirit'.)

This is good news. It was good news for Mary but also good news for us. Mary's role was quite unique and we should never underestimate that. But, like her, instead of our feeling worthless God also has 'favour' to give us. This was what the birth of Jesus is all about. Instead of loneliness there is the promise that God is with us. Instead of fear there is the command not to fear. Instead of feeling lost there is the presence of a father. God is not mean; he takes the lead in giving.

God is not powerless; he works through his Holy Spirit. He is God Almighty. This is the good news we celebrate.

Prayers of intercession

To reflect different styles of worship, there are two options for prayer:

Option 1
With: six black boxes from **Bible talk** Part 1

This prayer could be read by two people (A and B) as suggested. After each prayer section a person removes the relevant block from the wall built at the start of the **Bible talk**. Place the boxes around the Communion table/altar to suggest they have been handed over to God or, more dramatically, crunch them flat to suggest God has dealt with them and defused their threat. Then push them into a bin bag or large rubbish bin. The words in brackets are particularly relevant if you have young children in your service.

A: Lord, we pray for those who feel **undervalued** and **unvalued** (who feel that they are no good at anything); those who feel sidelined at work; those who feel ignored in school; those who feel they are invisible.
B: Father, in your sight each of us has value and worth. Help us to look for good things in others.
A: Lord, we pray for those who feel they are **alone** (with no one to play with or talk to); deserted by friends and family; deserted by you.
B: Father, you have promised that you are with us (wherever we go, whatever we're doing). We can never escape from your presence.

A: Lord, we remember those who are **afraid** (of people, events or the unknown).

B: Father, drive away their fears and comfort them with the assurance of your love.

A: Lord, we pray for the **lost**; especially those who see no purpose to their life (who can't see what their life is all about); those who are addicted to something harmful.

B: Father, help them to know your love. Place them in the warmth of families and the family of the church.

A: Lord, we remember those who have been hurt by **mean** words and unkind treatment from other people.

B: Father, give us the opportunity to treat them with kindness, generosity and love.

A: Lord, we sympathise with those who feel they are **powerless** and have no influence (nobody listens to them, or cares about what they say).

B: Father, give us all a sense of how great you are. You are God Almighty.

A and B: We ask these prayers in the name of Jesus who showed us that God has not left us lost and alone, but showered his generous love upon us. Amen.

The wall has been dismantled. Our fears are calmed. Our worries lifted.

Option 2

This activity maintains a celebratory tone and uses verses from Psalm 89. In four groups, ask each group to suggest things to praise God for in one of the following areas: creation, Jesus, family and friends, church. Try to name precise examples. The leader from each group leads the praise for their section and the congregation joins in the refrain below.

Creation: Lord, we declare your goodness. You stretched out the heavens like a tent and set the earth on its foundations. We praise you for the wonders of nature. Especially we thank you for those things in nature that amaze us. We think of…
We will sing of the Lord's great love for ever.

Jesus: Lord, we declare your goodness. You sent Jesus to die for us, to lead us in your ways. We thank you especially for…
We will sing of the Lord's great love for ever.

Families and friends: Lord, we declare your goodness. You have put us in families and given us friends. Thank you for those who unselfishly care for us, those who companion us, those who freely give us their time. We thank you for…
We will sing of the Lord's great love for ever.

Church: Lord, we declare your goodness. You have given us our church family, our leaders, musicians and teachers. Especially we thank you for…
We will sing of the Lord's great love for ever.

All the leaders together: With our mouths we will make your faithfulness known through all generations. We declare that your love stands firm for ever.
We praise you Father, Son and Holy Spirit. Amen.

The congregation could listen to 'I could sing of your love forever' by Delirious?.

Ending the service

If you did not reflect on all the Advent colour themes in **Beginning the service**, do so now. Firstly, gold for the promise of a king's return, then green for hope, followed by red for John the Baptist, the herald of God (or white for purity). And today, blue is for Mary. She received the good news that her son would be the Saviour. In a few days' time we celebrate Christmas Day and the birth of Jesus. Come dressed for the party – the birthday of Jesus.

A prayer of blessing based on Romans 16: And now may all nations believe and obey the eternal God, the only wise God to whom be glory for ever through Jesus Christ. Amen.

Helpful extras

Music and song ideas

These suggestions include the following celebratory phrases: Thank you – 'There is a Redeemer'; O yes – 'The virgin Mary had a baby boy' (for this song in particular, percussion instruments can be handed out); Rejoice – 'O come and join the dance'. Also: 'The angel Gabriel' is a celebration piece for a choir; 'Longing for light' (the hymn for Advent, see page 14); 'Tell out my soul'; 'Heaven shall not wait'; 'Let it be to me'; 'Long ago prophets knew'.

Three songs are suggested to be used as follows: after the **Bible reading** 'Let it be to me'; after the **Prayer activity** (option 2) 'I could sing of your love forever'; as a meditation 'Mary, did you know?' (see **Notes and comments**).

Notes and comments

The **Bible talk** is in two parts, which should help with attentiveness and recall. Print the reading Luke 1:26–38 (TNIV) so everyone has a copy. In the second part of the **Bible talk**, when the questions are asked, encourage the congregation to circle the answers in bright felt-tip pens. Older members can help younger children to search for the answers. Alternatively, make sure that there are plenty of Bibles available.

'Mary, did you know?' has words which celebrate Jesus as the one who made the blind see, the deaf hear, the dead live again. The congregation could listen to this as a **Prayer of meditation**. It has been recorded by several musicians, including Amy Grant.

Many of the suggested **Music and song ideas** can be found in *Carol Praise*, published by HarperCollins*Publishers*.

It may be that there is a nativity play this week. This play could be split in two so that the first scene of Mary and the angel comes early on and is followed by the **Bible talk** and activities. Then the whole play is given later in the service.

For an outline for a nativity service see Scripture Union's *All-Age Service Annuals*, Volumes 1–4).

Online resources

All suggested downloads are available at www.scriptureunion.org.uk/light. Visit www.lightlive.org for additional activities for children, young people and adults.

CHRISTMAS DAY

READINGS: **Titus 3:4–7; Luke 2:(1–7),8–20**
Isaiah 62:6–12; Psalm 97

Bible foundations

Aim: to celebrate the birth of Jesus

The story is well known, but it's worth noting the economy with which it is told. There is a lack of embellishment, which has encouraged the adding of embellishments which aren't in the original and which mask the narrative beauty, and hide the reality and theological significance. It is impossible to underestimate the theology in Luke's brief account.

The angel speaks of 'good news', a term rich in Old Testament overtones (see Isaiah 52:7; 61:1) and here used to describe a military victory or the birth of an heir to the emperor. 'in the town of David', is the fulfilment of prophecy, 'Saviour' is significant in that saving was the defining activity of God in the Old Testament (as Isaiah 62:11 and 12 reminds us), 'Messiah' means the promised anointed King and 'the Lord' was the term used for God in the Old Testament. Every word is richly significant. No wonder the angels sing 'Glory!' And then in the middle of all this richness the startling truth – the subject of the good news, the Saviour of the world, the Lord, the promised Messiah, is lying in a feeding trough. Glory and humility, 'Meekness and Majesty'; 'this is our God the Servant King'.

Today is a day for joining the shepherds in wonder and praise, the angels in singing 'Glory' and Mary in quiet reflection. It is a tragedy that much of this will be lost in the celebration and that even our worship may be invaded by the superficial focus on the presents we have received rather than the wonder of the incarnation. Paul helps us in our reflection as he points out exactly what God has done, underlining the message of Luke; in his love God has sent Jesus to ensure that we can be his friends. This is the truth to grasp today – and it can be appreciated, albeit in different ways, by all ages.

Beginning the service

Find out whose birthday is the nearest birthday to today. If it is someone who has recently had a birthday, ask them how they celebrated. Did they have a party, cake or friends round? Were they sung to, did they blow out candles, or were they totally ignored and everyone partied as if they weren't there? If it's someone who has a birthday in the next few days or weeks, ask similar questions relating to how they plan to celebrate.

Draw out the point that when it's your birthday, you tend to be the centre of attention. Most of what happens revolves around you. Is that how we will celebrate Jesus' birthday today or will we leave him out of our planning and thinking?

This service gives a wonderful opportunity to put Jesus and his birth right at the centre/start of our celebrations.

Bible reading

Ask a competent young reader to read Luke 2:8–20, especially emphasising verse 11 'today'.

As introduction, ask the congregation why, with everyone so busy and excited, we have come to church, 'today'. Draw out the fact that this day only 'exists' because of Jesus, the baby born in such squalor over two thousand years ago. Without him we have nothing to celebrate – yet so many people celebrate today giving no thought for Jesus at all. Suggest that as people listen to this reading, they think about the range of emotions felt by the shepherds. (Fear v 9; excitement/purpose vs 15,16; wonder/thrill v 20.)

Conclude by asking if we feel any of these feelings as we come to worship today?

In introducing the reading from Titus 3:4–7, make the link that it's the same Jesus, whose birth we celebrate today and who we read of in this passage. He is our Saviour – and all because of God's great mercy. You may prefer to place this reading in the middle of the **Bible talk** as suggested.

Bible talk

With: three or four parcels, beautifully wrapped and increasing in size (the largest should be a large tin of sweets, the second and third (smaller) are packets of sweets/chocolates, and the first just one small sweet). Be aware of nut allergies.

The story from Luke's Gospel is familiar to everyone. It's about the birth of Jesus which was announced to the shepherds. God's gift of his only Son to the world was happening in a very ordinary (or perhaps extraordinary) place, very near to them. It was not extravagant or plush or rich, just very basic. Yet the announcement was so amazing that the shepherds felt compelled to go and see for themselves. They found the baby just as they had been told.

Talk about how, just as God gave the most amazing gift in Jesus at that very 'first Christmas', so today, at Christmas time, we give gifts too. With a sense of excitement announce that you have got some lovely gifts with you today to give to others.

The smallest gift

Choose people to open the gifts, one at a time. Three gifts are essential, but you could use more if you wish to involve more people. First, invite someone to open the smallest gift. Raise the sense of excitement as they come forward with phrases such as 'Small packages are often the best.' Encourage the individual to hold the unwrapped present up for all to see before they open it. Commiserate with the person when they see it's not much. Emphasise the fact that at least it is a gift and better than nothing. Send them away to enjoy it anyway! Talk about whether this was how the shepherds might have felt when they found the baby. Then read Luke 2:20 which would suggest they were not disappointed, since they left praising and glorifying God.

The larger gift

Invite a second person to open the slightly larger gift. As it is opened, build a sense of expectancy that this parcel is a bit bigger, but once again commiserate that it's probably not the most amazing present they will receive today. Repeat this as many times as necessary.

The largest gift

As you prepare to give away the final, much larger present, be excited that at last this may be something more exciting! But first, hesitate and ask someone to read Titus 3:4–7. Reiterate verse 6: God poured his love on us generously through Jesus Christ our Saviour. Talk about how amazing God's love is for us in sending Jesus – it was 'over the top', extravagant. Invite someone to open the largest present and be 'wowed' by the size of the tin! Open the tin and ask the volunteer (preferably a child) to hold out their hands. Pour sweets into their hands until they overflow and go all over the floor!

This person didn't deserve the 'biggest and best present' any more than the first two or three people deserved the smaller presents, but this is what God's love is like. He sent Jesus, our Saviour, into the world, as a baby, not because of anything we had done, not because we deserved it, but because of his great love… that he pours out generously like the sweets overflowing. That's why everyone has come today and why this is the day we celebrate, because the birth of Jesus was the most amazing outpouring of God's love to us. Emphasise the enormity of God's love which overflows even more than the sweets pouring out of the child's hand! But unlike the empty tin, God's love is limitless and without end!

Finish by challenging people to think about God's amazing gift to us – undeserved because of his mercy. Challenge them to think about this today, as Mary did in Luke 2:19.

Prayer activity

With: prepared red, gold and green strips of paper (about A4 length, 4 cm wide) for making paper chains; pens/pencils

Make sure every person receives one strip of each coloured piece of paper. You may wish to play music while this is going on.

This activity can either be done individually or in small or family groups. Ask people to draw or write 'thank you' prayers on the red strips of paper. Encourage them to think of all that they have through their relationship with Jesus today and also all that they have in this world in terms of material possessions.

Particularly focus on how much we have as we celebrate Christmas. Remind everyone that all good things are a gift from God.

On the gold strips ask people to write or draw those things for which they are sorry. Focus on the past few days, thinking about important things that might have been left undone (as often happens when we are busy and preoccupied). Also think about things that have been done that were hurtful or about damaged relationships. Help children and young people to reflect on their last week. Explain to everyone that these prayers are just between them and God and no one is going to ask them about them, but they may be seen by others. At the same time explain that there may be situations brought to mind that may need to be put right, even today on Christmas Day – maybe, especially today!

On the green strips, ask people to write or draw something they want to ask God for, focusing on others in the world who do not know the truth about Jesus or do not have all the wonderful 'things' we may have and enjoy this Christmas Day. Highlight specific situations that you have focused on as a church over the past year, or situations in the news this week. There may be particular people in your church family that you need to remember, those unwell or sad at the loss of loved ones in the past year. Encourage people to name individuals if appropriate.

Everyone then brings their prayer strips to where there are people to link all the pieces together to make paper chains that can be displayed on the Christmas tree or somewhere else that is clearly visible. As

people are bringing their prayers, ask several people to share their red 'thank you' prayers with others, as appropriate. Conclude by drawing all of these prayers together on behalf of everyone.

Ending the service

As you wish everyone a very happy Christmas, remind them to remember God's amazing gift of Jesus to us. We need to keep Jesus at the centre of all our celebrations, just as we would treat the birthday boy/girl in our own family.

Encourage everyone to share something of God's amazing love that has been poured out to us with not only our families but others in our community.

Ask everyone to stand to pray:

Thank you, God, for the good news for all people that a Saviour has been born who is Christ the Lord.

Thank you that you save us, not because of anything we have done, but because of your great mercy, and that gives us the hope of eternal life.

Help us to live our lives in the reality of that truth today and in the coming year. Amen.

Helpful extras

Music and song ideas
Many people only come to church on Christmas Day and a few other festivals, so include traditional carols among your selection. Suitable songs/hymns might include: 'While shepherds watched their flocks

by night'; 'O come, all you faithful'; 'Hark! the herald angels sing'; 'Come and join the celebration'; 'From heaven you came, helpless babe'; 'God so loved this whole world'; 'See him lying on a bed of straw'.

Play 'From the squalor of a borrowed stable' as people are writing their prayers and making the paper chain.

Carol Praise, HarperCollins*Publishers*, contains many old but also many new or revised carols. It is well worth exploring this book.

Notes and comments

Many other ideas for Christmas services can be found in *Christmas Wrapped Up* and *More Christmas Wrapped Up,* and other Christmas Day services can be found in the *All-Age Service Annuals* Volumes 1–4, all published by Scripture Union.

There are likely to be a number of excited children (and adults) in church this morning. Build on that excitement for you are here to celebrate the birth of Jesus. Use that excitement to illustrate what an amazing event it is that we celebrate. You may wish to keep the service fairly short so select what you need from this service outline.

If in previous weeks you have followed the colour theme in Advent (see page 14), at **Beginning the service**, comment on the celebratory colours people are wearing. You could invite children to come to the front to show any gifts they have already unwrapped/ received. This could be a good link to talking about gifts being undeserved and given out of love, not because we have earned them or have a right to them.

The **Bible reading** from Luke 2 could be acted out by two or three shepherds, some angels and a Mary and Joseph. Ask the readers to really emphasise the reactions of the shepherds and Mary.

If in the **Bible talk** you are using sweets in the parcels to be unwrapped, be aware of nut allergies. How might you encourage the recipient of the largest gift to share their spilled-out sweets with everyone at the end so that no one is left out?

In the **Prayer activity**, the paper chains will be most efficiently and quickly linked together using a stapler. Ask someone in advance to do this as people bring forward their prayers.

If Holy Communion is included in this service, make links with the gifts of bread and wine that are brought to the front and the truth that Jesus freely gave himself for us. His death and subsequent resurrection are a great cause for rejoicing. In reality we cannot separate Jesus' birth from his death, as Mary was to be reminded by Simeon when he told her that a sword would pierce her heart. But more of that next Sunday!

Online resources

All suggested downloads are available at www.scriptureunion.org.uk/light. Visit www.lightlive.org for additional activities for children, young people and adults.

FIRST SUNDAY OF CHRISTMAS

READINGS: **Galatians 4:4–7; Luke 2:22–40**
Isaiah 61:10 – 62:3; Psalm 148

Bible foundations

Aim: to explore the greetings given to baby Jesus and then how we too greet God

We live in a world of instant everything. If we can't have it now, we don't want it. How different this is from what we have seen about waiting and expectation over the last few weeks. God works to a different timescale. Jesus came after many centuries of promise and waiting. Why should that be?

We don't have an answer, but Paul assures us that God knew exactly what he was doing – the time was right. Now, because Jesus became fully human, we can become the children of God, accepted, forgiven and brought home. And lest we should doubt all this, God has given us the Spirit, who assures us that God is our Father. The term Abba, the Aramaic word which Jesus uses to address God in the Garden of Gethsemane, has often been described as the equivalent of 'Daddy'; it is certainly a family name and one that speaks of intimacy, but not perhaps the familiarity that we would associate with Daddy – after all, patterns of family life in the first century were somewhat different and the father given rather more respect than in many Western societies today. Our prayer, inspired by the Spirit, will combine intimacy and respect.

It is no wonder that, as we saw on Christmas Day, the shepherds rejoiced, and also went and told others. The end of a year, and the start of a new one, is a good time to review how much we have celebrated and how many people we have told. How have we greeted Jesus throughout this year?

The *Common Worship* reading closes with Jesus being circumcised, a further indication of his complete identification with humanity living under the law of God. The *Revised Common Lectionary* reading, however, moves on to see Simeon and Anna recognising what God is doing and thus giving further confirmation of the fulfilment of the promises and the value of waiting for God's time.

Beginning the service

With: a collection of Christmas cards

Christmas is over but probably most people still have their cards on the bookshelf or wherever! How many people read the greetings on the cards they received? Ask a few people to come to the front to read out the greetings from the Christmas cards. Ask about the purpose of sending 'greetings'. You might also like to explore the purpose of sending Christmas cards at all. Talk about other sorts of cards that we send such as birthday, valentine, exam success, etc. Explain that in this service you are going to look at another sort of greetings card.

In addition, you could greet people in a variety of ways. Shake hands with some, hug others, wave to others, call out a cheery greeting to named people at the back and engage in conversation, even sing a song to someone! This is an example of the different ways of greeting people.

Bible reading

The reading from Galatians 4:4–7 could be presented as a choral reading as follows, also available as a download (Year B.Christmas1_1).

> Voice 1: But when the time was right
> Voice 2: God sent his Son
> Voice 3: and a woman gave birth to him.
> Voice 1: His Son obeyed the Law,
> Voice 2: so he could set us free from the Law,
> Voice 3: and we could become God's children.
> Voice 1: Now that we are his children, God has sent the Spirit of his Son into our hearts.
> Voice 2: And his Spirit tells us that God is our Father.
> Voice 3: You are no longer slaves.
> All 3: You are God's children, and you will be given what he has promised. Galatians 4:4–7 (CEV)

The reading from Luke 2:22–40 lends itself to people acting out the movements of the various characters in the narrative. Mary and Joseph could walk down the aisle holding a baby-sized bundle which very old Simeon, standing at the front, takes from them with delight. Jesus' parents look surprised at Simeon's words and then deeply shocked and saddened. Joy is restored when very, very old Anna appears, possibly shuffling up the aisle. Mary and Joseph leave in a different direction from the one in which they came.

Bible talk

With: a giant (A2 or bigger) greetings card with the words, 'Congratulations on your baby son' on the front; three cards that will be stuck on the inside of the big card with the following words: 'Hope and light', 'Pain and sadness', 'At last'; glue/sticky tape (The 'card' could be created as a PowerPoint presentation but a real card idea is more effective. Instead of sticking the words on the inside of the card, you could simply write appropriate words as the **Bible talk** proceeds.)

If anyone has recently had a new baby or grandchild, ask what sort of greetings were written on any cards they received. Alternatively, ask for suggestions as to what comments one might expect on such a card. (If it is New Year's Day you could expand on the sort of greetings you receive for the new year.) Explain that greetings cards were not around at the time of Jesus' birth although there were several people who might have sent them if they were! You are going to meet them now!

Show the giant card and explain that you are going to write on it (or stick inside it) three greetings that might have been written.

If you have had a dramatic presentation of Luke 2:22–40 as the **Bible reading** you will not need to fill in very much detail, but check that everyone knows about the four adults involved in the story – Mary, Joseph, Simeon and Anna. Joseph and Mary, in bringing Jesus to the Temple, were doing what was expected of them by Jewish Law. (This was not circumcision which had already taken place on the eighth day, but was to mark the ending of Mary's time of uncleanness after the birth. This had given her time to recover from the demands of the birth.) (Depending upon the congregation you may wish to omit the above section in brackets.)

Simeon's greetings

Joseph and Mary came into the Temple where they were met by Simeon, who really loved God and was longing for the arrival of the One promised from God. He had been told that he would not die until he had seen this person. Imagine his amazement when he saw this young family and God's Spirit told him that here was the One! Ask for suggestions of what greeting he would have given Joseph and Mary. (You are looking for words along the lines of 'Hope and light'. If someone gives you an answer that is not close to this, thank them and ask for other suggestions. Alternatively, if you have not written out the

words beforehand, you can adapt what you write on the messages to be stuck on the card.) Simeon knew that Jesus was going to bring the light of God to the whole world, including those who were not Jewish. He was amazed by what he was experiencing! (Add this greeting to the card.)

A greetings card for a new baby is not really for the child but for the parents and other family members. Simeon had a message for Jesus' parents too but it was not a joyful one. Ask if anyone can remember. You are looking for words such as 'Pain and sadness'. (Add this greeting to the card either by sticking on the pre-prepared card or writing a phrase from the congregation.) What an extraordinary thing to say, that Mary would suffer through being Jesus' mother! Of course, what he said was very true. We are told that Mary thought deeply in her heart about what she had been told about Jesus. God was preparing her for the future.

At this point, it would be appropriate to talk about hopes and fears for the new year.

Anna's greeting

Introduce Anna and then say that both she and Simeon might have said the same thing, after waiting so long for the promised One from God to come. When you have been waiting so long and eventually something arrives, what do you say? You are looking for words such as 'At last'. (Add this greeting to the card.) They knew that God had a plan for his whole world that would bring people back into a close relationship with him. Refer to the **Bible reading** from the epistle. Jesus' birth was no accident but the means by which God's plan for us to become his children could become reality.

If we are God's children, then we can enter into a warm, close relationship with him. We can speak with him, indeed we can greet him. There will be opportunities to explore that during the rest of the service but it would be appropriate to ask a couple of people to share a **Personal testimony** of what God means to them and how they speak with him.

Prayer activity

With: individual greeting cards for each person; pens/pencils/glitter pens/stickers/pictures to stick on the front of a card; glue

Just as Simeon and Anna greeted Jesus, there is now going to be a time to consider how we might greet God today. If necessary, split into small groups to decide what greeting you might want to give to God. Make suggestions such as 'Father/Daddy'; 'I love you!'; 'You are great'; 'Your plans are amazing'; or, on a more personal note, 'How much longer?' Write on, draw on or decorate the cards with the message inside and a drawing, pattern or picture stuck on the front.

Allow five minutes to complete this (some people will want 30 minutes but others will be finished before some have even started), then sing a song of thanks addressed to God, followed by a time when people address God and then talk silently with him.

Prayer of confession

Everyone is conscious that we often forget to greet God or we treat him disrespectfully. Ask people to think about times in the last week when they have just not bothered to think about God at all (especially as many

people are very busy at Christmas) or have blamed him for things that have gone wrong. Then after each of the following phrases, everyone joins in this refrain: **Lord God, we are sorry**.

We have been so busy that we have just not thought about you at all. *(Pause.)*
Lord God, we are sorry.
We are often so wrapped up in ourselves that we forget how great you are and treat you as very unimportant. *(Pause.)*
Lord God, we are sorry.
When things have not gone the way we wished, too often we blame you and treat you disrespectfully. *(Pause.)*
Lord God, we are sorry.
Lord God, we call out to you now, the God whose great plan to make us your very own children became possible when you sent Jesus. Forgive us and make us your own. Amen.

Ending the service

Greeting others has been part of this service, and the new year will soon be here, or it may even be 1 January today, so it would be appropriate to end with greeting each other with the Peace. Encourage people to use the name of the people they greet (if they know it) and to say:
……., may God's peace be with you into the coming year/in 2012/2015!

Helpful extras

Music and song ideas
Songs that address God to use in the **Prayer activity**: 'Abba Father'; 'My Jesus, my Saviour'; 'Who is this in yonder stall?'; 'God is good,

we sing and shout it'; 'Father, we love you, we worship and adore you'.

As Christmas is only just past, sing some Christmas carols. If possible also sing a version of the Nunc Dimittis, which is the song that Simeon sung. *Carol Praise*, published by HarperCollins*Publishers* contains several versions including Steve James' 'Oh, what a wonder you are' and Graham Kendrick's 'This child'. You could also listen to one of the many classical recordings of this often-used song.

Game

This wordsearch based on the TNIV is made up of words that Simeon said about Jesus, available as a download (YearB.Christmas1_2).

Making your own copy or using the PowerPoint one, ask children to identify the words that show what Simeon hoped would become of Jesus. What do the leftover letters say about how God viewed the arrival of Jesus as a baby? He was the fulfilment of _ _ _ ' _ _ _ _ _ (GOD'S PLAN). Use this game to recap on what Simeon said in his greeting to Mary and Joseph.

G	S	O	G	R	D	N
F	A	L	L	I	N	G
S	V	I	O	S	I	I
E	I	G	R	I	A	S
P	O	H	Y	N	P	P
O	U	T	L	G	A	N
H	R	E	V	E	A	L

SAVIOUR	GLORY	LIGHT
FALLING	REVEAL	SIGN
RISING	PAIN	HOPE

Notes and comments

For this Sunday, *Common Worship* uses the Christmas Day passage from Luke 2 about the shepherds, but includes verse 21 with the naming and circumcision of Jesus, whereas the *Revised Common Lectionary* takes the story on to the presentation of Jesus in the Temple in Luke 2:22–40, which is the passage that is the basis of this outline. If you wish to use the story of the shepherds again, refer back to the Christmas Day outline, which briefly explores the changing feelings of the shepherds, from fear, to hasty activity, to telling their story, to amazement and finally to praise of God. You could take each of these five emotions, to see how each of them is perfectly understandable, but then see how this connects with where we are, about to start a new year. In all five emotions, think what it might mean for a child as well as adults.

If Holy Communion is included in this service, encourage a sense of wonder at what God has done through Christ as people come forward to receive the bread and wine. By taking the idea that the shepherds greeted Jesus and responded appropriately, many of the suggestions in this outline could be adjusted to fit.

If using the outline as given, and a service of Holy Communion is included, make sure that the Peace is incorporated into the greeting theme.

Online resources

All suggested downloads are available at www.scriptureunion.org.uk/light. Visit www.lightlive.org for additional activities for children, young people and adults.

Epiphany

READINGS: **Isaiah 60:1−6; Matthew 2:1−12**
Psalm 72:10−15; Ephesians 3:1−12

Bible foundations

Aim: to recognise that just as the wise men came from the east to worship Jesus, so all nations can come to worship him

In the history of Israel, the Exile forms a counterpoint to the Exodus. During the Exodus, the people became a nation with the hope of the Promised Land and a place to serve God. By the time of the exile it had all gone wrong. Land and Temple, promises, covenant, self-respect and confidence, all seemed to have been torn from their grasp. Their failure to obey God and walk in his ways had brought judgement upon the nation. Isaiah's prophecy offers exhilarating hope to the exiles in Babylon (vs 4−6). Light is the main image. God's glory will rise to shine once again upon Israel (v 1) while the Gentiles will experience only darkness (v 2). They will recognise that Israel is the source of light and wisdom. The prophet urges Israel to look up to see not only their own sons and daughters returning from Exile, but also the arrival of the Gentiles bringing gifts and honour.

The arrival of the Magi in Bethlehem is clearly presented as a partial fulfilment of Isaiah's prophecy. There are unmistakable echoes of Isaiah in Matthew's account. The Magi, or wise men, bring gifts of gold, frankincense and myrrh (v 11 and Isaiah 60:6, though myrrh, which was used to embalm bodies after death, isn't mentioned in the Isaiah passage). The star which guides them echoes the prophecy of light (v 2 and Isaiah 60:1). Matthew twice uses the language of 'rising' (vs 2,9 and Isaiah 60:1). Tradition, though not Matthew, has it that they arrived on camels, which clearly echoes Isaiah 60:6. Tradition calls them 'kings' which also probably owes more to Isaiah 60:3 since Matthew calls them 'Magi'. They come to see the hoped-for king of the Jews (v 2), the Messiah (v 4), who was the realisation of Jewish hopes. Israel's hope is fulfilled in this child and the nations come to bring their wealth and gifts as they seek to participate in Israel's blessing.

Beginning the service

With: 'Jerusalem' printed on a large sheet of paper, a powerful torch

As the service starts, put out as many lights as possible to create a gloomy atmosphere. Read Isaiah 60:1–6, using the TNIV. Gradually switch on the lights during the first three verses. Alternatively, from verse 2 onwards focus the beam of a powerful torch on the word 'Jerusalem' displayed at the front. During verses 4 and 5 the torch could be directed around the church, but just above the heads of the congregation. If a nativity crib is still on display, focus the torch on it for verse 6.

You could follow this with the **Game** suggestion.

Bible reading

The main reading, Matthew 2:1–12, can be read from the CEV using different voices for the narrator, wise men, Herod and the chief priests.

Before the reading, explain that at Christmas when we read about the shepherds visiting Jesus, we are remembering that God's Son was first shown to Jewish people in his own community. By the time we come to Epiphany we learn that all people, not just the Jews, are called to worship him.

Bible retelling

Ask the congregation to think where they feel they fit into the reading from Matthew. Would they be one of the wise men, who has studied the stars for years before setting off to find the baby king for himself? Do they feel they are one of the chief priests and teachers of the Law who know the Scriptures well enough to be able to answer questions for other people? Could they play the part of Herod, being suspicious of both the wise men and the baby they are seeking? Or would they like to be in the house where Jesus is?

Ask as many of the congregation as are able to gather at one of the following places: by the door of the church if they see themselves as one of the wise men; halfway down the aisle if they are Herod or one of the chief priests; at the front of the church if they are going to be in the house with Jesus. Then slowly reread Matthew 2:1–12 while a 'stage manager' leads the group of wise men from the church door to meet Herod and the chief priests in the centre of the church. The wise men are then led to visit Jesus at the front. Finally, they are led back to the church door by a different aisle if possible. (This may mean they have to walk through a pew to ensure a different route.)

Bible talk

With: a variety of invitations to show, real ones and/or on a PowerPoint display, available as a download (YearB.Epiphany_1)

Invitations you have received
Show a number of invitations to the congregation. Hand out specific ones to any children present. Apart from obvious invitations to a wedding or birthday party, include invitations to gain double points at the supermarket if you spend more than £50, invitations to visit a stately home or visitor

attraction and invitations for a free session at a gym or spa. Ask everyone to think of the last invitation they received. What was it for? How did it arrive? Did they reply? Did they go?

Invitations come in all shapes and sizes. There are obvious ones like wedding or birthday invitations. Others are less obvious and personal such as supermarket offers. God invites people to worship his Son Jesus in different ways, and some of the invitations he uses are spectacular.

The shepherds' invitation

At Christmas, we remember that the first people invited to meet Jesus, and to worship him, were the shepherds. They got their invitation from a glorious, all-singing, all-praising army of angels. It was very personal and they accepted it. They went. They met Jesus and their lives were changed, even though they could not really understand it all. They went back from the encounter praising God.

The wise men's invitation

Now it is Epiphany when we think about the visit of the wise men to Jesus. Ask what form their invitation came in. (Posted in the sky, a special star.) It was there for everyone to see, but only the wise men who kept a sharp eye on the stars realised its significance. They accepted the invitation, though they had to travel a long way to do so.

The invitation to the shepherds was just to them – and they may have represented God's invitation to the Jews, to Jesus' own people. The invitation to the wise men was displayed in the sky, advertised to everyone. The wise

men remind us, just as Isaiah prophesied, that Jesus came to be the light of the world for all nations, not just the Jews. So that includes us, and everyone who lives around us. We are all invited to worship the Son of God, today and every day. Is this an invitation that you are going to accept?

Prayer activity

With: pictures of a treasure box on small pieces of card, enough for everyone present

Explain that everyone has the opportunity to worship Jesus today during the prayer activity. Give out the treasure box cards and ask everyone to imagine putting a worship offering inside this box to present to Jesus. Suggest some possible ideas such as money, time, a particular skill, a treasured possession, and then invite everyone to make their own choice during the song, 'I will offer up my life in spirit and truth'. This could be played to be listened to and reflected on, rather than sung. You could explain that this is more than a New Year's resolution and explore the difference.

After the song, invite everyone who is able to bring their treasure box picture (and whatever it represents) to the front of the church as an offering to Jesus. During this, sing (or play from a CD) 'King of kings, Majesty'. If there is a nativity crib in church, invite everyone to place their offering in front of it. Otherwise the pictures could be put into a basket in full view of everyone. Make sure that the pictures of those who are unable to leave their seats are taken forward at the same time.

Prayer of confession

This prayer of confession invites the response: **Father, forgive us.**

Father God, the wise men travelled far to worship Jesus. Forgive us for all the times we can't be bothered to make the effort to worship your Son.
Father, forgive us.

God of all nations, so many people cannot worship Jesus in freedom. Forgive us for not praying for freedom of worship for all your children.
Father, forgive us.

Father of all, so many people do not yet know Jesus as their friend and Saviour. Forgive us for not sharing the good news of his birth with people we meet.
Father, forgive us.

It would be appropriate to pray specifically for your community following this **Prayer of confession**, so that not only will you know God's forgiveness but seek to share the good news with others. As the new school term begins, you could also pray for those in school who have opportunities to share their faith.

Ending the service

Explain that Jesus is attractive. People are drawn to him and they are drawn to worship him – just like the wise men were, as was foretold by Isaiah the prophet. The wise men went home by another route, after they had worshipped Jesus and given him their gifts. Challenge everyone to go home after church by a different route – perhaps going down a different road or path from the usual one – as they think about how worshipping God today will have changed them. What difference will coming to church today make to how you all live tomorrow? Ask everyone to face the exit for a closing prayer or blessing, or for the singing of a final song such as 'O Jesus, I have promised' or 'You shall go out with joy'.

Helpful extras

Music and song ideas

During the **Prayer activity** use 'I will offer up my life' and 'King of kings, Majesty'. The most obvious choice for Epiphany would be the well-known 'We three kings of Orient are'. A suitable carol for those who want to sing Christmas music would be verses from 'O come, all ye faithful' as the chorus picks up the theme of coming to worship Jesus. A suitable song is 'Come, now is the time to worship'. For a final song use 'O Jesus, I have promised' or 'You shall go out with joy'.

Game

To underline that God's invitation is for everyone, play 'Pass the Parcel' with a different invitation in each layer. If you play this game with a children's group, ensure there are enough layers for each child to have a go. In an all-age service setting, aim for a maximum of seven layers to avoid boredom. Adapt these invitation suggestions to personalise the game for the people in your church. As each category of invitation is read out, invite everyone who fits in that category to come to the front. They can either sit down after each invitation or see if everyone can end up being at the front.

Everyone who lives in a corner house
Everyone who lives in a flat [or thatched property]
Everyone who lives with more than four other people
Everyone who lives on [Main Street]
Everyone who lives on their own
Everyone who lives near enough to church to walk
Everyone who has travelled more than two miles to church
Everyone else in church

Once everyone is standing out at the front, emphasise that God invites each of us to worship him. If you are going to use this game, it would be a good activity to follow the reading from Isaiah at **Beginning the service**.

Notes and comments

This service outline uses the Bible readings for Epiphany rather than those for the Second Sunday of Christmas. This enables service leaders to explore the significance of the visit of the wise men. Although this story will probably have been told many times over the previous weeks, its significance may have been overlooked.

If you are using this material with a children's group, give out various invitations in envelopes for them to open or look at during the **Bible talk** (rather than using PowerPoint illustrations). Being able to open and handle them will help children to make links with invitations they have received, as well as providing assistance for those who learn through using physical actions. With slightly older children, discuss how they might decide who to invite to a birthday party. Remember that most children under 7, as well as some adults, are not strong readers so do not expect them to read out any invitations that you hand around. Focus the activity on the opening of the invitation. Finally, discuss what sort of invitation they would create to invite someone to come to worship God.

As this service focuses on people responding to an invitation to worship Jesus, it provides an opportunity for someone to share their **Personal testimony**. Using suitable language, they can talk about how they were invited to worship God, why they decided to accept and what they did next. It is best to organise this with someone beforehand so they have a chance to think about what they want to say. After they have shared their experience, invite everyone else to reflect on their own experience of being invited by God.

Online resources

All suggested downloads are available at www.scriptureunion.org.uk/light. Visit www.lightlive.org for additional activities for children, young people and adults. For your convenience, the following activities are available as downloads: YearB.Epiphany_2 Adult sermon; YearB. Epiphany_3 Imaginative Bible meditation; YearB.Epiphany_4 Wise man journey for 5s and under; YearB.Epiphany_5 Bible story, making, circle rhyme and prayer.

Baptism of Christ

READINGS: **Acts 19:1–7; Mark 1:4–11**
Genesis 1:1–5; Psalm 29

Bible foundations

Aim: to recognise the importance of the Holy Spirit at the start of Jesus' ministry – important for any ministry

Why did Jesus go to meet John at the Jordan? Why did the Holy Spirit have to descend upon the one who was conceived by the Holy Spirit? Perhaps Jesus was simply identifying with the crowd, for it cannot be that he needed to confess his sins (Mark 1:4,5). Indeed he is never described as doing so and is clearly the one who, in his own time, will baptise others with the Holy Spirit (v 8). More likely he is identifying with John in his ministry of calling the people to repentance and preparation of the way of the Lord (v 3). Whilst John's baptism was simply in water, Jesus' ministry was to be characterised by the Anointed One (the Messiah) pouring out the Holy Spirit (vs 7,8). It is unsurprising that he should himself be baptised by the Father with that same Holy Spirit as he begins his messianic ministry.

When Paul arrives in Ephesus he clearly thinks that the people he meets are believers. Luke describes them as 'disciples' (Acts 19:1). Some commentators, consequently, read this incident as evidence of the need for a second experience of receiving the Spirit. It is likely, however, that Paul sensed that they were somehow deficient in their experience of the Spirit as he questions them about it (v 2). They resemble those people in Mark 1 who went to John at the River Jordan and had become John's disciples. They had received John's baptism, not as Christians. They had not received the Spirit from the one John had identified – Jesus. Paul puts that right. They are baptised into the name of Jesus as Paul lays hands on them and prays for them, with the result that the Holy Spirit now comes upon them with prophecy and speaking in tongues. Like their master, Christians need an experience of the Holy Spirit to be able to serve God.

Beginning the service

Place a table where it will be a visible focal point. (If your Communion table is in the body of the church, use that instead of a separate table.) Cover it with a large white or pale blue cloth. Gather together various items relating to baptism, including a large clear bowl of water. If you have one, a small portable font would work very well. Other items might include strips of blue and white voile (symbolising the River Jordan), anointing oils, a 'dove', a candle (unlit), symbols of the gifts of the Spirit, a picture of Jesus' baptism (a more traditional one would be appropriate – download from the Internet).

Give out these items to people of different ages (a family, perhaps). During the first hymn/song they should bring these items forward, one or two at a time, and arrange them on the focal table. The strips of voile, if used, need to be placed first and look particularly effective if allowed to drape exuberantly over the edge of the table.

Younger children could be given ribbons or streamers in blue, white and pale orange. Either during or after the table has been arranged, invite the children to swirl the streamers up and down in front of the table, like water tumbling along a riverbed or in a shower, depending on your space. (This is why it's very important that candles are unlit!) Let the children keep hold of the ribbons to twirl during other songs/hymns throughout the service.

Bible reading

The reading from Mark 1:4–11 could be mimed while it is read. At the point at which the Holy Spirit descends, children could circle 'Jesus' twirling blue, white and light orange ribbons or streamers over him. The streamers could be used elsewhere in the service, for example the children could swirl them during the hymns and songs.

Bible talk

With: a small microwave oven placed securely on a table near a socket (not plugged in, with rubbish such as a crushed paper cup, broken pen/toy, old envelopes, plastic bag, sweet wrappers inside); a rubbish bin; damp cloths; wipes; bags of uncooked microwave popcorn and enough bowls to pass popcorn round. (Practise making microwave popcorn before the service if you have not done so before and be very safety-conscious throughout!)

Ask if everyone likes popcorn. Explain that you have been asked to make some for everyone to share. You didn't have time before the service, so you're going to do it now. It won't take long in the microwave. Open the microwave door. Oh, dear! Look at this rubbish! No way to treat a microwave! Ask a couple of volunteers to clean it up and make it ready for cooking the popcorn. Give them the bin and damp cloths. Ask another volunteer to check the microwave is ready when they've finished.

Put the popcorn into the microwave oven, set the time and press Start. Of course, nothing will happen! Look puzzled. You've cleaned the oven, got it all ready, so what is missing? The power! Plug in, switch on and make the popcorn.

While it is cooking talk about how everything had to be clean and ready, but even then the oven couldn't do its work without the power. No power – no popcorn! In today's reading from Mark 1:4–11, we heard how people were made ready by John the Baptist for something big and new and exciting to happen – much more exciting than popcorn in church! But those new, exciting and extraordinary things could only happen when the Holy Spirit came.

First, the Spirit came on Jesus and gave Jesus the power to do and say wonderful and amazing things as he did God's work. Ask if anyone can remember some of the amazing things Jesus said and did. Lots of people followed Jesus to find out who he really was. He had power and authority like no one else.

After he died on the cross and rose again, Jesus sent the Holy Spirit to his followers. He baptised them with the Holy Spirit. The Spirit gave Jesus' followers the power to do wonderful and amazing things for God and to share the good news about Jesus.

Today's epistle was about some people the apostle Paul encountered in the city of Ephesus. They had received John's baptism, so they were all cleaned up and ready for Jesus, but they didn't know about the Holy Spirit. When Paul laid his hands on them they received God's Spirit. They were all powered up and some pretty amazing things happened! They started speaking in tongues and prophesying. Now they too could go out in the Spirit's power to do God's work and share the good news of Jesus.

When we get baptised we are cleaned up.

It is a sign that our sins are all washed away and we are made ready to do God's work. (You may wish to explain what this means in the different contexts of infants and adults, whatever is the practice in your church.) But we need more than that. We need the Holy Spirit to give us power and strength. So God gives us his Spirit too and baptism is also a sign of that. Jesus knew he needed the Spirit to do God's work. We too need God's empowering Spirit to do his work, and to share the good news about Jesus with others.

Ask what amazing tasks God might have for everyone here today. Remind them that the Holy Spirit gives us the power to do that work for God, reminding us that we know he is within us and enabling us to share the good news of Jesus with others.

Ask the children and young people to hand round the bowls of popcorn, and wipes if needed. Be aware of any possible allergies!

Prayer activity

With: paper hand shapes; paper dove shapes; a pencil or some coloured pens; glue sticks; a large sheet of paper with an outline of a dove, over the top of which are the words: 'Thank you, Lord, for your Holy Spirit at work in your church.'

Ask people to pick up their paper hand. Remind them that when Paul laid his hands on the people in Ephesus they received the Holy Spirit, enabling them to know God and be used by him. Ask everyone to look at their paper hand and think about one person they know who has helped them to know God and get closer to him – maybe when they were going through a tough time or just wanting to know God better. They can write the person's name or draw their face on the hand.

Invite everyone to come forward to stick their paper hand on the dove, forming the feathers of its wings. As they stick on their hand, they can say, 'Thank you, Lord, for your Holy Spirit at work in the name of _____ ___ (their person).' (Demonstrate this before people come forward.) When everyone has stuck their hand on the large dove, join together in saying 'Thank you, Lord, for your Holy Spirit at work in your church.'

Ask people to pick up and look at their paper doves. Just as the Holy Spirit came upon Jesus at his baptism (and the dove was the sign that the Holy Spirit was present), God wishes to give the Spirit to those who have turned to him. Baptism is a sign that someone has turned to Christ and is aware of their need of the Spirit. Invite people to think about how God gave/will give the Holy Spirit at baptism. Think about times when people have not let the Holy Spirit lead them, for example, when they have not shown God's love and care to someone, or passed by an opportunity to talk about God to someone ready to hear. Invite them quietly to say sorry to God, assuring them that God will forgive them.

Ask everyone to think about how the Holy Spirit helps them to share the good news about Jesus and suggest a variety of ministries that will include everyone. (Toddlers are very good at the ministry of hugging!) People could write or draw one of these ministries on one side of the dove. On the back write or draw a person or a situation they know currently needing that ministry. Invite people to hold up their doves as a silent offering of prayer for those people and situations.

Finish by saying, 'Come, Holy Spirit, and fill our hearts with the power of your love.' Suggest people take home their doves as a reminder of the importance of the Holy Spirit as they spread God's love.

Ending the service

Remind the congregation of the importance of the Spirit for God's work. Look again at the large dove with the Spirit-led people named on the wings, and then look at their own paper doves, their Spirit ministries and those who need them. Finish by saying the following responses, also available as a download (YearB.BaptismofChrist_1):

Jesus was baptised by the Holy Spirit when he came up out of the water.
By the power of the Spirit, Jesus did battle with evil
and showed God's love.
Jesus baptises his church and his people with the Holy Spirit.
He gives us power to do God's work.
In baptism we receive the Holy Spirit.
May the Spirit lead us to share God's love.
Go out in the power of the Spirit, to love and serve the Lord
In Jesus' name. Amen.

Helpful extras
Music and song ideas
There are several CDs available with

the sound of running streams or rivers, sometimes with music, the sound of birds, or wind in the trees. One of these could be used during the reading of the Gospel, during a period of silent prayer, or with the alternative idea for the **Prayer of confession** (see below).

Hymns/songs might include 'Spirit of the Living God' which would fit very well after confession/saying sorry; 'Breathe on me breath of God'; 'You've got to move when the Spirit says move'; 'For I'm building a people of power'; 'Filled with the Spirit's power'; 'Come, Holy Spirit, come'; 'Dance in your Spirit'; 'Lord of all life and power'.

Notes and comments

If you do not use a mime at **Beginning the service**, the theme of baptism and the coming of the Spirit would lend itself well to dance. A group of young people might enjoy choreographing a dance using blue, white, yellow and pale orange ribbons.

In the **Bible talk**, instead of microwaving popcorn, you could use an electric popcorn maker, or make drinks with a juicer or shake maker. The important thing is to retain the ideas of cleansing to make ready, the need

of power to make it happen, and a result of something to share with everyone. As always, be safety-conscious!

Instead of holding up the doves in silent prayer in the **Prayer activity**, you could have a time of open prayer.

As an alternative to 'saying sorry' as part of the dove **Prayer activity**, a **Prayer of confession** could form a separate element in the service, using similar words, but receiving assurance of forgiveness by coming forward and dipping hands in the bowl of water (towels will be needed), or the worship leader could sprinkle the congregation with water from the bowl, to remember the cleansing power of the Spirit. This could be done silently, or with background music or a worship song.

Online resources

All suggested downloads are available at www.scriptureunion.org.uk/light. Visit www.lightlive.org for additional activities for children, young people and adults. For your convenience, the following activity is available as a download YearB. BaptismofChrist_2 for 5s and under Make a dove.

Second Sunday of Epiphany

READINGS: **1 Samuel 3:1–10; John 1:43–51**
Psalm 139:1–6,13–18; Revelation 5:1–10

Bible foundations

Aim: to explore what it means to hear God calling us

Samuel is clearly a very special child. The book of 1 Samuel begins with the story of his parents, a so-far childless couple, Elkanah and Hannah. Hannah's grief and her prayer for a son are described in chapter 1. She promises that, if God grants her request, she will dedicate him to the Lord (1:11). This touching story is played out against the background of the corrupt and doomed priesthood of Eli and his sons. It begins with a stark but unsurprising observation about the rarity of words from God (v 1) – clearly a time of national spiritual decline.

Samuel, the much-longed-for son, is sent in due course to serve at the Temple alongside Eli. The priesthood of Eli and his family seems to continue the spiritually fetid atmosphere of the time of the judges. Samuel's family is different and his dedication to God is clear. He fulfils his mother's vow but we know little more about him at this stage, other than that he hears God speak to him three times without recognising God's voice (3:4,6,8). Eli at least still has the presence of mind to understand that it is God speaking (v 9). Samuel's godly heritage and his unassuming innocence seem attractive prompts to the persistence of God in calling his servant.

Unlike Samuel, Nathanael was found by Philip, whom Jesus himself had found. Unlike Samuel, Nathanael is not full of innocence and youthful naivety. He even seems slightly cynical (John 1:46) but that doesn't seem to put off Philip or Jesus. In fact, Jesus seems to appreciate his candour. Nathanael is open to listen and respond to the words of Jesus, and in this he resembles Samuel but not Jacob (otherwise known as 'Israel') who met with God at Bethel (Genesis 28:10–22; 35:1–15). Jacob was a twister and schemer by nature (Genesis 25:19–28; 30:25–43). Jesus promises Nathanael that he will be blessed with even greater divine revelations, this time just like his ancestor Jacob (John 1:50,51).

Beginning the service

With: pictures of different people whose appearance might suggest an occupation, eg slim woman, muscled person, clever-looking person with glasses, person with long fingers – either on PowerPoint or actual images, available as a download (YearB.Epiphany2_1)

Display the pictures. Ask which person is most likely to be a pianist, a builder, a ballet dancer or a scientist. Accept all answers, asking why anyone picked their candidate. Encourage people to disagree and make alternative suggestions. The person with the long fingers could be a ballet dancer or a scientist, for example. How we look is no way of knowing whether or not God will call us. In fact, he speaks with all sorts of surprising people throughout history. Explain that we are going to hear how God spoke with two very different people in the Bible and how they listened.

Bible reading

The readings from 1 Samuel 3:1–10 and John 1:43–51 both lend themselves to a dramatic reading. It would be useful to read 1 Samuel 3:1–10 partway through the **Bible talk**. The Gospel reading could come later in the **Bible talk**, or stand alone in a different part of the service. Psalm 139:1–6,18 is included in the **Prayer activity**.

Bible retelling

Ask an older man from the congregation to prepare this in advance. Use the following monologue script, available as a download (YearB.Epiphany2_2). Your actor could adapt it to his natural language. This could come in the **Bible talk** or towards the end of the service to reiterate the surprising nature of the call of God.

(The actor leans on a stick, led in by a young man or teenager who exits; the actor then sits down.)

Thanks Sam… My name's Eli. I serve as a priest in the place of worship. The routine there hasn't changed for decades… centuries even. I never expect anything to change. I just do my best to worship God. I am not sure if he ever hears! But I know he stopped speaking out loud to me and my people some time ago. When I was a lad I thought God was a bit of a chatterbox, he had so much to say, but not now. We just don't expect it any more.

Oh, I loved God… and I loved my boys! Too much, I suppose. They were always a bit wild, but as they got older they got more and more wild. They were cruel, and forced people to give them the best food. They were rude too. (*Sighs.*) I was in charge of a country, and I couldn't even handle my sons. The country was in a bad way too. And then God told me judgement was coming. I wasn't surprised that God should say that but I was surprised by the way he told me!

A few years ago a woman arrived for the festival with her young son. I had caught her pleading with God for this son to be born some years before. But now, here she was, with her young son and she wanted him to live with me so he could serve God. I couldn't say 'No', could I?

I was training this boy to take over the

routines for me. Good boy he was, too. One night he couldn't sleep. Kept coming in and asking what I wanted. 'Nothing,' I told him. 'Go back to sleep.' Afterwards I couldn't believe how slow I was. He came back twice more, asking what I wanted. And only after the third time did I realise he wasn't dreaming. Someone was actually calling him. And that someone was God. Now that did surprise me. God hadn't been talking much for a while. That poor boy had no idea it was God, until I told him. I had not prepared him to listen out for God. Sam was amazed that God might speak to him!

The next morning, he didn't want to tell me what God had said. I couldn't see why he didn't want to. But God was using him to tell me about my faults and those of my sons. I eventually got it out of him!

Now he's grown into a fine young man. He's gone on listening to God's voice. Sam! Sam! (calling) Is it time to blow out the lamps? (Sam enters and leads actor off stage.)

Bible talk

With: a clock with a second hand or digital face, large enough for everyone to see; a triangle or similar instrument to create a quiet, clear, single sound

Show the clock and explain that you are going to sit in silence for 30 seconds (or longer if people can take it!). During this time, someone, who is hidden, makes a quiet single sound on the triangle three times, separated by ten seconds. After this, ask what people heard (which will include sounds other than the triangle). When did they realise it was a triangle, the first, second or

third time? What stopped them from hearing things? What makes someone a good listener? Are children better listeners than adults? Be aware that people with hearing loss may not hear, but that is one of the answers to the question: What stopped people from hearing? – physical disability.

Listen to the reading from 1 Samuel 3:1–10. Alternatively, present the monologue from **Bible retelling**.

Samuel hears God call

Samuel was a young boy who lived in the place where people came to worship God. Eli, the priest, looked after this place and Samuel helped him. Explain how Eli's sons were bad men and how Eli seemed to have given up. In fact, people had just given up expecting God to speak. It was all very depressing!

But then, completely unexpectedly, God spoke. Check that people know the story. Samuel was asleep (v 3) and then he was listening but he did not immediately recognise that it was God (v 7). Ask why he might not have recognised God's call. You would not expect someone so young to be the first person God chose to speak to after a long time of apparent silence. You would probably have expected God to speak to Eli. But God speaks to all sorts of people, in all sorts of ways. Refer back to the discussion at **Beginning the service** about how God speaks to unexpected people.

If you have used Psalm 139 in any way earlier in the service, refer to that as an expression of how God knows us through and through and is with us, wherever we are; he's always ready to respond to us and to welcome our response. This psalm is part of the following **Prayer activity**.

Nathanael hears Jesus call

Read John 1:43–51 and ask people to listen out for what Jesus says to Nathanael. Ask what sort of person Nathanael was – proud of his Jewish background, sceptical, willing to give something a go. Jesus' first words to Nathanael have an immediate impact. Jesus knows him! This registers with Nathanael and he responds in making some amazing claims about Jesus which he could hardly have understood! He then went on to become one of Jesus' closest followers. Here is another person Jesus called. Maybe not the sort of person we would have expected to have mattered to Jesus!

What does it mean to listen out for God and respond to him? What stops us hearing? (We may be distracted with other things; we may not be used to recognising God's voice just as Samuel wasn't; or we may not be expecting him to communicate with us, just like the people of Israel weren't.)

We can hear God call

What helps us to hear God? (We may be with others who were thrilled about Jesus as Nathanael was; we may be helped by others to recognise God's voice as Eli did; we may just be listening carefully, expecting God to speak.) He speaks to all people, even the most unexpected, and is close to all people, as Psalm 139 emphasises. Sometimes he speaks in a way that we cannot miss (at this point clang the triangle several times) but sometimes it is a single sound.

If possible, ask someone to share their personal testimony of how they have known God communicating with them, maybe in a surprising way.

Prayer activity

To respond to God's call, we need to listen out for God's voice. Ask everyone to close their eyes as though asleep (but you want them to listen and not sleep!). Read Psalm 139:1–6,18 twice, asking everyone to listen out for one thing that the psalmist says about what God does. Allow for a short time of silence, as long a time as people are comfortable. Then invite people to call out the one thing that has struck them. This could be done in small groups.

Conclude with the following: Thank you, God, for always being with us, always near us and always willing to communicate with us. Help us to listen!

Ending the service

Ask everyone to think of one activity they are going to do this week – it need not be anything special. Then ask them to think of how busy they may be in that activity and what might stop them from being aware of God and listening to him. Remind people of how Nathanael was with Philip who was enthusing about Jesus, and how much we need to be with others who are expecting God to communicate with them. This will help us to listen out for God. Then lead in prayer and, after each silence, sound the triangle once.

Father God, thank you that you will be with us this week when we are… *(think of the activity)*. *(Triangle)*
Father God, we may be so busy that we

forget to listen out for you and do not expect you to be with us. (*Silence followed by the triangle.*)
Father God, help us to listen to you and respond. (*Silence followed by the triangle.*) Amen.

Helpful extras

Music and song ideas
Songs might include those about listening to and responding to God's call such as 'I the Lord of sea and sky'; 'Brother, sister, let me serve you'; 'Be still, for the presence of the Lord'.

Statement of faith
This is also available as a download (YearB. Epiphany2_3).

Creator God, we believe that you have made us.
Loving God, we believe that you love us.
Speaking God, we believe that you communicate with us.
Working God, we believe you equip us.
Living God, we believe you live in us.
Sovereign God, we believe you are our King.
Help us to listen to you and follow your call.
Amen.

Notes and comments

You will probably have at least one person in the congregation with a hearing disability. Acknowledge that they may not have heard the triangle in the **Bible talk** but this does not mean that they have not been listening. Hearing loss is one example of what stops us hearing others. Some people are spiritually deaf, which is a common theme in the prophets (Isaiah 6:9). And God speaks with us, whatever our hearing ability. If you use a triangle later in the service, you could accompany it by waving a flag too. Children could play other percussion instruments during the service.

If you are using the *Revised Common Lectionary* with 1 Corinthians 6:12–20 as a reading, comment on how the apostle Paul was implying that people were not listening and were questioning everything, as though they just did not want to accept how God wants us to live.

If there is a baptism during the service, it may be appropriate to focus on Nathanael and the initial call 'from darkness to light' along with the requirement this places on us to actively follow. If Nathanael had carried on sitting under the tree and not responded to what Philip had told him, he would never have learned more or become a disciple. Parents today have listened to God and if a child is being baptised, they need to help their child to learn to listen out for God.

If this is Education Sunday you may wish to pray for schools. You can download prayer material for schools and teachers from www.cte.org. uk. In the light of today's theme, you could especially pray for children with hearing loss.

Online resources

All suggested downloads are available at www.scriptureunion.org.uk/light. Visit www.lightlive.org for additional activities for children, young people and adults. For your convenience, the following options are available as downloads: YearB. Epiphany2_4 for 5s and under Joining in the Bible story; YearB.Epiphany2_5 Making puppets.

Third Sunday of Epiphany (Common Worship)

READINGS: **Revelation 19:6–10; John 2:1–11**
Genesis 14:17–20; Psalm 128

Bible foundations

Aim: to discover how Jesus came to the rescue in a family crisis

The first public event recorded in John's Gospel is a very homely affair. Jesus, the Word, really has come to share his life with ordinary human beings (John 1:14). The occasion is a wedding feast in crisis which he is abundantly able to resolve. His mother alerts him to the need (2:3), though the stakes are actually much higher than that.

Faithful Jewish families were looking forward to the feast when they would eat and drink with their ancestors in God's presence at the day of the Lord – the 'Messianic Banquet' (Isaiah 25:1–10, especially v 6), an expectation embraced by Jesus (Matthew 8:11; Luke 14:15–24) and most especially at the Last Supper (Matthew 26:27–29). It was expected that, when the Messiah came, Israel would experience great blessing and abundance. So there is an eschatological flavour here just as there is when Jesus feeds the 5,000 in John 6. John has, moreover, begun this account with a nod in the direction of Jesus' resurrection with his reference to the 'third day' in verse 1. Later, the first Christians couldn't miss the reference to this. No wonder the steward says '… you have saved the best wine till now' (v 10). John adds that Jesus had 'revealed his glory' (v 11).

This wonderful hope is taken up in the book of Revelation. It is alluded to in Revelation 3:20, as the risen Lord promises to enter and eat with those who open the door to him, and later on in the wonderful celebration in heaven. The great whore, Babylon, has been destroyed (Revelation 19:2,3). This takes place in the presence of God's people, his family, represented by the 24 elders and four living creatures (v 4 and in chs 4,5). A multitude of people worship God at the 'wedding supper of the Lamb' (v 9) as the Messiah receives his own bride, a pure and spotless church (v 8).

Beginning the service

Ask if anyone has seen the film *Shrek*. If yes, ask them to explain how Princess Fiona had to be rescued. If no, explain that the princess was locked up in a tower guarded by a dragon, waiting to be rescued by a prince. Suggest that although no one in the congregation has been rescued from a tower and fire-breathing dragon, we may all have had crises from which we needed rescuing. Ask if anyone will briefly share a situation where someone had to rescue them (eg from a spider in a bath or physical rescue when in danger or rescue from an embarrassing conversation at a party).

Explain that today we see how Jesus rescued a family caught up in a crisis.

Bible reading

The passage from John 2 is suitable for a dramatised reading. A dramatised version of the reading from John 2 is available as a download (YearB.Epiphany3_4).

The reading from Revelation 19:6−10 is filled with drama. The whole reading could be accompanied by a drumbeat which gets louder but stops sharply at the end of verse 9. The words of the crowd could be read by several people together. For maximum effect, both readings need to be practised.

Bible talk

With: episode 2 of *Wastewatchers* DVD (SU) or another video retelling of the wedding at Cana; several people dressed up to go to a wedding (at least two to be really smart and at least two to be wearing comfortable clothes rather than smart ones, because they know they will be on their feet for hours and may not be able to afford anything really smart − include children and young people)

Wedding guests

Invite the wedding guests to the front. Ask them how they chose what to wear and why. Those who are not smart should talk about how their mum/wife/friends had criticised them for wearing the clothes they chose. Brief at least one guest to talk about being embarrassed by what others are wearing or by what they themselves are wearing. Does it matter what we wear to a wedding? Ask the guests to comment on this. They can then sit down.

Wearing the right clothes or label really does seem trivial compared to issues of global warming, famine, war and refugees. On one level it doesn't matter what we wear at a wedding. Keeping up with the fashions or concern about our appearance can get out of hand!

At this point you could include the reading from Revelation 19:6−10 to put weddings into an eternal perspective.

Jesus at a wedding

But the story about Jesus at a wedding indicates that even the most insignificant things matter to God. We may sometimes limit our prayers because we feel we cannot bother God with something trivial. How do we know that God likes to be bothered with the apparently trivial details of our lives? Read John 2:1−11.

Retell the story briefly or show a

DVD retelling, such as episode 2 from *Wastewatchers* DVD (SU). Jesus was a guest at this wedding. Maybe there was a family connection, because the initial invitation seems to have been Mary's. Jesus doesn't appear to have been an usher, or the best man, and had no part in the proceedings except to be a good guest. But an embarrassing incident occurred. On the last day of the extended celebrations, the family ran out of wine. On the scale of living in an occupied land and being effectively under the rule of the pagan Romans, the problem was trivial. Few guests would have noticed or probably cared, but it was a social embarrassment. Mary asked Jesus to help them out.

Despite saying it wasn't yet time to reveal himself, Jesus acted. He miraculously supplied them with litres of the highest quality wine. Embarrassment reduced. Crisis solved. Face saved. Social standing maintained. Jesus was bothered by this small incident.

What was the outcome? His disciples put their faith in him. They saw he was more than just a great storyteller. What things about Jesus did they discover?
• Jesus even cared about trivial things.
• Jesus' generosity was overflowing – the guests weren't going to drink up all that wine. The family had months', if not years' worth of wine. This was no stingy half measure to provide 'enough', but a gracious outpouring of excess.
• God could do the miraculous.

So, what can we learn about God?
• God is bothered by even small, social crises in our lives.

• God is generous in the way he blesses us.
• God may choose to do something miraculous – if we will only ask him.

If possible, think of personal illustrations of this.

Prayer activity

With: three prayer stations for intercessory prayer – for a personal request; for a request for somewhere in the world/community; and for others – see materials for each station

Ask everyone to identify three things they want to ask God to do: a prayer for themselves, a prayer for a place (local or global) and a prayer for another person. Encourage everyone to move around the activities, pausing to speak with God as appropriate. (*Top Tips on Prompting Prayer* contains loads of ideas on leading interactive prayer. See page 64 for details.)

Personal request: A large sheet of paper with the outline of a person drawn on it, pens
Instruction: **Write your name or draw your face on this person as you talk to God about yourself.**

Place: A large map of the world on the wall, Post-it notes, pens
Instruction: **On the Post-it note, write or draw the place and what you would like God to do. Stick the note on the map.**

Others: Heart-shaped pieces of card, colouring materials
Instruction: **On the heart, draw something that reminds you of the person you are praying for. Take the card with you as a bookmark or put it**

in your pocket to remind you to go on praying for them.

Prayer of confession

Everyone joins in the response – **Help us to see you more clearly**.

Leader: Jesus, forgive us when we think you're not interested in what bothers us.
Help us to see you more clearly.
Leader: Father, forgive us when we forget how generous you are.
Help us to see you more clearly.
Leader: Spirit, forgive us when we don't expect you to come and work in our lives.
Help us to see you more clearly.
Leader: Gracious God, forgive us when we refuse to let you love us.
Help us to see you more clearly.

Ending the service

There was a crisis in the story of the wedding and Jesus did something about it. Sometimes we need to act to help others in a crisis. Challenge everyone to think about ways, small or big, that they can intervene or get involved in helping other people in crisis. Remind them that it is God who strengthens and equips us to do his work. If you support an agency that is working with those in some form of crisis, pray specifically for them. Then send people out with a blessing, so that they can go and bless others.

Bless us, Lord, in good times and sad times.
Strengthen us with your Spirit.
Inspire us through your example.
Challenge us through your Word.
Grant us the peace of knowing you are with us,
So that we might offer your peace to others in troubled times.
Amen.

Helpful extras

Music and song ideas
Songs about knowing God in crises could include: 'Blessed be your name'; 'We have sung our songs of victory'; 'Faithful God'; 'Guide me, O thou great Redeemer' and a version of Psalm 23.

It may be apt to offer to pray for people during a time of sung worship, if they are facing tough times. Make sure the pray-ers are experienced and know church guidelines on confidentiality and appropriate use of touch.

Statement of faith
This is also available as a download (YearB. Epiphany3_5). It is always good to remind ourselves and each other what God is like.

Oh, Lord God!
You are a God of miracles.
You are a God who gets involved in our ordinary lives.
You are a God who is bothered by what bothers us.
You are a God who rescues us and goes with us.
You are a God who will lead us in good and bad times.
You are a God whose love is so amazing we cannot understand it.
You are a God who chooses ordinary people to follow you.
You are a God who makes ordinary people

extraordinary.
You are our God and we love you.

Notes and comments

The miracle of providing wine at a wedding could also foreshadow the pouring out of Jesus' own blood like wine (and symbolised in a service of Holy Communion) as he pays the price of becoming our groom. If there is a celebration of Holy Communion within the service, this parallel could be drawn at an appropriate point.

In the **Prayer activity**, provide alternatives for those with mobility problems. They could be given an outline of a person, an image of a globe and a heart-shaped card, with space to draw or write.

If your congregation is used to sharing testimonies, you might extend the **Beginning the service** activity and even cut out the reference to *Shrek*. People could

be encouraged to share situations where God has rescued them.

The readings in the *Revised Common Lectionary* are completely different to those in *Common Worship*. A complete all-age session for these readings is available as download Year B.Epiphany3RCL. This session was written for *Light for the Lectionary January–March 2009*.

Online resources

All suggested downloads are available at www.scriptureunion.org.uk/light. Visit www.lightlive.org for additional activities for children, young people and adults. For your convenience, the following activities are available as downloads: Year B.Epiphany3_1 Discussion material for young people and adults; Year B. Epiphany3_2 Adult sermon; Year B. Epiphany3_3 Bible story and action song.

Top Tips on Prompting prayer
978 1 84427 322 5

What does the Bible say about prayer? How can you use all the senses to stimulate a relationship with God? This readable and practical guide is packed with wisdom and ideas that will inspire anyone wanting to strengthen children's and young people's conversations with God.

For more details, visit www.scriptureunion.org.uk

Fourth Sunday of Epiphany

READINGS: **Psalm 111; Mark 1:21–28**
Deuteronomy 18:15–20; Revelation 12:1–5a

Bible foundations

Aim: to recognise Jesus' uniqueness, seen in his powerful teaching and his authority over evil

The first step in real wisdom is to recognise that the Lord is to be feared (Psalm 111:10). Psalm 111 offers the reader many reasons to worship God. Firstly, the psalmist considers how great the works of the Lord are (vs 2–4). He then reminds us of God's provision and covenant love for his people (v 5). Next,, he rejoices in God's provision of a land (v 6) even at the expense of others, and that God can be relied upon in all that he says and does (vs 7,8). Finally, he speaks of how God has redeemed his people (v 9). All good reasons to cry out with wonder to the God of gods and Lord of lords! Although many psalms recognise the darker side of life, nothing clouds the horizon of our writer.

The passage in Mark presents a more troubling picture. Demonic power is present and powerful even in the synagogue as the people of God meet to worship (vs 21–24). The language, as well as the action, is violent: the man 'cries out' at the fear of destruction; Jesus rebukes and commands silence, and the man convulses and cries out again – this time with a 'shriek' (vs 24–26). No wonder the people are amazed (vs 22,27). However, the story makes clear that it is not just the violent and inappropriate happenings that amaze the crowd, but Jesus himself. Here is a man who speaks and acts with unparalleled authority and power. If they were amazed before the incident (v 22), they were even more so afterwards (v 27). Not the usual Sabbath worship! They had never seen anything so dramatic before; they regard his actions as a 'new teaching' (v 27). They are not yet at the point reached by the first disciples who asked, 'Who is this?', after Jesus stilled the storm (Mark 4:41), a question answered only gradually in the course of Mark's Gospel (8:27–30; 15:39).

Beginning the service

With: flip chart or other method of recording ideas

Invite people to talk about the teachers they most remember – in a good way. They could do this in small groups or as a whole congregation. Encourage children to participate fully, although young children will not have had many teachers thus far to be able to remember!

Ask why these teachers were important. It probably wasn't because they got their facts right or were particularly clever. The really significant teachers were often those who inspired us or made us feel special. Record people's answers on the flip chart.

Explain that today's Gospel reading is about an occasion when Jesus was teaching and then healing. People were amazed and told their friends and neighbours all about it. Ask the congregation why they think Jesus was an amazing teacher. Once again, record some of the answers and compare them with the previous comments about teachers.

Jesus was an incredible teacher: he was entertaining, told stories, spoke to individuals and said things that were astonishingly relevant and life-changing. As we shall see today, he also had an incredible authority. He spoke and things happened; people were freed from evil and lives were changed.

Give thanks for teachers and for the impact they have had on us. Ask God to teach us today through Jesus.

Bible reading

The reading from Mark 1:21–28 could be read as a drama. Psalm 111 is suggested as a **Statement of faith** available as a download (YearB.Epiphany4_1).

Bible talk

With: some volunteers and two boxes, each containing a different list of instructions on brightly coloured paper (see below)

Briefly retell the story of Jesus healing the man with the evil spirit, demonstrating his powerful and authoritative teaching (Mark 1:22) and his powerful authority to heal, even evil spirits (1:27). Comment on the contrast that people made between Jesus and the teachers of the Law.

Jesus' words had authority

Ask two volunteers to come to the front. They are going to help us understand why Jesus spoke and acted with such authority. Volunteer A represents what and how Jesus taught while Volunteer B represents the way the teachers of the Law of Moses (the scribes and the Pharisees) taught.

Place the appropriate box in front of each volunteer and tell Volunteer B that their box contains a sheet of paper but they are not to look inside. Invite Volunteer A to look inside their box. Ask both of them to tell the congregation what is inside their box, starting with Volunteer B, who still has not looked inside. Volunteer A should be able to comment on the colour and shape of the paper.

Ask how reliable these two volunteers are. One has first-hand knowledge – they've had a look. The other has only got someone else's word for it. This is the first difference between Jesus and the other teachers. The scribes and Pharisees learnt about God from books, but Jesus knew God personally. This made him a more reliable witness. His words therefore had more weight: more 'authority'.

Jesus knew God his father
Ask the two volunteers to open their boxes and show everyone what is inside, without revealing what is written on the instruction sheet. Both volunteers have a different set of instructions about how to follow a route around the building. Explain that the two volunteers now need to guide someone (Volunteer C) around the room following these instructions.

Volunteer B goes first, reading a set of written instructions to shout at Volunteer C, who attempts to follow them. The instructions on B's paper should be vague and complicated, making this a challenging task. Volunteer C tries to follow them.

Now ask Volunteer A to reveal what is on their instruction paper, which simply says 'Follow me' written in large letters. In much smaller writing on the sheet are some simple instructions around the building to guide Volunteer A, who then does what is said, taking Volunteer C with them. They should be able to do this easily.

Discuss this new challenge with the congregation. Was Volunteer A or Volunteer B in a better position to act as a guide? The answer should be that Volunteer A was a better guide all round! Jesus was like Volunteer A. He knew what it was like to

be human because he had lived an ordinary human life. He knew how to walk with God because God was his father and he spent time with him. It was not just head knowledge or complicated theory. This made him a better teacher and a real 'authority' on living God's way. The scribes and Pharisees just had their rules.

Jesus was God himself
Jesus had authority not just because he was a good teacher. He had authority because of who he was. He had the right to forgive sins or release people from evil because he was the Son of God. Jesus used his power and authority to set people free. Those who saw and heard him could not deny his authority or that he was uniquely different.

We live in a world where lots of people, organisations and religions claim to be right and to speak with authority. It can be very confusing and it undermines the confidence of Christians. But the ultimate authority can only be found in God the Father, the Son and the Holy Spirit. It is only in God that we can put our complete trust. Conclude this by singing at least two songs that state the basis of our confidence. Let people reflect on the words before singing them, to be sure that they mean them!

Prayer activity

With: paper strips; pens; other materials for making paper chains

Talk about the many forms of evil that can imprison or trap people, including crime, bitterness, hate, illness or injustice. Put this into child-friendly language by talking about being really unhappy or lonely or bullied. Jesus cast out evil spirits. He also died to set people free from evil and the effects of evil. Invite people to draw or write some of their ideas on the strips of paper. Encourage them to think of real situations that they know about in the news or in everyday life, but suggest they be discreet about sensitive details. This could be done in small groups if appropriate.

Turn the strips of paper into paper chains. Depending on the size or nature of your group, make them either into handcuffs or big chains trailing around the room. Once the chains have been made, invite people to hold them up. Explain that you are going to say, 'Jesus wants to set us free!' When this happens everyone should break the chains as dramatically (and safely) as possible. Do this in a prayerful way, with a pause for reflection and thought beforehand.

Invite people to take their broken links home as a reminder to keep praying for those who need to be released from whatever is binding them.

Prayer of confession

With: PowerPoint slides of things Jesus said: 'Be quiet'; 'Be still'; 'Be clean'; 'Be opened'; 'Your sins are forgiven'; 'Get up'; 'Follow me' – available as a download (YearB.Epiphany4_2)

Talk about the stories in which Jesus says some of these phrases: he tells evil spirits to 'Be quiet!'; he tells the wind to 'Be still!'; he tells people with skin diseases to 'Be clean!'; he says to the lips of a mute man, 'Be opened!' and to a lame man, 'Get up!'; he often calls out 'Follow me!'

These are words of authority that change the way things are because it is Jesus who is saying them. He still speaks to us through the Bible and through prayer. We need to listen to him, because these words still speak to us. Jesus is always present, willing to welcome, forgive and transform us.

Ask God to forgive us for all the times when we have not listened. Then run through the PowerPoint slides a couple of times while musicians play 'Be still, for the presence of the Lord' quietly and meditatively. Do this slowly with someone reading out Jesus' words with appropriate weight and warmth.

Alternatively, if you use a printed liturgy, ask members of the congregation to say the words of absolution to each other, catching the eye of those around them as they do so. This would be one way of allowing Jesus to speak to us – through our brothers and sisters. (Some congregations may be sensitive about asking lay people to 'pronounce absolution', so do what is appropriate for your group.)

Ending the service

Finish the service by discussing the final verse of the psalm: 'The fear of the LORD is the beginning of wisdom'. The psalmist doesn't say that we should be scared of God, but that we should be in awe of him; aware of his great power, authority and glory. That was how people responded to Jesus in the Gospel story. When we begin to appreciate how truly astonishing and significant God is, our whole life will be transformed.

Today, we have spent time thinking about the power and authority of God in Jesus. We can trust him. On the basis of that, say the Grace together, slowly and thoughtfully – each person can really trust that God will 'be with us all, evermore'.

Helpful extras

Music and song ideas

There are many songs that celebrate the power and authority of Jesus: 'Be still, for the presence of the Lord'; 'He is the Lord and he reigns on high'; 'My Jesus, my Saviour'; 'Show your power, O Lord'; 'Thou whose almighty Word'; 'When the music fades'; 'Our confidence is in the Lord'. Other songs that pick up the theme of his authority over evil: 'Great is the darkness'; 'He that is in us'; 'Jesus, we celebrate your victory'; 'There is power in the name of Jesus'; 'Victory is on our lips and in our lives'. You could choose a song based on Psalm 111 or a version of the psalm set to music.

Statement of faith

A statement of faith based on Psalm 111 is available as a download (YearB.Epiphany4_1) and could be printed on service sheets or displayed on a projector. Introduce it as follows: The psalms were often used in worship by the people of Israel. Some psalms are prayers; others are songs of praise. Some are very specific; others are quite general. These words, based on Psalm 111, give us an opportunity to thank God for all the things he has done for us as we make this bold statement that God does great things. We can trust in his authoritative words and actions! Ask people to think of specific things that they would like to give thanks for as you make this declaration.

Notes and comments

If you have not recognised Education Sunday this year, you could download prayer material for schools and teachers from www.cte. org.uk to use in **Beginning the service**. It might be possible to run a parallel activity for younger children. They could then make cards to give to those teachers. They could be encouraged to think of Jesus as a really special teacher.

The word 'authority' can mean power to control, judge, influence or limit others. It can also refer to someone who is an expert or a reliable witness. It would be worth looking at some dictionary definitions of 'authority' to reflect on the meaning of the word. A home group or youth group could be asked to look at the word 'authority' in relation to Jesus and present their thoughts in a creative way as part of the service.

The **Prayer of confession** builds on the concept of Jesus' authority and would fit well after the **Bible talk** or after the presentation suggested above. Some churches may choose to have the confession later in the service than normal, which is possible for most denominations, even in a service of Holy Communion.

Online resources

All suggested downloads are available at www.scriptureunion.org.uk/light. Visit www.lightlive.org for additional activities for children, young people and adults. The following activities are available as downloads: YearB.Epiphany4_3 Prayer response; YearB.Epiphany4_4 Adult sermon.

Third Sunday before Lent

READINGS: **Isaiah 40:21–31; Mark 1:29–39**
Psalm 147:1–11,20c; 1 Corinthians 9:16–23

Bible foundations

Aim: to acknowledge that God gives strength to the weak

The note of incredulity in Isaiah's voice is unmistakable. He has been challenging Israel to make comparisons between God and idols of wood and gold. It's almost laughable. There is no possible comparison. Israel, of all peoples, should know. God is incomparable. Isaiah reminds them, in case they have forgotten, that it is the God of all creation we are speaking of. The creator and sustainer of all that is (Isaiah 40:21–23). The power-brokers of this world are like chess pieces under his fingers (v 23). They are blown about like insubstantial plant life. When the people of Israel look up at the creation around them, they are to remember that it is their God who made it all.

So what is their problem? They think God has forgotten them and that their experience of exile indicates that perhaps, after all, he is not so powerful and great (v 27). They are downtrodden and weak. The people who had rejoiced in their deliverance from slavery in Egypt were now little more than slaves once again – exhausted, demoralised, weak, powerless and hopeless. It is to them that this message comes. The endlessly powerful God will give them strength to cope. Where everyone else would collapse, they would be given the strength of eagles, the swiftness and power of runners and the ability to persist when they want to give up in despair.

The description we have of Jesus' ministry is the counterpoint to Isaiah's majestic claims. It is domestic and small-scale. Simon's sick mother-in-law is taken by the hand and the fever leaves her (Mark 1:31). Queues of sick and demon-possessed people are healed and delivered (vs 32–34). The source of Jesus' power to heal the sick and weak is founded upon a cultivated and vibrant relationship with his Father (vs 35–39) – this is the same God of creation who helped Israel to cope in exile and who is with Jesus as he takes the gospel to neighbouring towns.

Beginning the service

With: a pole with two inflated balloons tied to each end, a pin

If possible, enact the following scenario, making it as amusing as possible:
A strongman (possibly dressed in a leopard skin) is seen flexing his muscles. In front of him is a pole with a large balloon fixed to each end. It is important that the strongman is not seen carrying the pole, so it should be placed there by someone else. The strongman is obviously gearing up to pick up the pole. He grasps it, tries to pick it up, but then lets go and pretends that was just a practice. After several attempts it is obvious to the audience that the pole is too heavy, but that the strongman doesn't want to admit it. While he flexes his muscles with his back turned, a child creeps up with a pin and bursts the balloons. The strongman turns back, makes a final attempt to lift the pole, which to his surprise he manages to do. In triumph he holds it above his head and walks off.

Explain that in today's service you will be thinking about someone who is very strong, who gives his strength to help us, the weak. See **Notes and comments** for an alternative way to begin the service.

Bible reading

The Bible reading from Isaiah 40:21–28 is about God's strength. The congregation joins in with a response after verses 22, 24, 26 and 28. This is, 'Lord, you are mighty and powerful and strong.' A PowerPoint version of Isaiah 40:21–28 using the CEV is available as a download (YearB.3B4Lent_1). Teach the response to the congregation. Verses 29–31 of this passage are also on the PowerPoint. Use these at the end of the **Bible talk.**

Read Mark 1:29–39, if you are not including the drama in **Bible retelling** below.

Bible retelling

With: the script below, also available as a download (YearB.3B4Lent_2)

Ask five people to enact this simple drama based on Mark 1:29–39. They do not need to learn the script (which can be on the back of A4 cards showing their character's name) but should rehearse it before the performance so that they can add actions as appropriate. The actors sit in a row on identical chairs. Each stands to speak and then sits down again.

Simon: I am Simon.
Family: I am Simon's family.
Mother-in-law: I am Simon's mother-in-law.
Jesus: I am Jesus.
Crowd: I am a crowd.
Simon: Please come to my house, Jesus.
Jesus: Thank you, Simon.
Simon: Here we are. Where's mother-in-law?
Family: She's ill in bed with a fever.
Simon: That is sad.
Jesus: I'll go and see her.
Mother-in-law: Oh dear, I feel hot and sticky and not at all well.
Jesus: Get up, my dear.
Mother-in-law: I feel better! I will cook dinner.
Family: Hurrah! Jesus has made Granny better!

Crowd: *(Use a different voice for each sentence.)* Jesus can make people better. Let's take our sick friends and relatives to him. Yes, let's.

Jesus: *(Stands and makes 'laying on hands' movements.)*

Crowd: They are all better! It's amazing! *(To indicate night time everyone rests their head on folded hands as if asleep. To make it more amusing, everyone could lean in the same direction and all move head and hands to the other side at the same moment. After a while Jesus sits up straight while the others continue to sleep. They then all sit up straight.)*

Crowd: *(Use different voices.)* Is Jesus here? Is Jesus here? Is Jesus here?

Family: He must have got up early.

Simon: I'll go and look for him. *(Pause.)* Ah, here you are, praying. Everyone wants to see you again.

Jesus: I must go on to other places and talk to them about God too.

Bible talk

With: a long, strong rope for a tug of war, knotted at each end; seven very large luggage labels to attach to the rope – labelled with the following words – Strong, Weak, Simon, Mother-in-law/Granny, Crowd, Jesus and one blank label (The 'Weak' label also has 'Strong' written on the other side), a whistle/bell/drum

Begin by saying we seem to be at the fairground today. Not only did we meet a strongman at **Beginning the service**, but now we also have an old-fashioned fairground game – tug of war.

Who is strong and who is weak?
Invite six people to come to the front and create two fairly balanced teams. Explain that each team needs to pull their end of the rope as hard as possible at the sound of a whistle/bell/drum roll. After one 'go', ask which of your volunteers is the strongest then rearrange the teams so that the strong person is against all the others. This should mean that the strong person loses because they are weaker than the combined strength of the others. Explain that we all want to be really strong people. But none of us is really strong. Even if our bodies are strong, we are weak in other ways. We might not be able to do as well at school as we would like or perhaps we find it hard to be truthful or feel we can't do things we want to do. Two of the volunteers (of about the same strength) then stretch the rope across the front of church. *(The rest can sit down.)* Fix the 'Strong' label to the end where the group of volunteers pulled and the 'Weak' label to the other end.

Granny/Mother-on-law is weak
Refer to the story from Mark. Read it aloud if you have not included the drama in **Bible retelling**, and ask who the characters were. Observe that most of these people were not strong. Show the 'Mother-in-law/Granny' label. Explain what 'mother-in-law' means, saying that as well as being Simon's wife's mother she was probably Granny to his children. We know she was weak as she was ill in bed, having a fever and not able to get up. Fix her label to the weak end of the rope.

Simon is weak
Show the 'Simon' label. He and the rest of his family were weak, not because they were sick but because they were powerless. They were worried about Granny's illness but there was

nothing they could do about it. Fix Simon's label to the weak end of the rope.

The crowd is weak

Show the 'Crowd' label. These were people who all had some problem. They were sick or worried or seeking help. They were weak and could not help themselves. Fix their label on the weak end of the rope.

Jesus gives strength to the weak

And there was another character in the story. Who was it? Jesus came to Simon's house and gave Granny back her physical strength. He took away the worries from Simon and his family by bringing his power into the situation. He gave strength to the weak and sick people in the crowd. Fix the 'Jesus' label to the weak end of the rope and turn the Weak label around. Now both sides are strong. Invite the two volunteers to have a go at pulling and it should be fairly evenly balanced.

If you have included the reading from 1 Corinthians 9, you could mention how God helped Paul to be strong.

Show the blank label and suggest people think about their own name being there. In a few moments of quiet, fix the blank label on the weak-now-strong end. Remind everyone that on our own we have no hope of reaching the strong position. Only with strength from God can we do that. Say that when you read the verses from Isaiah about God's strength you did not read them all. Now you are going to read the rest, reminding each other of God giving his strength to us, who are weak. Show the second part of the PowerPoint download

(YearB.3B4Lent_1) and read Isaiah 40:29–31 aloud together.

Prayer activity

With: a large cardboard hand (made from an A2 sheet); pens; Post-it notes

Display the hand and ask the congregation to suggest words describing God's strength, eg 'powerful', 'strong', 'creator'. Adults and older children could be asked to find words in Psalm 147, if you have used the psalm. Write these boldly all over the hand. Pray: 'Lord God, we praise you for your strength and power.'

Ask everyone to think of weak people they know or who are currently in the news, or those who are powerless or sick and in need of God's strength. Let everyone write the names (or younger children could draw the people) on Post-it notes and stick these on to the hand. Draw everything together with a prayer such as: 'Lord God, we bring to you these people who are weak, sick and powerless, to ask you to give them your strength.'

Prayer of confession

Teach the response **'Lord, forgive us… and help us to rely on your strength.'**

Divide the congregation into two halves. Suggest one side says the beginning of the response 'Lord, forgive us…' and the other side the second part '… and help us to rely on your strength.' Remind everyone that although they may only be saying some of the words with their mouths, they can say all of them in their heads.

Use the following or similar words, repeating the response in two parts after each section:

Lord, we know we are weak and in our daily lives we sometimes forget about you, go our own way and do things in our own strength.
Response
Lord, we know we are weak and in our daily lives we sometimes ignore your wisdom and think up our own ways of working things out.
Response
Lord, we know we are weak and in our daily lives we sometimes use our own words instead of asking you for the right words to say.
Response
Lord, we know we are weak and yet we so easily try to rely on our own strength.
Response

Finish with words of absolution or by thanking God for his forgiveness.

Ending the service

Remind everybody that as we leave we do not go in our own strength, but in God's. Give everyone a Post-it note or small slip of paper on which to write 'God's strength'. Suggest that everyone gives their paper to someone else to slip into their shoe. Ask them to pray for that person as you all read Isaiah 40: 29–31 again together (see **Bible talk** above). Finish with a prayer such as 'Lord, bless each one of us as we walk in your strength this week.'

Helpful extras

Music and song ideas
Sing hymns and songs that tell about God's strength and his support for the weak. 'Give

thanks with a grateful heart'; 'Praise, my soul, the King of heaven'; 'Come let us sing of a wonderful love'; 'Make way'; 'Safe in the shadow of the Lord'; 'Blessed be the name of the Lord' and 'God of grace and God of glory'. 'Strong Tower' based on Proverbs 18:10 from *Bitesize Bible Songs* (SU) is a *Learn and remember* verse to help everyone remember that God is strong and safe.

Notes and comments

An alternative **Beginning the service** could be the showing of a series of pictures of 'strong things'. These could include an athlete (eg a javelin or discus thrower); a very dark cup of tea; a mature tree; a piece of equipment in a children's play area (eg climbing bars) and a heavy vehicle such as a tractor, digger or tank. Challenge the congregation to discover the link between the pictures.

In *Pilgrim's Progress* there is the story of a fire that is in constant danger of being put out, but which somehow manages to keep burning brightly. Christian is shown that, behind the scenes, oil is continually being poured onto the fire. This illustration of God giving his strength to the weak could be used in the service, but should not be copied!.

Online resources
All suggested downloads are available at www.scriptureunion.org.uk/light. Visit www.lightlive.org for additional activities for children, young people and adults. For your convenience, the following activity is available as a download:
YearB.3B4Lent_3
Finger rhyme for 5s and under.

Second Sunday before Lent

READINGS: **Colossians 1:15–20; John 1:1–14**
Psalm 104:24–35; Proverbs 8:1,22–31

Bible foundations

Aim: to explore what it means that Jesus is the Word of God

Both passages today find their origins in the Jewish concept of God's Wisdom. The easiest place to read about this is Proverbs 8:22–31 where Wisdom is spoken of as an attribute of God, like his Word: something identifiable in its own right. God's Wisdom, his Word, was there and helped at the beginning of creation. This idea fed into both Paul's and John's presentation of the Lord Jesus Christ.

John 1:1–5 uses similar language to that of Proverbs to confirm not only that the Word was there at the very outset of creation but actually was God. We might speak of them separately but they are the same. The Word was both light and life – both identified in John's Gospel with Jesus (8:12; 14:6). Though God's Word was in the world, even his own people did not recognise or embrace him (1:10–13). The astonishing turning point of this passage comes in verse 14 with the announcement that this Word of God has become flesh and shared human life with ordinary beings. Jesus has brought grace upon grace (v 16). Indeed he is 'full of grace and truth' (vs 14,17). While God cannot be seen, his Son has made him known (v 18).

Colossians 1:15–20 echoes many of these insights. Like Wisdom, Christ is God's very image and was present at the very moment of creation (vs 15,16). All creation was intended for his pleasure and he holds all things together as he sustains the creation (v 17). So the Lord of all creation is now discovered to be the Lord of the new creation in the church (vs 18–20). He is the church's founder, being the first to be raised from the dead. Paul's hymn to Christ reaches its climax with the acclamation that all God's fullness dwells in him and that he has reconciled all things to God through the cross. All this goes well beyond what could ever have been said of Wisdom in the Old Testament.

Beginning the service

Before the service display the word code puzzle available as a download (YearB.2B4Lent_1) or have paper copies available for each person or small group. There are missing letters which spell out 'WELCOME TODAY TO OUR SERVICE'. Show the finished puzzle and say that a welcome is given today to everyone present. But words are more than marks on a page or a screen, so say that you welcome people with spoken words too. Actions also convey the message of welcome. You hope that by the end of the service you will all have met with and have more understanding of God's living Word, Jesus Christ.

Bible reading

In John 1:1–14, Jesus is called 'the Word'. Explain that we will be thinking about what it means that Jesus is the 'Word of God'. To help us understand the reading better, everyone is invited to say 'Jesus' each time 'the Word' is mentioned. A PowerPoint presentation of John 1:1–14 from the CEV is available as a download (YearB.2B4Lent_2). This includes 'Jesus' added at the relevant places. If using another translation, the reader should pause after 'Word' each time for the congregation to say 'Jesus'.

The **Statement of faith**, especially in its simplest form, version 3, could be used as the main reading – see below. This is based on Colossians 1:15–20.

Bible talk

With: a dictionary or encyclopedia and a person who can explain a difficult word or idea; a recipe book and a person to demonstrate a simple cookery activity in church, such as making a sandwich or decorating a biscuit with tube icing; a handwritten letter and a mobile phone with someone in the congregation ready to make a call; a Bible; three large labels saying 'Jesus'

Show the dictionary/encyclopedia, the recipe book, the letter and the Bible, and ask what they all have in common. The answer you are looking for is that they are all full of words. Say that in fact our whole lives are full of words. We come across them in different forms all the time. You are going to look at how words are used in four particular ways to see if they can help us understand about Jesus being the Word of God.

Words help us understand

Hold up the dictionary/encyclopedia. Ask what this type of book is for. It is full of facts and words to help us learn about and understand the world around us. Challenge someone in the congregation (primed in advance) to find a word or subject that puzzles them. Let them read out the word and part of the explanation. But however helpful these books are, they can still be difficult for us. How much better it is to have a real person to explain something to us. Bring on your expert and ask them to explain a pre-decided idea. Ask them more questions so that they simplify the answer even more. (For instance, they could be asked what a unicorn is. Answer: a mythical animal. Question: what does 'mythical' mean? Answer: imaginary, not real. Question: what is a unicorn supposed to look like? And so on.)

Say that having a real person can help us to understand much better.

Words and actions show us what to do

Hold up the recipe book. Ask if anyone has tried to use one and had a disaster in the kitchen. Agree that it's wonderful to be creative, but recipes are not always easy to follow. You could read out some cooking terms such as 'fold in' or 'a moderate oven'. How much better it is when someone actually shows us what to do. At this point your cookery expert demonstrates their very quick recipe. Do not allow this activity to be a distraction. For those who cannot see, the expert could talk into a microphone as they demonstrate.

Words communicate that we are loved

Hold up the letter. Ask who has received one like this recently and agree that it's great to know that we are loved and remembered. At some point here, mid-sentence if possible, your collaborator in the congregation should be ringing the phone so that you stop to answer it, exclaiming with delight how good it is to talk to your friend. Don't carry the one-sided conversation on too long, but point out that letters are great but it is even more precious to be able to talk to our loved ones. Real people are more than just words on paper.

Ask a child to come forward and hold up the dictionary/encyclopedia again. Remind everyone that this is a book of facts. Ask another child to hold the recipe book, reminding everyone that this is a book about creating things. Ask a third child to hold the letter, reminding everyone that these are words of love.

The Bible and Jesus himself are God's Word

Hold up the Bible and point out that this book is all of these things: a book of facts about God and how he deals with people, a book telling us that he is the Creator, and above all, a book with a message of love. But the Bible is not just a collection of long and short words. Like every book there is a person behind it. Jesus is the Word of God. He is the one who gives us understanding (indicate the dictionary); he is the one who spoke and the world was created (indicate the recipe book); he is the one who showed how much God loves us by dying on the cross for us and rising again (indicate the letter). As you point to each book, give the child holding it a label saying 'Jesus'.

Finish by pointing out that none of us can fully understand what it means for Jesus to be the Word of God, but just as we learn new words all through our lives, so Jesus, God's Word, can help us to learn more and more about him. End by reading John 1:1–3,14 adding 'Jesus' each time the Word is mentioned.

Prayer activity

With: a balloon for each group of five to six people (tie helium-filled balloons to a chair or pew, with the long string looped to keep them at a suitable height, and if using ordinary air-filled balloons provide a long garden cane for each group); pens to write on the balloons; flip chart or OHP (optional). (It would be sensible to have spare balloons in case some burst.)

Remind everybody that the service is all

about Jesus, the Word of God and about how great and wonderful he is. Challenge everyone to think of some of the phrases about Jesus that have been said (perhaps from the Bible) or sung in one of the songs or hymns. Ask them to call out these phrases in praise of Jesus. If you wish, write some of these on the flip chart or OHP.

Ask each group to write words of praise to Jesus on their balloon. They could refer to the flip chart or OHP, if you have used it. Young children could draw patterns or pictures instead of writing. Each member of the group should have the chance to write or draw something in praise of Jesus. When all the groups have finished, the balloons should be prepared for 'take off'. Air-filled balloons should be tied to the end of the cane and the loop on the string should be loosened for the helium-filled ones (although the end should remain tied). At a signal, all the balloons should be held up high or released as far as the string will allow.

Bring all your praises of Jesus together with words such as the following: Lord Jesus, we praise you for your creative power, for your love of us that took you to the cross, and for your resurrection life. We praise you that you are the Word of God.

Ending the service

Refer back to **Beginning the service** when you prayed that everyone would have more understanding of God's living Word, Jesus Christ. You hope this has happened, but understanding on its own is not enough. You also prayed that everyone would have met with Jesus, the Word of God. Say that a

passage in Proverbs, all about Wisdom, is also thought to be about Jesus, and this is what Wisdom says: read Proverbs 8:35 from the CEV or NIV. Pray together that everyone will find Jesus, God's Word, and will continue to walk with him. End with words of blessing.

Helpful extras
Music and song ideas
Many favourite songs and hymns exalt Jesus and he is often referred to as the Word. Among traditional hymns are 'At the name of Jesus'; 'Crown him with many crowns' and 'Come let us join our cheerful songs'. More modern hymns include 'Christ triumphant, ever reigning'; 'Jesus is king and I will extol him'; 'Jesus is Lord! Creation's voice proclaims it'; 'Meekness and majesty'; 'Name of all majesty'. 'The Word' based on John 1:14 from *Bitesize Bible Songs* (SU) is a *Learn and remember* verse to help everyone remember Jesus is God's Word.

Statement of faith
This statement of faith has the reading from Colossians 1:15–20 as its basis and could be used in several ways. Several versions are available on PowerPoint as a download (YearB.2B4Lent_3). They include a CEV version and NIV with individual or congregational responses, with version 3 as a simplified statement for children. In a fourth version, not downloadable, the leader can read the statements below while the congregation reads the verses from Colossians 1 from church Bibles as follows:

We believe that Jesus is God.
Read verse 15.
We believe that Jesus is the Creator.

Read verses 16,17.
We believe that Jesus lives in heaven now and is leader and guide over us, his church.
Read verse 18.
We believe that Jesus came to earth to live and die for us, so that we can have life through him.
Read verses 19 and 20.

Notes and comments

With a subject as immense and deep as 'Jesus the Word of God' you can only scratch the surface. It is important that children can engage with the subject and so the writer has deliberately kept to examples of 'words' that they will understand, and also has not confused them by using the word 'Logos'. But it is also important that adults and young people deepen their understanding of, or even think for the first time about, Jesus as the Word of God, so quite difficult Bible passages have been quoted at length. The service is meant to work as a whole: on its own the **Bible talk** can appear quite shallow and it needs the support of the other elements of the service and particularly the **Bible reading** and **Statement of faith** to bring out the teaching about Jesus as the Word of God.

Online resources

All suggested downloads are available at www.scriptureunion.org.uk/light. Visit www.lightlive.org for additional activities for children, young people and adults.

The four service outlines for Palm Sunday, Maundy Thursday, Good Friday and Easter Day suggest setting up a series of prayer stations as part of the journey of Holy Week. These are incorporated into each service. They take time to prepare and require the imagination and commitment of church members (of all ages!). Consider providing an all-age service or even an all-age Passover meal on Maundy Thursday if you do not normally do so.

If you set up a series of prayer stations in the church during Holy Week, you could invite members of the local community to visit the church building to travel on this Easter journey. In particular you could invite local schools to participate. For details and ideas of what churches have done during Holy Week visit http://www.scriptureunion.org.uk/MakingChurchSchoolLinks/SeasonalEvents and http://www.scriptureunion.org.uk/HolidayandMidweekClubs/Otheroutreachideas.

Top Tips on Explaining the cross

Helen Franklin, Steve Hutchinson and Robert Willoughby
32pp £2.99
How do you explain the meaning of the cross to people of
all ages in your congregation? This book will provide you
with invaluable fresh insights as you prepare for Lent and
Easter.

Easter Cracked

£9.99
A resource book packed full of craft, drama, all-age service
ideas and much more, to help you prepare for Easter!

Easter Bible Comic

£1.99 each or £15 for pack of 20
Discover the story of Easter with this great comic-strip
retelling of the Bible story. Uncover the real meaning of
Easter through the puzzles, quizzes, facts and information. A
great accompaniment to Easter events, a Sunday school prize
or Easter present for children aged 8 to 11.

To find out more, visit your local Christian bookshop, call 0845 0706 006 or go to
www.scripturunion.org.uk/shop

Sunday before Lent

READINGS: **2 Kings 2:1–12; Mark 9:2–9**
Psalm 50:1–6; 2 Corinthians 4:3–6

Bible foundations

Aim: to reflect on the character of God as shown in the stories of the death of Elijah and the transfiguration

Transcendence, the common theme of today's Bible readings, is that which is beyond ordinary, common human experience. We find it hard to grasp, so we tend to concentrate on the material aspects of faith. Yet, as Paul wrote in 2 Corinthians 4:3–6, God shines light into our hearts, the good news of Christ, so that we can begin to grasp what is beyond our human existence.

We say that God moves in mysterious ways, beyond what we can think of or imagine. Psalm 50 attempts to describe God in his mightiness and awe. The fiery chariot which carried Elijah to heaven and the dazzling brightness of Jesus on the mountain are more than the mind can take in, and are only two of the many examples that the Bible gives us of the awesome nature of God. See also Moses' experience in Exodus 3, the dedication of the Temple in 2 Chronicles 7 and the commissioning of the prophet in Isaiah 6.

We need not shy away from transcendent experiences but should welcome them, even seek them since, throughout history, God has spoken in and through them. He spoke to Elisha through the prophets who clearly anticipated that Elijah was about to die. By permitting Elisha to see Elijah's departure, God bestowed his Spirit on him. There are clear parallels when the terrified disciples witnessed the dazzling display of brightness and cloud on the mountain top and heard God speak. It was an event which deeply affected them and is significantly recorded in the three synoptic Gospels (Matthew 17:1–8; Mark 9:1–8 and Luke 9:28–36, and is perhaps referred to by two of the witnesses in 2 Peter 1:16–18 and John 1:14). In both events, the almighty God stepped into the lives of individuals giving them an awareness of his amazing power and authority which in different ways he had bestowed on Elijah and Jesus.

Let us bring an element of wonder and awe into today's worship.

Beginning the service

Ask the congregation to sit quietly to listen to a recording of orchestral music, while thinking about the character of God. Afterwards, let them call out words to describe the music such as 'strong', 'mighty' or 'mysterious'. Suggested music might be Gustav Holst: *Planet Suite*, 'Jupiter'; Richard Strauss: *Thus Spoke Zarathustra (2001: A Space Odyssey);* or Gounod: 'Judex' from *Mors et Vita*. Fade out the music after a minute.

Bible reading

The Old Testament reading from 2 Kings 2:1–12 lends itself to a dramatic reading. It is also available as a download (Year B. SunB4Lent_1). Ideally this requires six readers but it could be done with four or five.

Reader 1: Not long before the LORD took Elijah up into heaven in a strong wind, Elijah and Elisha were leaving Gilgal. Elijah said to Elisha,

Reader 2: The LORD wants me to go to Bethel, but you must stay here.

Reader 1: Elisha replied,

Reader 3: I swear by the living LORD and by your own life that I will stay with you no matter what!

Reader 1: And he went with Elijah to Bethel. A group of prophets who lived there asked Elisha,

Readers 4,5,6: Do you know that today the LORD is going to take away your master?

Reader 3: Yes, I do. But don't remind me of it.

Reader 2: Elisha, now the LORD wants me to go to Jericho, but you must stay here.

Reader 3: I swear by the living LORD and

by your own life that I will stay with you no matter what!

Reader 1: And he went with Elijah to Jericho. A group of prophets who lived there asked Elisha,

Readers 4,5,6: Do you know that today the LORD is going to take away your master?

Reader 3: Yes, I do. But don't remind me of it.

Reader 1: Elijah then said to Elisha,

Reader 2: Now the LORD wants me to go to the Jordan River, but you must stay here.

Reader 3: I swear by the living LORD and by your own life that I will never leave you!

Reader 1: So the two of them walked on together. Fifty prophets followed Elijah and Elisha from Jericho, then stood at a distance and watched as the two men walked toward the river. When they got there, Elijah took off his coat, then he rolled it up and struck the water with it. At once a path opened up through the river, and the two of them walked across on dry ground. After they had reached the other side, Elijah said,

Reader 2: Elisha, the LORD will soon take me away. What can I do for you before that happens?

Reader 3: Please give me twice as much of your power as you give the other prophets, so I can be the one who takes your place as their leader.

Reader 2: It won't be easy. It can happen only if you see me as I am being taken away.

Reader 1: Elijah and Elisha were walking along and talking, when suddenly there appeared between them a flaming chariot pulled by fiery horses. Right away, a strong wind took Elijah up into heaven. Elisha saw this and shouted,

Reader 3: Israel's cavalry and chariots

have taken my master away!
Reader 1: After Elijah had gone, Elisha tore his clothes in sorrow.
2 Kings 2:1–12 (CEV)

Bible talk

With: whiteboard or large paper and pens; three round circles of card with faces on – A: two wide eyes and open mouth, B: ordinary eyes and downturned mouth, C: ordinary eyes and a straight, determined smile

Ask children and young people to suggest something really big and then ask for a suitable suggestion with something even bigger. Write sentences such as 'Gorillas are really big; whales are bigger'. Repeat each statement, this time finishing off with 'But God is even bigger/higher/greater/more wonderful!'

In today's Bible story about the death of Elijah and the transfiguration of Jesus, we hear how some quite ordinary people were completely amazed by the greatness of God. It was a bit like a crash course in learning things about God. Ask if anyone has ever been on a crash course, for example, to learn to type or ski. Why are crash courses needed? It's no good going on any course though, unless what is learnt is put into practice. Elisha and Jesus' disciples discovered some wonderful things about God but they needed to discover what it meant in practice.

Elisha discovers God's greatness
Look at Elisha first. Check that everyone has heard the story and its details. Elisha knew something unusual was about to happen and he wasn't very happy. *(Show face B.)* What was

he unhappy about? (Two groups of prophets had told him that his master Elijah would soon be taken by God.) He would have preferred not to talk about it. Yet he was determined to be there when the inevitable happened, in spite of his conflicting emotions and sense of confusion.

Elisha was so worried that he refused to let Elijah out of his sight for a moment. Then came the terrifying chariot and horses of fire, accompanied by a whirlwind. *(Show face A.)* What was God doing? Elisha cried out in a mixture of wonder, terror and grief. He had lost the man who was like a father to him.

Elisha's greatest wish was to take up Elijah's role and do the same things Elijah had done. He asked Elijah to give him twice as much of his power. But this was not a gift that Elijah could give. It could only come from God. Elisha was left completely alone. After weeping with sorrow, he picked up the cloak that Elijah had left behind, and immediately tested whether Elijah's God had given him the power he had asked for. At the very first attempt, he succeeded in repeating one of Elijah's miracles (parting the waters of the River Jordan). This crash course was just the beginning of Elisha's service for God. *(Show face C.)* From now on, Elisha expected God to do great things!

The disciples discover God's greatness
Turn now to Peter, James and John. Check that everyone is aware of what happened. Jesus had gone up the mountain with his disciples and Jesus changed right there in front of them. His disciples simply did not know what was happening, or why. *(Show face A.)* Peter was so terrified when Moses and Elijah appeared on the mountain

that he started to say things he did not quite understand. He was scared. *(Show face B.)* This encounter, often called the transfiguration of Jesus, was something of a crash course. What on earth were Moses and Elijah doing? Actually it would have made some sense to Jesus' Jewish disciples. The Jews were waiting for the Messiah. They knew all about these two most important characters in the history of the Jewish faith. The appearance of Moses and Elijah was like a sign of approval of Jesus.

On the way down the mountain, Jesus explained to the disciples that they were not to tell anyone what they had seen, not until after he had come alive again. He was preparing them for his own death, something they could not understand. It only began to make sense after Jesus had died, risen and returned to heaven. For now, they were aware that there were things that they had to do and they went on expecting Jesus to do great things. *(Show face C.)*

Many things about God may confuse or even upset us. *(Show face B.)* There may be things about God that amaze us. *(Show face A.)* As Elisha, Peter, James and John discovered, God does not do what we expect. They were caught up in awe and wonder at his power and might and what we might call 'transcendence'. As they had to learn, we too can't try to freeze what we have discovered, seen or experienced. We have to take in what we have learnt about God (as part of what we might call a crash course) and then put it into practice. *(Show face C.)*

Remind everyone that God is bigger, greater and more amazing than the limited pictures we have of him and he wants to communicate wonderful things to us.

Prayer activity

With: a set of slides of awe-inspiring scenes from nature as a background to the meditative prayer, available as a download (YearB.SunB4Lent_2)

Ask the congregation to sit quietly and look at the images while you read the following aloud.

I ask the sun, 'Who is your father?'
I ask the lightning, 'Who put you in the sky?'
I ask the distant sea, 'Who causes you to spread so far?'
I ask the stars, 'Where do you end?'
I ask the depths of the earth, 'What secrets do you hold?'
I ask the volcano, 'Who has awoken you?'
I ask the storm, 'What message do you have for me?'

They all answer, 'God is our beginning. He designed us and made us move. In each of us you see his glory, power and love.'

O God, my Father! Although I am so small and helpless, I lift my head to you. Let me encounter you in your greatness, glory and majesty. I am here because you want me here. You have given me life. Tell me what you want me to do and let your name be glorified in me. Amen.

Ending the service

The doxology from Jude 24 and 25 may be particularly appropriate as a means of ending the service. It can be read by the leader to the congregation in the second person (you), as it appears in the Bible, or it can be said by everyone together in the first person (we). The text for the latter is available as a PowerPoint download (YearB.SunB4Lent_3).

You may like to read aloud the testimony by Blaise Pascal, the famous French mathematician and philosopher, who lived in the 17th century, which is available as a download (YearB.SunB4Lent_4).

Helpful extras

Music and song ideas
Choose hymns or songs which speak of God's greatness, such as 'All heaven declares'; 'The Lord is King!'; 'When I look into your holiness'; 'He is exalted'; 'Be still, for the presence of the Lord'; 'My God is greater than…'; 'Jesus is greater than the greatest hero'; 'Our God is a great big God'; 'Our God is so big, so strong and so mighty'; 'Immortal, invisible, God only wise'.

Statement of faith
The congregation makes the following response after each statement in this statement of faith: **But we trust in you.**
You are a great God who made a wonderful world.
You are far beyond what we can ever understand.
But we trust in you.
You work in ways that we do not expect.
You are far beyond what we can ever understand.
But we trust in you.
You make yourself known to us in all sorts of ways, as we speak with you, as we read about you, as we meet with others, in our dreams

and in the silence.
You are far beyond what we can ever understand.
But we trust in you.
You know all people by their personal name, all across the world.
You are far beyond what we can ever understand.
But we trust in you.

Notes and comments
The word for 'transfiguration' used in the New Testament is the word translated by the English word 'metamorphosis' which can mean 'transformation' or 'transmutation'. The word is used four times in the New Testament. It is translated twice as 'transfigured' and twice as 'transformed'.

This is a challenging story for young children who experience life very literally. You will need to reassure them that God was with Elisha as he began to serve God, and Jesus tried to help his disciples understand what had happened as they went down the mountain.

Online resources
All suggested downloads are available at www.scriptureunion.org.uk/light. Visit www.lightlive.org for additional activities for children, young people and adults. For your convenience, the following activities are available as downloads: YearB.SunB4Lent_5 Alternative prayer activity; YearB.SunB4Lent_6 Illustrations for adult sermon; YearB.SunB4Lent_7 Bible engagement for 8 to 11s.

First Sunday of Lent

READINGS: **Genesis 9:8–17; 1 Peter 3:18–22**
Psalm 25:1–10; Mark 1:9–15

Bible foundations

Aim: to see how God made and kept his promise to Noah

Genesis 3 records the first sin and subsequent judgement by God. As the human capacity for sin is not reduced in any way, God determines to wipe out humanity from his creation (Genesis 6:5–7). Noah, however, has God's approval and is instructed to build an ark to survive the ensuing flood (Genesis 6:8–22). God intends to begin again with Noah, to make a new covenant with him (9:9). This covenant embraces the whole of creation which has survived the flood. His covenant promise is to never again destroy the earth by flood (9:11). Covenants always have signs and in this case it is the sign of the rainbow (vs 12–17). God commits himself to this sign. It is not to be simply a reminder for Noah and his family, for when God sees the rainbow he too will be reminded of the promise.

1 Peter 3:18–22 has been described as one of the most obscure and difficult passages in the New Testament and many interpretations have been proposed. However, the main point must be why Peter sets off on this exposition at this point in his letter. It comes in the middle of a passage about Christian attitudes to persecution. The outcome of Christ's death (v 18) was that he atoned for sin. When he was raised he went to preach to rebellious fallen spirits from the time of Noah before God judged the world with the flood (vs 19,20). At that time, as now, a small minority remained faithful while the rest persecuted them. Noah and his family were saved by water; baptism, as a symbol of God's grace, saves us now (v 21) and acts as a sign of God's promise of ultimate salvation, however harsh the persecution might be. The risen Christ who now sits at the right hand of God is ample reassurance (v 22), better even than a rainbow in the sky.

Beginning the service

With: a line, or hooks, on which to hang up (football) boots and (boxing) gloves

Begin by welcoming people to the service. Then ask, 'Can anyone tell me what it means when someone hangs up their boots?' It means retirement. *(Hang up the boots.)* Ask, 'What does it mean when someone hangs up their gloves?' They have finished with their boxing career. *(Hang up the gloves.)* In our service today these ideas will be developed as we think of the peace that God offers to us.

Bible reading

For the reading from Genesis 9:8–17 use the NIV or TNIV. The reading is linked to five pictures on a screen (to be reused as a focus for prayer later) – pictures of: a family (v 8); birds/animals (v 10a); ark/boat (v 10b); river or coast (v 11); rainbow (vs 12,13). These are available as a download (YearB.Lent1_1). The reading is prefaced by the following introduction: God promises never to destroy the earth again. He gives the rainbow as a sign of this agreement. The word 'covenant' means a binding agreement or promise.

Psalm 25 is used in the **Prayer of confession**.

The reading from 1 Peter 3:18–22 has three images, also available on a download (YearB.Lent2_1): a cross (v 18); a baptismal pool/font (whatever style is used in your church) (v 21); an empty tomb (v 22). There is the following introduction: Peter thinks of the good things achieved by Christ's suffering on the cross. He not only secured resurrection

life but is now in authority in heaven.

Bible talk

The talk, split into two sections to encourage concentration and recall, is based on the fact that the Hebrew word for 'rainbow' is the same word used to refer to a bow as a military weapon. The *Learn and remember* suggestion in **Notes and comments** could follow on from the talk.

Part 1
With: three objects: a globe (or a stamp album, or a cross, or compass with the four points of the compass on display); an Easter egg; a bow and arrow (toy or real one from an archer)

God of the entire world
Remind everyone of the story of Noah and then take the globe/album/compass and explain how God was now making an agreement not just with Noah's family but with the whole world, every living creature, bird and animal. God is the **God of the entire world**. This was the news to north and east and west and south.

God of new life
Then take the Easter egg. Talk about why we have Easter eggs, as a sign of new life. Check how many eggs anyone has already eaten in anticipation of Easter! Explain that in Genesis 9:11 God is the God of **life**. He promises never to destroy the earth with a flood again. After the flood there is **new life**.

God of peace
Finally, take the bow and arrow. Ask if there are arrow references in the reading. No! God

has put away the arrows of anger. He has decided to hang up his bow as well. You could make reference to the fact that he displayed the bow in the sky. Link this to hanging up boots and gloves (see **Beginning the service**). It isn't that God has retired but that he has put away his anger. He is a God of **peace**, a God who **loves** his creation.

Part 2

After other activities (such as the **Prayer activity**) recap the first part referring again to the visual aids (the entire world, new life and peace). Look now at how Jesus fulfils these, picking up the emboldened words in Part One.

God made his agreement with all living creatures, **the entire world**. Where is there evidence that Jesus came not just for Jews but for all people? Is there evidence that Jesus had control of nature? (The miracle of the loaves and fishes and calming the storm.)

God promised **new life** on earth. What do we associate with Easter Sunday? New life, not just on earth but after death. **Resurrection life.**

God hung up his bow to assure us of his **love and peace**. Where do we see Jesus assuring us of God's love and peace? He welcomed outsiders such as women, Samaritans, people with skin diseases, tax collectors and non-Jews. He came to bring peace between God and all people who have disobeyed God. The apostle Paul referred to Jesus as the Reconciler. We worship the God of the world, the God of resurrection life, the God of peace. Our God keeps his promises.

Prayer activity

With: the pictures from the Bible reading from Genesis 9; card; pens

Individuals or small groups have a card and pen on which to write the following five categories from the story of Noah: a family (Genesis 9:8); birds/animals (v 10a); ark/boat (v 10b); river or coast (v 11); rainbow (v 12) and to write down their own suggestions for intercession. This will also serve as a takeaway reminder of the main points from the reading. Alternatively five representatives can lead each section using their own suggestions, or use the following:

(Picture of family.) Lord, we thank you that you saved the family of Noah at the time of the flood. We pray for our own family: our parents, grandparents, uncles and aunts, nephews, nieces, godparents and godchildren and the church family here today. We pray especially for... Help us to live happily together, putting others first instead of ourselves.

(Picture of birds/animals.) Lord, we thank you that you have given us a beautiful world. We thank you for the birds, the animals and the insects. Especially we thank you for... Help us to take care of your world.

(Picture of ark.) Lord, you are a God who works to save us, just as you saved Noah in the ark. We remember all those who teach others about how you want to save all people, those who teach adults and younger members in our church. Especially we name...

(Picture of coast.) Lord, we thank you for the coasts, seas and waterways. We pray for

those who sail on the sea, transporting goods and people. Keep them safe when the sea is rough and stormy. We remember especially...

(Picture of rainbow.) Lord, thank you for your promise of peace. You declared that you would never destroy and flood the earth again. We pray for areas of the world where there is little peace. Especially... Help us to work for peace among our family and friends.

Lord, you are a God of promise, a God of peace and a God of power. May we walk in your ways and become more like Jesus. Amen.

Prayer of confession

This prayer is based on Psalm 25 using two voices. Ideally it is spoken in a measured but urgent way from opposite parts of the worship space.

Voice 1: Remember not my sins, O Lord, remember them not.
Voice 2: Remember not the sins of my youth, O Lord, remember them not.
Voice 1: According to your love remember me.
Voice 2: Remember your great mercy and love, for they are from of old.
Voice 1: To you, O Lord, I lift up my soul.
Voice 2: In you, O God, I put my trust.
Voice 1: Show me your ways, O Lord, and teach me your paths.
Voice 2: Guide me in your truth and teach me.
Voice 1: Good and upright is the Lord.
Voice 2: Therefore he instructs sinners in his ways.
Voice 1: He guides the humble in what is right.

Voice 2: He teaches them his way.
Voice 1: You are God.
Voice 2: You are God, my Saviour
Voice 1: and my hope is in you.
Voice 2: My hope is in you all day long.
Voice 1: You are God, my Saviour
Voice 2: and my hope is in you all day long.
Voices 1 and 2: You are God, our Saviour, and our hope is in you all day long.
Psalm 25 (NIV)

Ending the service

The environment and green issues are often talked about in our society. We must look after our world and protect it as best we can. To close the service everyone says together the *Learn and remember* verse in Genesis 9:13, as suggested in **Notes and comments**. God keeps his promise.

Helpful extras

Music and song ideas

A theme hymn for the next three services of Lent could highlight the theme of covenant promise. 'Amazing grace' includes the line 'the Lord has promised good to me'. 'Great is your faithfulness' is also apt for learning about covenants. The modern version includes the line 'You have fulfilled all your promise to me'.

The following hymns fit in with the biblical teaching, another opportunity to reinforce the main teaching. 'Lord of our life' picks up themes of life, every nation and peace. 'Love is his word' picks up the ideas of life and love. 'Peace is flowing like a river' stresses 'Peace to you'; 'Who put the colours in the rainbow?' ties in with the rainbow in the passage.

Notes and comments

Be sensitive. God promised never to destroy the earth through flooding but there are local floods and tsunamis. These are sometimes the result of our own greed and poor management of the world, but not always.

If there is a local Rainbow group, invite them to come to the service and interview a leader about the work of Rainbows. If there is a local Rainbow Hospice, feature their work in bringing peace and love and healing and hope.

One way of ending Part I of the **Bible talk** is to read the version of the story from page 29 of *The Street Bible* (Rob Lacey). To conclude the **Bible talk**, encourage everyone to learn and remember Genesis 9:13 to help them remember God's promise. You might prefer to shorten it as follows: The rainbow will remind you that I will keep my promise forever.

Even if this is not your usual practice, sharing the Peace could be built into part of the service. People used to wear swords down their left side. To draw out the sword, the right hand was used. If we were to punch someone most of us would use our right fist. To shake hands with our right hand we are showing we are people of peace. We are not using our right hand to draw a sword to attack them. We are extending our hand (not clenching it in a fist) to show we are people of peace.

The colours of the rainbow are named so you could create your own rainbow. Select a child/adult wearing something red, others with orange, yellow, green, light blue, dark blue (indigo) and violet. Line them up in order at the front. (Take in your own supply of coloured T-shirts!)

Online resources

All suggested downloads are available at www.scriptureunion.org.uk/light. Visit www.lightlive.org for additional activities for children, young people and adults. For your convenience, the following activities are available: YearB.Lent1_2 Adult sermon; YearB.Lent1_3 for 5s and under Bible story and prayer; YearB. Lent1_4 for 5s and under Rainbow fun.

Second Sunday of Lent

READINGS: **Genesis 17:1–7,15,16; Romans 4:13–25**
Psalm 22:23–31; Mark 8:31–38

Bible foundations

Aim: to see how God made and kept his promise to Abraham

This is the point at which God confirmed his repeated promise to Abraham with the sign of circumcision. The relationship between God and Abraham develops over the course of Genesis 12–24. In chapter 12 God calls Abraham to leave Ur and makes general promises to him; in chapter 15 God develops his promises with reference to the son who will be born to his wife, Sarai. In chapter 17 God confirms those promises again and expands them. This is a relationship based upon promise, not what Abraham can do for God but what God will do for Abraham. Abraham simply had to believe. See Genesis 15:6 and Romans 4:3,22.

Genesis 15:6 is crucial to Paul's argument in Romans 4. In the previous three chapters he has demonstrated that God has no favourites; neither Jew nor Gentile can consider themselves righteous before God. Paul then settles down to show that this has always been the case. Some Jews had seemed to think that they were considered to be righteous before God on the basis of obeying the Law of Moses. We cannot be sure that they all thought this, but certainly some did. This is likely since human beings tend to seek to justify themselves. For Paul, Abraham was a crucial example. He preceded the giving of the Law to Moses by hundreds of years and it was clearly his faith that pleased God, not what he did as such. God's promise was simply based on Abraham's faith (Romans 4:13). God's promise, based on his grace, operates by means of human faith (v 16). So Abraham's descendants cannot only be those who possess the Law (the Jews) but everyone who is able to exercise faith (v 17) – many nations, huge numbers of descendants. God's promise includes all today who exercise faith in that way (vs 23–25).

Beginning the service

Explain that last week you looked at the promise God made to Noah, and today you will be looking at the promises God made to Abraham. We worship God. He is a God of promise. He not only makes promises but he keeps them as well.

Ask everyone to think imaginatively about what they would expect in the following situation: a friend of the family promises that something special will happen on your birthday. Ask for suggestions for what this might be. This makes you think of the sort of things this friend has said and done before. Ask for more imaginary suggestions. Just before your birthday this friend falls ill. What might this mean? *(Pause for suggestions.)* You get home from school on your birthday and still nothing special. *(Pause for suggestions.)* Just before bedtime, the phone rings. It is the friend, calling from his hospital bed. He says he has not forgotten the promise and if you look outside the front door at 9pm, you will find something special. At nine o'clock exactly, you cautiously open the door and there is a cat carrier containing one small kitten – for you! It's what you have always wanted. The promise has been kept. Ask how you would feel about the friend now and the promise that was made!

Bible reading

Introduce Genesis 17:1–7,15,16 by saying: God makes a number of promises to Abraham. He does this in what is called a covenant or solemn agreement. Listen carefully and see how many promises you can notice. The reader should speak the relevant

verses of promise with greater emphasis and deliberation. Note verse 4b ('father of many nations'); verse 6c ('kings will come from you'); verse 7c ('be your God and the God of your descendants'); verse 16 ('I ... will surely give you a son by her'). After the reading ask people to pick out and name the promises. Alternatively this could be left until the **Bible talk.**

Introduce the reading from Romans 4:13–25 by saying: Paul explains how Abraham pleased God. It was not because he kept the Jewish Law, which did not exist in Abraham's time. It was because he was a person of faith. He trusted totally in God and in the promises of God.

Bible talk

With: four visual aids – a baby's toy or item of baby clothing; a globe; a crown; a symbol of a personal relationship with God, perhaps a confirmation book, hymn book or a well-used Bible – pictures available as a download (YearB.Lent2_1)

Begin with a demonstration of faith and trust. Blindfold someone and direct them round the worship space, perhaps around obstacles. The speaker, or person who directs, promises to guide reliably. The blindfolded person needs to trust. Alternatively, refer back to the imaginative **Beginning the service**.

God made a series of staggering promises to Abraham.

The promise of a son
He was 99 years old and had no children from his marriage with Sarah. Sarah herself

was 90 (Genesis 17:17). Ask if there is anyone present who is around that age. Yet God told Abraham he would be a father and his wife would have a son. *(Display the baby item and comment that 99-year-old people do not normally need this for a baby.)* Imagine making such a promise to an old man. If it were anyone other than God making the promise it would seem cruel and a joke in bad taste. (Even Abraham saw the apparent absurdity in v 17 which is not included in the lectionary reading.)

The promise of nations of descendants

Abraham was in a marriage without children yet God went further. He would not just have a son. He would be the father of nations, even many nations and he would have numerous descendants. *(Display the globe and explain the astounding scope of this promise.)* Imagine making such a promise to a couple who as yet have no child. It would seem like fantasy land. In order to confirm this promise God changes Abram's name. He is to become Abraham. Abram (father) becomes Abraham (father of many).

The promise of kingly descendants

Abraham was a kind of wealthy desert nomad. Yet God said that kings would come from him (v 6). *(Display the crown.)* Not the usual headdress that is associated with a wanderer. If it were anyone other than God making the promise it would seem preposterous that someone who travelled around with goats and camels and with his relatives should be the ancestor of a king. God promised he would be the father of kings. As a token of this, Abraham's wife Sarai was renamed Sarah (princess, a royal name suitable for the mother of kings).

The promise of God's personal commitment

Abraham lived a life of movement and uncertainty. Yet God said he would be his God and would be the God of his descendants after him. *(Find the item that is a symbol of a personal relationship with God. A member of the congregation may have brought it with them. Display the symbol, ask the owner about it and explain the significance of this.)* This is another staggering promise. The God of the world and the nations was interested in, and committed to, a nomadic person like Abraham.

These were four great promises: Abraham would be a parent with Sarah, but more than that, a father of nations, and more than that, the ancestor of kings, and even more than that, he would have a personal God. Why should Abraham believe this? It is because it was not just anyone making these promises. It was God. Moreover God revealed himself as God Almighty, Almighty God. Sometimes that phrase is used as an insult or swear word. But it is a true description of the true God. He is God Almighty, and with him there is no power shortage.

It is one thing to make promises. God also kept these staggering promises to Abraham. 1 *(Display the baby item.)* Abraham and Sarah had a son called Isaac. The Lord did as he had promised (Genesis 21:1). Abraham became a father.

2 *(Display the globe.)* Abraham has become a spiritual father to many. Whenever and wherever we trust in God and have

faith in him we are sharing in the family characteristic of Abraham. (The apostle Paul pointed this out in Galatians 3:7: 'Those who believe are children of Abraham.') We trust in God's promises.

3 *(Display the crown.)* Abraham's descendants include the kings of Israel such as David and Solomon. Abraham's descendants eventually included the King of kings, Jesus (Matthew 1:1–16).

4 *(Display the symbol of personal faith.)* God is the God of the world and cosmos yet he proved to be the God of Abraham. In the same way God is the creator, the God of the stars, yet he is my God and your God.

We need to have faith. Sometimes it is needed in a game where a person is directing us around a space. Sometimes it is in a very real-life situation. For us as Christians, throughout life, we trust in God Almighty as he guides us through the obstacles and challenges that we face. Sometimes that may mean a lot of waiting. But Abraham knew all about that! He had to wait a very long time.

Prayers of intercession

With: a version of the following chart in the appropriate format (a chart with two columns and four rows. In the left column draw a symbolic illustration of the four items used in the **Bible talk**: a baby's toy or item of baby clothing; a globe; a crown; a symbol of a personal relationship with God, perhaps a confirmation book, hymn book or a well-used Bible. This chart is available as a download (YearB.Lent2_2).

The following can be done corporately where suggestions are gathered by the leader at the front and added to a large chart. Alternatively it can be completed in groups where each of four groups takes one of the lines on the chart and a leader collects and incorporates ideas into the relevant prayer. Or individuals can be given a piece of paper containing the chart.

Next to the baby item write a suggestion for a prayer topic dealing with children and families. Next to the globe record a prayer concern from world news. Next to the crown write either a need for the royal family or someone in government or leadership. Next to the symbol of personal faith pray for those who help others to grow in their faith in God. Activities like prayer and Bible study groups can be mentioned.

If the chart is not used in this **Prayer activity**, it can still act as a summary of the Bible talk and is a prayer reminder for the coming week. You could give out copies as people leave. Alternative prayers are available as a download (YearB.Lent2_5).

Ending the service

Abraham had faith in God. He trusted him. We all have faith in various people and things. Is our faith placed on a sure foundation which is God Almighty? Join in the following prayer:

Go out into the world with the power of God Almighty within you.
Offer the compassion of God Almighty to all those you meet.

And this week, may your faith in God
Almighty grow.
Amen.

Helpful extras

Music and song ideas
As last week, 'Amazing grace' celebrates
God's promise and faithfulness; 'King of kings,
Majesty' celebrates promise and stresses
God who is eternal, faithful and true; 'King
of kings and Lord of lords' (sung as a round)
points to the fulfilment of the promise to
Abraham to be the forefather of kings, and
ultimately to the King of kings. 'The God of
Abraham praise' might seem rather heavy
for an all-age service but contains some
strong statements of truth; the choir, music
group or soloist could be asked to present
it. 'Father God, I wonder' speaks of our
never being alone; 'Father, I place into your
hands' is a hymn of trust and faith. See also
the suggestion for 'El Shaddai' in **Notes and
comments**.

Game
Choose a leader for the young people (eg
the person with a recent birthday). Prepare
a route round the church, such as going from
the font to the pulpit, to the altar and lectern,
making sure that it is as visible for everyone
as possible. Leave a message in each place
or have a person at each staging post with
directions. The leader leads all the young
people along this route. Comment that they
don't know where they are travelling or what
lies ahead. At the final destination there is
a promise box with copies for everyone of
a verse of scripture such as Matthew 28:20,
where Jesus says, 'I am with you always, to the
very end of the age' or Genesis 17:7, where

God says, 'I will… be your God and the God
of your descendants after you.' The children
distribute the verse to everyone present.

Notes and comments

Paul emphasises the family of faith. The
point is further stressed if a godparent from
the congregation is invited to speak or be
interviewed about their personal testimony.
They could stress the fact that they are not
the literal parent of their godchild but they
pray for them, give them presents and take an
active interest in their spiritual growth. This is
an opportunity to model godparenthood!

To illustrate the subject of a personal
relationship with God, before the **Bible
talk**, arrange for a more mature Christian to
bring a precious memento that is a symbol of
their personal faith. Is there someone who is
almost as old as Abraham?

As an alternative **Prayer activity**, listen to
the hymn 'El Shaddai' which celebrates God's
name given in the reading, looking forward to
when Abraham's faith in God was tested to
the point of being asked to sacrifice his son.
Make the words available. As an introduction
explain that the Hebrew term 'El Shaddai'
means God Almighty.

Online resources
All suggested downloads are available
at www.scriptureunion.org.uk/light. Visit
www.lightlive.org for additional activities
for children, young people and adults.
For your convenience, the following
activities are available: YearB.Lent2_3
Alternative ending to the service; YearB.
Lent2_4 Adult sermon.

Third Sunday of Lent

READINGS: **Exodus 20:1–17; Psalm 19**
1 Corinthians 1:18–25; John 2:13–22

Bible foundations

Aim: to reflect on the wonders of God and the goodness of his guidance for living

Exodus 20 is a climactic moment in Israel's history. After the call of Moses (Exodus 1–6), the plagues (chs 7–11), the celebration of the Passover (chs 12,13) and their eventual escape from slavery in Egypt (chs 14,15), God leads his people through a number of adventures to the foot of Mount Sinai (chs 16–19). Through Moses, he announces the standards (called 'words', better known as the Ten Commandments) by which they will live their lives as his people. They are not just rules and regulations. Chapters 21–23 record an unsystematic collection of other laws and the rest of the book outlines norms for proper worship.

It is crucial to remember that obeying the law does not make them God's people. They are God's people because God himself chose to make them his and to bring them out of slavery (Exodus 20:1–3). That is why he must be the only object of their worship (vs 4–7). It all starts with God, not what they must do. It is God who will make a lasting covenant with them in due course (ch 24). The fourth commandment equally ties the day of rest to God's action as creator (not because they needed a rest!). The fifth commandment explicitly connects respect for parents with God's promise of the land. The five remaining commandments are to characterise their behaviour towards each other.

Psalm 19 (like Psalm 119 – which is at much greater length) celebrates the wonder of God's law. Some knowledge of God may be discovered in the creation (vs 1–6) but knowledge of his moral perfection and beauty comes chiefly through his revealed word. It revives and gives joy (vs 7,8) and mediates truth (vs 9,10). If believers know and obey God's law, they will not sin. The law is not a burden but a joy, something to be grateful for and enthusiastically studied.

Beginning the service

Display an open Bible on a table facing the congregation. It is open either at Exodus 20 or Psalm 19. Explain that this is the practice in some churches (the French Protestant Church for example) where the Bible is always left open. Everything that is said from the front is to be judged by the Bible's standards, by you, the listener. Introduce the theme of the service.

Bible reading

Exodus 20:1–17 is read in an encouraging voice, not a grim authoritarian one. Preface it with this introduction: God gives his people ten pieces of advice. Here is God our Father wanting the best for us. Two of the commands are worded as things to do rather than things to avoid. Can you spot which they are? After the reading, or during the **Bible talk**, check that 'Remembering the Sabbath Day' and 'Honouring your parents' have been recognised as positives.

Psalm 19 is read by two voices: verses 1 to 6 by one voice and verses 7 to 14 by another. Introduce it as follows: The psalmist delights in the fact that creation reveals something of God. However, God is revealed more personally in the law he has given his people. Such commands show his moral nature. In the first section the general name 'God' is used; in the second part of the psalm, God is addressed with his more personal name, 'Lord'.

Alternatively, the following, taken from Psalm 19, could be presented by two voices or by two halves of the congregation and used as a prayer to celebrate God's law, also available as a download (YearB.Lent3_1).

> Father God, we thank you for your creation;
> We marvel at the stars and moon by night.
> **We delight in the sun and clouds by day.**
> **Above all we admire your wisdom.**
> We thank you for giving us your law and instruction.
> **Your advice lights our ways and shines on our paths.**
> Your law is perfect.
> **Perfect, Lord, for it revives the soul.**
> Your instructions are trustworthy, Lord,
> **Trustworthy, Lord, and they make the simple wise.**
> Your standards are right;
> **Not only right, Lord, but they give joy to our hearts.**
> Your commands are radiant
> **And they give light to our eyes.**
> Your guidance is sure
> **And it is altogether sound.**
> Your law is more precious than gold;
> **More precious than much pure gold.**
> Your law is sweeter than honey;
> **Sweeter than the honeycomb.**
> Lord, you are our rock.
> **Lord, you are our rock and our redeemer.**
> From Psalm 19

Bible retelling

If you have a video version that tells the story of the Ten Commandments, you could show it during the **Bible talk** to bring a fresh slant on the story. For example, episode 2 of *Megaquest* (Scripture Union) or the relevant section from *Prince of Egypt*. Alternatively, you could read the story *The Big Clean Up* from *The 10 Must Know Stories* (Scripture Union) which has been especially written to be read out loud to children.

Bible talk

With: a car manual instruction booklet or a How-to-use leaflet that accompanies a well known brand of children's medicine – adapt what you say; something gold; some toast with honey on it (or honey cake). It may be possible to have a large toaster(s) to prepare small pieces of toast and honey to give out at the end of the service, or use honey on bread or cream crackers. (Check if anyone is allergic to honey.)

God's law is there for our good and the good of others

When you buy a car or get a prescription for a child's medicine you should get an instruction booklet or a How-to-use leaflet in the box/bag from the pharmacy. *(Hold up one of these and look through it.)* There is a command that if your car runs on petrol you need to use unleaded fuel. You may feel that you are not going to be dictated to by anyone, so you ignore the original instruction and fill up with diesel. Some people in the congregation may admit this has happened to them by mistake but would anyone admit to doing that deliberately? If you take too much medicine at the wrong times, the medicine will not help you get better as quickly as it might and may even harm you. All board games, radios, washing machines and DVD players come with sets of instructions so that they work trouble-free and effectively. Explore what might go wrong

if they are ignored. Lots of advice and lots of instructions are all there so that you get the best out of a product. You would be silly to ignore them.

It is the same for us. God our maker gave his people in the desert a set of instructions, the Ten Commandments. He wanted them to live life to the full, and avoid problems, living safe lives. The Ten Commandments deal with areas of life that need to be handled with care.

We can get into trouble in our relationships with other people. Advice is needed and the last six commands provide it. Our parents – they deserve to be respected. Human life is valuable – we must not kill. Marriage is precious – don't take someone's partner. God has given us possessions – don't take what belongs to someone else. We need to trust people – don't lie to them. God gives us enough to live on – don't get distressed by becoming discontented and envying what others have got.

But the first four commands aim to put us right with God himself. Being right with God comes before being right with people. Put God first. Avoid images of God which limit our understanding of him. Treat his name with respect. And keep his day special. (We do not need images of God because human beings are made in God's image.)

These Ten Commandments are advice from a loving father. They are not commands from a dictator determined to spoil our life. The advice is there to ensure we get the best from life. God's law is for both our good and for the good of other people. We might be unaware of the mayhem that breaking God's law can cause other people.

God had already saved his people from slavery in Egypt when he gave them the Ten Commandments. They did not have to earn his favour; they already had his love. But these instructions were given for their own good and well-being. In the UK we are told to drive on the left side of the road. This is for our own safety and everyone else's too. Problems arise when someone makes an error of judgement and finds themselves going the wrong way up a motorway.

God's law is there to delight us
God's people compared God's law to something precious. *(Hold up something gold.)* Why is gold precious? It is rare, valuable and doesn't rust. The psalmist says God's law is like this. No one else has a set of guidelines like it. It is permanently relevant. Read Psalm 19:9 and 10. The commands of the Lord are 'more precious than gold, than much pure gold'.

Then hold up toast with honey/honey cake/ honeycomb. Why is honey special? It tastes good. It protects our health. For example a report in December 2007 stated that: A clinical trial has found that honey is more effective at soothing a sore throat than a common active ingredient in children's cough medicines. It is the same with God's law. The commands of the Lord are 'sweeter than honey, sweeter than honey from the honeycomb' (Psalm 19:10). Jewish children were encouraged to act out this truth. When they first began to learn the Law for themselves they were given a slate on which were written some verses about the

Law (or 'Torah' in Hebrew meaning 'fatherly instruction'). The teacher put some honey on the slate and the child licked the honey from the letters. It symbolised the fact that the child, often as young as 5, was going to study the law and take delight in it. We are not going to be so unhygienic but later we are going to share some toast (or whatever) and honey to remind us of God's goodness to us and the sweetness of his law.

Prayers of intercession

Many young people struggle to see the law in society or rules in school as anything positive. It would be appropriate to pray for them. Ask a group of young people to prepare prayers to read out loud – for young people in school and in the community and also for those who enforce the law.

An alternative would be to use a very large sheet of paper as a graffiti wall. In advance ask a few people to scrawl or draw on this something they want to say to God about those who are caught up in violence and criminal activity. Ensure that this is not an opportunity for judgemental comments on the 'youth of today' but to ask for God's compassion on and action with all those who are victims, young people in the process of dropping out, and those who enforce the law, including workers in schools! Key phrases could be 'be compassionate', 'give purpose', 'strengthen the weak', 'support the frustrated', 'all have sinned, forgive us', 'free those influenced by drugs', 'challenge prejudice'. Follow this by a prayer asking God to take action.

Prayer of confession

This is based on Psalm 19. It would be appropriate for this to occur after the **Bible reading** from Exodus 20 or after the **Bible talk**.

Lord, nothing is hidden from you.
You have shown us what is right:
What is right in our words – to honour your name and not to lie;
What is right in our actions – not to steal or kill, not to disrespect our parents;
What is right in our thinking – not to long for what our friends have.
You have told us what we ought to do – for example, keep your day special.
You have told us what not to do – for example, take another person's partner in marriage.
Forgive our faults.
Keep us from sinning.
Protect us from rebellion against you.
In the name of Jesus take our sin from us and make us new.
May the words of our mouths and the thoughts of our hearts be pleasing in your sight, O Lord, our rock and our redeemer. Amen.

Ending the service

At the start of the service we thought of how the Bible is our standard to judge truth. This Bible stays here in church. You have your own Bibles. You can also take the truth away with you in your hearts and minds. (If appropriate, the honey cake or toast/bread with honey is distributed.) Together the congregation says: Lord, your words are sweeter than honey. Help us to feed on your truth.

Helpful extras

Music and song ideas

Use the theme song for the past two weeks to highlight the theme of covenant promise; 'Amazing grace' includes the line 'the Lord has promised good to me'; the modern version of 'Great is your faithfulness' includes the line 'you have fulfilled all your promise to me'; 'Lord for the years' celebrates God's Word in the second verse; 'Lord, thy Word abideth' celebrates the lasting value of God's Word; 'Love is his word' stresses the motivation behind the law; 'O Lord, the clouds are gathering' speaks of God's laws of love being scorned.

Statement of faith

This is based on the Ten Commandments. It could be prefaced by groups looking at the Ten Commandments and talking about how they show God's love for family, how they protect his own reputation, how they show his love of truth and justice, and how they show he is a God of life. This is available as a download (YearB.Lent3_2).

Notes and comments

You could interview a person involved in the law – a policeman, solicitor or judge. They could stress the difficulty of being just and compassionate at the same time.

Online resources

All suggested downloads are available at www.scriptureunion.org.uk/light. Visit www.lightlive.org for additional activities for children, young people and adults. For your convenience, the following activities are available: YearB.Lent3_3 Pebble praise for 5s and under; YearB. Lent3_4 Bible story for 5s and under; YearB.Lent3_5 Adult sermon.

Fourth Sunday of Lent

READINGS: **Numbers 21:4–9; John 3:14–21**
Psalm 107:1–3,17–22; Ephesians 2:1–10

Bible foundations

Aim: to appreciate that God's salvation is available to anyone who trusts God and looks to him

John 3:16 is frequently referred to as 'the gospel in a nutshell'. It comes towards the end of Jesus' famous conversation with Nicodemus in which Jesus has stressed the need to be born again (3:3,7). This might be better translated 'born from above'. Nicodemus fails to understand and fades out of the conversation. Jesus expresses surprise at his ignorance, but recognises that only the Son of Man (Jesus himself) is likely really to understand such deep teaching (v 13).

At this point Jesus makes reference to the strange incident in the wilderness wanderings recorded in the reading from Numbers 21. The people of Israel are grumbling once again and in a desperate plight. God judges them and they are attacked by poisonous snakes. God tells Moses to lift up a poisonous snake on a pole and get anyone who has been bitten to look at the snake in faith and they will be miraculously healed.

Jesus compares the Son of Man (himself) to the snake. In John, the language often has double meanings and 'lifting up' has particular reference to Jesus being lifted up on the cross (12:32–35). When he has been crucified he will give eternal life, not just temporary healing, to any believer who looks to him. John 3:16 encapsulates this truth. In his love, God has made an offer of eternal life to absolutely anyone who puts their faith in the crucified Christ. The sad thing, highlighted in verses 17–21, is that although God did not send Jesus into the world to condemn and enact judgement (as he did with the snakes in the wilderness) but to save people, people condemn themselves by failing to believe. They prefer darkness to light (vs 19–21) as we have already been told in John 1:9–13.

Beginning the service

Some people spend their lives looking down at the ground and never look upwards. Talk about the sort of things that a ground-studier would miss, such as trees moving in the wind, planes, cloud formation, a full moon in the sky, interesting rooftops on tall buildings and adverts on the side of a double-decker bus. Small children will have some interesting insights since they always see things from a lower height than everyone else. Explain that the theme of this service is that God invites everyone to look up to Christ to be saved, but some may choose not to! This could be humorously introduced by someone walking to the front studying the floor, refusing to look upwards and even addressing people by the wrong name because they don't see people's faces.

Bible reading

With: a group of people to mime; a pole with an imitation snake fastened to it

The reading of Numbers 21:4–9 lends itself to something really dramatic. At the start of the reading, a group of people, including children, begins to walk to the front. As prompted by the text, they begin to huff and puff because of the heat, and grumble under their breath. As the snakes weave their way into the group (and these could be small children holding their hands one on top of the other at mouth level, with the lower hand darting out every now and then, as a snake's forked tongue) the group begins to cry out and drop to the floor; some are even dead. 'Moses' steps forward to hold up the pole and some of the people on the floor make a show of looking at the pole and then get up, smiling.

During the reading of John 3:14–21 show the pole with the snake as above and, at the appropriate time, replace the snake by the word 'Jesus'.

It is suggested that Ephesians 2:1–3 is read during the **Bible talk** and Psalm 107 is used in the **Prayers of intercession**.

Bible talk

With: make a recording of voices (or it could be done live) that grumble and grumble (which increases in volume during the first part of the Bible talk) and a set of sounds of singing voices that increases in volume during the second part of the **Bible talk**. A drum roll could be played to separate the two parts.

The people forgot what God had done

God had done so much for the people of Israel. He had rescued them from Egypt where they had been slaves for years and years. He had given them Moses as a leader. He had given them water that miraculously began to flow from the rock when they were thirsty. He had given them food in the form of manna, sweet-tasting flakes, and wild birds that they had to gather first thing in the morning.

(Grumbling begins.) But this was not enough for God's people. They had bad experiences in the past and thought that life should be better. They had forgotten just how bad it had been in Egypt. So they grumbled. But by doing this they were insulting the God who

had cared for and protected them. They did not trust him. And this was, and is, sin. The snakes came to bite them as a punishment. *(Grumbling stops and there could be a drum roll every time the word 'sin' is mentioned.)*

We forget what God has done

Reflect on how often we forget about God and what he has done for us, and how often we try to do things or go places that we know, deep down, are not good for us. This is sin!

And sin needs to be punished. But even though God's people suffered because of their sin, God provided them with a way to be rescued. *(Singing begins.)* But they had to do what Moses told them. They had to trust that what God had said would come true. If they looked at the snake they would get better. Looking at the snake was an act of faith and trust in God.

Jesus explained to his disciples that having faith in him was just like what happened in this story, even though his listeners did not understand what he meant at the time. Jesus meant that people grumble and ignore God. *(The grumbling sounds begin again.)* They have always done this; all people have sinned and disobeyed God.

But God forgives and heals us

If you have not done so already, you could read part of the epistle, Ephesians 2:1–3. (Drum roll.) But when Jesus was nailed to the cross, he was giving people the opportunity to be freed from the effects of sin. Anyone who looked to him and had faith in him would be saved. *(Singing voices begin again.)*

The writer of John's Gospel talks a lot about followers of Jesus walking in the light, not in the dark. God's people in the desert discovered what it meant to be healed and saved. It was as though they were walking in the light. So too, anyone now who looks to Jesus, trusting him to save them, will be healed, saved and walking in the light.

The sobering thought is that some people in the desert chose not to look up and presumably they died. There were those in the time of Jesus who chose not to look to him to be saved. There are people today who choose not to look to Jesus to be saved.

Prayer activity

With: a cross or a large photo of one (or a crown if using the symbolism of the crown of thorns); pairs of gardening gloves; a collection of thorns or enough copies of a picture of a thorn for everyone to have one or see one close to them. (One image is available as a download (YearB.Lent4_3). (Be careful of sharp thorns!)

Ask a few people wearing gloves to scatter the thorns or pictures of them on the ground around the church or give everyone or small groups their own copy of a thorn. Invite everyone to look down at the thorns which stand for the times when we have grumbled against God or failed to remember all he has done for us. Pause for reflection and then say the following:

Lord God, you have done so much for us and we know we should be thankful. But so often we just forget or we deliberately ignore you, the God who made us, cares for us and guides us. Please forgive us.

Invite everyone to look upwards as you hold the empty cross. Explain that the cross is empty because, although Jesus hung on it, he came alive again, so the empty cross is a sign of his victory. However, if you wish to use a crucifix, comment on how Jesus hung on the cross for six hours and how excruciatingly painful it was. (If you want to use the symbolism of the crown of thorns, anticipating the Passion narrative in two weeks' time, explain its meaning and then the significance of the crown as a sign of Jesus' victory.) As we look to Jesus, trusting him to save us and rescue us, we need to be thankful. Pause to reflect on what each person wants to thank Jesus for, then pray:

Thank you for dying on the cross, Lord Jesus, so that everyone who has faith in you will have eternal life. As we look up to you, help us to be grateful for all you have done for us.

Prayers of intercession

People forget and have bad memories so it is important to pray together for some matters that may have dropped off the radar or which people just get so used to praying about. Use the adaptation of Psalm 107 which is available as a download (YearB. Lent4_1). Ask one person to read the verses from Psalm 107 and others to lead prayers as suggested.

Conclude by singing a song of praise.

Ending the service

You could conclude the service by playing the wordsearch **Game** below. Or you could

invite everyone to stand up straight with their chins up, looking upwards, ideally to focus their eyes on a cross. After each of the following phrases, everyone says as a response: **We trust in you and are saved**.

This week, when we are afraid, we will look to you;
We trust in you and are saved.
This week, when we know we have done wrong and need forgiveness,
We trust in you and are saved.
This week, when we face opposition from those who do not love you,
We trust in you and are saved.
Amen.

Helpful extras
Music and song ideas
There is a *Learn and remember* verse song based on John 3:16, in *Bitesize Bible Songs 2* CD (SU); 'Lift high the cross' is a stirring but not well known song appropriate for this theme. The chorus goes: 'Lift high the cross, the love of Christ proclaim, till all the world adores his sacred name.' Other songs include 'For God so loved the world'; 'When we walk with the Lord'; 'When I survey the wondrous cross'; 'What love is this? (I surrender)'; 'Above all powers'.

Game
Below is a wordsearch, also available as a download (YearB.Lent4_2). There are clues to work out seven people in the Bible who trusted God, in the order they lived. Work out who they are (asking the children first), then find them in the wordsearch grid and finally work out the message from the leftover letters.

1. He trusted God and built a boat.
2. He trusted God even if that meant risking the life of his son.
3. She trusted God to give her a son when, broken-hearted, she had prayed.
4. He trusted God and built a barbecue.
5. He trusted God and ate only vegetables.
6. He trusted Jesus and walked on water.
7. He trusted God and walked off into the desert to race with a chariot.

Answers: Noah, Abraham, Hannah, Elijah, Daniel, Peter, Philip

H	A	N	N	A	H
T	B	R	E	U	P
S	R	T	L	P	I
D	A	N	I	E	L
G	H	O	J	T	I
O	A	A	A	E	H
D	M	H	H	R	P

The eight leftover letters spell TRUST GOD

Notes and comments

John 3:16 is one of the best-known verses in the Bible. If appropriate, encourage everyone to learn and remember it. For some younger people and those new to the Christian faith, this will be something new, and for older people it will remind them, lest they forget, as God's people did in the desert.

This Sunday is also Mothering Sunday. You may wish to expand the service to include prayer for mothers who have to trust God as they bring up their children. You could also pray that mothers and fathers will pass on their faith to their children so that the next generation will trust in God and be saved. Other ideas for Mothering Sunday can be found in the next service outline, or in the *All-age Service Annual* Volumes 1–4 (SU).

Online resources

All suggested downloads are available at www.scriptureunion.org.uk/light. Visit www.lightlive.org for additional activities for children, young people and adults.

The service outlines leading up to Easter focus around the journey that Jesus went on, as he travelled to the cross. Suggestions are made for setting up a series of interactive stations for people to spend time engaging with what Jesus went through. You will need to begin preparing for this some weeks before Easter, especially if you are going to invite members of the community (including schoolchildren) into the church to spend time at the prayer stations. See page 117 for suggestions.

Mothering Sunday

READINGS: **1 Samuel 1:20–28; Psalm 127**
Colossians 3:12–17; John 19:25–27

Bible foundations

Aim: to explore the fact that, like God, we give to others and, like God, we also receive from others, with gratitude

A great many women identify with Hannah. In 1 Samuel we read of her exultant joy on giving birth to a son. She is also no stranger to the pain of childlessness. Chapter 1 tells of a woman who, especially given the culture of the time, was utterly desolate. She turns her grief into prayer, beseeching God to meet her need, and he answers with the birth of Samuel. No one has a right to children and Hannah is not the only woman in Scripture to be childless (though that does not lessen her pain). So great is Hannah's gratitude to God, who is ultimately the only real source of human life, that she dedicates her young son to God's service. She makes sure he has every chance to fulfil her vow by sending him off to serve God with the priest Eli (v 28). Her psalm of acclamation in chapter 2:1–10 demonstrates some of the theological depth to which this woman aspires. Not sentimental or over-possessive, she places herself and her son in the centre of God's purposes – a good, wholesome and secure place to be!

Psalm 127 reflects the same kind of vigorous theology. A secure, prosperous and happy home belongs chiefly to people who put God first. Wealth, security, connections and a good education may play their part, but the psalmist is quite clear that in real terms God is the source of well-being (v 1). As Jesus said, 'Seek first his kingdom and his righteousness, and all these things will be given to you as well' (Matthew 6:33). The psalm cautions against excessive work and worry (v 2). Jesus also does this just before the passage cited from Matthew. Ironically, the psalm is very male-centred, speaking of 'sons' and 'men' in a way that contemporary society may reject, sometimes editing out a man's role in the family. But both men and women can rejoice in God's gracious provision of children and the blessing of a secure and happy home.

Beginning the service

Ask how many people have given something to someone today. For example, children giving a gift to their mother, including breakfast in bed! Probe a bit further. Did the person receiving the gift say thank you?

We may enjoy giving to others but it is really satisfying if the person who receives the gift is grateful. Explore examples of disappointment and how it feels when someone is not grateful when they receive a gift. The theme of this service is that, like God, we give to others and, like God, we also receive from others and should be grateful.

Bible reading

The reading from 1 Samuel 1 lends itself to a narrative reading. Ask people to listen out for the word 'give'. **Who** gives **what** and **to whom** in this story?

Psalm 127 could be presented using actions or signs, which the congregation could work out together or a group of children and young people could devise before the service. Draw attention especially to verse 3. In the **Game** there is an alternative suggestion for engaging with verse 3.

Bible talk

With: a large set of traffic lights, with the three colours clearly marked; three cards with the words 'Yes and go', 'Wait a bit' and 'Stop and no' to be stuck underneath or close to each traffic light, also available as a PowerPoint download (YearB.MothSun_1)

Hannah had been desperate for a child. Her husband, Elkanah, had two wives and the elder one had had several children. Hannah had come to worship God in the holy place and had pleaded with him to give her a child. Her pleading had been so over-the-top that the priest, Eli, thought she was drunk! But God had heard her request. She became pregnant and gave birth to a boy whom she called Samuel which means 'someone from God'.

But does God always give us what we ask for? *(Show the traffic lights.)*

Yes and go!
Sometimes God gives us what we want, as we ask for it. *(Draw attention to the green light and attach the phrase 'Yes and go'.)* Like a good father, God loves to bless us and give us things that will please us. Obviously, God knew what Hannah wanted and what would be best for her. Her relationship with him was strengthened as a result of his gift to her. When we ask God for something we need to ask: *will this help us to get to know and love God better?*

Wait a bit!
(Point to the amber light and attach the phrase 'Wait a bit'.) Sometimes what we are asking for is a good thing for us but now is not the right time. We have to wait, and waiting, for impatient people (which most of us are) is a challenge. There may be things God wants us to learn as we wait. Ask the children what things they have to wait for and how they feel about having to wait. The first time we read about Hannah asking for a child was when she was praying in the holy place. But this cannot have been the first time she ever asked God for a child. All the other times

before then, God heard her request but he said, 'Wait a bit'. He wanted her to learn to wait and ultimately to trust him. If you have read the Gospel reading, refer to the fact that Mary not only waited for Jesus to die at the foot of the cross but for much of her life she had been waiting: for Jesus to be born, for 'the sword to pierce her own soul' (a sorrow which Simeon had told her about soon after Jesus' birth), for Jesus to come alive again (and did she expect that?) and for the Holy Spirit to come. Much of life is about waiting and it is in the waiting that we often encounter God.

Stop and no!

(Point to the red light and attach the phrase 'Stop and no'.) Sometimes what we are asking for is not what would be good for us and God knows that. He says 'Stop and no', but we may not want to hear that. We have to accept that he knows best and we have to listen in case 'No' is the answer. It is not that he is any less generous, just that he is loving and knows what is best for us and others. For Hannah this was not the answer on this occasion. (The supreme example of someone asking God for something to which the answer was 'Stop and no' was when Jesus did not want to die and pleaded with God in the Garden of Gethsemane. But God said 'No'. Jesus accepted this.)

We give to God in return

God gave Hannah a son and she gratefully received him. But she had also promised to make a gift to God. When she prayed in the holy place, she promised that, if she had a child, she would give her child to God. She kept her promise. When Samuel was old enough, she left him with Eli the priest. Every year she went to see him but this was her way of giving to God. Samuel was to become God's man in Israel, a great leader.

God gives to us, and children are one way in which we see his generosity. That is what we celebrate on Mothering Sunday. Parents are to thank God for their children. They can also ask God to be generous to their children. We can also give to God. Hannah showed her gratitude in a very unusual way. God certainly does not expect every child to be left by their parents in the care of someone else! But we need to show our gratitude to God in whatever ways are possible and appropriate. One way is to give to others. And that is another part of what we are doing today – giving to others to show our gratitude to God.

For visitors in church today the idea of listening to God and having a personal relationship with him may seem rather strange. It might be appropriate to invite someone to give a personal testimony about what this means to them. Make sure that what they say is free of jargon and makes sense to younger people present.

Prayer activity

With: a large gift-wrapped box; Blu-tack or glue; a gift tag for everyone present (plus some spare ones) on which are simply drawn one of the following: a face with a smile (ability to welcome); a hand (ability to help); a pile of money/£10 note (money); a glass with a straw sticking out (hospitality); a guitar and a paintbrush (gifts and abilities); thought bubble (ability to pray) These illustrations are available as a download (YearB.MothSun_2).

Give out the gift labels (people can make their own if possible) and explain that these are all examples of things that we can give to others as a means of giving to God. People choose which label they have, can swap with others around them or take an alternative one from a spares box. Invite everyone to be quiet to thank God for who he is and what he has given us. Everyone then brings their label forward to stick on the large gift box as a means of expressing their thanks to God. You will need to give everyone a tiny piece of Blu-tack or use glue.

Afterwards, talk about how these gifts and abilities are things that everyone, whatever their age, can give to others.

Prayers of intercession

Mothering Sunday can be a tough day for those with unhappy experiences of being a parent or being parented or for those who have lost a mother, just as it can be especially hard for those who long to be a parent but for various reasons cannot. Be especially sensitive towards these people.

In advance ask several parents and children to prepare prayers for each other. At the front, the parents stand together on one side and the children stand on the other. Their prayers could be read alternately. The prayers could focus around the following issues: thanks to God for all children and all parents, grandparents and carers; thanks to God for specific things that parents can do for children and vice versa; requests for parents and children in the future – wisdom, health,

spiritual life – asking that both parties will learn to listen to what God is saying.

Ending the service

With: a large thought bubble, like the one on the gift label, on a whiteboard or acetate; appropriate pens

Ask everyone to think of one thing they plan to thank God for throughout this week, then ask for people to call out their thoughts. Write these in the thought bubble. Alternatively, give out pens and a thought bubble for each person to complete before leaving church. This can act as a reminder all week.

Close with the following prayer:

Thank you, God, that you are a generous God and answer prayer.
Thank you especially for mothers, fathers, grandparents and carers.
Thank you that you welcome our thanks and gifts.
May we be grateful this week, in what we say and do, and may we give to others.
Amen.

Helpful extras

Music and song ideas
'Father God, I wonder'; 'Give thanks to the Lord, our God and king'; 'Praise my soul the king of heaven'; 'For the beauty of the earth'; 'God forgave my sin in Jesus' name'; 'Thank you, Jesus'.

Game
With: nine large jigsaw pieces with the following words on them: Children are a

blessing and a gift from God (Psalm 127:3 from the CEV), also available as a download (YearB.MothSun_3); Blu-tack; board

This is an alternative way of engaging with Psalm 127 and is a *Learn and remember* verse. Hide the pieces of the jigsaw around the church, invite children to find them and then stick them on the board at the front. 'Children', the first 'a', 'gift' and 'God' should be the four corner pieces, if they need a clue. Ask the children what the word 'blessing' means and in what ways they might be a blessing to their parents. Then ask parents in what ways they think their children are a gift from God to them.

Notes and comments

This Sunday, Mothering Sunday or Mothers' Day, as it is more often called, is also the fourth Sunday of Lent. An alternative service is available for this Sunday in the previous service outline. The readings that have been used in this Mothering Sunday service are those recommended in *Common Worship*.

Mothering Sunday is not a specifically Christian festival. Many churches, however, recognise that there are opportunities for welcoming mothers and families to church on this Sunday which may not normally occur. This service has been written with this in mind.

If this service includes Holy Communion, make reference to the fact that God said to Jesus in the Garden of Gethsemane 'Stop and no' when Jesus asked God to save him from the cross.

Online resources

All suggested downloads are available at www.scriptureunion.org.uk/light. Visit www.lightlive.org for additional activities for children, young people and adults. For your convenience, the following activities are available as downloads: YearB.MothSun_4 Bible story with actions for 5 to 8s; YearB.MothSun_5 Bible story for 5s and under.

The service outlines leading up to Easter focus around the journey that Jesus went on, as he travelled to the cross. Suggestions are made for setting up a series of interactive stations for people to spend time engaging with what Jesus went through. You will need to begin preparing for this some weeks before Easter, especially if you are going to invite members of the community (including schoolchildren) into the church to spend time at the prayer stations. See page 117 for suggestions.

Fifth Sunday of Lent

READINGS: **Jeremiah 31:31–34; John 12:20–33**
Psalm 51:5–10; Hebrews 5:5–10

Bible foundations

Aim: to recognise that Jesus chose to suffer and give up his life

Jeremiah's is a prophecy of new covenant (31:31). Judah needed that reassurance. Jeremiah's message was not generally one of encouragement. He lived and prophesied at a time of national spiritual decline. The nation had failed and Jeremiah, often called 'the weeping prophet', told God's people that they would be taken into exile. This did not make Jeremiah popular. He did, however, deliver this remarkable prophecy of a new covenant. It will be different, he says, from what their ancestors had experienced (v 32) when they were led out of Egypt. Previously the emphasis of the covenant had been national (Exodus 24). This new covenant would be with them as individuals, as in Ezekiel 34:25–27. The nation had failed and now God would focus upon an individual response and renewal of heart. No one need depend upon others for instruction (v 34). Potentially all people would have a knowledge of God and it would not be merely a matter of external obedience but would be written on their hearts (v 33). In case they are concerned at the loss of Temple sacrifices, Jeremiah reassures them that forgiveness of their sins will come as an integral part of this new covenant.

John 12 records the moment when Jesus knows that, in fulfilment of the promised new covenant, he must give up his own life and he does so willingly. He knows that there are no covenants and no release of new life unless a seed falls into the ground and dies (John 12:24). The time has come for him to be glorified. As with the language of 'lifting up', which points to the crucifixion in John (John 3:14), 'glory' is what happens to him at the cross. It crosses Jesus' mind that he could ask to be saved from this (vs 27,28). The other Gospels record a similar moment in Gethsemane (Matthew 26:36–46; Mark 14:32–42; Luke 22:39–47). But Jesus' calling is to seal the new covenant with his own sacrifice – a moment of glory.

Beginning the service

Use these opening sentences, based on Jeremiah 31:33, also available as a download (YearB.Lent5_2).

Leader: God says: I will write my law on your hearts.
All: Help us to serve you, to follow you and to love you.
Leader: God says: I will be your God, and you will be my people.
All: You are our God and we are your people.
Leader: God says: You will all know me – from the greatest to the least.
All: To know you is to find peace in our hearts and purpose in our lives.

Bible reading

Jeremiah 31:33 forms the suggested **Beginning the service** and Psalm 51 is part of the **Prayer of confession**.

John 12:20–33 could be read as a choral reading and is available as a download (YearB. Lent5_3).

Bible talk

With: some seeds (individual grains from a piece of wheat); a piece of wheat (if available – alternatively use a picture); a bag of flour; water; dried yeast and a loaf of bread (preferably one which looks home-made)

What's bread for?

Show the loaf of bread and offer some of it to eat. Emphasise how important bread is as a basic food staple. Comment on how long people have been relying on it (but comment on other staple foods across the world such as rice or maize). Point out that in the prayer Jesus taught us, the Lord's Prayer, he tells us to ask for 'daily bread'.

What's flour for?

Ask what bread is made from and wait for the answer 'flour'. Show the bag of flour on being told the right answer. Then ask what flour is made of and wait for the answer 'wheat'. Show the ear of wheat. Ask where wheat comes from and wait for the answer 'a grain of wheat' or a 'seed', then show the grain you have. Say that you would like to go through this again, starting from the beginning rather than the end, thinking about the purpose of each one.

What's a grain of wheat for?

Show the grain of wheat and ask what it is for. Acknowledge that this may sound like a strange question, but allow people freedom to suggest different answers (such as food for birds, or wheat in next year's harvest), before settling on a final answer such as 'to become something else'. Grains of wheat cannot stay as they are. God created them to be planted and to grow. They die, in the sense that they do not remain themselves any more, but from them comes something new and different. Sum up by saying that the purpose of wheat grain is to grow wheat.

Wheat becomes flour

Show the ear of wheat. Express wonder at how complicated and perfectly designed a thing it is to have come from one small grain. Pass the piece of wheat around (if you have a real one) and ask people to look closely at its detail. But if the wheat was allowed to stay in the field until it faded and died it would not have achieved its purpose. Sum up by saying that the purpose of wheat is to be harvested and taken to the mill to make flour.

Flour becomes dough

Show the bag of flour. Point out that people have been grinding wheat to make flour for many thousands of years. Windmills used to do this, although now most flour is made in factories. Pour some flour out of the packet and then point out that the seed and the ear of wheat did not exist just to make flour. What is the flour for? It makes papier mâché and playdough but what else? Mix some water with the flour, add some yeast and invite some volunteers to mix them together to make some dough while you continue talking (although you would need to add other things too, such as oil, salt and seeds, and this is only a demonstration to show the early stages of bread-making). If your volunteers can get to the point of kneading the dough, all well and good! You could have prepared a piece of dough which has been allowed to rise during the service to show what happens in the second stage of bread-making. Volunteers could give this a second knead!

Dough becomes bread

A grain of wheat is crushed, yet ends up as part of a loaf of bread. Read Jesus' words from John 12:24. Jesus was using a grain of wheat to make an important point about himself. He knew that the time he had spent with his friends was coming to an end, and that having entered Jerusalem (this passage comes straight after the triumphal entry) he would soon be put to death on the cross.

Jesus' death becomes new life

Take hold of the grain of wheat again. Jesus knew that his death was to be like planting a grain of wheat in the ground. The wheat would no longer remain as it had been, but it would achieve the purpose for which it had been designed. In the same way, Jesus' life had been leading towards this point, so that he might not only show people how to live their lives, but also die on a cross. This is what he meant when he talked about being 'lifted up from the earth'.

Jesus' one death led to new life and enabled him to come alive again. This meant that people could discover that God could forgive them and that their sins could be dealt with. One thing followed on from another. Just as the grain led to the ear of wheat which led to the flour which led to the bread, so Jesus' death led to his resurrection, led to the hope of forgiveness of sins, and ultimately led to the Holy Spirit bringing new life. Jesus said '… if it dies, it produces many seeds.' His death would bring many people to know God for themselves.

Jesus' death was no accident, which is something that we will discover in the following two weeks as we enter Holy Week. His death was part of God's plan for the whole world.

Prayer activity

With: a good number of coloured balls, in four colours which are the colours of food such as red, orange, green, yellow, white or purple (circles of coloured card would be as effective)

This prayer activity is designed to be near the beginning of the service. It focuses on adoration, praise and thanksgiving but introduces the idea that the fruit of the earth leads to other things, such as providing us with food. Before the service, place the balls all over the church. Ask people of all ages to find one ball and then see if they can find any more of that same colour. After a minute or two, ask people to move to one of four different areas of the room, according to colour. You will need to indicate which colour is in which corner!

Everyone thinks of a food that is in their particular colour, something for which they can give thanks and praise. For example, if they are in the red corner, they might thank God for juicy tomatoes; in the purple corner, thanks for blackcurrant yogurt or blackberries. Explain that these fruits and vegetables have been created by God for several purposes, including making us strong. They are a means to an end. One person can say something like 'Thank you, God, for juicy tomatoes', which the whole group then repeats, or everyone in the group in turn can express a one-sentence prayer of gratitude for the food they have thought of. Duplicating prayers are not a problem for God.

After a few minutes, interrupt the prayer time and pray a general prayer of thanks for God's plan for the world.

Prayers of intercession

With: cut-up strips of OHP acetate for each person to have one or more; soluble felt-tip pens; bowls of water around the church (Check in advance that the pens write on the acetates, and are easily washed off the acetates when dipped in water.)

The prayer of confession is based on Psalm 51 and uses images of being made clean. Explain that King David had chosen to do some bad things which spoiled the lives of other people, as well as his own relationship with God. In this psalm he tells God how sorry he is, and asks to be forgiven. Read verse 2 of the psalm: 'Wash me clean from all of my sin and guilt.' David felt dirty and needed God's forgiveness to make him clean again.

Invite everyone either to write or draw something on their piece of acetate to represent something that they feel has spoiled their relationship with God and maybe hurts others too. When they have done this, they can take their acetate to a bowl of water, dip it in the water and wash away what they had written or drawn. Ask them to think about verse 2 of the psalm, making it a prayer for themselves.

Sum up this time of confession by using the following prayer which is available as a download (YearB.Lent5_1). The response is: Wash us clean, make us new, by your grace, by your love.

Leader: Generous God, we have spoiled our lives by our selfishness and greed.
All: Wash us clean, make us new, by your grace, by your love.
Leader: Loving God, we have spoiled the lives of others by our ignorance and weakness.
All: Wash us clean, make us new, by your grace, by your love.
Leader: Forgiving God, we have spoiled our

relationship with you by our pride and hard-heartedness.

All: Wash us clean, make us new, by your grace, by your love.

Leader: Ever-patient God, we have hurt you by our distance from you.

All: Wash us clean, make us new, by your grace, by your love.

Leader: Hear our prayer, touch our hearts, heal our lives.

All: In the name of Jesus, who died as a seed dies in the ground, so that we might have eternal life.
Amen.

Ending the service

If possible, provide enough bread for everyone to have a piece each and to share the bread together. This will remind everyone that a grain has to 'die' just as Jesus had to die quite literally in order to bring new life! Be aware of anyone requiring a gluten-free product.

Helpful extras

Music and song ideas

'God forgave my sin in Jesus' name'; 'Thank you for the cross'; 'From heaven you came helpless babe'; 'I cannot tell'; 'My Lord, what love is this'; 'Lord, I lift your name on high'; 'Above all powers'; 'In Christ alone'; 'You chose the cross'.

Notes and comments

You may need to make sure that anyone with a wheat allergy knows about the content of the service in advance, although wheat allergy is not common in the UK (Source: Food Standards Agency www. eatwell.gov.uk/healthissues/foodintolerance/ foodintolerancetypes/wheatallergy/) and does not usually affect sufferers by contact, rather by being consumed, which of course they do not have to do.

The importance of broken bread would be very significant if Holy Communion is included in this service.

Online resources

All suggested downloads are available at www.scriptureunion.org.uk/light. Visit www.lightlive.org for additional activities for children, young people and adults.

The next four service outlines leading up to Easter Day focus around the journey that Jesus went on, as he travelled to the cross. Suggestions are made for setting up a series of interactive stations for people to spend time engaging with what Jesus went through. You will need to begin preparing for this some weeks before Easter, especially if you are going to invite members of the community (including schoolchildren) into the church to spend time at the prayer stations. See page 117 for suggestions.

Palm Sunday

READINGS: **Psalm 118:1,2,9–24; Mark 11:1–11**
Isaiah 50:5–11; Philippians 2:5–11

Bible foundations

Aim: to contrast Jesus' expectations as he entered Jerusalem with those of the crowd

State visits are regular occurrences in most countries. They normally involve the visiting dignitary disembarking from their plane and waving to the receiving throng – a pretty standard formula.

In a similar way, military giants such as Alexander the Great and Judas Maccabeus entered a city as leaders, or self-proclaimed leaders. They came with pomp and ceremony, cheered (or jeered) by the crowds and, quite often, finished with an approach to the Temple. When Jesus entered Jerusalem it was a similar situation. But this wasn't just someone taking a trip to the big city. The events of Palm Sunday proclaim Jesus as King, and start a week that sees him crucified as king of the Jews.

Although Mark doesn't include a direct reference, there is a clear allusion to Zechariah 9:9 with Jesus riding on a colt. Matthew and John pick this up in their Gospels. But Mark does allude to Psalm 118:25,26, with the crowd's shouts of praise. This psalm is one of the royal psalms, in which the king asks to be admitted into the Temple to sing his royal song of thanksgiving. This was acted out as a processional song or prayer. As the years passed, it gained Messianic importance. In Mark 12:10,11 Jesus applies Psalm 118:22,23 to his coming rejection, of which the triumphal entry is the beginning.

When Jesus arrived at Jerusalem he knew what awaited him, and yet he continued. He let the crowds shout their praise, while knowing that the Messiah would be rejected. He was both an awesome and triumphant king, and an awesome and triumphant servant.

Holy Week prayer stations

For services taking place during Holy Week, it is suggested that, around the building, you set up a series of prayer stations for all ages. One station per session has been highlighted, although you may wish to create more than four. (Of course, the services can be easily adapted if you decide not to set up these stations.) You may not usually have an all-age service on Maundy Thursday, but this year you might consider holding one.

These stations can be used during a service but also during the week. The church may be left open for visitors to travel with Jesus on his journey to the cross, making use of the prayer stations. Many churches in Holy Week invite a local school to visit during the school day, as part of their provision for Religious Education. This helps to build relationships within the community. Children could be given a bag or container to collect and take home various objects from the stations. (Offering refreshments may be possible but that may take up too much time.) Of course, you need to consult fully with the school to ensure that what is available complies with the school curriculum and with plans for end of term activities. Health and safety requirements must be followed. Throughout the day, someone will need to be around to welcome and provide security. For more information on working with schools read *Top Tips on Developing partnerships between church and school* (SU) or visit www. scriptureunion.org.uk.

To open up a church like this has proved a valuable way to present the Easter event to people who may not be familiar with the story. In one church recently, several children visited the prayer stations with their teacher and then dragged parents and grandparents to the church on the way home from school. You could move the stations around as the week proceeds so that the relevant one is on show throughout a specific service. There are suggestions in each session for creating the stations, but use to the full your imagination and the gifts of the congregation. Different family groups could work together on creating a station.

The four suggested key stations are:
1. Palm Sunday (use on Sunday)
2. Last Supper (use on Maundy Thursday)
3. Crucifixion (use on Good Friday)
4. Resurrection (use on Easter Day)

Beginning the service

Draw attention to the Palm Sunday station which should be in a prominent place. Introduce what is going to happen during the rest of Holy Week.

Palm Sunday station

With: an arch of branches inviting people to enter; behind this, rugs on the floor, a low table covered with a cloth and objects such as a crown, balloons and flags placed on it;

Mark 11:7,9 reproduced and placed on the station; instruction card for visitors 'Write down one thing you want to thank God for and then tie it to the palm arch.'; home-made luggage labels cut out of coloured card as 'Shout' bubbles; pens.

Jesus' entry into Jerusalem is essentially a joyful event for everyone, except for Jesus' enemies and presumably Jesus himself, who knew he would have to suffer. The Roman authorities, responsible for maintaining law and order, might also have been alarmed.

Remind people of a recent local or national celebratory event such as the return of a successful football team or award-winning Olympic athletes. What happened and was everyone in the crowd joyful? Why might some people be unhappy – such as personal sadness, supporting the team that lost, angry at the money spent on the celebrations? Sometimes we can be in a cheering crowd but cannot share everyone else's joy. Jesus was most probably not happy on this day and his enemies certainly weren't.

Bible reading

Psalm 118:1,2,9–24 is a celebratory psalm. It could be read with the congregation split into two, reading alternate verses, or read by two people who walk together into church, proclaiming what God has done.

Mark 11:1–11 lends itself to a dramatic reading with a narrator and other readers taking the different parts.

Bible talk

With: objects that make the following sound

effects: clopping, swishing branches, shouting/party poppers; the final three statements on display, also available as a download (YearB.PalmSunday_1)

The aim of this **Bible talk** is to walk through the story again and show that Jesus knew what was happening, even though others in the crowd would not have known and had mixed reactions.

Give out the sound effect objects or instruct people to make different sounds as you tell the story. At the time of Jesus, a victorious military leader might return to the city riding on a horse. Everyone would cheer him. Jesus chose to ride into Jerusalem on a very young donkey which no one had ever ridden on before. (*Make the clopping sounds.*) He was acting as a victorious king, except the donkey was not exactly what people expected. Was this the Messiah they were all waiting for?

At the time of the Romans, the success of athletes and victorious army commanders was recognised by the waving of date palm branches. (*Make the swishing sounds of branches.*) Whose idea was it for the crowd to wave such branches as Jesus rode into Jerusalem? We don't know, but the Romans, seeing Jesus caught up in this, might have thought he was challenging their authority.

The excitement spread. The crowd got bigger. Jesus' disciples must have wondered if this was the time they had all been waiting for. (*Shouting and cheering!*) Refer back to the earlier discussion of crowds. What do the people who are being applauded by a crowd usually do and say? (Smile, wave, make a speech, get big heads!) Jesus gave no explanation and said nothing. He sat on the donkey (notice he knew it was going to be there; he wasn't surprised at what was happening) and then, as Mark's Gospel tells us, he went into the Temple in Jerusalem. Then he went to stay at his friends' home. That's all.

Invite everyone to make their sounds. Then call for silence. (*Allow for a long pause.*) For Jesus, this was the start of his final journey to the cross; this was what he had ultimately come to earth to do – to die. Introduce the following set of three statements and ask two people to read them, pausing after each statement.

The crowd was excited at being part of a celebration.
Jesus knew he was going to die.
The crowd was thrilled to cheer for their new king.
Jesus knew that they were not cheering for him as God the king.
The crowd did not think at that time that Jesus' enemies were plotting his death.
Jesus knew he was going to die.

Prayer activity

With: the home-made luggage labels from the prayer station, cut out as 'Shout' bubbles (speech bubbles!); pens

Because of its celebratory note, this would best follow on from the **Bible reading**, before the **Bible talk**. What would you want to shout out to Jesus if you had been in Jerusalem the day Jesus rode on the back of a donkey? Ask everyone to write or draw the best thing they would want to say to

Jesus. They can come forward to tie the shout bubble/label to the palm branch arch. You could distribute branches of trees (real or made of paper) so that younger people especially can wave them as they come to the prayer station. They could bring balloons and flags too. Comment on some of the things that people have written and conclude with a prayer of praise.

Prayer of confession

With: a large cross, or palm crosses if you will be distributing them

(*Everyone turns to the right.*) When Jesus rode on a donkey into Jerusalem, people shouted out cries of welcome. A few days later they were shouting for his death.
Forgive us, Father God, for the times when we have not faithfully followed you, when one moment we have said we love you, but the next moment have behaved as though we did not know you. (*Pause*) **Please forgive us**

(*Everyone turns to the left.*)
Forgive us, Father God, for the times when we have got caught up with what everyone else is doing and just forgotten about you and how you want us to live. (*Pause*) **Please forgive us**

(*Everyone looks up at the cross or holds their palm cross.*)
Forgive us, Father God, for the times when we have forgotten just how important it was, and is, that you sent Jesus into this world and that he came to die. (*Pause*) **Please forgive us.** Amen.

Ending the service

With: a large cross, or palm crosses if you will be distributing them

As the church community enters Holy Week, ask what people expect God to do for them this week. Suggest five or six different groups that describe where people might be located during part or all of the week. These could be: the schools group, the being-on-holiday group, the workplace group, the visiting-family group, the staying-at-home group. Everyone goes to one of these groups and pauses to think what they expect to be doing this week. Talk with smaller children about what they might be doing.

Everyone either holds their palm cross or looks to the large cross with their hands open to receive. Silently people ask God to remind them during this week what Jesus faced as he prepared to die, wherever they are. Then pray this prayer:

Jesus Christ, this week help us not to forget what it cost you to come to this earth to die. Amen.

Extra: If you have given out palm crosses, ask everyone to think about where they might strategically place their cross, so that it prompts curiosity and questions from their friends, colleagues and acquaintances in the week ahead.

Helpful extras

Music and song ideas
'From heaven you came, helpless babe'; 'All glory, laud and honour' (or a modern version); 'Hosanna, hosanna, hosanna to the king of kings'; 'Make way, make way'. Ending on a more solemn note with 'Ride on, ride on in majesty' or 'You laid aside your majesty'.

Notes and comments

You could take this service, or part of it, outside. Churches have been known to bring a donkey into church or at least into the church grounds. The story of Palm Sunday is a dramatic outdoor story!

Children from a non-church background coming to the prayer station will need to hear the story told briefly, explaining that the crowd shouted and cheered for Jesus who they thought was the Messiah, the person God would send to rescue them from the Romans. Help children to decide what they want to thank God for. In a school setting you need to introduce the activity by explaining that Christians regularly thank God for what he has given us and done for us. Can they think of something that they would like to thank God for? If they would like to, they can fill in a 'Shout' bubble label, thus they are given the choice of whether or not to join in. They could take home the luggage label or a celebratory balloon.

Online resources

All suggested downloads are available at www.scriptureunion.org.uk/light. Visit www.lightlive.org for additional activities for children, young people and adults. For your convenience the following activities are available as downloads: YearB.PalmSunday_2 Extra ideas; YearB. PalmSunday_3 and YearB.PalmSunday_4 Activities for 5s and under.

Maundy Thursday

READINGS: **Exodus 12:1−5,11−14; 1 Corinthians 11:23−26**
Psalm 111:1,2,12−19; John 13:1−17, 31b−35

Bible foundations

Aim: to recognise the symbolic importance of the Passover and the Last Supper

When the Lord spoke to Moses in Egypt, he commanded Moses and the people to participate in the rite of the Passover. The Passover was a one-off event as God's people escaped from Egypt, and ever after, could only be a memorial event. The Passover was a new beginning that they were commanded never to forget. (The only other things the people of Israel were told always to remember were the Lord's name and the Sabbath Day.)

Sacrifice had been a long-established tradition and played a part in covenantal agreements (Genesis 4:4; 15:9−18). It was to play a major part in the Passover with a carefully chosen lamb, providing the blood to be splashed on the doorposts. This provided protection and salvation for the people. The lamb had to be perfect, which links to the suffering servant of Isaiah 53:7−9, 1 Peter 1:19 and alluded to in Luke 23:41.

Paul, in his letter, reminded the Corinthians of the Last Supper because it was a tradition they were not keeping in the right way (1 Corinthians 11:2,17,22). Paul emphasised the word 'remembrance'. They were supposed to remember Jesus. What Jesus did was the whole point of the celebration.

Jesus reinterpreted the Last Supper as a Passover meal, using the bread and wine as symbols of his body and blood that were broken and poured out in his death on the cross. The Last Supper was part of the church's tradition, just as the Passover meal was to the nation of Israel. It was received from Jesus and passed on to the church as an act to be performed and drawn into until Jesus himself returned. It draws together the past (the Exodus and Jesus' death), is an action for the present and looks to the future.

See page 117 for details of setting up the Holy Week stations.

Beginning the service

Draw attention to the Last Supper station which should be in a prominent place, if relevant. Pick up a bowl of water and comment on the symbolism of water as a sign of cleansing. It would be appropriate to retell or read the story of Jesus washing the disciples' feet, reading from John 13:1–11. This could be followed by the **Prayer of confession** and/or by gently sprinkling water over the congregation.

Last Supper station

With: laid out on a low table a bowl of water and a roll of paper towel; a chalice-shaped cup to be filled with blackcurrant juice; pitta bread; if appropriate small cups for the 'wine'

The following Bible verses reproduced and placed on the station:

> Jesus took some bread in his hands. 'This is my body, which is given for you. Eat this and remember me.'
> Jesus took a cup of wine in his hands. 'This is my blood, and with it God makes his new agreement with you. Drink this and remember me.' 1 Corinthians 11:23–25 (CEV)

An instruction card for visitors:

- Break off a piece of bread and look at the jagged edge. Jesus' body was torn like this. Eat it and remember Jesus' death.
- Hold up the cup of juice. Jesus' blood was poured out just as the blood of the lamb was splashed on the doorposts which protected God's people when they were escaping from Egypt. Take a sip of the juice and be thankful for what Jesus did to save and protect his people.

- Wash your hands slowly and remember that, as a servant, Jesus washed the disciples' feet.

Note that the instructions for visitors do not assume any commitment to the Christian faith. You might want to amend these if only members of the church community are going to visit the stations.

Bible reading

The reading from Exodus 12 contains many visual images. If people have a clear view, you could collect symbols of the objects in the passage and show them as appropriate, or show the PowerPoint version of these verses available as a download (YearB.Maundy_1). This should be incorporated into the **Bible talk**.

John 13 could be included in **Beginning the service**. The reading of 1 Corinthians 11:23–26 could be incorporated in the **Bible talk**.

Bible talk

With: two people holding a pre-prepared conversation about forgetting; objects from the prayer station or materials to use in Holy Communion; the PowerPoint version of Exodus 12 (see above)

This talk could be part of a service of Holy Communion as you demonstrate what Jesus did in his Passover meal with his disciples. Obviously you will need to adapt it to the accepted practice in your church and the role children take in Holy Communion.

Two people walk into church talking loudly. The words 'forgotten' and 'remember' should frequently be spoken. One of them is telling the other about an appointment they should have kept but they had forgotten – such as an invitation to a party, or the date of a birthday of someone they love. The other verbally chastises them and suggests all sorts of things they could do to make sure they don't forget again, such as writing it in the diary, asking someone to remind them, putting a reminder on their mobile phone, even taking a photograph. Conclude with the statement: 'But I always forget!'

We all have trouble with our memories. You could ask for suggestions. God knows that that is how we are. Fortunately he never forgets anything but, of course, he doesn't hold grudges about anything we have done wrong. There is one really important thing that he wants us to remember. Briefly tell the background story of the Exodus including the visual reading from Exodus 12:1–4, 11–14, available as a download (YearB.Maundy_1).

God wanted his people to remember that they had been rescued from Egypt. It was the blood on the doorpost that had identified them as God's people. Blood was to become a symbol of God's act of saving and protecting his people.

But then, many centuries later, even before he had died, Jesus gave his disciples two symbols that would help them remember his death. Indeed, this was for all those people who were to follow him for all the centuries to come. Jesus' death mattered. It is the most important thing that has ever happened in all of history. How could we forget? The trouble is, we do. We have poor memories.

At this point, if you are having a Communion

service, lead into that, breaking bread and drinking wine together. You could do this by inviting everyone to come to the prayer station, allowing time for people to break a piece of bread, to look at the jagged edge, to eat and to drink. Alternatively, follow your normal practice of celebrating Communion.

If, however, you are not celebrating the Eucharist, take the bread and wine/ blackcurrant juice from the prayer station and tell the story, using Jesus' words from 1 Corinthians 11 as a framework. Tearing the bread and pouring out wine are bold, dramatic actions.

Conclude by asking how people are going to remember the importance of Jesus' death. Remind them that we need regularly to take part in a Communion service. (You will need to adapt this statement if children do not usually play any part in Communion.) We also need to make a point of regularly thanking God for Jesus' death and often to read the account of what Jesus did on the cross.

Prayer activity

People across the world and down through the ages have used the symbols of bread and wine to remember the significance of Jesus' death. It would therefore be appropriate to pray for Christians in other parts of the world. If you have links with mission partners in another country, pray for them and the country where they are living and working. If you do not have such links, choose a country in the news at the time and pray for Christians there, this Holy Week. Make sure that children know where the country is. It would be appropriate for them to pray for children and young people in that country. These prayers could be prepared in advance. Encourage children's spontaneity.

Prayer of confession

It would be appropriate to use this prayer immediately after **Beginning the service**.

Take the bowl of water from the prayer station and let the water run through your fingers. Explain that as we come to worship God we need to confess our sins and come with a pure and cleansed heart. Read Hebrews 10:22: Let's come near to God with pure hearts and a confidence that comes from having faith.
Invite people to reflect on when and where they have wronged God in the past week. Then read out these words of promise, fulfilled in Christ, from Ezekiel 36:25 that God said to his people, long before the time of Christ:

I will sprinkle you with clean water, and you will be clean and acceptable to me. I will wash away everything that makes you unclean.

Then sprinkle the water over the congregation. Warn people what you are going to do if you think there will be squealing or other adverse reactions.

Ending the service

A dramatic memorable ending to the service would be to place some white paper upon a board, with a plastic cloth on the floor. Darken the room but ensure there is sufficient light shining on the board. In the silence, throw some dark red paint or tomato sauce at the board and watch it slide down. You will need to check that it is the right consistency to run smoothly but thickly. Say: 'Jesus' blood was poured out so that we might be saved and protected.' After a pause, invite people to say that again, together.

Helpful extras

Music and song ideas
'Do this, do this, and remember me' is a song about the Last Supper that was written for the *Xpedition Force* holiday club programme (SU). It is available with words and a recording as a download: (YearB.Maundy_2); 'Thank you, Jesus'; 'Broken for me, broken for you'; 'You led me to the cross'.

Play some suitable recorded music as people come to the prayer station or take Communion.

Statement of faith
We believe that God saved his people in Egypt by the blood that was splashed upon the doorposts, so that everyone inside was kept alive.

By his blood we are saved

We believe that God saves us by the blood of his Son which was poured out as a sacrifice for us as he hung on the cross.

By his blood we are saved

We believe that we must never forget, now and in the future, that Jesus died to save and protect us.

By his blood we are saved

Notes and comments

Not many churches hold all-age services on Maundy Thursday and yet it is wholly appropriate that children and young people should be included in a re-enactment of what happened in the Last Supper. Obviously the custom in your church with regard to children taking part in Communion will affect what you are able to do. But it is important to remember that the drama of the event speaks powerfully to children (and people of all ages). If appropriate, the service could be followed by a church family meal or, at the very least, hot cross buns.

Alternatively, you could hold an all-age Passover meal, which incorporates elements of this outline. Suggestions for this can be found in *Easter Cracked* (SU).

Children from a non-church background coming to the prayer station will need to hear the story told briefly, explaining the significance of the Passover. This could be done by a rolling PowerPoint presentation of the reading from Exodus 12, available as a download (YearB.Maundy_1). They then need to hear how Jesus was preparing his disciples for his death. He wanted them to remember it as he joined in his last Passover meal. He gave the meal a new meaning by giving them the symbols of bread and wine. In a school setting you need to introduce the activity by explaining that Christians regularly take part in a service of Holy Communion or Eucharist, taking seriously Jesus' words to go on remembering. Invite them to tear off a bit of bread, looking at the rough edge and eating it. (Be aware of allergy issues.) They can then drink some of the blackcurrant juice which should be made available in small cups. They should be given the choice of whether or not to join in. Children could take home a broken piece of bread.

Many churches incorporate foot-washing or hand-washing into a Maundy Thursday service. This can be very powerful but bear in mind personal sensitivities.

Online resources

All suggested downloads are available at www.scriptureunion.org.uk/light. Visit www.lightlive.org for additional activities for children, young people and adults. For your convenience the following activity is available as a download: YearB. Maundy_3 Other ideas.

Good Friday

READINGS: **Isaiah 52:13 – 53:12; John 18:1 – 19:42**
Psalm 22; Hebrews 4:14–16; 5:7–9

Bible foundations

Aim: to identify with the suffering and purpose of Jesus' death

'Goals', 'objectives' and 'vision' are key words in contemporary management jargon. Many of the most productive businesses are driven by these. It is important for us to see that Jesus had a clear vision of the purpose of the events that unfolded on Good Friday. He was not a victim of the mob, who clamoured for his blood, nor was he a pawn in the hands of the religious leaders of the day. Isaiah 52:13 – 53:12, when applied to Jesus as the servant, makes it clear that Jesus' death is no accident. Similarly, parallels to Jesus' crucifixion are clear in Psalm 22. His death was planned from the beginning of time. As Isaiah presented it, this death was essential to take away the sin of the world.

From the beginning of John 18, Jesus sets the events in motion. Jews observing the Passover had to stay within a certain distance of the city. Judas would have known this. All four Gospels record that Jesus knew what was going to happen, for example John 18:5,9. John emphasises that Jesus was voluntarily giving up his life in obedience. When Peter raised his sword, Jesus stopped him. Throughout the trial Jesus answered without attempting to escape the inevitable outcome. Crucifixion was a horrendous form of capital punishment. Already weakened by the beating, Jesus' pain would have been intense. His final words are best rendered: 'It is accomplished.'

The writer of Hebrews presents Jesus as the high priest, whose purpose was to suffer every human weakness but then to pass into heaven (Hebrews 4:14–16). This is not the language of a victim or a pawn! Helping children (indeed people of all ages) to understand the cross is a challenge. You would benefit from reading *Top Tips on Explaining the cross*. For more details see page 80.

See page 117 for details of setting up the prayer stations.

Beginning the service

As people arrive, communicate something of the bleakness and hopelessness of this day for Jesus' followers 2,000 years ago, by displaying a picture of Christ on the cross. You could darken the room slightly. Play music that communicates something of the sorrow of Jesus' death eg Bach's 'St Matthew Passion', 'Message of the cross' (Delirious?) or 'How deep the Father's love for us'. You could sing this latter song at the beginning of the service.

If you are using the prayer station, draw attention to it and comment on how the stations have been used during the week.

Crucifixion station

With: laid out on a low table a crown of thorns (or a picture of one); a large vertical empty cross; a box of tissues; pieces of string and piles of small twigs; blank sheep-shaped pieces of card, template available as a download (YearB.GoodF_1); white thin candles; pins or glue to attach to the cross

The following Bible verses reproduced and placed on the station:

> Jesus was nailed to a cross, and on each side of him a man was also nailed to a cross.
> Jesus knew that he had now finished his work.
> After Jesus drank the wine, he said, 'Everything is now done!' He bowed his head and died.
> John 19:18,28,30

Above the cross write these words:

> All of us were like sheep that had wandered off. We had each gone our own way, but the Lord gave him the punishment we deserved. Isaiah 53:6

An instruction card for visitors:

> - Jesus died on the cross to take the punishment for the wrong we have done. With a white candle on the sheep-shaped card write one wrong thing you have done that you would like Jesus to take away. No one will know except God since it is invisible writing. Pin your sheep to the large cross. (The prophet Isaiah called us all sheep.)
> - Touch the crown of thorns and imagine that being pushed over your eyebrows. That is what happened to Jesus.
> - Take two of the twigs and bind them together to make a cross.

Note that the instructions for visitors do not assume any commitment to the Christian faith. You might want to amend them if only members of the church community are going to visit the stations.

Bible reading

Isaiah 52:13 – 53:12 could be read in the **Prayer of confession**. (If you think that the reading is too long for an all-age service, you could end after 53:6.) Isaiah 53 is available as a download (YearB.GoodF_2). Introduce by explaining that one way of understanding the identity of God's servant is to see him as Jesus. Listen out for all the ways that Isaiah is speaking about Jesus who lived many centuries after Isaiah. Readers 1 and

2 describe what the servant has done while Reader 3 reads how others are affected by the servant. Reader 3 could stand separated from the other two.

Summarise John 18, then read John 19:1–42 as a drama. You may choose to read only part of the chapter.

Psalm 22:5 could be used as a *Learn and remember* verse. Display the whole verse for everyone to read out together several times. They could shout it out and then whisper it. As confidence in remembering it increases, take away a word at a time. Ask if any individuals can speak the verse out on their own. A game version of the first half of the verse is available for younger members as a download (YearB.GoodF_5).

Bible talk

With: a picture of a giant roller coaster available as a download (YearB.GoodF_3); PowerPoint of the six stages/slides of the disciples' roller coaster ride (YearB.GoodF_4)

Recap the summary of John 18,19 up to where Jesus was taken away (19:16). Invite everyone to imagine they are going on a giant roller coaster. *(Show picture.)* How might you feel if you were about to go on this? Refer to a local or well-known roller coaster such as the Junglecoaster at Legoland or the Stealth at Thorpe Park. You may be excited and scared stiff all at the same time! Once it starts, there is no return. The feeling in your stomach can't get worse as you swoop down, but suddenly it starts over again as you ascend to the heights only to plummet again. (Let children really enthuse about this!)

That may have been how the disciples felt. Ask what happened on Palm Sunday. *(Show PowerPoint slide 1.)* How might they have felt? But what happened next? *(Show next three slides.)* Jesus talks of his death, is arrested, put on trial! Could it get worse? Surely he would do something to stop it all! What was going to happen next? They couldn't get off, just as you can't get out of the roller coaster once you're strapped in! They would have to go through with it. Ask how people would have felt if they had been the disciples – desperate, disappointed, scared, humiliated and confused. Count how many words people can suggest.

(Show slide 5.) Things had got worse. Briefly pick out three things that happened at the actual crucifixion as Jesus hung on the cross. So why did this have to happen? How could it have all gone so wrong? Reread Isaiah 53:10a and comment on the sheep-shapes **Prayer of confession.** This was no mistake. The prophet Isaiah had prophesied this hundreds of years before.

(Show slide 6.) The best was yet to come. Jesus did indeed die and the disciples thought this was the end. But it wasn't. And on Easter Day we celebrate the fact that he came alive again. But on Good Friday we leave the disciples confused and sad and wondering where God is in all this. They were learning what it means to trust that God knows best! And that is a hard, hard lesson for anyone to learn.

Refer to Psalm 22:5 as the *Learn and remember* verse. This is what the disciples needed to discover about God at this time of despair. You could learn the verse as this point – see **Beginning the service** and the **Game** in **Helpful extras**.

Prayers of confession

With: enough blank sheep-shaped sheets of card/paper for everyone (as on the prayer station) available as a download (YearB. GoodF_I); thin white candles

Give everybody a blank sheep-shape with access to a candle. Read Isaiah 52:13 – 53:12 or just up to verse 6, preferably using the version on the download 2. Draw attention to verse 6 and comment on what sheep are like and in what ways we can be like sheep. Ask people to write on the sheep-shape where they have gone their own way this week. Make suggestions and give prompts such as being selfish, being unkind to a younger brother or sister, doing things they shouldn't have done or leaving undone what should have been done. How have others been upset by our action or lack of it this week? Comment that writing in invisible 'ink' means that no one except God knows what is being written.

Invite people to bring their sheep-shape to pin or stick on the cross that forms part of the prayer station. Explain that by doing this they are asking God to forgive them – which he will do because of Jesus' death. Play some quiet music while people come forward. Declare that God has heard our requests and has forgiven us. Jesus has taken our punishment on the cross!

Prayers of intercession

Use Psalm 22:4 and 5 (verse 5 has been the *Learn and remember* verse) as the basis for these prayers. Encourage people that God is trustworthy. There are many examples in the Bible of our forefathers trusting in God and in his deliverance. He answers our prayers today too.

- Focus on the needs of the world that seem hopeless. Display news headlines from the past week as a focus. Pray into these situations. Close this section by reading Psalm 22:5b.
- Focus on specific local situations that seem hopeless. Remind people of Psalm 22:4. Name specific situations and pray that God will use individuals from your church family to bring hope, trust and his deliverance.
- Ask people to pray for specific individuals in need and encourage them to trust God to care for them. Remind them that they will not ultimately be disappointed. Read Psalm 22:5a.
- Close by encouraging people to think how the disciples must have felt as they saw Jesus crucified. Yet three days later they heard or saw that he was alive again. Ultimately, we can have hope that God will act. He hears and answers our prayers.

Ending the service

Either ask a few people to do the following at the front, or encourage anyone to join in. You could show the six PowerPoint slides again.

Stand on the seat to say loudly: JESUS IS KING!
Stand on the floor and say quietly: JESUS TALKS OF DYING!
Bend down as though about to sit down and say quietly: JESUS IS ARRESTED
Sit down and say quietly: JESUS IS PUT ON

TRIAL
Kneel on the floor and whisper: JESUS IS PUT TO DEATH
Stand on the seat and shout: THE BEST IS YET TO COME!

Encourage people to return on Sunday to celebrate that Jesus lives, the best has come! Use this weekend as an opportunity to share the greatest news history has ever known.

Helpful extras

Music and song ideas
'When I survey the wondrous cross'; 'From heaven you came'; 'How deep the Father's love'; 'Consider Christ'; 'Jesus Christ I think upon your sacrifice (once again)'; 'The price is paid'; 'Led like a lamb to the slaughter'; 'Oh to see the dawn of the darkest day'; 'Christ on the road to Calvary'; 'When I think about the cross'.

Game
A PowerPoint game suitable for 8s and under to unpack the Learn and remember verse is available as a download (YearB.GoodF_5).

There are ten hidden pictures of the three crosses, split into identical pairs. Can younger members of the congregation match them up? When they get one pair right, some words from the Learn and remember verse will appear. Use this game to help reinforce the verse and its meaning.

Notes and comments
Good Friday is a sad and reflective day. Christ died a real and brutal death and real people who knew him and were close to him were affected by this. We need to encourage everyone to appreciate the reality of what happened but at the same time to appreciate that, unlike the disciples, we know that the best was yet to come. There is a balance here that needs to be struck! Many people know what it means to be full of despair and asking what there is to be hopeful about. Where is God? The reflections of today can be most helpful to anyone whose life is like this.

You may want to emphasise something of the brutality of Jesus' death, perhaps visually using a video. The Jesus Film or the children's version of this, The Jesus Quest, does this well. This may not be appropriate, however, if there are very young children present.

Children coming on a school visit can make up a cross with twigs and string/wool to take home with them as a souvenir. You will need to tell the relevant part of the story and/or show part of the video.

Online resources
All suggested downloads are available at www.scriptureunion.org.uk/light. Visit www.lightlive.org for additional activities for children, young people and adults. For your convenience the following activity is available as a download: YearB. GoodF_6 Adult sermon.

Easter Day

READINGS: **1 Corinthians 15:1–11; Mark 16:1–8**
Isaiah 25:6–9; Psalm 118:1,2,14–24

Bible foundations

Aim: to celebrate the amazing effect of the resurrection on the first disciples

To say that the world is a little crazy could be an understatement. On Easter Day Christians celebrate the culmination of the Easter story, the resurrection of Jesus. On the other hand, shops pile their shelves high with chocolate Easter bunnies.

Paul's letter to the Corinthians was probably written during the AD 50s, about twenty years after the events of the first Easter. In today's passage Paul is appealing to the tradition that was central to the Corinthian church, namely that Jesus had died, was buried and was then raised to life. What's more, many people still alive at the time of his writing had seen Jesus. It was this belief that had saved them. Possibly the only creedal saying that was common to the whole church can be found in verses 3–5. Notice the importance that Paul places on the fact that these events were the fulfilment of the Scriptures. He wanted them to be confident in their faith. But unfortunately the Corinthians were wavering in their understanding. Paul points out in verse 2 that salvation is found in the gospel which he has received and passed on. This resurrection is a real fact.

From the moment of his resurrection (strengthened by the events of Pentecost), Jesus' followers were transformed from being scared and reticent. Mark's account of the empty tomb is important because the empty tomb was crucial in convincing them that Jesus was alive! Without it, all accounts of the resurrection appearances could be interpreted as ghost stories. Remarkably it is initially the account of women which adds authenticity. Anyone seeking to cover up the truth would not have relied on women whose testimony in court would not be accepted.

Belief in the resurrection transforms lives. May that be true for all those worshipping with you this Easter Day, just as the lives of the first disciples were transformed!

Beginning the service

Introduce the fourth Easter Day prayer station and share how the stations have been used this week. See page 117 for details.

Easter Day calls for everyone to celebrate the resurrection of Jesus from the dead! Stand for a proclamation 'praise shout'. Split the congregation into two, one half to read the first bold 'shout' followed by the others with the second bold 'shout'. The leader reads the first line. This is also available as a download (YearB.Easter1_2).

Jesus Christ, the Son of God, conquered death for us!
Hallelujah! Praise the Lord!
Hallelujah! Thank you, Lord!

Jesus Christ, the Son of God, rose triumphant from the grave.
Hallelujah! Praise the Lord!
Hallelujah! Thank you, Lord!

Jesus Christ, the Son of God, is seated in heaven at the Father's side.
Hallelujah! Praise the Lord!
Hallelujah! Thank you, Lord!

Jesus Christ, the Son of God, will return in power and majesty.
Hallelujah! Praise the Lord!
Hallelujah! Thank you, Lord.

Easter Day station

With: objects that will make this into a garden; short-stemmed spring flowers each wrapped in a damp kitchen towel (to make them last as long as possible); large boulder (made out of cardboard); Easter/paschal candle; tea lights (be aware of safety issues: provide a firm, heatproof base for them!); a basket of small chocolate eggs. This could be made more interactive by putting this inside a tent with a wide entrance or a side chapel or a baptistery used for adult immersion.

The following Bible verses reproduced and placed on the station:

> Very early on Sunday morning, just as the sun was coming up, [the women] went to the tomb ... they saw that the stone had already been rolled away. And it was a huge stone! The women went into the tomb, and on the right side they saw a young man in a white robe sitting there. They were alarmed. The man said ... 'God has raised [Jesus] to life and he isn't here.' Mark 16:2,4–6 (CEV)

An instruction card for visitors:

> - Jesus came alive again and that brings new life and hope to everyone. Take a spring flower and think of a sad place where you would like God to bring hope. Speak to God about this.
> - At first the women were afraid. When they had met Jesus and really knew he was alive they did not need to fear. Light a tea light and ask God to shine his light and take away fear.
> - Take an Easter egg to remind you that, just as an egg stands for new life, so Jesus came alive again.

Note that the instructions for visitors do not assume any commitment to the Christian faith. You might want to amend that if only members of the church community are going to visit.

Bible reading

Read 1 Corinthians 15:1-11 using CEV or TNIV. The reader could learn this by heart to present to the congregation as if he is the apostle Paul and they are his friends. He wants them to remember the message that Jesus is alive! Introduce as follows: The apostle Paul sent this long letter to the Christians who lived in Corinth. They were a group of believers who had had lots of growing pains as Christians but Paul had helped them. Above all, he wanted them to be absolutely certain that Jesus had died but was now alive.

Alternatively it could be read as a **Statement of faith**.

Mark 16:1-8 could be read as a drama script, available with music suggestions as a download (YearB.Easter1_1). Allow a short time to reflect, after the music has finished. Comment that even after they had heard Jesus was alive, people were afraid or unbelieving, as the reading points out. You could refer to Thomas too. It was only after people had met Jesus that their fear changed.

Bible talk

With: three groups of witnesses to the fact that Jesus is alive; a witness box – conversation with the witnesses should be as natural as possible and a rehearsal is strongly recommended

1 Corinthians 15:1-11 should be read as suggested above to introduce the **Bible talk**. Make sure that people know who the apostle Paul is. Remind everyone about the sadness of Good Friday. Two days later everything had changed. Jesus had come alive! Over the next few weeks loads of people met Jesus so they were witnesses to that fact that he was alive. We are going to meet some of them. Invite the groups of witnesses to the witness box. Each could place their hand on the Bible to promise to tell the truth. Interview each of them asking them the following questions:

- Who are you?
- What is your connection to Jesus?
- How do you know he is alive?
- How has your life been changed as result?

Check that everyone knows what a witness is. Expect responses along the lines of 'someone who was there', 'someone who has seen the evidence'.

First witnesses: the three women in the Bible reading.

- Who are you? (Mary Magdalene, Salome, Mary the mother of James)
- What is your connection to Jesus? (Friends and relatives of Jesus)
- How do you know he is alive? (They watched him die on the cross, they knew he was buried in the tomb in the garden, it was a rush to get him buried because the Sabbath began, and his body was not properly prepared. Recount in their own words what happened according to Mark 16:1-8 (and not any other Gospel!).)
- How has your life been changed as result? (Initially they were afraid until after they met Jesus. Then they walked and talked with him. He is alive, for ever. That means he is always with them.)

Second witness: Peter

- Who are you? (Simon, but Jesus renamed him Peter or Cephas which means 'Rock')

- What is your connection to Jesus? (One of Jesus' closest followers, who saw him feed thousands, walk on water (even help Peter walk on water), saw him arrested and then denied knowing who Jesus was three times (said shamefacedly).
- How do you know he is alive? (The women said that an angel had specifically told them to tell Peter that Jesus was alive, he met Jesus on the day he came alive, on the beach early in the morning and other times. He knew it was Jesus and not a ghost!)
- How has your life been changed as a result? (Jesus has forgiven him for letting him down and has given him a new task to help others become followers of Jesus.)

Briefly, comment that Paul had also mentioned the 'Twelve' in his letter. The 'Twelve' were identified as Jesus' companions which included Peter. Comment that the identity of the 'more than five hundred' is uncertain but they may have been the followers Jesus met in Galilee. Mention 'James', the half-brother of Jesus who did not believe until after the resurrection. 'All the apostles' was an inclusive term taking in the twelve and others involved in the spread of Christianity.

Third witness: Paul
- Who are you? (Known as Saul who had a name change, came from Tarsus in Syria)
- What is your connection to Jesus? (A very intelligent and religious man who persecuted the early Christians)
- How do you know he is alive? (Briefly recount Saul/Paul's encounter with Jesus on the road to Damascus.)

- How has your life been changed as a result? (Refer back to the Bible reading verses 10,11. His life has been transformed!)

All these people had met Jesus and were convinced that he was alive. None of them was expecting this. But after they met Jesus, they were never the same again. We do not meet Jesus in quite the same way as they did but this church is full of people who have met Jesus and have been changed. We can have hope and need not be afraid. Invite someone to share how meeting Jesus has changed them. Make sure they have prepared what they say, not using jargon but child-friendly language, making sense to those who have not yet met Jesus themselves. This leads into the **Prayer activity**.

Prayer activity

With: the flowers on the prayer station; Easter eggs; small candles which could be lit from the paschal candle (be safety conscious!)

Give people a choice of what they bring to the prayer station – a daffodil to be put in the 'garden' or a tea light they can light and leave on the table in front of the empty cross. They can either ask God to bring hope to a place where the hope of Jesus is needed such as a country where there is hunger or someone they know who is sad, or they can light/hold a candle and ask God to take away fear, thinking of someone they know who is scared or is facing something difficult in the future. Give some specific suggestions. Everyone takes an egg as they leave the station as a sign of new life and hope.

Conclude by reading Isaiah 25:6–9 and then I Corinthians 15:3b,4. Musicians play/sing as people come forward to make their prayer requests.

Ending the service

Conclude with the declaration used at **Beginning the service**, followed by a celebratory song. 'Peace to you' (see **Music and song ideas**) could be a benediction to sing to each other.

A feast after the service would continue the celebratory theme. If this is not practical, offer some special things to eat with tea and coffee – chocolate cake is always a winner!

Helpful extras

Music and song ideas
'Thine be the glory'; 'Christ the Lord is risen today, Hallelujah'; 'From heaven you came'; 'There is a redeemer'; 'Sing a song, sing a joyful song (Celebrate)'; 'Low in the grave he lay'; 'Here is love vast as the ocean'; 'How deep the Father's love for us'; 'King of kings, majesty'; 'Above all powers'; 'Light of the world'; 'Oh to see the dawn'. 'Peace to you' (Graham Kendrick) could be sung as a blessing to each other at the end as this echoes Jesus' words when he appears after his resurrection.

Statement of faith
Read I Corinthians 15:3b–7 as a statement of the things that we are sure about. It could be read antiphonally or each section could be read and then repeated.

Notes and comments

The **Prayer activity** flows from the **Bible talk**. Some supervision will be needed to give out flowers and candles, light candles and hand out eggs. You could fix the daffodils to the cross itself (using chicken wire). This is very effective but will also need supervision.

If the service includes a baptism, draw comparisons between Jesus' death and resurrection and the symbolism of baptism – the baptised person witnesses that they have died to sin and live in the resurrection power of Christ. A child is being baptised on the basis of what Jesus has done.

Incorporate the words of the praise shout or the **Prayer activity** into a Communion service.

Online resources
All suggested downloads are available at www.scriptureunion.org.uk/light. Visit www.lightlive.org for additional activities for children, young people and adults.

Second Sunday of Easter

READINGS: **Acts 4:32–35; John 20:19–31**
Psalm 133; 1 John 1:1 – 2:2

Bible foundations

Aim: to experience the impact of the resurrection on the first disciples

We believe that if a series of specifically-shaped pieces of metal are put together using the right methods, powered by the right sort of engine and driven by a qualified pilot, we have before us an aeroplane. We can fly. We get on board a plane and fly around the world. Our belief leads to action.

In Acts 4:32–35 we have an account of how the early church operated together after the events of the resurrection and ascension. These early believers have been empowered by the Holy Spirit and we read how their faith and belief work out practically in the way they live as a community.

Luke's phrase in verse 32 that describes the togetherness of the community is common in Greek thought. Similar language can be found in Euripides, Aristotle, Plutarch, Plato and Cicero. Luke places the apostles at the centre of events. The 'great power' of the sharing of the good news to others by word of mouth is matched in the collection and distribution of the community goods. By living this way they are being blessed by God, a similar phrase to a Septuagint reading of Exodus 3:21.

This is in stark contrast to the disciples' behaviour in John 20:19, when they hide from the authorities. The resurrection was about to become very real to them. Jesus' greeting, 'Shalom', perfectly follows the 'It is accomplished' that were the last words some of them may have heard him speak. Thomas is not present at the initial appearance but when Jesus returns the following week, he responds with praise, making his profound theological statement on the status of Christ.

All that was written in John's Gospel is there so that we may believe (20:31). The resurrection was believed by the apostles and it changed their lives. Expect God to change the lives of everyone in church for this service!

Beginning the service

Ask everyone to imagine they have a friend who plays in a local football/sport team. You spend weeks and months telling everyone about how great this team is and bragging about the friend who is in the team. The team sails through the qualifying rounds of the FA Cup (or another equivalent big sporting tournament). You have persuaded a bunch of friends to support the team. Describe the team's incredible victories in the early rounds. Pick a few big name opponents and try to rally a cheer from the congregation each time you announce that this local team has beaten an opponent. It is real David and Goliath stuff!

Now imagine this team makes it into the final. You sell a few tickets to your friends, all on the basis of your confident predictions of great success. The team is facing (name a mega-team and encourage boos etc). Describe the match as your team gets trounced 5–0. How do you now feel, facing all those friends you've boasted to? What kind of jokes might you face? Some of those people you sold tickets to even want their money back.

Imagine all of this multiplied dozens of times over. You might be getting somewhere close to how the disciples felt after Jesus' death. But then… something changed!

Bible reading

Read John 20:19–31 using different people for each of the following 'voices': Narrator, Jesus, Thomas, Disciples. People should practise this in advance. The 'Disciples' only have one easy line, suitable for a less confident reader. Alternatively, the whole congregation could speak this line. The reading is available as a download (YearB. Easter2_1).

Display the reading below from Acts 4:32–35 (CEV), also available as a download (YearB. Easter2_2). Explain that you are going to read out the passage, but you want them to speak out all the words in bold. Use this at the start of the **Bible talk**.

The group of followers **all** felt the same way about **everything**. **None** of them claimed that their possessions were their own, and they shared **everything** they had with each other. In a powerful way the apostles told **everyone** that the Lord Jesus was now alive. God greatly blessed his followers, and **no one** went in need of **anything**. **Everyone** who owned land or houses would sell them and bring the money to the apostles. Then they would give the money to **anyone** who needed it.

Bible talk

With: Acts 4:32–35 on display – see **Bible reading**; flip chart paper divided into two columns with a vertical space down the middle; pens

Display Acts 4:32–35. Using a flip chart (or OHP), ask people to suggest words that describe the disciples in this passage. You may need to explain that this describes the disciples soon after Jesus had gone back to heaven. Write suggestions on the right-hand side of the flip chart. If necessary, prompt for descriptive words such as: united, sharing, selfless, generous, empowered, bold, radical, enthused, committed, convinced.

137

Ask if anyone can think of examples before this time when the disciples hadn't been like this. Refer back to last week. You should get some of the following examples: Peter denying Christ (afraid, embarrassed); James and John asking to be the greatest in the kingdom of heaven (selfish/disunited); Judas stealing from the disciples' money bag (greedy, selfish); asking for signs (doubting). Use the **Bible reading** from John 20 for examples, eg the disciples hiding away in a locked room. Write up some of these opposite descriptions on the left-hand side of the flip chart, trying to place them directly opposite their counterparts.

Explain how hard it is to believe that these are descriptions of the same group of people just a few weeks apart! What has happened to change these greedy/selfish/disunited/scared people into the sharing/united/selfless/generous ones? Something really big and unimaginably enormous must have happened to make this kind of change. What could it be? Dramatically, write RESURRECTION down the middle of the chart.

The 19th-century poet, Gerard Manley Hopkins, in *That nature is a Heraclitian fire and of the comfort of the resurrection*, captured something of the wonder, amazement and life-changing nature of the resurrection as follows. Younger members of the congregation may not understand some of the terms and references, but the language and rhythm can still strike a chord. You could also take time to discuss some of the meanings and images!

'... the Resurrection,
A heart's-clarion! Away grief's gasping, joyless days, dejection.
Across my foundering deck shone
A beacon, an eternal beam. Flesh fade, and mortal trash
Fall to the residuary worm; world's wildfire, leave but ash:
In a flash, at a trumpet crash,
I am all at once what Christ is, since he was what I am ...'

Through the resurrection, which ultimately led to the coming of the Holy Spirit, the disciples were able to become like Christ. That can be our experience too. The unity and togetherness that the disciples found is a reflection of the unity that Jesus had with his heavenly Father and the Holy Spirit. The resurrection has the same power to change lives today as it did 2,000 years ago. But we need to tell others, just as the first disciples were to discover.

Prayer activity

Read 1 John 1:1 – 2:2, then pray for people to **HEAR** God through us, to **SEE** him in us, to **FEEL** his touch through us. Divide the congregation into at least three groups, and assign each group to be either A, B or C.

- Group(s) A: discuss ways in which people might **HEAR** God, or hear about him. (For example: music, talking to Christians, reading the Bible, God speaking directly, eg a voice from heaven, still small voice, as a human voice, through non-Christians/elements/creation.)
- Group(s) B: discuss ways in which God can be **SEEN**. (For example: nature, art, church buildings, physical manifestation, actions of Christians, visions.)

- Group(s) C: discuss ways in which God can be **TOUCHED** or **FELT**. (For example: through Christian actions, through their conscience, through experiencing love.)

Pray in each group that we and others would SEE, HEAR and FEEL God in these ways. You could ask one person from each group to share one of their prayers with the congregation. Make sure that children are included in your discussions/prayers.

Ending the service

An appropriate way to end this service would be to have some form of shared, community activity to reflect the actions of the disciples in Acts 4. This doesn't mean convincing everyone to sell their houses and pile all the cash up in the font! But you could:

- have a bring and share lunch
- organise a litter-picking expedition in the town centre
- clear up a local park
- arrange a friendly football match with a nearby church, mosque or other local organisation
- work with others to arrange a sponsored activity to raise money for charity.

All of these require forward planning, but are a very practical way of cementing the message of this service. Before embarking on the activity, close the service by reminding the congregation to think about how the resurrection of Jesus overcame all the differences within the disciples. Encourage everyone to remember that ultimately this still binds all Christians in the world together,

irrespective of whatever other quibbles and disagreements we may have. Think how this week they could work to put aside differences they have with other Christians (whether individual Christians, or a particular group or denomination that they disagree with) and instead focus on the unity they have in the resurrection of Jesus.

Helpful extras

Music and song ideas

A selection of songs and music celebrating the resurrection include: 'Thine be the glory (Risen conquering son)'; 'He has risen' (Noel Richards/Tricia Richards/Gerald Coates); 'Easter (Rise, heart, thy Lord is risen) by George Herbert; 'Brother, sister, let me serve you'.

You could also use Mahler's *Resurrection symphony*, with or without an introduction, to begin or end the service (or both!). The words to the libretto in his fifth movement are especially pertinent and can be found by using a search engine on the Internet. These could be used as a meditation, or the English version read out before or after playing the piece.

The song 'In the light' (DC Talk/Charlie Peacock) is an extremely powerful evocation of I John I and is a good starting point to talk about what 'living in the light' means in practice. Either play this or display the lyrics to use as a starting point to talk about the way in which we all fail to live up to our own standards – let alone God's.

Statement of faith

Display this statement of faith on OHP/

projector or print on service sheets. It is also available as a download (YearB.Easter2_3). The congregational response is in bold.

There is a life that comes from God.
He is the resurrection and the life.
There is a Spirit who breathes in us.
His Spirit is with us and within us.
There is a truth that sets us free.
God is truth. In him there is no falsehood at all.
There is a love that fills our hearts.
God is love. In his presence there is peace.
We believe in a living God, a risen Saviour.
May we bring the light and life of Jesus into a dark and dying world.
Give us gladness in sharing good news and fill us with fearlessness.
Let us be true disciples; touch our lips that we may speak of you.

Notes and comments

The resurrection brought the disciples together in unity in a way that couldn't have seemed possible before Jesus' death, with all the squabbles and struggles for positions of status that were going on. Sadly, one of the things that turns many people from the church and Christianity today is the division and arguments between denominations, and even within them. If you think younger members of the congregation may not understand talk about 'unity' try using synonyms such as 'togetherness', 'agreement' or even 'being friends'.

For more in-depth discussion or with older groups, you can delve deeper with some of the following:

It's not that the importance of unity wasn't recognised until the resurrection – as today's psalm, Psalm 133, makes very clear, as it expresses a deep, heartfelt yearning for unity. David, who probably wrote this, knew intimately the effect of factional divisions and splits between God's people. Look at what happened before and during his reign as king – civil war and conflict between Israel and Judah and also within his own family. Yet David foresaw a time when 'God's people live together in unity' and 'the LORD bestows his blessing… for evermore'. This is David's vision of the kingdom of God, finally fulfilled through Jesus' resurrection.

The 'dew from Mount Hermon, falling on Zion's mountains' is an image of unity. Mount Hermon was at the northern boundary of the Promised Land, whereas Zion was on the edge of Jerusalem – two of the most disparate parts of the kingdom sharing blessing from God. More specifically, Mount Zion and Jerusalem are relatively dry areas, whereas Mount Hermon has the highest precipitation in the country. David's vision of divine unity among God's people, with the sharing of unequally distributed resources, is prophetic, as he foresees the way in which the disciples in Acts live out the kingdom of God after the resurrection.

If Communion is included, comment on the community element, as people come to break bread and drink wine together and share the Peace together.

Online resources

All suggested downloads are available at www.scriptureunion.org.uk/light. Visit www.lightlive.org for additional activities for children, young people and adults.

Third Sunday of Easter

READINGS: **Acts 3:12–19; Luke 24:36b–48**
Psalm 4; 1 John 3:1–7

Bible foundations

Aim: to understand how the first disciples talked about the meaning of Jesus' life

Following his resurrection, Jesus revealed himself to his disciples on several occasions. In Luke 24, Jesus explains that the significance of what has happened is to be found as a fulfilment of the Scriptures. His expression 'The Law of Moses, the Prophets and the Psalms' (verse 44) is meant to be a summary of the whole Hebrew canon. The Jews divided the Scriptures into three sections: The Law (the first five books of the Bible), the Prophets (including the historical books, the so-called Former Prophets), and the Writings.

The early Christians frequently used the Scriptures in their preaching of the good news. For example, Peter does this in Acts 3, where he not only states that Jesus as the promised Deliverer has fulfilled the Scriptures (v 18) but gives a particular example – Jesus is 'the Prophet like Moses', a promise based on Deuteronomy 18:15,18 and 19. To his audience, who revered Moses, this would have been very effective. Clearly the disciples had an infectious joy (a parallel to Psalm 4:7) based on their assurance that Jesus was truly alive, and that he would return in glory (1 John 3:2). Their assurance was based on an understanding that Jesus fulfilled the Scriptures.

It is important for us to stress that the real Jesus is the biblical Jesus, and we neglect the Old Testament at our peril. People must be called to do a U-turn, from a self-centred lifestyle ('repentance'), to accept the most precious and amazing gift there is – the forgiveness of sins (Luke 24:47). This is the heart of Peter's preaching (Acts 3:19), all based on the prior revelation in the Scriptures. As you lead worship in this service, ask the Holy Spirit to illumine the minds of everyone so that they can grasp the scriptural significance of Jesus' death and resurrection, and share it powerfully and relevantly with others.

Beginning the service

As you begin the service, somebody dressed like a government official, carrying a briefcase and looking important, walks up to the front of the church looking around critically. Ask them what they are doing. You have a dialogue along the following lines:

'I'm from the newly formed Ministry for Beliefs. I've been sent to your church to find out what you believe about Jesus.' *(Opens briefcase and gets out a file and pen.)* 'Can you tell me what you believe, please?'
'What, me personally, or all of us?'
'All of you… I'm waiting.'
'Well, perhaps you'd like to join us for our service and then you might find out.'
(Official looks anxiously at watch.) 'Oh. Um. OK. I suppose I've got the time. Where shall I sit?'
(During the service he could take notes.)

This service is all about what we believe. And our aim at the end will be to satisfy our friend here and to help each other understand what it is we believe about Jesus. *(Make reference to their presence throughout the service.)*

Bible reading

Both readings need some introduction to put them in their context.

Before reading Acts 3:12–19, the event of the healing of the paralysed man which precedes Peter's speech could be acted out. The person playing the part of Peter could then read Acts 3:12–19 as if he were making the speech. Alternatively the person reading Peter's speech could retell the story in their own words before reading.

Introduce Luke 24:36b–48 by explaining that it is the evening of the first Easter and, although some disciples have met the risen Jesus, there is still confusion over what happened. This could be read with a narrator and a voice for Jesus.

Bible talk

With: a coded message displayed prominently (containing instructions such as: turn around, touch the ground, wave your hand in the air) and, to be shown later, the code breaker; a second coded message: 'but God' with the same code breaker – either invent your own simple code, such as A=1, B=2 or suggestions are available as a download (YearB.Easter3_1)

Ask for three volunteers who can read. Show them the coded message, asking them to follow the instructions. Look confused and ask them why they aren't doing it. Expect a response along the lines of them not understanding the message. Look confused again. Then apologise that you haven't given them the code breaker. Show this and then see who can be the first to decode and obey it. (You may need to supply them with pen and paper or a whiteboard for them to work it out.) Alternatively work out the instructions as a whole church activity and then ask for volunteers to follow the instructions.

Explain that once they know the code they can understand the message. The disciples spent a lot of that first Easter Sunday being confused. It hadn't dawned on them that the Scriptures were coming true in Jesus. So when they met the risen Jesus, they weren't sure who he was. They thought he was a ghost and were afraid. Jesus asked them, 'Why do you doubt?' He recounted to them the Scriptures that explained that he would suffer and, three days later, rise from death. And then the code was cracked. They got it!

They probably spent the next few days chatting to each other about things Jesus had done and saying, 'Remember when he... Why didn't we get the message?' and so on. And in that time they were chatting with Jesus, rereading the Scriptures until, just after Jesus had returned to heaven, they were ready to voice it for themselves. The Holy Spirit had come upon them in power at Pentecost giving them the courage to tell others what they knew and the confidence to obey Jesus' final command to tell everything that had happened.

They didn't waste any opportunities and they didn't waste any time, as can be seen by Peter's speech in Jerusalem after the healing of the lame man. Peter told it straight. He told the Jews that they had rejected Jesus, they had been responsible for his crucifixion (with some help from Pilate), and they had disowned the holy one of God and asked for a murderer to be released in his place. And then Peter said two words that mattered more than anything:

(Show second coded message with words 'but God' and allow time for people to work it out.) The important thing was not what Peter had understood but what God had done. Jesus was rejected and disowned by the people he came to save, but God had brought honour to him.

The Jews might have put Jesus to death, but God raised him from the dead; Peter and John might have told the lame man to walk, but God had compassion and gave them the power to make it happen; Jesus' resurrection, the new-found confidence and assurance of the disciples, the healing of the lame man – it was all to do with the power of God; no human being could do any of these things, but God could. Finally, the Jews might have had Jesus crucified; their sin caused the Messiah to suffer but, if they came to him in repentance, God would forgive them.

This is what the disciples had worked out and discovered since that first Easter. All the things that had happened to Jesus were part of God's plan. They could see what the life of Jesus was all about in relation to that plan. Now they were being obedient to God by telling others what they had learned.

The command Jesus left with his disciples wasn't just for his first-century friends and it wasn't just for Jews either. In the power of God's Spirit, we too need to carry on the work of the disciples by telling everything that happened. But before we can share the story of Jesus, we need to be sure of it ourselves, just like the disciples had to be. In some ways it's a lot easier for us because we have the whole of the New Testament to refer to, as well as the various creeds that the church has formulated over the centuries working out how to understand the Christian faith.

Like the disciples we can think and talk with Christian friends and pray through what we believe so that we're ready to answer anyone who says to us: Tell me who Jesus is! What happened to Jesus? What has God done and what is he doing in the world?

Turn to the 'official' who has been sitting taking notes all though the service and ask if this has helped to answer their questions.

Prayer activity

With: a Bible; a globe/map of the world/map of your local area/telephone directory

Show the Bible and the globe/map/directory and explain that you are going to pray for yourselves and for others who are sharing the truth about Jesus as he explained it using the Scriptures. Lead prayers for mission partners who are engaged in sharing the gospel with others. Then pray for yourselves in your own communities, homes and places of work or study. Invite different people of all ages to lead in prayer.

Confession

This needs to take place after the **Bible talk**. Use your code from the **Bible talk** to put the following phrases hidden round the room or on a board/screen. They are available as a download (YearB.Easter3_1). Different groups/people can crack the code and discover the phrases which were all said by Jesus and Peter in today's readings.

Turn to God
Give up your sins
You will be forgiven

Lead everyone, after a time of quiet, in the following prayer:
Lord, we don't always do the right thing. Sometimes we say unkind things *(Pause.)*; sometimes we do things that hurt others *(Pause.)*; sometimes we don't help when we should *(Pause.)*. All these things turn us away from you. We are sorry. Help us to turn back to you, stop doing wrong and instead, do what you want. Thank you for forgiving us. Amen.

Ending the service

Invite your 'government official' to give you some feedback. They should express delight that you are so clear about what you believe. The official could issue the church with a 'Certificate of authenticity' or something similar. Finish with them saying: 'Oh, by the way, don't forget: Jesus challenged his disciples to tell others about what happened to him. I'm challenging you to do the same. Goodbye.'

Helpful extras

Music and song ideas

Use any hymns and songs which tell the Easter story, such as 'See what a morning, gloriously bright'; 'Low in the grave he lay'; 'How deep the Father's love for us'. Also encourage each other to go out and tell the good news using hymns such as: 'Go tell it on the mountain'; 'Go tell everyone (God's Spirit is in my heart)'; 'Our God reigns'; 'Go forth and tell'; 'You laid aside your majesty'; 'Peter and John went to pray'; 'O what a gift'.

Statement of faith

Explain that the followers of Jesus were working out what they believed as they came to understand Jesus' death, resurrection, ascension and the coming of the Spirit. Over the centuries, the church has written down various creeds which Christians say together as a statement of faith. In this service, either emphasise the significance of the saying of the creed that you usually say or use the following. It could be read in two parts by the congregation. It is based on Peter's speech in Acts 3 and is also available as a download (YearB.Easter3_2).

> **All: We believe that God keeps his promises.**
> A: We believe the prophets said that God would send his servant to suffer for us.
> B: Amen, God kept his promise.
> A: We believe that Jesus lived and worked on earth among us.
> B: Amen, God kept his promise.
> A: We believe that he was handed over to Pilate to be crucified.
> B: Amen, God kept his promise.
> A: We believe that Jesus was crucified even though he was holy and good…
> B: … So that we could be forgiven for our sins.
> A: Amen, God kept his promise.
> B: We believe that God raised Jesus from death.
> A: Amen, God kept his promise.
> B: We believe that God has brought honour to his servant Jesus.
> A: Amen, God kept his promise.
> B: We believe that God will make all things new.
> **All: Everything that God tells us comes true. Praise him.**
> Acts 3

Notes and comments

As an alternative activity to the **Statement of faith,** put everyone into small groups for a few minutes to write a statement of faith of no more than 50 words. They can only say things about God and Jesus that they've read in the Bible. Share these 'creeds' with each other. Alternatively, set this as a challenge for home groups or families during the week, or for your youth and children's groups.

As an alternative **Ending the service,** stand in a circle facing each other and say the following words to each other or split into two halves with one half saying it to the other and vice versa.

'Jesus challenges us to go and tell others about him.
With God's help, we will.'

If you are having a Communion service remind people that Jesus called us to go and tell others about him (Luke 24:48). One way to remember what Jesus did is to share bread and wine together, obeying his command. In the same way, a baptism is a sign that we want to pass on what we know of Jesus to our children and godchildren.

> ## Online resources
> All suggested downloads are available at www.scriptureunion.org.uk/light. Visit www.lightlive.org for additional activities for children, young people and adults. For your convenience the following activities are available as downloads: YearB.Easter3_3 Adult sermon; YearB. Easter3_4 Prayer response; YearB. Easter3_5 Balloon fun for 5s and under.

Fourth Sunday of Easter

READINGS: **Psalm 23; John 10:11–18**
Acts 4:5–12; 1 John 3:16–24

Bible foundations

Aim: to explore the image of Jesus as the Good Shepherd

As a boy, David had, of course, worked as a shepherd (1 Samuel 16:11). The image of the Lord (the covenant name for the God of Israel) as a shepherd was deeply meaningful as would be the image of God as the Shepherd (or the Ruler) of Israel (see also Psalm 78:52; 80:1). In Psalm 23 David makes it very personal.

The psalm begins with the assurance that God will meet the needs of his sheep, satisfying their hunger and quenching their thirst, restoring them when weary and leading them along right paths. But this peaceful pastoral picture suddenly changes. David had had to rescue his sheep from the paw of the lion and the bear (1 Samuel 17:37), taking his life in his hands. The Judean hill country contained numerous slopes to the valleys below, where robbers and wild animals presented many dangers for unsuspecting sheep. But if the shepherd was there to protect with his club as well as guide with his staff all would be well. As John Stott in *The Canticles and Selected Psalms* (Hodder, 1966) helpfully comments, 'My security then, lies not in my environment – whether green pastures, still waters, right paths, or the deepest valley – but in my shepherd. In his presence there is neither want (verse 1) nor fear (verse 4).'

The Hebrew word 'follow' (v 6) could also be translated 'pursue'. When we wander from the shepherd he sends out his sheepdogs of goodness and mercy to bring us back to him again! One day we will be safe from every danger when in the heavenly fold – a wonderful image.

Of course, talk of danger reminds us that Jesus, our good shepherd (John 10:11,14), not only faced danger of death but for our sake actually sacrificed his life to save us. We must trust this wonderful shepherd, come to know him, follow him and listen to his voice every day (John 10:14,16,27).

Beginning the service

Ask this question: If you were an animal, what sort of animal do you think you'd be?

Let a few people tell you, giving their reasons. Ask for a show of hands if anyone thought sheep. Explain that, even if nobody thought sheep, according to the Bible, we are all very like sheep.

Alternatively, use the shepherd quiz (see **Game**).

Bible reading

Instead of being read, Psalm 23 could be sung (see **Music and song ideas**). A choir or music group could sing it while the words are displayed. Alternatively, play a CD version.

Or you could ask six people to stand up where they are to read one verse each. Use a version which is refreshingly different.

John 10:11–18 lends itself to a reading with mimed drama. Any version of the Bible works well but the NIV is used below, also available as a download (YearB.Easter4_1). You will need a narrator; several 'sheep', ideally wearing woolly hats; a 'wolf' (W), perhaps wearing a large cowboy hat; a hired hand (HH), with magazine to read, and a good shepherd (GS).

The action and reading should happen simultaneously.

> *(The sheep assemble at the front in a chaotic cluster.)*
> Jesus said, 'I am the good shepherd. The good shepherd lays down his life for the sheep.'

> *(GS enters to one side and makes a cross shape with his arms, hanging his head.)*
> The hired hand is not the shepherd and does not own the sheep…
> *(HH puts a chair near the sheep and sits down to read a magazine. The sheep tap him on the shoulder but he shrugs them off and takes no notice. GS can walk away unobtrusively.)*
> So when he sees the wolf coming, he abandons the sheep and runs away.
> *(W enters in a threatening way. Sheep begin to panic, HH leaps up, gathers his chair and runs off!)*
> The wolf attacks the flock and scatters it. The man runs away because he is a hired hand and cares nothing for the sheep.
> *(Sheep scatter throughout worship space.)*
> I am the good shepherd; I know my sheep and my sheep know me – just as the Father knows me and I know the Father – and I lay down my life for the sheep.
> *(GS beckons to the scattered sheep, who regroup happily around him.)*
> I have other sheep that are not of this sheep fold. I must bring them also.
> *(GS starts walking round the worship space touching others [who have been prepared beforehand]. They don woolly hats and make their way to the front too.)*
> They too will listen to my voice, and there shall be one flock and one shepherd.
> *(All gather for a group hug!)*
> The reason my Father loves me is that I lay down my life – only to take it up again.
> *(GS again makes a cross shape with his arms in front of the sheep but looks up to heaven rather than hanging his head this time.)*
> No-one takes it from me, but I lay it down of my own accord. I have authority to lay it down and authority to take it up again. This command I received from my Father.
> John 10:11–18

Bible talk

With: a set of sheep-shapes with the following words and symbols on them: Refreshing (water), Giving (food/clothing), Guiding (shepherd's crook), With us (large hand holding a smaller one), Welcoming (outstretched pair of arms), Knows us (the word 'Me'), Saving (sheep and a cross), available as a download (YearB.Easter4_2) (The sheep-shapes are hidden around the worship space in a random order except that the 'Saving' sheep should be last so hide this one where only you can find it!)

In this talk we will unpack what the Good Shepherd is like and how he cares for us, his sheep.

Sheep and shepherds were a familiar sight. People knew how sheep behaved (ask for suggestions), so when Jesus talked about people being like sheep, everyone listening would have known what he meant! People also knew how shepherds cared for the sheep and led them to good pasture. So when Jesus described himself as the Good Shepherd his hearers would understand. Explain that there are some hidden sheep in church who will help us understand how Jesus is a Good Shepherd and how we can respond to him.

Ask for volunteers to find and then bring each sheep to the front. In no particular order the meanings behind each sheep are:

Refreshing

Sheep need to rest. We too need rest and refreshment. Jesus provides us with physical rest. He also gives us peace. He invites us to tell him what troubles us and he will refresh us. Whether life is going badly or is going well, the shepherd can lead us into quiet places.

Giving

A shepherd makes sure his sheep have the best pasture and clean water – everything they need. Jesus makes sure we have all we need. He supplies us with what we need, when we need it. This isn't just about physical things; it could be a solution to a problem or a helpful call from a friend when we feel alone. He even gives us things that we don't know we need!

Guiding

Life can be confusing (give some examples). Jesus will show us the best way to go if we ask him. His plans are not always what we want, and sometimes he takes us to places we'd never dreamed of. But because he is the Good Shepherd, if we listen carefully, we can be sure he will lead us on the right paths, sometimes to unexpected places! We need to trust.

With us

Jesus, the Good Shepherd, doesn't abandon us when life gets tough which is what a bad shepherd might do. He travels with us into the dark places, keeping us close by his side, and sometimes carries us when life is too much to bear. Often we grow in our faith after we have walked through 'the valley of the shadow of death'. Jesus encourages us not to be afraid in these hard places.

Knows us

Jesus knows each of us, personally; the good bits and bad bits; the happy bits and the sad bits. There's nothing about us that Jesus doesn't know. He has watched over us day by day. Not like the hired hand who just wants the money! Jesus knows, cares and loves.

Welcoming

Jesus is a shepherd for everyone, not just a few chosen sheep. He longs to see everyone coming to love him. He won't turn anyone away. Not only does Jesus welcome us all, but he welcomes us all to a party! (Comment on the last part of Psalm 23.) He treats us as his special guests in his kingdom for ever.

Saving

(This final shepherd characteristic needs to come last): Jesus is the Good Shepherd because he cares, knows, loves, gives, refreshes, guides and travels with us, but most important of all he gave his life for us. He loves us so much that he willingly died so that we might be forgiven. He rose again and is preparing that great party for us in heaven! This makes him not just the Good Shepherd but the greatest shepherd there can ever be!

Prayer activity

With: sheep-shapes (A5 size) – one per person (use any left over from Good Friday); pencils; a sheepfold (either drawn on paper or 3D from card or building bricks); Blu-tack

During the prayers people can write or draw on their sheep-shape the name of a person or a situation that they would like to pray for. Gather all the sheep together and put them in the fold to offer to God with words such as: 'Loving Shepherd, we bring all these sheep to you. Please help them. Please guide them. Please be close to them. Amen.'

Encourage everyone to pray for one of the following:

- someone who needs God's peace or refreshment
- someone who needs help or guidance about something
- someone who is facing dark times because they are ill or in danger
- someone whom we want to tell about Jesus (reflecting John 10:16).

Alternatively, ask four people to lead in prayer for each of these types of people, referring to the sheep in the **Bible talk**.

Prayer of confession

This is also available as a download (YearB. Easter4_3).

Leader: Like sheep, we are sometimes silly.
All: Good Shepherd, forgive us for the silly things we do.
Leader: Like sheep, we sometimes follow a leader without thinking. We don't always follow the right person, which can lead us to do wrong.
All: Good Shepherd, forgive us for times when we have followed the wrong person.
Leader: Like sheep we are easily frightened and panic.
All: Good Shepherd, forgive us for times when we don't put our trust in you.
Leader: Thank you that as the Good Shepherd you chose to die to forgive us for all the wrong we do.
All: Good Shepherd, we thank you. Amen.

Ending the service

If possible, encourage your congregation to huddle as close together as possible, as if in a sheepfold, and then use the words of blessing from Hebrews 13:20,21.

Helpful extras

Music and song ideas

Many hymns and songs accurately reflect Psalm 23, such as the one to the tune Crimond or the version by Stuart Townend, or the choral version by Howard Goodall; 'The King of love my shepherd is'; 'The Lord is my shepherd, I'll follow him always' could be sung as a round; 'Led like a lamb to the slaughter'; 'How sweet the name of Jesus sounds'; 'O let the Son of God enfold you'; 'I'm special'; 'Hold me, Lord, in your arms'; 'Do not be afraid for I have redeemed you'; 'When the road is rough and steep'; 'Be bold, be strong'.

Game

There are lots of shepherds in the Bible. Use the quiz 'Who am I?' available as a download (YearB.Easter4_4). Award three points if a team gets the answer on clue 1; two points if they need two clues and one point if they need all three. The answers are: Abel, Moses, Jacob, David, Amos and Reuben.

Notes and comments

There are opportunities for personal testimony during the **Bible talk**. Children may be willing to talk or be interviewed about their experience of seeing Psalm 23

as real to them. Alternatively they could write down their testimony for you to read out loud. Make sure that whoever speaks uses inclusive, jargon-free language and that if someone is talking about a 'valley of the shadow of death' experience they don't say anything that might disturb children!

One church recently ran the Psalm 23 challenge, when individuals and family groups were challenged to learn Psalm 23 over several weeks. Younger children learnt the first part only. Devise your own ground rules, such as Bible version, whether singing it is an option and so on.

If there is Holy Communion during this service, make the connection between the bread and wine and the shepherd willingly laying down his life for the sheep. You could use words from Psalm 23:2,3a to introduce the Peace.

The reading from 1 John 3 reminds us that we need to behave as good shepherds to our fellow-sheep.

Online resources

All suggested downloads are available at www.scriptureunion.org.uk/light. Visit www.lightlive.org for additional activities for children, young people and adults. For your convenience the following activities are available as downloads: YearB.Easter4_5 Retold story on John 10 for 5s and under; YearB.Easter4_6 Responsive activity to Psalm 23 for all ages.

Fifth Sunday of Easter

READINGS: 1 John 4:7–21; John 15:1–8
            Acts 8:26–40; Psalm 22:25–31

Bible foundations

Aim: to explore the image of Jesus as the true vine and his followers as the branches

In the Hebrew Scriptures, Israel was frequently likened to a vine that God had planted (Psalm 80:8–16; Isaiah 5:1–7; Jeremiah 2:21). But this vine had, sadly, only produced bad grapes despite all that had been done for it. So when Jesus describes himself as the true vine, (John 15:1), this is deeply significant.

Anyone who wishes to belong to God's people must 'remain in the vine' (v 4). It is only through staying in relationship with him that we can 'bear fruit' as God intends we should (vs 2,4,8). Whether we think of 'the fruit of the Spirit' (Galatians 5:22,23) or acts of mercy and justice, we are reminded that God has not put us on earth to twiddle our thumbs but to live out the life of Jesus in the nitty-gritty challenges that life and relationships bring.

Of course the model for living a life of love is God himself. His love was shown once and for all in that he sent 'his one and only Son into the world that we might live through him' (1 John 4:9). Imagine the cost to the Father of making the Son 'the atoning sacrifice for our sins' (v 10)! This is costly, sacrificial love that takes the initiative and carries the blame and the shame so that others may be free of it. We are called to be like this in our relationships with one another. As it says in John 15, it is as we allow his words to remain in us (v 7), especially his command to love one another as he has loved us (v 12), that we will remain in the vine (v 4), experience wonderful answers to prayer (v 7), and bear much fruit to the Father's glory (v 8).

Beginning the service

Display this message at the front of the church as people are arriving and see if anyone can work out what it says:

ISATMATYHJEOTIRNUEEDVTIONMEE

Miss out every other letter to decode the message: I am the true vine, stay joined to me. Who said it? Explain that today you will be exploring this theme.

Alternatively, if people don't already know the song, 'You are the vine, we are the branches' teach it at the start so that you can use it later in the service.

Bible reading

1 John 4:7–21 explores the theme of love. Split the reading between various members of the congregation who could call out one verse each from where they are sitting as if they were having a conversation with one another about love. The CEV works well for this.

John 15:1–8 could be read as a 'living parable'. You will need a branch with several strong twigs on it (but no leaves) in a pot at the front of the church, and a gardener. As the verses are being read, the gardener 'sculpts' the branch. They cut away a couple of branches, clean up some others, throw the 'dead wood' into a compost bin (or something similar) and hang some 'grapes' on the pruned branches. This is not meant to be funny, but is a visual aid to the reading. It would work best if done by someone known by others to be a good gardener.

Bible talk

With: a healthy, woody plant in a pot (it could be the same one used in the **Bible reading**) with some grapes hanging from it (this is optional); a person pretending to be a plant (dressed in brown, wearing a green hat); a large pot-shaped piece of card with 'Jesus' written on it; a watering can; a large Bible; some un-inflated balloons, preferably green; a balloon pump (or a good pair of lungs!); a marker pen; string in lengths of about 50 cm; sticky tape; scissors; a gold envelope with a gold certificate inside, like a winning one at the Chelsea Flower Show

Bring out the plant in its pot so that everyone can see it. Admire its stem and branches. Bring out the 'plant' person (PP). Ask for suggestions as to how we might be like plants. Draw out answers such as: created by God; we grow. Then ask for ways we are not like plants, such as we don't grow flowers. If someone says that we don't grow fruit, look as if you're about to agree and then ask whether actually we do. Remind everyone that the Gospel reading talked about producing fruit. This cannot be fruit like bananas or grapes. (*You could hang some grapes on your plant in the pot.*)

What fruit do we grow?

What sort of fruit should we be producing? Ask for suggestions (not necessarily the fruit of the Spirit as that hasn't been one of the readings). If people are stuck, remind them that there was a big clue in the first reading. (*Write suggestions on the balloons, with the neck at the top. When you've written down several, blow up the balloons so that they look like over-sized grapes. You could have had them* ready-inflated as long as you can write on them! The words should be big enough to read. Attach string to the neck of the balloons and stick them to PP using sticky tape. They should look like a healthy plant!)

Highlight all the 'fruits' that are growing on them. Talk about when and how we should display the fruits: such as being helpful at home; loving people even when they are unkind to us; looking after lonely people.

What aids growth?

What conditions are needed for real plants to grow? Light, water and soil. What conditions do we need for the fruits of love, kindness, goodness to grow in us? We have to stay joined to Jesus. Bring in the large pot shape with 'Jesus' written on and lean it near to PP. PP coughs. You do a double-take and ask if there's anything the matter.
PP says: My fruit is wilting.
You: Why?
PP: Because I'm not in the right place. What did it say in the reading?
You: Stay joined to Jesus.
PP: So…?
(Move the pot so that PP is attached to it by holding it in some way.) Staying in the same area as Jesus won't help our fruit to grow. Staying near to Jesus won't help either. Jesus said we had to stay **joined to him**, because he is the true vine, who will give us all that we need to help us to grow. He is the source of all the goodness, kindness and love. (Read your balloons again.) It's not just a question of us not producing much fruit. Without him we cannot produce any fruit. Without him we cannot do anything.

If we decide to go our own way we become

like useless branches with wilting fruit. (Cut the neck of a couple of your balloons at this point, this should make them shrivel dramatically rather than burst). Wilting fruit is not very attractive, so don't be tempted to go your own way. Ask what happens to gone-off fruit and dead branches.

(Pick up the watering can and make as if to water PP, who looks nervous!) Of course, Jesus doesn't feed us by pouring water over us! How does he feed us? Ask for suggestions, but make sure you include reading God's Word (hand PP the Bible), prayer and spending time with other Christians. Jesus said that if we stay joined to him, his words become part of us.

When all this happens, we grow fruit, we stay joined to Jesus, he may prune us and his Word becomes a part of us. Then the best part happens. (Someone comes to the front bearing a gold envelope. PP looks excited.) It's a Gold award for beautiful fruit and it's awarded to: God. He's the one who made all this fruit to grow on PP and this good fruit has brought honour to God.

Prayer activity

With: a large picture of a vine, just a wide main stem with lots of branches leading off it

Display the large vine (or several smaller ones) and explain that it is a picture of your church. Write JESUS sideways down the stem. Gather round the vine picture in a series of branches stretching from the stem, with everyone holding onto at least one other person next to them. Explain that you will all pray in silence for the people on either side of you. Check that people know the names of those around them. Then lead a prayer with words such as:

'Lord, we thank you that you want us to be fruitful branches with you at the centre of our lives. We pray for each other now.' *(Pause to pray silently for the person. They can just say the person's name to God.)*

'Help us, Lord, to be good fruit, serving each other for your glory. Amen.'

If appropriate, pass a squeeze around like a Mexican wave, each person squeezing the hand of the person on either side of them in a chain, only squeezing when they have been squeezed! This could go off in several directions, as do the branches of a vine!

Prayer of confession

With: strips of brown paper (enough for one each) which represent branches from a vine; several rubbish bins; the prayer of confession, also available as a download (YearB.Easter5_1)

Everyone gathers around a rubbish bin and is given the brown paper. (This could precede the **Prayer activity** when people gather around a picture of a vine.) Begin by saying: Jesus said, 'I am the true vine, and my Father is the gardener. He cuts away every branch of mine that doesn't produce fruit.' Explain that the brown strip of paper is like a fruitless, dead branch of a vine. Ask people to think of ways in which they are rotten, like branches that do not bear good fruit. As you read out the following sentences, encourage people to tear off a piece of their branch each time, throw it into the bin and then respond with the words: **Forgive us, and help us stay**

joined to you.

Leader: Lord Jesus, we are like this dead branch. Sometimes we are unkind or unhelpful.
All: Forgive us, and help us stay joined to you.
Leader: Lord Jesus, sometimes the things we say are cruel or rude, like sour fruit.
All: Forgive us, and help us stay joined to you.
Leader: Lord, we are sorry for the times when we are selfish, thinking that our way is better than yours.
All: Forgive us, and help us stay joined to you.
Leader: Lord Jesus, every time we do wrong things we fail to bring glory to God.
All: Forgive us, and help us stay joined to you.
Leader: Jesus said, 'If you stay joined to me, and I stay joined to you, then you will produce lots of fruit.'
All: Lord, thank you for forgiving us. Help us stay joined to you.

Ending the service

With: seedless grapes (enough for one each), other slices of fruit or raisins

Put the fruit on several plates. Be aware of allergies. Hand the fruit round and ask people to hold it. Divide the congregation into A and B facing each other. Holding their grapes they say to each other:
A: Stay joined to Jesus
B: And he will stay joined to you.
B: Bear lots of fruit
A: And bring God glory.
Then eat your fruit!

Alternatively, if you haven't already done so, sing 'You are the vine', as a song of affirmation and commitment.

Helpful extras

Statement of faith
The words from Psalm 22:25–31, especially in the CEV, make a good creed. This could be read antiphonally, or read by one or two people, pausing at the end of each statement for everyone to say 'Amen'.

Music and song ideas
'You are the vine, we are the branches'; 'Father God, I wonder' has the thought of us not being able to exist without God; 'Jesus, take me as I am' has the final line, 'Giving glory back to you' which reflects the honour good fruit brings to God; 'In my life, Lord, be glorified' mirrors this theme; songs on the theme of letting Jesus' teachings become part of us include 'Seek ye first'; 'May the mind of Christ my Saviour'.

Notes and comments

If you serve refreshments, encourage people to get to know better those they prayed for in the **Prayer activity**. They could find out something they specifically want prayer for, or an interesting fact that they didn't know before.

There is an obvious link between Jesus the vine and his blood being the wine. If you have a Communion service, have grape juice available for any who would not normally take the wine.

If there is a baptism, link in with the importance of staying close to Jesus and how the parents and godparents have a vital role in helping the child to do this.

Online resources

All suggested downloads are available at www.scriptureunion.org.uk/light. Visit www.lightlive.org for additional activities for children, young people and adults. For your convenience the following activity is available as a download; YearB. Easter5_ 2 Retold story for 5 to 8s.

Sixth Sunday of Easter

READINGS: 1 John 5:1–6; John 15:9–17
Acts 10:44–48; Psalm 98

Bible foundations

Aim: to explore how Jesus loves us and wants us to obey his commands

In 1 John the Christian life is made gloriously simple. It simply involves loving God. We love God by keeping his commands. This is not hard because those who have been born of God, who are his sons and daughters through believing in his Son, have overcome the world (5:1–5). But what is it that God commands us to do?

Before the coming of Christ, God's people would have turned to the Law, especially the Ten Commandments, for an answer to that question. But since Christ, we understand more clearly that the essence of God's Law is a call to love others in all relationships. Jesus stresses the call to 'love each other as I have loved you' (John 15:12 repeated in v 17) as his most important command, which holds all the others within it. So how has Jesus loved us? His love was sacrificial – he laid down his life for his friends (v 13). It was also a sharing love – Jesus shared with his disciples all that he heard from his Father (vs 14,15). It was also a sending love. Jesus took the initiative to call his disciples to follow him, and now appoints us to 'go and bear fruit', be his witnesses and live out this life of love in the world.

Of course we cannot do this in our own strength. But all Christians have received 'the gift of the Holy Spirit' (see Acts 10:44–47). So in 1 John we can be described as having been 'born of God' – the very life of God is within us. Confident that we are 'on the victory side', let us love the Father's children as well as the Father (1 John 5:1,2), however difficult that may be!

Beginning the service

Present different views of God that explore love and command. If appropriate use images or film clips: for example, an uninvolved old man on a cloud, a loving grandad who spoils his grandchildren by giving out sweets, a wise guru offering advice in obscure sayings, a strict headmaster dealing out rules and punishments. Film clips could include: a scene with Miss Trunchbull, the strict headmistress in *Matilda*, contrasting this with a scene about the friendly teacher Miss Honey; a scene from *Shrek 2* that involves the king as an overprotective father figure; a scene from the beginning of *Mrs Doubtfire* in which the indulgent father throws an excessive birthday party for his son, completely overshadowing the little cake and present that his wife brings home. Ask people in small groups or on their own to consider which image is most like their view of God, or whether they would use another image or character.

Explain that in this service we will be looking at God's commandments and love, exploring ways in which God loves and relates to us. Is he strict or loving, or both?

Bible reading

To bring out the theme from 1 John 5:1–6 and John 15:9–17, ask everyone to listen out for the words 'love' and 'command' in both readings. In the NIV, 'love' appears five times in the epistle and nine in the Gospel, while 'command' appears three times in the epistle and five in the Gospel. You could teach a sign for each word, perhaps in British Sign Language, that the congregation could make whenever the words appear.

Bible talk

With: PowerPoint images or pictures to represent Love and Commandment such as a heart; a stone tablet (as Moses used); school rules; a red rose; a No Smoking sign; a red man at a pedestrian crossing; Mother Teresa; somebody helping a homeless person; a wedding invitation and an image of a cross available as a download (YearB.Easter6_1)

Recall the two key words in the **Bible readings**: Love and Commandment. Using PowerPoint or printed pictures, show a variety of images and ask people whether they represent Love or Commandment and then sort them into the two groups. Include a mix of obvious symbols and subtler ones – there should be an element of discussion about some of the less obvious images. This could be done all together by vote, or in small groups.

Explain that these readings, like the images, show that the boundaries between love and commandments are thinner than we may sometimes think. In 1 John 5:3 John writes, 'This is love for God: to keep his commands.' In John 15:10, Jesus says, 'If you keep my commands, you will remain in my love'. There is a danger of thinking that these verses mean that God's love is somehow conditional on us 'getting it right'. But God's grace is not like that. Instead they show something about the nature of the loving relationship between us and Jesus.

Ask the children how they show that they love their parents, and ask a few married people how they show that they love their spouses. It would be very strange to say

'I love you' but then never do anything that the other person wanted, or take any advice from them. To show that we love Jesus, we need to find out what he wants us to do.

Jesus' commandment in verse 12 is, 'Love each other as I have loved you.' He says it again in verse 17. He wants us not just to love him, but to act as people of love in the wider community, inspired by his example. To follow this command, we need to understand how Jesus loved us, so that we can love each other in the same way.

Jesus tells us what we need to know in verses 13 and 14a, 'Greater love has no one than this: to lay down one's life for one's friends. You are my friends…' Go back to the images you used at the start of the **Bible talk** and the image of the cross. In which group did people place the cross, Love or Commandment? It is in fact an image both of Love and Command. By dying on the cross Jesus showed his love for us, but the sacrifice that it represents is also the way that Jesus commands us to love each other. We must love sacrificially and wholeheartedly, ready to give anything up for each other. After all, Jesus referred to following him as 'taking up your cross'.

Prayer activity

With: four prayer stations set up as described below; if providing the suggested option for teenagers, a printed version of John 15:12 and 16

This naturally follows the Gospel reading and/or **Bible talk** by offering prayer for love to exist in situations where love is needed. This is motivated by Jesus' commands to

'Love each other as I have loved you' and also to 'Go and bear much fruit' as we consider practical ways to show God's love in the situations we are praying for. We can also remember his promise that 'Whatever you ask in my name the Father will give you'. Explain this in your own words or read out the verses as an introduction. If there are plenty of older children and teenagers present, introduce the activity as a quest to follow Jesus' commandment by printing out the two verses from John 15 as 'instructions' or in the style of a treasure map which also shows the different stations around the church.

Set up prayer stations around the church as follows and encourage people to visit at least one station as they simply talk with God. Provide for people who are less mobile. Play background music such as Taizé 'Ubi Caritas' or Iona's 'A Touching Place'.

- Love between God's people
  Display pictures of churches in the local community, along with any prayer requests you have been able to get from them. Include pictures of their leaders.
- Love between families
  Display details of local community issues, schools, community groups run by the church or in the parish. Do this with newspaper cuttings, school notice sheets or local event advertisements. You could include pictures of families in need – people about to get married, having a baby or moving home, or names of those recently bereaved. It would also be appropriate to pray for any child or family-related organisation that the church

supports.

- Love between countries
Display a world map, newspaper cuttings and headlines of areas in need around the world. You could run a short news film or have a PowerPoint playing with pictures from the areas you have identified.
- Love between people and God
Display pictures and news from any mission your church is involved with, such as Alpha, or mission partners abroad. This could include somewhere in the local area where the church is seeking to share the good news.

Prayer of confession

The invitation to confession often begins with a reading of the two greatest commandments. Read John 15:12–14. Allow time for reflection, then sing or play the Taizé chant 'Ubi Caritas' (see **Music and song ideas**). The words, '*ubi caritas et amor Deus ibi est*' mean 'wherever there is charity and love, there is God'. Having sung through or listened to the chant, continue to use it as a response between the prayers.

Lord Jesus, you commanded us to love each other. We are sorry for the times that we have been impatient, bitter and angry, and the times that we have hurt each other. Please forgive us.
Ubi caritas…

Lord Jesus, you commanded us to forgive each other. We are sorry for the times that we have borne grudges and been resentful, and the times that we have broken off friendships because of hurt. Please forgive us.
Ubi caritas…

Lord Jesus, you commanded us to look after each other. We are sorry for the times that we have turned away from those in need, and have not done all we can to help those who are suffering. Please forgive us.
Ubi caritas…

Lord Jesus, you laid down your life for your friends. Thank you for doing that so that we could be forgiven. Help us to live the way you asked us to.
Ubi caritas…

Ending the service

John 15:16 and 17 could be used as part of the dismissal, in the context of reminding everyone that the **Bible reading** contains some of Jesus' last words to his disciples before returning to his Father in heaven. Verse 17 brings together the twin themes of Love and Commandment with the words, 'This is my command: Love each other.' This could be used as a *Learn and remember* verse as well as a dismissal, or printed out on cards, badges, fridge magnets or other keepsakes for people to take away to remember throughout the week.

Helpful extras

Music and song ideas
'Love divine, all loves excelling'; 'What a friend we have in Jesus'; 'O Jesus, I have promised'; 'Give thanks to the Lord (His love endures forever)'; 'A new commandment'; 'When I was lost (There is a new song)'; 'For God so loved the world' (by John Hardwick, downloaded from johnhardwick.org.uk).

Taizé music: '*Ubi caritas*' and '*El alma que anda*

en amor'. (Many Taizé songs can be found in sheet music form online at www.taize.fr/en_article503.html, while some can be heard on podcasts. Taizé music is good to sing with a few instruments and a strong leader, but can also help create a meditative atmosphere when played in the background during prayers or a time of silent reflection.)

Iona music: 'A touching place' speaks of Jesus' love coming into situations through prayer and through the actions of his followers and would be appropriate to play during the **Prayer activity**. The verses are intercessory and could be printed out separately to place in a relevant prayer station.

Statement of faith

Invite everyone to declare their faith using words from 1 John 5:4b–6. Either introduce your regular liturgy with the verses given here at the beginning and end, or use the whole of this alternative statement which makes other direct references to the same passage. It is also available as a download (YearB.Easter6_2).

Leader: This is the victory that has overcome the world, even our faith. Who is it that overcomes the world? Only he who believes that Jesus is the Son of God.
Do you believe in God the Father, who is Love?
All: I believe in God the Father.
Leader: Do you believe in Jesus Christ, the Son of God?
All: I believe in Jesus Christ.

Leader: Do you believe in the Holy Spirit, who testifies to the truth?
All: I believe in the Holy Spirit.
Leader: This is the victory that has overcome the world, even our faith. Who is it that overcomes the world? Only he who believes that Jesus is the Son of God.

Notes and comments

This service has focused on the epistle and Gospel readings, but if the service includes a baptism, you may wish to make more of the Acts reading, Acts 10:44–48, which includes the baptism of the Gentile believers who have already received the Spirit. This reading carries the message that God noticed and loved even those who seemed to the disciples to be unlikely candidates for baptism. The people getting baptised today can expect the same acceptance and love from God. You may also wish to focus in the **Prayer activity** on the candidates for baptism by creating a station for the family of the church of which they are now a part.

If the service includes Communion, you could focus on John 15:13 and 14 making it clear that Jesus has laid down his life and that by sharing in this we are counted among his friends.

Online resources

All suggested downloads are available at www.scriptureunion.org.uk/light. Visit www.lightlive.org for additional activities for children, young people and adults.

Seventh Sunday of Easter

READINGS: 1 John 5:9–13; John 17:6–19
Psalm 1; Acts 1:15–23

Bible foundations

Aim: to explore how Jesus prayed for his followers

The prayer of Jesus in John 17:6–19 is frequently called Jesus' high priestly prayer. In it Jesus acts like the high priest of Israel, coming to God on behalf of his people, his disciples. He asserts their identity (vs 6–12); they have obeyed God's Word and know that Jesus has come from God. Indeed, they have been given to the Son by the Father (vs 6,9). Thus they belong to the Father because of the intimate relationship of unity between Father and Son which enables Jesus to make the extraordinary statement that 'All I have is yours, and all you have is mine' (v 10a). This is more intimate than the closest marriage. Incredibly, true believers share this amazing spiritual unity (vs 21,23), being 'one as we are one' (v 22).

Jesus then prays for their sanctity. They need to be protected from the evil one, who will attack them because they do not belong to 'the world' which is under his control (1 John 5:19). The world hates them because they constitute a rebuke to the world's ways by being different. Above all they need 'to be sanctified by the truth', that is by God's Word (v 17). They need to be those who meditate on God's Word 'day and night' (Psalm 1:2) so that it comes to define who they are. As those sent into the world (v 18), it is essential that their attitudes, values, priorities and goals are godly, as they shine as a light in the darkness, turning their backs on 'the way of sinners' (Psalm 1:1).

If we live this way, fully aware of our new identity, and committed to true holiness that reflects the life of Jesus, we will 'know that [we] have eternal life' (1 John 5:13), because we will already be living the life of heaven here on earth.

Beginning the service

Ask everyone what would be the one thing that they would ask for right now. Take a few suggestions, then ask what they would ask for someone else right now and who would it be for. Explain that the theme of this service is prayer, in particular, exploring Jesus' prayer for his disciples – what he asked God for, on their behalf.

Bible reading

John 17:6–19 is very dense. One person could read it from the NIV or CEV, pausing at the end of each sentence. Introduce the reading by explaining that it comes at the end of several chapters containing Jesus' last instructions to his disciples after the Last Supper, just before his betrayal and arrest. Many of the more complicated sayings of Jesus in the prayer stem from his teachings in these earlier passages.

One way of placing it in context would be to have a disciple as a 'witness' telling the congregation about that night. They could begin by saying, 'I remember being there, after the meal was finished, and listening to Jesus teaching well into the night...' and insert the reading in its entirety as part of the 'memory'.

A dramatised suggestion, which brings out the points in the **Bible talk** and **Prayer activity**, is given below in **Bible retelling**.

Bible retelling

This is an introduction to and brief explanation of John 17:6–19.

I remember being there, after the meal was finished, and listening to Jesus teaching well into the night. That was nothing new, of course. We were used to sitting around the fire, listening to his stories until the sun came up. But that night seemed different. Looking back, we should have guessed what was going to happen. He certainly knew. There was a new urgency in what he was saying. He was speaking like a mother, halfway out of the door, about to leave her teenage son in charge of the house for the first time. He kept repeating some things. 'Love each other' seemed to be the one thing most on his mind. He told us that he was going away, and coming back again, and that we knew where he was going, and that we had to follow him there. We were bewildered. We were sleepy.

And then – it must have been very nearly the last thing that happened before we went out to that dreadful place where they came to arrest him – we suddenly became aware that he was no longer talking to us. His tone of voice hadn't changed, and neither had the kind of things he was saying, but he was looking upwards towards heaven and addressing his Father, the way he had taught us to do. Instead of talking to us, he was talking about us. He was praying about us. For us!

I don't recall it word for word, but he prayed that we would be kept safe, protected from the evil one, and that we would remain one, in unity with each other. The memory of those words kept me going in the dark days that followed. He said that he was praying so that we would have the full measure of his joy within us, words that started to make more sense four days later. He prayed for us to be set apart, made holy, like him.

If we hadn't guessed it already, I'm sure we would have worked it out then. Something huge was about to happen, and we were being entrusted with an enormous, important task that we didn't fully understand. But we weren't being left alone. That was what he had been trying to tell us all evening. With Jesus praying for us, we had the Father's protection, his joy and his holiness. We also had each other. We were going to be all right.

Bible talk

With: a football supporter's bag containing the following objects with the appropriate word written on card: Unity (two identical football scarves or shirts), Joy (a football rattle or something that represents cheering), Protection (thick gloves which protect the hands if cold or the hands of the goalkeeper), Holiness and Truth (a ticket to enter an expensive spectator box in the stands)

Explain that when Jesus prayed the prayer in the reading in John 17, he asked God to give some important things to his disciples, things that would equip them while Jesus was away. As you talk about each word, produce it from the supporter's bag along with the object. Illustrate with real-life examples from football fans if such are present!

Unity

Jesus asks God that his disciples may be one as he and God are one (v 11). He prays for unity a few verses later on, this time for the people who will come to believe in him through the disciples. It's obviously very important to him, as he has repeatedly told the disciples that they must love one another. But he prays for something more than love – for the disciples to be one as Jesus and the Father are one, means they have to agree so much that they act as the same person! Show the identical shirts/scarves and talk about how football fans are often passionately in agreement about the fate and/or brilliance of their team. They wear the same kit to show they belong to each other. They often behave in the same way. Similarly, if we all start acting like Jesus, then we must also be acting like each other.

Joy

Jesus says that he is praying this prayer while he is still in the world so that his disciples may have the full measure of his joy within them (v 13). He must have known the terrible, frightening things that were about to happen. The disciples did not know about the happy ending yet, nor of the tough times that would follow as they took the good news of Jesus everywhere! Show the football rattle or ask some fans to demonstrate their cheering skills. Ask what makes people happy at a football match. Why do fans cheer? Sometimes following Jesus is tough, but his prayer for joy is an encouragement. Jesus' hope and desire is still that we should be able to find joy in him. That is a joy that lasts a lot longer than the joy of the successful football result!

Protection

Jesus says that his prayer is not that 'you take them out of the world but that you protect them from the evil one' (v 15). Jesus doesn't pray for an easy life for the disciples, because there is work to be done which may not be easy. But he does pray for them to be protected against evil, which is what he taught them to do in the Lord's Prayer. Show the gloves and talk about how gloves protect hands during a cold football match or how the huge gloves protect and facilitate a goalkeeper. Jesus doesn't take his followers right out of harm's way, but he does give them the right defences to continue following him.

Holiness and Truth

Jesus asks for the disciples to be set apart by the truth (v 17). Set apart is a meaning of holiness, put to one side for a special purpose. The disciples are set apart by their belief in the truth of God's Word – and so are we. Show the ticket which gives its holder the right to privileged seats, set apart from the vast majority of other fans. (Acknowledge that this only partially illustrates what holiness and truth means.) Sometimes 'set apart' can be a special and important place to be, but at other times it can feel very lonely and we need to hang on to the truth that we are following. In verse 19, Jesus makes it easier by explaining that he is going there himself first: he is the Way and the Truth, and his prayer equips us to follow him.

The **Prayers of intercession** follow on immediately from this.

Prayers of intercession

With: enough cards, one for everyone, with the words used in the **Bible talk** and the symbol of football objects in the supporter's kitbag, available as a download (YearB. Easter7_1)

Give out one card per person. Have a 'spares' box if someone wants to swap their card. Ask people to pray for themselves or someone they know who needs to know joy, God's protection, unity with other Christians or knowing that they are special to God and set apart to serve him in some unique way. You could ask someone to give a brief personal testimony about one or more of the topics. People could pray on their own or in small groups. You could play some Taizé music during this time of prayer.

Ending the service

Remind people of the four symbols in the **Bible talk** and **Prayers of intercession** then pray for people as they go out into the world, sent out by Jesus, as he was sending out his first disciples. You could use the following prayer based on John 17:18:

Jesus prayed, 'As you sent me into the world, I have sent them into the world.' Go out now in unity with one another, sanctified by his truth, filled with his joy, and protected by his hand. Follow in his way now and for ever. Amen.

Helpful extras

Music and song ideas

'Praise to the holiest in the height'; 'Father, hear the prayer we offer'; 'The day thou gavest' (for an evening service); 'Thy hand, O God, has guided'; 'Lord, who the night you were betrayed did pray' (for a Eucharist); 'You never let go (Matt Redman)'; 'Bind us together'; 'For I'm building a people of power'.

Taizé music: 'Bleibet hier und wachet mit mir' which in translation means 'Stay with me, wait here with me, watch and pray, watch and pray.' (Many Taizé songs can be found in sheet music form online at www.taize.fr/en_article503.html, while some can be heard on podcasts. Taizé music is good to sing with a few instruments and a strong leader, but can also help create a meditative atmosphere when played in the background during prayers or a time of silent reflection.)

Music specific to each of the four sections of the **Bible talk** are Joy: 'Joy, joy or joyful, joyful'; 'Oh happy day', or other gospel music; 'How can I keep from singing?' (in any version from Eva Cassidy to Aled Jones); Protection: 'Faithful One'; 'He's got the whole world in his hands (Tim Hughes)'; Holiness: 'Holy, holy, holy, Lord God Almighty'; 'Purify my heart'; 'It is you (Newsboys)'; Truth: 'The voice of truth (The Casting Crowns)'.

Statement of faith

As an introduction explain that Jesus prayed that we might be one. You could read verse John 17:11b and then say that you are now joining together to state your shared belief in him, a statement that unites Christians across the globe. Either use one of the creeds from your own liturgy, or if there are many young children, ask people of all ages to lead the following, based on 1 John 5:9 to 13 (CEV), also available as a download (Year B. Easter7_2).

Speaker 1: If we believe what people tell us, we can trust what God says even more.
Speaker 2: This is what God says:

Speaker 3: That he gave us eternal life
Speaker 4: And that it comes to us from his Son, Jesus.
All speakers: Do you believe it?
All: We believe it!
Speaker 2: This is what Jesus says:
Speaker 3: That God is our Father
Speaker 4: And that he hears our prayers
Speaker 1: And he loves us.
All speakers: Do you believe it?
All: We believe it!
Speaker 1: To you who have faith in the Son of God:
Speaker 2: You may know that you have eternal life.
All: We have faith in one God: Father, Son and Holy Spirit. Amen.

Notes and comments

For a Communion service, the hymn 'Lord, who the night you were betrayed did pray' (see **Music and song ideas**) could become a focus for prayer and contemplation, leading to a further emphasis on unity expressed through the sharing of Communion.

Some churches may wish to include the possibility of prayer ministry during the **Prayer activity** or after the service following on from the personal nature of the prayers.

Pentecost

Ezekiel 37:1–14; Acts 2:1–21
Psalm 104:24–34,35b; John 15:26,27; 16:4b–15

Bible foundations

Aim: to celebrate the coming of the Holy Spirit and what the Spirit makes possible

Ezekiel prophesied from 593 to 573 BC. He lived in Babylon with others from Jerusalem who had been taken into exile. By the time we get to chapter 37, Jerusalem has fallen and the Temple destroyed. With it, the exiles' hope was also destroyed because the Temple expressed God's presence with his people. Verse 11 shows the people feeling like dry bones with no hope for the future. When the Lord asked Ezekiel if the bones could live (v 3), Ezekiel replied that only God himself could answer that, leaving the way for the answer to be 'Yes!'

The Lord tells Ezekiel to prophesy to the bones, telling them to come together, to be made into bodies. The bones weren't arranged neatly. They were lying around, all higgledy-piggledy. Imagine Ezekiel's surprise when he hears a rattling noise, and realises that the bones are coming together. But the bodies were still lying lifeless. Ezekiel prophesies again, addressing the Holy Spirit. The word used throughout this passage is the Hebrew word '*ruach*' which refers to the Spirit, breath and the wind. Now the bodies come to life and there are so many of them, they form a vast army. Seeing the bones become living bodies, the people begin to hope again that the Lord is still with them and that one day he will take them home to Jerusalem.

Peter in Acts 2:17 and 18 speaks of God's promise through Joel, to pour out his Spirit on everyone. This was the equivalent of God breathing his Spirit into the dry bones. Because of Jesus' death and resurrection, the Holy Spirit can be given to all who believe in Jesus. At Pentecost we say to the Lord that we don't want to be like dry bones. We want to be like the disciples: full of the Spirit, new life and power to share God's love with others.

Beginning the service

Ask what is the most essential thing we need in order to live. (You're looking for the answer, 'oxygen'. You'll probably get other answers which will be correct which you can affirm, but keep asking until someone says 'oxygen' or 'breath'). Introduce the theme by saying that, as Christians, we need the Holy Spirit to live as God wants us to, just as much as we need oxygen. Today is Pentecost, when we celebrate the gift of the Holy Spirit to Christians. We'll be thinking about how the Holy Spirit helps us.

Use this opening response:

God says, 'I will pour out my Spirit on everyone.'
Come, Holy Spirit and pour out your power on us.

Bible reading

Ezekiel 37:1–14 is very visual. Use the CEV to read it, ideally with a narrator, Ezekiel and the Lord. More dramatic would be to dress six children in black with one of six large bones stuck to them – two arms, two legs, a spine and a skull. At the start they lie down in a pile at the front or down the aisle. As verse 7 is read they clack together to become a body but they then lie down, lifeless. As verse 10 is read they stand up and dance around, but still all joined together. It will look odd but its meaning will be obvious. They freeze during the reading of verses 11–14 and then dance back to their seats. A glockenspiel could be played early on to give the effect of bones or the 'fossils' extract from Saint-Saëns' *The Carnival of the Animals*.

Acts 2:1–21 also lends itself to a narrative reading with a narrator, a crowd and Peter. Sound effects could be introduced in the early part, or swirling ribbons to give the effect of wind and fire.

Bible talk

With: a large outline drawing of a human skeleton, with all the major bones separated (a good skeleton drawing can be found at www.lessontutor.com/jm_skeleton.html); a flip chart stand; Blu-tack

The skeleton would work best if reproduced on black sugar paper, using white poster paint. It needs to be big enough for everyone all over the building to see it. Cut out the skeleton into separate bones. Don't worry about having individual bones of the hands and feet, but the whole hand needs to be separate from the two arm bones, and the whole foot separate from the two leg bones.

Before the service hide all the separate parts of the skeleton around the building. Count how many pieces you have before hiding them, so you can tell whether you've got them all once the younger children have finished the bone hunt.

A pile of bones
Begin by asking the younger children (those under 7) to move around the building to hunt for bones. Tell them to bring any bones they find to the front. Encourage everyone else to call out where they can see bones. Once you have all the bones, ask people to help you put the skeleton together, sticking it on the flip chart. Working downwards would be the best way. Ask what you need to start

with. Involve older children by asking for several to help you search through your pile of bones to hand you each bone as you ask for it. You may want to 'ham it up', by playing thick about which bone you need next and deliberately putting them in the wrong place, so that people can call out to tell you the correct way of doing it.

Dry bone people

Explain the situation that Ezekiel was in, living in exile with others from Jerusalem. The city was taken by enemies as God's punishment for the people ignoring God. Everyone felt that God had deserted them. They felt hopeless, like dry bones. Ezekiel's picture from God, of bones getting back together again with life breathed into them, was a picture of God breathing life into his people. It was his promise that, one day, he would rescue them and take them home to Jerusalem. It was something that only he could do with his Holy Spirit.

Life into old bones

Left to our own devices, we are like dry bones: lifeless and powerless because we ignore God. But when we say sorry to God for ignoring him he forgives us and breathes his Holy Spirit into us. Peter's speech on the very first day of Pentecost (Acts 2:1–21) reminds us that because Jesus died for us, we can all have God's Holy Spirit living in us. We need him to help us to live as God wants us to, just as we need oxygen for our bodies to live. But just as Ezekiel needed to ask the Spirit to breathe into the bodies to make them come to life, so we need to ask the Spirit to breathe into us to help us to live as God wants us to.

Prayer activity

With: enough balloons for every 2 to 3 people; some wool, string or gift ribbon in order to hang the balloons up; jumbo marker pens with very thick tips (enough for every 2 to 3 people)

Hold up a deflated balloon. Explain that everyone will use a balloon in the prayer time. Try to write something on it. Point out that you can't when it's deflated. Ask what you need to do to the balloon to make it possible to write on it. (Answer: blow it up.) Blow the balloon up, tying a knot in it to keep it inflated. Make the point that Ezekiel's bodies without God's breath were useless. Explain that when we pray, we need the breath of the Holy Spirit to help us. Show that once the balloon is blown up, it is possible to write on it. Ask for some suggestions for prayer topics, based on the subject of our need of the Holy Spirit to fill us so that we can live as God's people.

Ask the congregation in pairs or family groups to blow up their balloons, tying knots in the necks of them, and then tying a length of wool to the neck. Ask an adult in each small group to carefully write on the balloon a short prayer based on the subjects discussed.

When everyone has finished their own prayer, ask people (children, where possible) to bat their balloon across the building to someone else. When people have a new balloon, ask them to pray the prayer on the new balloon. Repeat this two or three times, according to the time available and people's responsiveness. When you have finished, ask a couple of adults to gather up the balloons, then bunch them together so they can be suspended around the building. People can see the prayers they've prayed.

Prayer of Confession

When we ignore you and go our own way, Lord, have mercy: **Lord, have mercy**.
When we forget your presence with us, and become like dry bones,
Christ, have mercy. **Christ, have mercy**.
When we do things in our own strength and not yours,
Lord, have mercy. **Lord, have mercy.**
Father forgive us
through the death of Jesus, your Son,
and strengthen us to live in the power of your Holy Spirit
today and every day.
Amen.

Ending the service

Remind people that Ezekiel's bones became bodies but didn't live until they were filled with the Holy Spirit. As Christians we need to be constantly filled with the Holy Spirit. The closing prayer helps us to ask God to fill us with his Holy Spirit, so that we can live as he wants us to. Ask everyone to join in with the closing prayer, also available as a download (YearB.Pentecost_1).

Heavenly Father, thank you for the gift of your Holy Spirit.
Please fill us with your breath and power every day,
So that everyone may see through us that Jesus Christ is the Saviour of the world. Amen.

If appropriate, give out six deflated balloons to each family group and ask them to create another Holy Spirit prayer for each day of next week, asking God to give them new life as individuals and as a family, so that they can live as God wants them to. You could also give a balloon to those who are sad or feeling hopeless, as a reminder of the hope that God gave to his people in exile. This would need to be handled sensitively.

Helpful extras

Music and song ideas

General music to play might be Saint-Saëns' 'Fossils' from *The Carnival of the Animals* (see **Bible reading**) or the song 'Dem Dry Bones'. These can both be downloaded from iTunes for less than £1 each.

'Breathe on me, breath of God'; 'Come down, O love divine', 'O Thou who camest from above'; 'Rejoice, rejoice, Christ is in you'; 'Send us the rain, Lord' by Dave Wellington (the third verse picks up on the Ezekiel passage); 'These are the days of Elijah' (the second verse speaks of Ezekiel); 'Like a gentle breeze' (Holy Spirit, come); 'Holy Spirit, we welcome you'; 'Spirit of the Living God' (there are two forms of this song which are both suitable but only use one as they're very similar).

Notes and comments

You may want to refer to the passage from John 15. This is a difficult passage for children to grasp because the concepts are quite abstract. Collect a few photos of people who you know will be at the service. Show the photos and ask if anyone knows the names of the people whose photos you're showing. Photos are reminders of what people are like. They don't tell us everything, but they show us enough to help us to remember the people or the occasion. Photos are especially important reminders when members of the family live a long way away, or are apart from each other.

Jesus was promising to give the disciples the Holy Spirit because he had to go away and leave them. In one sense, he was like a photograph of Jesus. The Holy Spirit would comfort them when they were sad. He would also help them to know when they went wrong, just as Jesus had done when he was with them. It was important that the disciples should have the Holy Spirit with them to help them to live as Jesus had taught them and to tell others about Jesus. But whereas Jesus could only be with a few people at a time because he was a human being, like we are, the Holy Spirit can be with any number of people all at the same time.

At Pentecost we thank Jesus for giving us his Holy Spirit to help us to live as he wants us to. We ask the Holy Spirit to make us more like Jesus every day.

Online resources

All suggested downloads are available at www.scriptureunion.org.uk/light. Visit www.lightlive.org for additional activities for children, young people and adults. For your convenience the following activity is available as a download: Year B. Pentecost_2 Song for 5s and under.

Trinity Sunday

READINGS: **Isaiah 6:1–8; Romans 8:12–17**
Psalm 29; John 3:1–17

Bible foundations

**Aim: to appreciate something of the mystery and wonder of God –
Father, Son and Holy Spirit**

Isaiah 6:1–8 brings into sharp focus the theme of holiness which has been present
from the opening chapters. God is 'the Holy One of Israel' (1:4). The people, called
holy, have been corrupted by the dishonest practices of their leaders, have engaged
in misguided worship and suffered social injustice. King Uzziah, bypassing the priests,
had made an offering in the Temple, and was struck with a skin disease (see
2 Chronicles 26 and 2 Kings 15). After Uzziah's death, Isaiah has this vision of
God enthroned in the Temple.

The scene is full of movement and fire and smoke – images reminding us of the
guiding presence of God (Exodus 13:21) and of sacrifices offered in the Temple
(Leviticus 1:4). Isaiah's response to the overwhelming holiness of God is an
awareness of his own and his people's sinfulness. Only when he is cleansed by a
Seraph ('fiery one' in Hebrew) touching his lips with a fiery coal, can he hear the
call of God himself, and respond.

Paul's sense of being caught up into the life of God lies at the heart of Romans
8:12–17. Paul often uses the much-debated term 'flesh' (in Greek 'sarx'), but not
always with the same meaning. The GNB's choice of 'human nature' is a good
translation here. Paul contrasts two ways of living – not the physical versus the
spiritual, but life centred on God or not centred on God. He contrasts the images
of being slaves or being children. This is not about degrees of freedom (sons were
obliged to their fathers just as much as slaves were to their masters) but about the
future: only sons can expect an inheritance from their 'master'. Through the death
and resurrection of Christ, we too can be part of the glorious life of God. The Spirit
of God working within us enables us to recognise, rejoice and live this.

Beginning the service

It is important to convey the fact that thinking of God as Trinity is exciting. In this service we will see something of what it is like to be caught up in the circle of God's life and love. The ideas in **Notes and comments** may help you find the best way to express this. Start with a strong hymn or song of praise, with instruments and shakers available – especially for young children who are not able to join in with the words.

Bible reading

What Isaiah describes in Isaiah 6:1–8 is very vivid. Suggest that people listen with their eyes closed, imagining the scene as it is read.

Romans 8:12–17 could be read as follows (from the CEV) to show the contrast between life with God and life without him.

Reader 1: My dear friends, we must not live to satisfy our desires. If you do, you will die.
Reader 2: But you will live, if by the help of God's Spirit you say 'No' to your desires. Only those people who are led by God's Spirit are his children.
Reader 1: God's Spirit doesn't make us slaves who are afraid of him.
Reader 2: Instead, we become his children and call him our Father. God's Spirit makes us sure that we are his children. His Spirit lets us know that together with Christ we will be given what God has promised. We will also share in the glory of Christ, because we have suffered with him.
Romans 8:12–17 (CEV)

Bible talk

With: symbols of Isaiah's experience in the temple such as strips of red, orange and yellow crêpe paper; pieces of gold and red foil to represent the Seraphim; a lump of coal (wrapped in cling film); some incense (either grains of 'ecclesiastical' incense and a piece of charcoal in a suitable heatproof container or suitably scented incense sticks); about twenty tea lights (with a suitable heatproof container or sand to stand them in) with matches and a taper available; music to accompany the dance

The aim of the **Bible talk** is to reflect on God as Trinity, and what that means for us. When we speak of the Trinity, it is not some sort of abstract description of God. The Trinity bears witness to the fact that the life of God is shared life, embracing the world he has created. The readings both point to the fact that, as his people, we are involved with God in the world, energised by eternal life. The talk has three parts. In advance, hide the symbols around the church.

The circle dance
Explain that you are going to show what God is like. It is something in both readings that people might have noticed. Ask for two volunteers to join hands with you in a circle. Explain that you are going to dance. Play some music such as the tune of 'Lord of the dance'. After dancing round in a circle a few times, break the circle and invite others to join in. Dance round for a short time. Hopefully this will be done with enjoyment and not reluctance! Ask whether anyone noticed the bit about the dance in the readings. The link is not obvious, so most

people will be puzzled but be prepared to respond to someone who says yes! Say that you are going to think about someone who was called to join God's dance.

Isaiah called to join God's dance

Point out that there are some unusual things hidden round the room. Invite people to find them and bring them to the front. (Children may enjoy doing this but adults can join in too.) As the objects are brought forward, talk about Isaiah's experience in the Temple. What did he see, smell, and feel? Arrange the things on a table, lighting the incense and tea lights. Ask what God looked like. We can use the visual aids as a small reminder of the fiery creatures and the smokiness, but we don't know what God looked like. The impression Isaiah had was just huge and mysterious. Point out that fire and smoke were signs of God's guiding presence for his people in the past, and Isaiah would have known this.

The piece of coal is a reminder of what happened to Isaiah. He had an overwhelming sense of God's holiness. There he was, in the Temple and suddenly he saw just how unworthy he was – and not just him but his community too. He felt lost; what could he do about it? He could do nothing, except to allow himself to be cleansed by God – which one of the fiery heavenly creatures does with the coal from the altar.

Point out that Isaiah didn't just have an amazing vision, which ended with him being cleansed. It was only when he had been cleansed that he could hear the voice of God calling him to be involved with God among his people. He was being drawn into God's dance. Straight away he said, 'Send me'. He had a tough message to proclaim.

We are part of God's dance

Ask for three volunteers to join hands and stand a little to one side, out of the way. Point out that God is not like that. He wants us to join in too. Ask the three to come to the centre and loose hands so that others can join them. If we feel unworthy, if we don't feel like dancing, remember that God makes the first move. He can cleanse us. Paul reminds us that God has given us his Spirit, to work within us. The Spirit helps us to know that we are God's children and we share the life of God that we see in Jesus.

Remind everyone that, like Isaiah, we need to allow ourselves to receive what God gives, to admit our need and be touched by God. As a 'thought for each day', suggest this: every morning, when we wake up, think that today we are going to dance with God.

If appropriate, encourage as many as can to join hands in a large circle (taking care of the candles on your table). Point out that those who cannot easily do this can remain seated, contained within the circle, part of the life it represents. Another verse of 'Lord of the dance' could be played as you dance round, or you could use the **Statement of faith** at this point.

Prayers of intercession

Encourage a time of silent adoration, much needed as we live in such a noisy world. How this is done will depend on what you usually do as a congregation. Music is a good way into a time of silence (see **Music and song ideas**).

After this, offer prayers of intercession. These should be short and to the point, not a change of activity, but demonstrating that the awareness of the presence of God frees us to bring before him the needs of the world. Members of the congregation could be encouraged to pray out loud.

Prayer of confession

Isaiah was aware not just of his own sinfulness but that of his people. Remind everyone that when we confess together we are not just praying for ourselves as individuals, but bringing before God our wider human responsibility for the things that spoil his world. The confession is based on Isaiah 6. It is available as a download (YearB.Trinity_1).

Ending the service

End with 'Lord of the dance', singing it with hands joined in the big circle as before. Use percussion instruments if available.

Helpful extras

Music and song ideas

To appreciate the mystery and wonder of God, play music which enables people to 'tune in' to a time of stillness with God. The 'Duo Seraphim' from Montiverdi's 'Vespers' is a very atmospheric setting of this vision of heaven. You can hear the seraphs calling to one another. It lasts six and a half minutes so you may only wish to play part of it. You could display the following translation of the Latin words: 'Two seraphim called to one another, "Holy, holy is the Lord God of Hosts. The whole earth is full of his glory." There

are three that testify in heaven, the Father, the Word, and the Holy Spirit; and these three are one. Holy is the Lord of Hosts. The whole earth is full of his glory.' This could be played during Communion or as people are coming in to church.

'Holy, holy, holy, Lord God Almighty' (Heber); 'Holy, holy… Lord God Almighty' (Jimmy Owens); 'Holy, holy, holy is the Lord' (author unknown); the Taizé chant 'Adoramus Te Domine'; 'Lord of the dance (I danced in the morning…)' emphasises the way in which we participate in the life of God – use this in the **Bible talk**: 'I the Lord of sea and sky'; 'Will you come and follow me' (John Bell) picks up on the invitation to share in the life of God. 'God's love is like a circle' complements the circle dance image and could be used with younger children, sung during the dance.

Statement of faith

This is also available as a download (YearB. Trinity_2).

We believe in God!
In love you created the earth,
made us your children,
and we call you Father.
We believe in God!
Jesus, you show us your love:
forgiving, healing, restoring,
transforming.
We believe in God!
Through you, Holy Spirit,
we share in the life that you live,
and show your love in the world.
Amen!

Notes and comments

It is a great privilege to lead worship on Trinity Sunday. The Trinity is not about God being remote and self-contained, but is all about the dynamic relationship God has with the world from the beginning of creation. Bear the following points in mind.

- It is easy to fall into the way of thinking that says, 'the doctrine of the Trinity is difficult and complicated.' This can happen if we think it is about trying to define God. There is a danger of getting stuck with words and concepts, as if talking about something static, like a picture or statue in an art gallery.
- The Trinity is about how God continues to be involved in the world, and we are caught up to share in his life.
- We do not find the doctrine that God is Trinity in any one biblical text; it comes through many texts as we understand what God is like through his dealings with his people. The experience of Jesus did not suddenly reveal God as triune ('three in one'), but in the light of Jesus' ministry, death and resurrection, and in the coming of the Spirit, it was easier to see that this is the nature of God.
- We cannot 'do the Trinity' simply by expounding one of today's readings. The aim of the **Bible talk** is to explore the idea that because God is Trinity, we are involved with God in the world, energised by eternal life.
- One of the best images for the Trinity is a circle: God is love; the relationships within the Trinity are of reciprocal love; the creation of the world is an act of overflowing love, so we, as created beings, are caught up in this 'dance of love' within God.

It might be effective for younger children to stick the coloured paper and foil onto a pre-drawn outline of a seraph. If the worship space is big enough, this could happen in the same room during the **Bible talk** and be hung as a banner when finished, as a reminder. These heavenly creatures remind us of the holiness of God, and God's initiative in cleansing and calling us. Alternatively they could do this during the **Prayers of intercession**.

Many Christians have recently read the novel *The Shack* by William P Young which sheds some refreshing light on the Trinity. You may not agree with everything in the book but if appropriate, refer to it.

Online resources

All suggested downloads are available at www.scriptureunion.org.uk/light. Visit www.lightlive.org for additional activities for children, young people and adults.

Top Tips on Explaining the Trinity to young people

This book helps youth workers explore the Bible's teaching on the Trinity and the Christian understanding of this mystery. Packed with practical ideas of pictures and images to aid understanding, the reader discovers how belief in the Trinity affects worship, mission and community.
For more details, visit www.scriptureunion.org.uk

Proper 5

READINGS: 1 Samuel 8:4–11,16–20; Mark 3:20–35
Psalm 138; 2 Corinthians 4:13 – 5:1

Bible foundations

Aim: to accept the challenge to make living God's way the top priority and not to conform to the expectations of those around us

Being different from those around us, peers, colleagues or just the norms of our culture, has always been a challenge. The people of Israel wanted to be like neighbouring nations in their worship but also, as we read in 1 Samuel 8, in how they were governed. God had made allowance for them to have a king (see Deuteronomy 17:14–20), but even here there is a recognition that the king could lead them astray. He was to be subject to God and his law.

Samuel warned the people (1 Samuel 8:10) recognising that ultimately they were rejecting God himself in their demand for a king to rule them. They were not to be deterred, so Samuel (and God himself) gave into their insistent request. Saul was appointed king (11:15). This was not the ideal path to follow, but as has happened throughout time God gives people the freedom to choose to do the right thing but goes along with those who opt for a lesser path. However, such a choice cannot hamper God's ultimate way of salvation.

Jesus' family wanted Jesus to behave as an eldest son. Not understanding nor accepting the path he had chosen, they gathered outside the place where he was (Mark 3:31–35). Jesus did not concur with their ambition. Ultimately they came to accept him, as seen by Mary's and his brothers' commitment to being one of Jesus' disciples (Acts 1:14). The grand plan meant that anyone who did the will of God was Jesus' brother, sister and mother.

In this service there is the challenge to make what is ultimately right in God's eyes a top priority, even though this may result in standing out from the crowd. He offers forgiveness if we get it wrong, but, as the people of Israel discovered, there are always consequences.

Beginning the service

Two women (A and B) act out the following sketch, both wearing a bright-coloured scarf or something as a sign that they are acting in character. The sketch could be adapted to be two children with bikes, or men with car magazines, or two people planning a holiday etc to make the same point.

A: I have just got to have that new kitchen, with the Grecian marble work surfaces, expanding drawers, and super-sized sink unit. (*She waves her arms around to demonstrate smoothness of surfaces and size of the drawers and sink.*) Everyone in the reading group has got one. I have to have a new kitchen. I am so embarrassed with mine. I could never invite any of them in the group to my home. Trouble is, we can't really afford it. But I suppose if we didn't give so much away… (*she sighs*)

B: But you promised to support the new play group. You very generously said you would buy the climbing frame and soft play shapes that we needed to get started. Will you not get them now?

A: (*looking cross*) It is all a matter of priorities… I am so embarrassed and feel so different from everyone else. It makes me feel so bad. What will they think of me? Maybe I could buy one play shape and give the rest next year…

Introduce the theme of this service outline and then sing a song which recognises God's omnipotence such as 'Guide me, oh thou great redeemer' or 'God of glory, we exalt your name'.

Bible reading

I Samuel 8:4 to 11 and 16 to 20 lends itself to a narrative reading with a narrator, the elders of Israel, the Lord and Samuel. Conclude, after a pause, with the words from 11:15: Everyone went to the place of worship at Gilgal, where they agreed that Saul would be their king. (CEV)

The verses in Mark 3:31–35 tie in closely with the theme of this service. This could also be read as a narrative reading with the same people reading as above: the narrator, 'the elders' could be Jesus' mother and brothers, while 'the Lord' could be Jesus. Draw attention to what the characters had in common in the two readings.

Psalm 138:7,8 are used in **Ending the service**.

Bible retelling

This simple retelling of I Samuel 8:4–11 should be read as follows:

A: 'We want a new leader,'

B: some men told Samuel.

A: 'We want a new leader…

B: because you are getting old. We know you tried your best to teach them what's right, but your sons never listened to what they were told.'

A: 'We want a new leader,'

B: the men told Samuel.

A: 'We want a new leader…

B: but this time we want a king. All the countries near here have kings to rule them. We're sure a king for Israel would be the best thing.'

A: They want a new leader,'

B: Samuel said to God.

A: They want a new leader…

B: because I am getting old. Although I've tried my best to teach them to love you, your people rarely listened to what they were told.'

A: Don't worry,'

B: said God, 'you've been a good leader.'

A: 'Don't worry,'

B: said God, 'leave the problem with me. They can have a king if that's really what they want, but I'm going to choose the man who it will be.'

A: 'Meet your new leader,'

B: Samuel told all the people, 'Saul is the person God has chosen for you.'

© Kathleen Crawford and adapted with permission

Bible talk

With: three people dressed in red and a fourth person in another colour, who are all prepared to mime; four crowns

You may have played the **Game** just before this talk.

We know best

Begin with this imaginary tale; those miming will need to have practised:

It was the fashion in a faraway town to wear red clothes (*three people walk to the front wearing red*). Admire their clothes and fashion consciousness. Anyone not wearing red felt an odd one out. But not everyone wanted to wear red. Ask for suggestions why this might be so, such as they supported a football team with blue shirts, they had ginger hair

and red does not suit them, they like to be different. (*The fourth person walks to the front wearing any colour but red and the three in red deliberately turn away.*) Ask the fourth person how he feels (and he will need to want to be like the others) and then ask the congregation to comment. What would he have to do to be like the others?

(*Each red person then puts a crown on their head and forms a tight circle.*) Explain that the countries next door to God's people in Israel all had kings. But God's people did not have a king. They were led by their leader Samuel and he was in touch with God and knew how to lead the people. But the people really, really wanted to be like everyone else. (*The fourth person tries to break into the circle formed by the red people, but is shunned.*) God's people felt left out. So they asked Samuel to give them a king.

God knows best

God did not really want the people to have a king. He knew that in reality the people were rejecting him as their leader when they said they did not want Samuel as their leader. He knew that they were influenced by the nations around them. But the people were so insistent, despite Samuel's warnings. Refer to the **Game** if you have played it.

So God told Samuel to appoint King Saul as their king. (*Fourth person puts on a crown and is accepted into the red people's circle.*) But the people were to find out that having a king was not a happy thing for them. Saul may have begun well as a king but things went wrong. David followed Saul as king but there was lots of fighting and the people were not always faithful in worshipping God. In fact, there were only three kings who ruled Israel and then the country was split in two with two kings. And the other nations did not accept God's people. (*The red people throw the fourth person out of the circle.*)

Making the best choices

We make choices, often because we want to be like others, and this may not be the best choice for us or for others. With every choice we make (and this is probably not talking about the choice whether to have a chocolate or strawberry ice cream!) we need to ask if there is a right way that God wants us to take. If we ask him and wait for an answer, we are likely to make the right choice.

But even if we make the wrong choice, God is still with us and will help us to live with the consequences. That was what God's people discovered. It would be appropriate to follow on with the **Prayer of confession**.

(If appropriate, you could make the parallel with Jesus' family – see **Bible foundations**. The three people in red [without their crowns] hold their arms out towards the fourth person, opening out the circle. But he steps back to hold his arms out to include everyone. The red people then turn their backs away from him. They do not want to accept what was the right way for Jesus and ultimately the right way for the whole world. Note that later on, Jesus' family did accept him.)

Prayer of confession

We sometimes make choices from the wrong motives or just get things wrong because we have not cared enough about what God thinks. Ask everyone to think how the people of Israel would feel when some years later they realised that they had made a mistake. Then lead into the time of responsive prayer, which is also available as a PowerPoint download (YearB.Proper5_1). Show the PowerPoint before you begin so that people have time for reflection.

Lord God, sometimes leaders of nations make mistakes. They get bad advice, or they are dishonest, or they want to keep themselves in power, or they do not consider what will happen to others as a result of their decisions. (*Pause for a time of reflection.*)
Thank you, Lord God, that you long to forgive. Thank you that even when mistakes are made, you can still make a difference for good.

Lord God, sometimes we make mistakes and make wrong choices. We get bad advice, or we are dishonest, or we are selfish, or we do not think what will happen to others as a result of our choice. (*Pause for a time of reflection.*)
Thank you, Lord God, that you long to forgive. Thank you that even when mistakes are made, you can still make a difference for good.

Father God, forgive us.
Father God, forgive us.

Father God, help us to be strong when we have made mistakes.
Father God, help us to be strong when we have made mistakes.
Amen.

Prayers of intercession

It would be appropriate to pray for anyone making choices at this time, whether about big changes in life, such as changing schools, moving home or job or lesser things that might be equally significant. This could be in small groups or led from the front all together.

Ending the service

Verses 7 and 8, from today's psalm, are appropriate to end the service. God is so trustworthy that it makes sense to make it our top priority to choose to do what's right with him. Ask for suggestions for hand or body movements, before you read out these words (with the last line amended) in a final dismissal.

> I am surrounded by trouble (*arms around the head*),
> but you protect me against my angry enemies (*palms outwards to form protection*).
> With your own powerful arm you keep me safe (*clenched fists raised in front of face*).
> You, LORD, will always treat me with kindness (*a smile as hands held out in welcome*).
> Your love never fails (*hands clenched together*).
> You have made us what we are (*forefingers traced from head to toe*).
> **You will never give up on us, Lord** (*shouted twice*).
> Psalm 138:7,8 (CEV)

Notes and comments

Many people make choices and live to regret them, without ever knowing the forgiveness and sustaining nature of God. Encourage any people affected by the theme of this service to seek prayer from someone before leaving.

Helpful extras

Music and song ideas

'Guide me, oh thou great redeemer'; 'God of glory, we exalt your name'; 'When you make a mistake, don't worry' (from *Reach Up! CD*, Scripture Union); 'God forgave my sin'; 'King of kings'.

Game

Create sets of six crown-shaped cards, each set a different colour. A set contains six cards with the following phrases, possibly with simple pictures: declare war on other nations; command men to fight in his army; employ women to work in his palace; take the best fruit for himself; take one tenth of the grain for himself; take the best cattle for himself.

Give out these cards as people arrive. Just before the **Bible talk** ask people to find the other cards that make up their set, explaining that each set is a different colour. When they have done so, discuss what is written on the cards. This is what God said a king would be like if the people of Israel were given a king (see 1 Samuel 8:12–18, which you have probably not read.) The people of Israel had been warned!

Online resources

All suggested downloads are available at www.scriptureunion.org.uk/light. Visit www.lightlive.org for additional activities for children, young people and adults.

Proper 6

READINGS: **Ezekiel 17:22–24; Mark 4:26–34**
Psalm 92:1–4,12–15; 2 Corinthians 5:6–10,14–17

Bible foundations

Aim: to understand that God's way of working is not what we might expect

Verses 22–24 form the third message of Ezekiel 17. Unlike the other messages, here is a message of salvation. Judah and the exiles in Babylon, having been devastated in 587 BC, receive a message of hope.

The metaphor of a cedar tree bearing fruit points to God working out his punishment on Judah through the hand of King Nebuchadnezzar. There is also an ongoing promise to the Davidic line through whom the promise would be developed. The language reminds the reader of that used in the royal psalms. The effect is to recall the promises of worldwide rule found in these psalms. Since King Zedekiah (the last king of the exiled people) broke his vassal oath to Nebuchadnezzar (an oath made in God's name), he had invited retribution from God. But God's pledge was a guarantee that things would change.

In Mark 4, Jesus explains the kingdom of God using parables. In 4:30–32 he describes the mustard tree growing from a small seed. This has echoes with Ezekiel's cedar tree. In Jesus' series of parables about seeds he shows the kingdom germinating, growing and maturing of its own accord without human assistance. It is all of God. Some of Jesus' followers may have thought that the kingdom could be brought in by force, but this parable disproves it.

After the first Easter, the disciples may have wondered at the smallness of what God was achieving in and through them. They had learnt to be surprised at how God worked! At times today we may struggle to see God's kingdom in the world. But the promise is that the kingdom will grow into something large. At the appointed time he will bring the kingdom to its fullness, in his way, not ours!

Beginning the service

As people arrive, display a picture of a Lebanon cedar tree (an Internet search will provide some images) on the screen or on a large roll of paper. At the start, welcome everyone and explain the identity of the tree that is on view. Comment that you will refer to it later.

Use Psalm 92:1−4 as an opening prayer. The whole congregation could read the verses out loud. Encourage each person to share something of God's goodness to them with the next person before you sing your first hymn or song.

See **Notes and comments** for an alternative **Beginning of service** suggestion.

Bible reading

As you read Ezekiel 17:22−24 show the image of the cedar tree again and ask people to look at it as the verses are read. Explain that God is showing that he can bring down the strongest tree (which to the original hearers living in exile far from their home, meant Zedekiah the king of Judah) and grow something even taller. You may wish to read this during the **Bible talk**.

Mark 4:26−34 lends itself to a retelling which involves sound effects. This passage reflects the same themes as those raised in the **Bible talk**. If you have percussion instruments, choose the most appropriate for this retelling. Alternatively, you might use body sounds and sounds made from everyday objects.

Jesus went on to say, 'The Kingdom of God is like this. A man scatters seed in his field. *(Shake empty margarine pots filled with broad beans.)*

He sleeps at night, *(All rub hands together or yawn.)* is up and about during the day *(Tap empty jam jars with a pen.)* and all the while the seeds are sprouting and growing. *(All click fingers together, getting louder and louder.)* Yet he does not know how it happens.

The soil itself makes the plants grow and bear fruit; first the tender stalk appears, then the ear, and finally the ear full of corn. *(If there is a drum kit, shimmer the cymbal, quietly at first and then getting louder. If not, do the same with a large pan lid using a wooden spoon wrapped in a tea towel as a beater.)*

When the corn is ripe, the man starts cutting it with his sickle, because harvest time has come.' *(Scrape a cheese grater with a fork.)*

'What shall we say the Kingdom of God is like?' asked Jesus. 'What parable shall we use to explain it? It is like this. A man takes a mustard seed *(Take a potato snack tube filled with rice and shake gently.)*, the smallest seed in the world, and plants it in the ground. *(All stand and stamp feet together.)*.

After a while it grows up *(Shake the potato snack tube more loudly or fill milk bottles with different amounts of water, so that they make a scale, and tap each one gently using a pen or pencil, so that each note increasingly becomes higher.)* and becomes the biggest of all plants. It puts out such large branches that the birds *(Make cooing bird noises by blowing into a cupped hand.)* come and make their nests in its shade.' *(Scrunch empty crisp packets in your hand.)*

Jesus preached his message to the people, using many other parables like these; he told them as much as they could understand.

Mark 4:26–33 (GNB)

Bible talk

With: a thriving plant from which you can make a cutting; garden shears; compost; smaller plant pots; plastic sheeting; watering can and water; photos of children in the church three years ago and now, for comparison (with parents' permission)

Ensure that the picture of the cedar tree (mentioned in **Beginning the service** and shown in the reading of Ezekiel 17:22–24) is displayed. Begin by explaining that you will be exploring trees and how they grow but, more importantly, seeing how God uses the picture of a tree to tell his people what is important as his kingdom grows.

Growing new plants

Invite volunteers to help you with some gardening! Take a couple of cuttings from the main plant and replant them into other pots using compost and water. Ask people to tell you what you must now do to ensure that the new plants will grow (such as water regularly, put in a sunny place, talk to them!). Each volunteer can take their plant home. Invite one of the volunteers to read Ezekiel 17:22–24.

Explain that in the verses just before what has been read from Ezekiel 17, God, through Ezekiel, is telling his people living in exile in Babylon how the mighty, who are disobedient (in this case, the king of Judah), will be punished. They will be humiliated and killed in battle. However, the future of God's kingdom will be built by those who are seemingly unimportant.

It is possible in verses 22 to 24 that Ezekiel is referring to Jesus, who the Bible presents as coming from an insignificant background. For example, he was like a small twig (Isaiah 53:2a), from a lowly family born in a lowly town (Micah 5:2), was not attractive or handsome (Isaiah 53:2b) and from a place despised (John 1:46). Yet he was the one who would bring about the fulfilment of God's work. In God's kingdom all peoples would find a place, regardless of class, race, gender, age and religious heritage. God's kingdom would be made up of the small, the weak, the sinful and the vulnerable.

Remind people of the reading from Mark 4. Comment on how plants are growing at this time of year and how often people may need to cut their grass or prune their tomato plants! You could invite a gardener to talk about the plants they are nurturing.

Growing taller children

Show some photographs of children who are in the congregation, as they were three years ago and as they are now. Marvel at how they have grown and then ask how it is that all this growth has happened! Of course, they have eaten food and exercised their bodies (and these things are important) but we don't really know! It is a mystery.

Growing God's kingdom

We don't know how God is bringing in his kingdom. But we do know that that is what is happening and he is doing it through people like us. No matter how insignificant, weak or vulnerable we feel, God sees our potential. He wants to use us so that others might come to be part of his kingdom. With the Holy Spirit, we are all given the power and strength to live for him.

Turn back to the plants. For the potted cuttings to grow and bear fruit, they must be watered and tended to. In turn they will develop roots which will allow for growth. In the same way, Christians need to develop roots, for without them Christians become flimsy and flaky. (It is like growing children eating well and exercising lots!) To develop strong roots we need to:

- Spend time reading God's Word, the Bible. Describe different ways to do this, for adults, children and young people.
- Spend time in praise and worship, with others and on our own. Give some suggestions and personal preferences.
- Spend time being with God in stillness and quiet, listening and 'being'. You could refer back to the stillness suggested for the service on Trinity Sunday.
- Spend time with other Christians developing relationships that are honest and real.
- Spend time in prayer; for the world, for others and for yourself.

Strong roots ensure that we will bear fruit. From small beginnings, God fulfils his plans.

Prayer activity

With: a leaf-shaped green piece of paper;

a 'branch' of a tree or the outline of a tree drawn onto lining paper; pens and pencils; packets of mustard seeds; cotton wool; plastic trays (from ready meals); sticky labels

Set up a table or area where children can 'plant' mustard seeds. Place a square of cotton wool on a plastic tray. Sprinkle some mustard seeds on top of the cotton wool and water carefully. On sticky labels, write '_____' is important to God. Each child can write their name in the blank space to stick on the tray. Pray for the children in the light of this.

Other members of the congregation will be given a leaf shape and a pen. On the leaf, each person writes a short prayer asking for God's strength to do whatever he has called them to. As a sign of unity, each person sticks or hangs the leaf onto the branch or tree outline. If you have a large congregation, you may need to place several 'trees' around the worship area.

Ending the service

To draw the service to a close, use the words from 'Carmina Gadelica' as a final prayer (an Internet search will provide the words) or from one of the contemporary songs which acknowledge that God is with us at all times and in all places such as 'May God's blessing be upon you now' or 'May the Lord bless you'. This will sum up a commitment to God for the week ahead.

Helpful extras

Music and song ideas
'How great thou art'; 'Give thanks with

a grateful heart'; 'God made you and me (from Light for Everyone); 'Lord, I come to you (The power of your love)'; 'God in my being'; 'God be in my head'; 'Faith as small as a mustard seed'; 'May God's blessing be upon you now' (*Spring Harvest Kids' Party Praise 3*); 'May the Lord bless you' (*Spring Harvest Praise 2010*)

Game

With: a grid with 12 squares (3x4) containing pictures of six small things and the same six things as they have reached their full potential, all placed face down on the 12 squares – eg a baby – a man; an acorn – an oak tree; a tadpole – a frog; a raindrop – a waterfall; a spark – a fire; a chick – a hen; a caterpillar – a butterfly. An electronic version of this game is available as a download (YearB.Proper 6_1).

This game of pairs links up pictures of small things with their fully-grown counterpart. Split the congregation into two teams. Invite players to take two pictures at a time. If the two correspond to each other, they can keep the pair and have another turn. If not, they place the pictures back in the same place, for the next player. The winning team is the one with the most pairs.

After the game, read Psalm 92:12–15. Remind people that God works differently from the way the world works. Each of these small things has the potential for great beauty and strength. Similarly, God does not always begin with the strong and the big. He often chooses to begin with the small and weak but, in his strength, they will become those who fulfil his big plan for his world and for his people.

Notes and comments

Alternative **Beginning of service**: In advance of the service (the week before), set the congregation a challenge to fit as many small items into a matchbox as is possible. Provide the matchboxes for all who are willing to take part. At the start of the service, check the matchboxes and give out a prize for the person with the most. Explain that in the service you will be learning about how, in God's eyes, small things are the beginning of his big plans for his world and his people.

If there is a Communion service, you could draw attention to the smallness of bread and wine which are symbolic of the vastness of what Jesus achieved in his death and resurrection.

Online resources

All suggested downloads are available at www.scriptureunion.org.uk/light. Visit www.lightlive.org for additional activities for children, young people and adults.

Proper 7

READINGS: **Job 38:1–11; Mark 4:35–41**
Psalm 107:1–3,23–32; 2 Corinthians 6:1–13

Bible foundations

Aim: to encourage people to have faith in God, even when facing problems

The story of Job is well known – the man who had everything and lost it all, including his health and happiness. Yet he hung onto his faith in God, despite the urgings of his supposed friends to blame God. His words have a strongly contemporary feel in a world where there is so much that is wrong and so much we cannot understand and have no power to rectify. God speaks from a storm in powerful poetic language. Job is reminded who God is and what he has done. God the creator has placed limits on the forces of nature (38:11). Ultimately, Job is stunned to silent trust.

Psalm 107 picks up this theme of God present in the tempest. All seemed lost in the storm but, in crying out to God, those in danger were rescued (vs 28,29). The apostle Paul had discovered what it meant to live in close communication with the God who rescues those in need. His list of disasters that he gives to his readers in Corinth resonates with trust in the One who has kept him safe. He writes as '… sorrowful, yet always rejoicing' (2 Corinthians 6:10).

Jesus' disciples were discovering what it meant to trust Jesus. What was going on in their minds as he slept in the boat as the storm brewed? They had seen Jesus perform miracles of healing (Mark 1:31; 3:5) and miracles of amazing provision at the wedding (John 2:1–12), but it was early days. Who was Jesus if he was able to command the forces of the natural world to obey him? Their trust in him was challenged and no doubt grew through this incident. May the faith of each person in church today, whatever their age, grow as a result of encountering God who is with us in the tough times, transforming both us and the circumstances.

Beginning the service

Introduce the aim of the service, explaining that everyone needs to provide sound effects several times in the service to emphasise this message. Half the congregation makes the noise of a storm. This 'storm' represents problems and difficulties faced in life. The noise of wind, rain and thunder can be made using fingers drumming on chairs, feet stomping on the floor and loud blowing. The other half of the congregation represents faith in God by chanting 'God is great! God is powerful!' repeatedly. Practise the two sound effects, using a clear gesture to indicate when each side should start and stop. These sound effects can be used during the **Bible readings**, the **Bible talk** and at **Ending the service.**

Bible reading

The recommended translations for these readings are from either the NIV or the CEV.

Use the 'storm' and 'God is great! God is powerful!' chant within both of these readings to help the congregation engage with the events described (see **Beginning the service** for an explanation of these sound effects). Before reading Job 38:1, gesture for their storm noises; and at the end of verse 11 gesture for the 'God is great! God is powerful!' chant. During the reading of Mark 4:35–41 gesture for the storm noises after verse 37 and for the 'God is great! God is powerful!' chant after verse 39. Warn the readers that this will happen!

Bible retelling

With: two narrators; one silent actor; a chair; the 'Riches to rags' drama script available as a download (YearB.Proper7_1) (The drama 'Riches to rags' places the reading from Job 38 into the wider context of Job's suffering, struggles and faith. It describes the crisis that God was responding to, and also shows what Job's reaction to this encounter was.)

Bible talk

With: images with appropriate words as follows: two of a storm cloud; two of sunshine; one of the sun appearing behind the cloud to be seen on a screen or on a board. The following are examples of what could be written beside the weather images: Storm cloud 1: illness, losing a job, money worries, unkind friends, horrible teacher, scary exam; Sunshine 1: God is with us; Storm cloud 2: angry, confused, rejected, worthless, hopeless; Sunshine 2: God is powerful; Sunshine and cloud: faith. These are available as a download (YearB.Proper7_2).

Remind everyone of their two sound effects (a 'storm' and 'God is great! God is powerful!' chant). They will be asked to make these noises during the **Bible talk**.

Focus on 'storms' people face in life. (*Gesture for half the congregation to make their storm noises.*) Give appropriate examples of what sort of problems in life there might be such as a horrible teacher, an unkind friend, someone you love being sick, or worries about money. (*Reveal Storm cloud 1.*) Refer to the story of Jesus in the storm and explain that the disciples and the people in the other boats with them were in great danger. Storms on Lake Galilee could start very quickly and become very dangerous. Emphasise that the boats were being thrown about and big waves were coming into the boat; the boats might capsize and the passengers all drown.

Next, focus on the fact that God was present in the middle of the problem. (*Gesture for half of the congregation to chant 'God is great! God is powerful!' Reveal Sunshine 1*.) Ask people to imagine God standing next to them when they meet a bully, do a hard exam, visit someone sick or have a difficult conversation at work. God was present with the disciples. As Jesus, he had become a human being, and in the middle of this story he was asleep in a boat. As he was woken up he would have been soaked to the skin and maybe even feeling sick. He experienced what his friends experienced although he was not afraid. God is still with us now through the Holy Spirit. He knows exactly how we're feeling. God is not far away when we face a storm; he is very close.

Turn your attention to the people's responses to problems. (*Gesture for the storm noises.*) Ask people what they feel about God when they face problems such as: 'God doesn't care'; 'God can't help me'; 'My problems are too small for God'; 'I can't ask God for help'; 'I don't understand why God isn't helping me.' (*Reveal Storm cloud 2.*) Refer again to Mark 4. Although the disciples were skilled and experienced fishermen, they couldn't cope with this storm. The problem was too big for their skills and they thought they were going to die. Refer to the disciples'

question to Jesus, when they ask whether Jesus actually cared about them. It would appear they doubted Jesus' love.

Focus on God's response to the problem. (*Gesture for the chant 'God is great! God is powerful!' Reveal Sunshine 2.*) Sometimes God takes our problems away completely and stops us from being hurt, but at other times, for reasons we can't always explain, he doesn't. Instead he gives the courage, wisdom and patience to face the problem. Refer back to Mark 4:39, where Jesus shows he's so powerful that all he has to do is give an order and the storm stops. The trouble disappears. Jesus was able to do this because he was not only an ordinary human being; he was God. He had made the whole world. God reminded Job that he was speaking to the one who had made the world and controlled the sea.

Encourage people to have faith in God even when facing difficulties. (*Gesture for both sound effects to be made at the same time. Reveal Sunshine and cloud.*) The disciples and Job had their faith challenged. Jesus asked the disciples, 'Do you still have no faith?' and Job clung on to his faith in God, even though life was really tough. Having faith in God means believing that he exists, that he is good, that he is close to us and that he is powerful, no matter what happens. It means asking him for help, trusting he will help, even though that might not mean taking the problem away.

If possible, ask someone to share a short testimony about a time they went through difficulties but went on trusting in God. Make sure they speak in language that people of all ages can understand.

Prayer activity

With: four children prepared to read out loud; a pencil or pen per person; at least one per person of A6-sized storm shapes – raindrops, clouds or lightning bolts – a photocopiable version is available as a download (YearB.Proper7_3); at least one roll of blank paper (eg the back of a roll of wallpaper); one piece of string for each roll of paper used; a copy of the prayer below, also available as a download (YearB.Proper7_4)

Before the service begins, distribute the storm shapes and pens and give the four young readers the storm shapes on which are written the names of people who are known to be facing difficulties, relevant topics from the church prayer diary or the names of countries in crisis. Make sure you don't break confidences. This activity allows people to bring their personal and wider concerns to God and to see them being placed in his care.

Explain that the storm shapes contain the words or pictures of things that people are concerned about. Invite the volunteers to bring up the storm shapes you gave them earlier. Ask them to read out what is on the shape and then to place it on the roll of paper which is stretched down an aisle or across the front of the worship area. Invite everyone to write or draw on their own storm shape a concern that they have which they'd like to bring to God. They then place their shape on the roll of paper. If they want to keep it private they can place it face down.

Instead of returning to their seats, everyone stands to watch as someone rolls the paper up, making sure all the storms shapes are contained in the roll. Tie a piece of string around the roll so that it doesn't open up. Everyone joins together to say the following prayer as the roll is carried to the Communion table or placed at the foot of a cross or in some other significant place.

Father God,
We believe you are a powerful and loving God.
We bring to you the things that make us sad and worried.
Give strength to everyone who has just brought to you something that troubles them.
Help them to know you are near.
Help us all to trust you.
In Jesus' name. Amen.

Ending the service

A song to express a commitment to stay faithful to God even when life is hard would be an appropriate conclusion such as 'O Jesus, I have promised' or 'Lord, reign in me'.

The two sound effects of the storm and the 'God is great! God is powerful!' chant could be used for a final time in tandem. Both begin quietly and then gesture for them to get louder rising in a crescendo. When the noise reaches an appropriate volume, gesture for the storm to be silent and then, several seconds later, silence the other chant.

Helpful extras

Music and song ideas
Music could accompany the sound effects made by the congregation. For example, cymbals clashing in the storm or a drum beat as a rhythm for the chant.

During the **Prayer activity**, background music could create a reflective mood. Using recorded music frees the musicians to participate. 'You never let go' by Matt Redman would be suitable.

'Jesus is Lord'; 'O Jesus, I have promised'; 'Lord, reign in me'; 'Our God is a great big God'; 'Our God is so big' (this could be sung in two parts with two halves of the church singing alternate sentences back to each other); 'Be bold, be strong' (this could be performed in a reggae style).

Statement of faith

This would fit effectively after the **Bible talk** or towards the end of the service. A leader speaks out each phrase and the congregation echoes this loudly and positively. Four simple actions shown in italics emphasise the message and help people to remember the statements. Try a slow practice run with the congregation before trying a more confident declaration.

Leader: We believe God is mighty. *(Flex the arm muscles.)*
All: We believe God is mighty. *(Flex the arm muscles.)*
Leader: We believe God is good. *(Thumbs up.)*
All: We believe God is good. *(Thumbs up.)*
Leader: We believe God made the world. *(Draw a circle with a finger.)*
All: We believe God made the world. *(Draw a circle with a finger.)*
Leader: We believe God is with us. *(Hug arms around self.)*
All: We believe God is with us. *(Hug arms around self.)*

Notes and comments

Before the service, images of storms interspersed with statements describing God could be projected onto a screen to provide a visual focus for the service. Complementing this could be 'Storm' from Beethoven's Symphony No. 6 (The 'Pastoral' Symphony).

If the church is familiar with praying aloud within the service, during the **Prayer activity** encourage people to pray for some of the specific matters they see before them. If appropriate provide an opportunity for people to have one-to-one prayer after the service.

The simple **Statement of faith** could be incorporated into a baptism or Communion service, but alternatively could be replaced by the creed that is normally used. Consider using three or four actions within the creed to emphasise the key points.

Online resources

All suggested downloads are available at www.scriptureunion.org.uk/light. Visit www.lightlive.org for additional activities for children, young people and adults.

Proper 8

READINGS: **Lamentations 3:23–33; Mark 5:21–43**
Psalm 30; 2 Corinthians 8:7–15

Bible foundations

Aim: to wonder that God comes to those in need

The story of the two healings in Mark 5:21–43 are frequently remembered as the story of Jairus' daughter with the healing of the woman inserted almost as an interruption. This would suggest the story of the raising of Jairus' daughter is seen as the more important of the two. But is one more important than the other? Mark presents four miracle stories – in nature (4:35–41), an exorcism (5:1–20), a healing (5:25–34) and over death (5:21–24,35–43). He puts the story of the woman within the frame of the raising of the dead girl. This technique, sometimes known as the Markan sandwich, is also seen when he framed the overturning of the moneychangers' tables within the conversation about the fig tree (Mark 11:12–26). In both cases, he is focusing upon the central story as the more significant and using the surrounding story to act as a sort of comment on it.

It could also be argued that Mark, presenting Jesus' divine character, wanted to offer a different way of determining who is or who is not important. Those in need are both women, less important in society. The woman has been sick for 12 years from a gynaecological condition and, according to the Law of Moses, was ritually unclean.

Significantly, the girl was 12, the age when she too might begin menstruation and therefore regularly be identified as ritually unclean. Jesus, as ever, accepted the marginalised, the sick, the poor and women – those who were unaccepted in religious ritual. This he compounded by actually touching a dead body! He ascribed importance in different ways to the accepted norms. He responded to all and accepted all.

Today's other readings present God always listening and always accepting. In Lamentations 3, the prophet, grieving over the state of Jerusalem, acknowledges God's great mercy. Psalm 30 echoes a similar message. In 2 Corinthians, Paul urges the believers to be generous to the less well off, taking the overwhelming generosity of Jesus as their model. Jesus came to this world for all people.

Beginning the service

Ask the congregation to put up their hands if they would like a treat. Choose one or two younger children to come to the front. Show them some treats (such as chocolates, or pieces of fruit), and say that they can either have one now or wait until the end of the service and then have two. Depending on what they choose, draw out that it's sometimes difficult to wait for things, but it's often worth waiting, if we can be confident that what we look forward to will be better than what we can have now. Today's theme is that of Jesus' coming to those in need, which did involve some waiting. But, however long people waited, Jesus treated them all as equally important. It was worth the wait. (Whatever your volunteers choose, be sure to honour your promise!)

Bible reading

Lamentations 3:23–33 can be read by two readers. The first reader should read verses 23–26, the second reads verses 27–31. Then the first reader reads the last two verses.

Both should be visible to the congregation and have the Bible open in front of them. This reading has a poetic feel to it, and is best read from a more traditional version such as the NIV.

The Gospel reading is a narrative story and benefits from the less formal treatment of the CEV.

Bible retelling

The first part of Mark 5:21–43 can be retold dramatically, from the points of view of Jairus and the woman. It needs minimal staging. The two actors simply stand a little apart, facing the congregation. You'll need someone to walk to the front to whisper in Jairus' ear and a male voice to read the words of Jesus from offstage. (If you do not have the Sam Cooke recording, you'll need a third person to read or retell the first part of the story.)

Play a recording of 'Touch the hem of his garment' by Sam Cooke. See **Music and song ideas** for details. Fade it out after the first half of the second verse, that is, begin fading at the line, 'When she touched him the Saviour didn't see'. As the music fades rapidly to silence, a voice is heard offstage…

Voice (*offstage):* Who touched my clothes?

Woman: Oh no! He felt me touching his cloak! What's he going to say? I feel so stupid now. I didn't want to disturb him. They say he's a great teacher and a healer. He must be important, he has lots of people with him, and one of them is a synagogue ruler! They seemed to be in a hurry too. I thought if I could just touch his clothes, I would be healed, without even bothering him. But now I've got to explain why I touched him. And he'll be angry when he finds out why I needed healing. Religious leaders won't have anything to do with blood. (*She sinks to her knees, and sadly says these words from Psalm 30.)* Hear, LORD, and be merciful to me; LORD, be my help.

Jairus: What's he doing? Who is this woman who's made us all stop? Doesn't she know that my daughter is dying? And why is Jesus so bothered about someone touching his cloak? It's not even a particularly expensive

cloak! Come on Jesus, there are more important things to worry about!
(As Jairus has been speaking, a man has been walking towards him from the back of the church. When he reaches the front, he whispers in Jairus' ear.) It's too late now… She's gone. *(Jairus sinks to his knees, and sadly says these words from Psalm 30.)* LORD, when you favoured me, you made my mountain stand firm; but when you hid your face, I was dismayed.

Voice *(offstage):* You are now well because of your faith. May God give you peace! *(The woman stands and exits. There is a pause as Jairus remains kneeling.)* Don't worry. Just have faith! *(Jairus stands and exits.)*

Bible talk

With: three people to interview, who take on the following roles: one has an important role in the church or community, one has done something important, such as winning a race or a prize or meeting someone important, and one is an only child and loved by their mum; if used, a flip chart with two columns, one for the details of Jairus and one for the woman; marker pens; a display of the summary points are available as a download (YearB.Proper8_1)

The talk is in three parts, each emphasising that God's love is unconditional.

God will come whether you are a ruler or a child

Explain that you are going to have an 'Importance Inquest', a competition to decide who the most important person is. Invite the three people to the front. They should

be in costume or holding something that emphasises their importance, such as their prize or certificate, something that their mum has given them. Ask what they have done and why they think they should win. The one who is loved should give no reason other than the fact that their mum thinks they should win!

Then ask the congregation to vote. Be as noisy as you like. Ask for reasons why voters have made their choice. What criteria do we use for judging importance?

In the story from Mark's Gospel, Jesus responded to the requests of two people. One was someone whom everyone thought was important. Ask why Jairus might be important (his job, his status in society, his confidence, his religious faith, he was a man, he was at least 30 so was older, his small daughter was ill so an emotional pull on Jesus). You could write down the details on Jairus in one column of a flip chart and the details of the woman in a second column. Remind everyone about the woman. Ask why people thought she was unimportant (poor, sick, a woman, probably not married, ritually unclean, no obvious friends and supporters, shy).

If Jesus had conducted an 'Importance Inquest', who would have got the first prize out of these two? (You want to come to the conclusion that Jesus accepted both of them!) Remind the congregation that every one of them is equally important to God. Whatever their age or status, if they call on God, he will answer. You could sing 'Everyone in the whole wide world' at this point.

God will come whether your problem is big or small

The prophet who wrote Lamentations, which was one of the readings, said, 'I am finished! I can't count on the LORD to do anything for me' (Lamentations 3:18 CEV). But then he went on to say that God could be trusted! But are there some things that are too big to talk about with God, or some things that are too small to bother God with? Divide people into small groups to discuss the sort of things that we talk with God about. Are they big things or little things? Subjects might include: illness, job interview, broken iPod, money worries, school, an evening out with friends, lost keys, work, football match, car MOT and anxiety. Ask for comments on what might be seen as too big or too small for God.

Say that sometimes we don't like to trouble God with seemingly trivial concerns, because we feel that he has more important things to worry about. Consider how Jairus might have felt when Jesus stopped to see who had touched his cloak, and when the news came that his daughter had died. Was this too big or too small a matter?

Jesus did not have to choose between two people. He helped them both. The fact that he stopped to ask who had touched him shows that he was always in control. We can talk to God about anything that concerns us, in just the same way that we would talk about it with our friends. Nothing is too big or too insignificant for God!

God will come whether you have been good or bad

Point out that the readings from Lamentations and Psalms have a slightly different emphasis: they suggest that it is God himself who has caused the writers' distress, and that God has turned away from them. But both passages have a message of hope: read Psalm 30:4 and 5 and Lamentations 3:31 and 32 as examples. Ask whether sometimes people feel that they have wronged God, and that as a consequence they have no right to call on him. Remind them that his anger lasts only a moment, but his favour lasts a lifetime (Psalm 30:5a).

Sum up with the following points which could be displayed.

God will come:
- Whether you are a ruler... or a child
- Whether your problem is big... or small
- Whether you have been good... or bad.

Prayers of intercession

Use the refrain 'Come, Lord Jesus' to pray together. Pray for international issues, then for national concerns, your own community and finally for your own church and its people. Each subject will be introduced and responded to as follows:

Leader: Lord, we pray for... asking that you will...
All: Come, Lord Jesus.

As an alternative congregational response, use a few lines from an appropriate song. The chorus from 'Great is the darkness' is particularly effective.

Ending the service

Ask for suggestions of ways in which God helps us when we call on him. Refer to

2 Corinthians 8:7–15, and remind them that the Church is Christ's body on earth, empowered by the Holy Spirit to do God's will. Pray that God will come to you all, and to the world. Then send the congregation out into the world!

Helpful extras

Music and song ideas

The backing for the alternative **Prayer activity** can be a secular recording, such as 'Hope of deliverance', by Paul McCartney, or 'Things can only get better' by D:Ream, or a Christian song such as 'Great is the darkness'; 'Faithful One'; 'Jesus never, never, never' clearly presents Jesus as welcoming all; 'Everyone in the whole wide world (Everyone matters to Jesus)' fits with the first part of the **Bible talk**, and could be sung in the middle of the talk, with simple actions; for the **Bible retelling** play the song 'Touch the hem of his garment' by Sam Cooke (for details with a version to listen to, see www.last.fm/music/Sam+Cooke/_/Touch +the+Hem+of+His+Garment).

Notes and comments

Another way to read Lamentations 3:23–33 is to use pauses to emphasise the themes of waiting and silence. The reader would pause for longer than usual between verses 24 and 25, verses 25 and 26, and verses 27 and 28. Contrast the tone of the passages with our modern 'Instant' society, in which everything from food to written messages

can be received instantly. God will come, but 'it is good to wait quietly for the salvation of the LORD'.

As an alternative to the reading from 2 Corinthians in **Ending the service**, remind people that God will come to them when they call him, and then offer the opportunity to pray with somebody if there is something that concerns them.

As an alternative **Prayer activity**, explain that sometimes it is appropriate to pray with our eyes open. Play some suitable music (see **Music and song ideas**) and display on a screen pictures from the recent news, some local, some national and some international. The pictures should serve as prompts for prayer. If you have enough time, you may be able to prepare this so that the pictures synchronise with the music, both rhythmically and thematically.

Don't forget to give out the treats to those who chose to wait until the end.

Online resources

All suggested downloads are available at www.scriptureunion.org.uk/light. Visit www.lightlive.org for additional activities for children, young people and adults. For your convenience the following activity is available as a download: YearB. Proper8_2 Story for 5s and under.

Proper 9

READINGS: **Ezekiel 2:1–5; Mark 6:1–13**
Psalm 123; 2 Corinthians 12:2–12

Bible foundations

Aim: to understand the challenges for those who bring God's Word to reluctant hearers

Ezekiel receives his commission as a prophet; these are the first words he hears from God. The potential difficulties of being a prophet are mentioned straight away. The people of God will not accept Ezekiel's words, even though they will acknowledge that he is a prophet! Referring to the time before the Exile started (note Ezekiel 1:1,2), God accuses the people of continuing to rebel against him. Whatever the discouragement Ezekiel experiences, he must proclaim God's message to them (see further 2:6,7).

Jesus gets no better a hearing than Ezekiel was led to expect. The local people can't quite shake off the image of the precocious 6-year-old lad around the village, or the 16-year-old learning the craft of a carpenter (presumably from his father). The sheer ordinariness of Jesus as a member of a local family gets in the way of them accepting him. Wisdom and miracles are not what would be expected, and so they cannot believe it. Yet the need remains to ensure that the message reaches as wide an audience as possible. Jesus sends out the 12 disciples. They are challenged to rely on the hospitality they are offered (Mark 6:8–10). They also face rejection and disbelief (v 11).

The challenge for Paul is of a different nature: controlling his pride. The temptation to boasting, though, does not come from his achievements as a missionary but from his mystical experiences. Note that he closes by mentioning the privations of his lifestyle (2 Corinthians 12:10); preaching about Christ brings him frequent suffering. He does not view this as a challenge, though. He has so thoroughly accepted the fact that this will happen that he is not discouraged by it. In the 'weakness' of relying on Christ, he finds strength. In the lament of Psalm 123 the writer looks to God for mercy, for relief from the challenge of this situation.

Beginning the service

Start with a clapped question and response; clap the rhythm and say the chant at the same time.

Leader: Are you listening? (Crotchet, crotchet, quaver, quaver, crotchet)
All: Yes I am! (Crotchet, crotchet, crotchet)

Prime the music group with the required response. Practise this a few times until everyone has the idea. At random moments through the rest of the service clap this question, and chastise a lazy congregation for not listening! Explain that today's service is all about listening and hearing what God has to say to us. Joke that there will be a test! In particular we're going to think about people who don't want to hear what God has to say to them.

Bible reading

Each reader should preface their reading with the chant: Are you listening? Yes I am!

The readings from Ezekiel 2:1–5 and Mark 6:1–13 include people who refuse to listen. At least two people could mime the refusal to hear by blocking up their ears and turning their backs on the reader. Other 'actions of refusal' might include waving an angry fist, shrugging shoulders in disbelief or waving someone away. Explain that Ezekiel, who was from a priestly family, was in exile in Babylon with God's people who had been taken away from Jerusalem, their home. The people longed to return home.

Bible talk

With: a large rock; a small hammer (wooden or plastic toy hammer, not a metal one)

Ask for a child volunteer to do a job for you. (As you are effectively setting somebody up to fail, choose your volunteer carefully.)

Are you listening?

Show the congregation the hammer and say that you want someone to hit the stone with it. Give the toy hammer to the child telling them to keep hitting the stone until you tell them to stop. Be very careful not to tell them that you want them to break the stone, just to hit it. Clearly the hammer is inadequate for breaking stone, and if they object along those lines ask them if they're listening to you or not. (Are you listening?)

Once your volunteer is hammering, address the congregation with a comment about the service theme of listening and not listening. Often listening is hard to do, especially with the sound of hammering in the background. (Are you listening to me, not him/her?)

What things are we reluctant to hear, especially when it's something important? Ask for suggestions such as, 'I've got good news, and bad news'; 'If you don't tidy your room you'll get no pocket money this week'; 'You're going to need an operation'.

Check up on the child with the hammer. How are they doing? Whatever they answer, just tell them to hit the stone (but do so encouragingly).

Are you listening to God?

These important things that we don't want

to hear about can be like not wanting to hear the good news of Jesus. People don't want to hear about him, even though it's so important. Check that everyone has understood what was happening in the Gospel reading.

When we think about reluctant hearers of God's Word we tend to assume this is referring to non-Christians. But all of the people in the different Bible readings were Israelites, people who were supposed to belong to God. Note that Ezekiel, Jesus, Jesus' disciples and Paul were all sent to their fellow Israelites, people who were supposed to believe in God. But these people were reluctant to hear from God. (Paul later took the good news of Jesus to those who were not Jews.)

Are other people listening?
Some people think of themselves as Christians. They tick that box on hospital admission forms, they come to church for baptisms, weddings and funerals and they might come at Christmas. But the idea of being with God's people and listening to him regularly doesn't seem important. In addition, note that many people now think of themselves as 'spiritual', but see no reason to come to church in order to be 'spiritual' – whatever that might mean. In our multi-cultural, multi-faith society, many other people are not interested in Jesus or are even offended by him. Others just have not heard anything about him. No one has told them.

Conclude by asking your volunteer how they're doing. If they don't mention being unable to break the stone, do so yourself.

Ask about the original instructions. Affirm that they weren't asked to break it, so if they kept on hitting it then they did exactly what you asked them. Make sure they don't feel stupid as a result of their 'failure'.

God asks us to preach the message of the gospel. People will be reluctant to hear, and we may well not get anywhere, just as the child got nowhere with the stone. We may even encounter a hostile response, which the disciples did. So what? If we're hearing what God is saying to us, we'll just talk to people about Jesus, and leave the results to God.

Prayer activity

With: a map of the world projected on a screen or displayed on a board around which are pictures of people from your church who are sharing the gospel with others (If possible, contact them in advance to see if they can email current prayer needs.)

Choose a member of the congregation to prepare prayers for those pictured around the map. You could even attempt a conversation with these people over Skype, especially if you both have access to a video link. Ask them about their work and the challenges they face, especially when people do not want to hear.

Alternatively, create the following three places: pictures of people the church supports on one wall; words that describe God on another (or a graffiti wall for people to add such words) to act as a place for praiseful worship; a candle to act as a focus for people's own prayers. Explain that these are prayer stations that people should move round, praying as prompted by the items displayed. People could form three groups or move freely as individuals or family groups. Encourage everyone to listen out for what God might be saying to them.

Ending the service

End with a variant of the chant and this blessing based on Matthew 28:18–20.

Are you listening?
Yes I am!
Were you listening?
Yes I was! (Repeat that if the congregation clearly didn't listen to you the second time and replied with the present-tense response.)

Jesus says, 'All authority in heaven and earth has been given to me. Therefore go and make disciples of all the people from different nations who live in this country, teaching them to listen to and obey everything I have commanded. And surely I am with you always, today and to the very end of the age.' Amen.

Helpful extras

Music and song ideas
Songs relevant to the themes of this service (including that of our willingness to hear God speak) include: 'Here I am, wholly available'; 'I, the Lord of sea and sky'; 'Master, speak, your servant's listening'; 'Open our eyes, Lord'.

Game
With: paper and pens for recording answers; optional prizes for the winners

Are you listening? **Yes I am!**

How well were people listening through the

Bible readings? Split the church up into groups or teams with between six and 12 in each, appointing a leader of each team to write down the answers. Read out the questions. Each team discusses their answers before recording them. Check the answers (swapping sheets with a different team); there are 15 points available. Which team was listening best? Comment that there are some trick questions and some are really quite hard. This is also available as a download (YearB.Proper9_2).

1. Q: Who was the prophet in the Old Testament reading?
A: Ezekiel.

2. Q: Did the person speaking to Ezekiel ever use his name?
A: No. Ezekiel is called 'son of man' or 'mortal' (or whatever your translation used).

3. Q: Will the people know that Ezekiel was a prophet?
A: Yes, both those who were willing to hear what he had to say and those who were unwilling to.

4. Q: Which Gospel did the New Testament reading come from?
A: Mark.

5. Q: What were the names of Jesus' four brothers?
A: James, Jose (or Joseph), Judas and Simon. (One point for each name.)

6. Q: Were Jesus' father and mother both mentioned?
A: No, only Mary is included.

7. Q: At the start of the reading, where was

Jesus teaching?
A: In the synagogue of 'his hometown'.
(Award a bonus point for the phrase 'his hometown', but not for Nazareth, which is not mentioned in the reading.)

8. Q: Did Jesus perform any miracles here?
A: Yes (but not many).

9. Q: There were three things the disciples were not allowed to take. What were they?
A: Bread, a bag, and money in their belts. (One point for each item.)

Statement of faith
This is also available as a download (Year B. Proper9_1). It is adapted from Romans 10:13 and 14 and can be used as a response to the **Bible talk**. Note the incorporation of the chant towards the end.

All: We believe that everyone who calls on the name of the Lord will be saved.
Leader: But how can people call on Jesus if they haven't believed in him?
All: They can't.
Leader: And how can they believe in Jesus if they haven't heard about him?
All: They can't.
Leader: And how can they hear about Jesus if nobody tells them about him?
All: They can't.
Leader: Are you listening?
All: Yes I am!
Leader: Who will go and tell people about Jesus?
All: I will. We believe that Jesus calls us to tell anyone and everyone all about him. We will go and tell them.

Notes and comments

Superficially, there is a connection between the Ezekiel and Corinthians passages from the visions that feature in both. That is coincidental to the aim of the service.

You might want to encourage different sorts of listening. At **Beginning the service**, sit in silence for 30 seconds and ask what people can hear once they get used to the silence. Musicians could play something a little different from normal and you could then ask if anyone noticed anything different.

It would be very appropriate to ask someone in the congregation to talk about how they share the good news of Jesus at work or in the community, especially as you do not want anyone to leave thinking it is only the professionals who may share the good news with those who may or may not listen.

It would also be appropriate to pray for those who are going to be starting at a new school in the next few weeks, or those who are moving on to somewhere new. There are many opportunities to make it clear to others that we are followers of Jesus when we first start something new. Acknowledge that this often takes courage.

Online resources

Proper 10

READINGS: **Amos 7:7–15; Mark 6:14–29**
Psalm 85:8–13; Ephesians 1:3–14

Bible foundations

Aim: to appreciate the personal cost to those who speak out God's truth

Amos learns that God has lost patience with his people in Israel (the northern kingdom), where he has been sent as a prophet (Amos 7:1–9). God is going to bring punishment on them, and Amos' prayers will not be effective any more, as they once were (vs 2,3,5,6). It was about fifty years later though before the Assyrians took Israel into exile (2 Kings 17:5–23).

In addition, Amos has a confrontation with Amaziah, the priest at the shrine in Bethel (7:10–17). We don't learn if the priest's appeal to the king is successful (vs 10,11). Amaziah probably hoped that the king would intervene and deport Amos. He certainly tries to prohibit Amos from declaring any more prophecies (vs 12,13). In response, Amos belittles his own status (vs 14,15), but effectively replies that he has no option but to do what God commanded of him (compare this with Acts 4:18–20). By denying that he is a prophet, Amos is probably distancing himself from those who appear to have had the official status of 'prophet'. We would probably call those people 'false prophets'.

John the Baptist's fate is sealed with an act of petty vengeance. Herodias, the wife of King Herod Antipas, instigates John's murder. John's preaching was not just publicly uncomfortable for the king, it was also personally embarrassing for Herodias (Mark 6:17,19). She was not just a divorcee (as was Herod) but she had initially been married to Herod's half-brother Philip. John focuses on the theological issue of the incest violation this produced. Without any sort of trial, John was executed for proclaiming God's values.

The designated portion of Psalm 85 starts with a statement of a willingness to hear what God has to say. Neither Amaziah, nor Herod, nor Herodias was willing to hear God speak to them. The psalm expresses the benefits that come from being a willing hearer.

Beginning the service

With: the theme music from *Chariots of Fire* (the track can be bought from iTunes)

Play the theme music from *Chariots of Fire*. You might choose to imitate the slow motion running from the film as you walk in! If possible, display downloaded pictures of Ian Charleson in the role of Eric Liddell (and of Liddell himself) to make the connection with the music. Introduce the theme for today's service: the inconvenience of speaking out the truth for Jesus.

Bible reading

With: an improvised plumb line

Before the reading of Amos 7:7–15, introduce and explain what a plumb line is. You could construct one in the **Prayer activity** but have one to demonstrate at this point. Leave it tied to the pulpit or lectern as a visual aid. A picture of the Leaning Tower of Pisa would also help. A **Bible retelling** of these verses is suggested to use just before the **Bible talk**.

The reading of Mark 6:14–29 is not easy because the story of the murder of John the Baptist is gruesome and could be disturbing. Assess what is appropriate for your congregation. You may wish to avoid the description of the method of execution in verse 28. A PDF of this reading from the CEV without verse 28, with three voices, is available as a download (YearB.Proper10_1).

It might be appropriate to show one or more of the range of classic paintings of the event downloaded from the Internet. These could

include:

- Caravaggio, *Salome with/receives the Head of St John the Baptist*
- Caravaggio, *The Beheading of St John the Baptist*
- Fabritius, *Beheading of St John the Baptist*
- Spinello, *Feast of Herod*
- di Paolo, *The Head of John the Baptist brought to Herod*
- Dürer, *Beheading of St John the Baptist*

Bible retelling

With: an actor

This should take place just before the **Bible talk**. The actor co-operates with you to tell the whole of Amos 7 in the style of a first person narrative. The actor takes the role of a prophet who has come to your church to tell everyone about the successive visions they have received over the past few nights. Alternatively, if there are usually times in the service when people share things that have happened, the actor could adopt that style.

Introduce the actor who is going to share something from God.

The actor tells the congregation they have had a series of visions over the past few nights. The disasters in the first two visions (Amos 7:1–3 and 4–6) have been averted, because of the effectiveness of prayer. (Since locusts are unknown in the UK, the first disaster could be a drought, and the second a forest fire.) Aim to make the congregation feel positive about all of this: the coming disaster is not going to happen. With the third vision, however, everything is different. Prayers have not been heard by God. The people of this church have been found wanting and God is going to punish them. Lay this on thick.

You (or a church leader) break into this 'speech' to tell the actor off for frightening the children. Threaten them with the bishop, or similar high-ranking church official. Tell them they're not welcome here. What makes them think they have the authority to deliver such a disturbing message?

The actor must respond by saying that they have no option but to talk about the things they've seen and know God is saying. Dismiss the actor and apologise to the congregation for what's just happened.

Bible talk

With: any of the following – a carving knife (be careful in carrying blades in public); a clock; a TV remote and/or a games console (such as a Wii) controller; a football team scarf; your wallet or purse; a mobile phone

Start by rapidly introducing your items, one by one. These items will help to focus on what it might cost to speak out the truth for God.

Thinking back to the **Bible readings**, what did it cost John the Baptist? The carving knife is a reminder that it cost him his life. He told the king and queen, Herod and Herodias, that their marriage was wrong. The queen was angry with that, and she made sure that John was executed for it.

Even today there are people who die for being Christian. However, in most countries (but certainly not all), there is generally little

chance that we will die for speaking out God's truth.

What about Amos, though; what did it cost him? What do members of the congregation think? (You could include the reading at this point in the service.) Invite responses and interact with comments.

Amos didn't die. The priest threatened to have him kicked out of the country, but not that he would be killed. Amaziah told Amos to stop preaching. That was awkward, but not dangerous. What it really cost Amos, though, was inconvenience. Amos probably wanted to do something else instead of go preaching. He wasn't a professional prophet, he was a farmer. God told him to go to a different country, and to preach to ungrateful people.

In a very similar way, the most likely thing for us in speaking out the truth for God is inconvenience. How might that work?

Speaking out for God might cost time
The clock reminds us of this. To speak out for God might mean that we miss out on things we might prefer to do. We might need to: write a letter to our MP, instead of watching the TV (brandish the remote); go on a protest march, instead of standing on the football terraces; come to the prayer meeting instead of getting exercise on the Wii; phone or spend time with friends who don't know God so that our friendship can develop (show mobile) instead of playing a computer game. Speaking out the truth may be inconvenient. It will cost us time, and cause us sometimes to have to forgo our personal preferences.

Speaking out for God might cost money

We might choose to: support agencies such as Christian Aid, or Amnesty International or missionaries and mission agencies. These organisations are dedicated to speaking and acting out the truth.

Speaking out for God might cost friendships and reputation

The high priest tried to get rid of Amos. What will your friends think if you speak out for God? Are you going to lose friends? Will your behaviour make you stand out, not because you are odd (which might be the case!), but because behaving as God would want, you might challenge their behaviour – such as being honest, befriending outsiders? Will there be fewer people to text or talk to? Will you be ostracised at the school gate or playground? God expects us to stand out, no matter how inconvenient it might be, or how much of a killjoy it makes us. Standing out for the truth, and speaking out the truth, runs the risk of losing us friends and reputation. That is quite a price to pay.

How willing are we to hear it when God speaks truth to us? It was the priest who tried to silence Amos. Recall the **Bible retelling** when the person speaking God's message was shut up. God calls us first to hear what he has to say to us, before we try and take his truth to others.

Prayer activity

With: lengths of cord (or laces) in various colours; a number of large chunky nuts (as in nuts and bolts); fittings to make a mobile phone pendant (from a craft shop)

As a reminder of their willingness to pay the cost of speaking out God's truth, invite the congregation to create a plumb line. Ways of doing this include: tie the cord onto a key ring; make a mobile phone pendant; tie the nut to the cord. Hang the 'plumb line' somewhere prominent, such as by the kitchen sink, the front door, the bedroom door handle or workplace locker. When everyone is finished, ask them to hold up their plumb line to say together the following prayer, also available as a download (YearB. Proper10_2).

Heavenly Father, you have set up a plumb line.
You measure all our words and behaviour by it.
You want us to speak out for you by what we do and by what we say.
Today, we affirm our intention to live an honest and true life for you.
We will speak out your truth when you ask us to.
We will act out your truth in everything we do.
Help us to remember this every time we see this plumb line.
Amen.

Ending the service

A blessing:
The leaders in Jerusalem once commanded Peter and John not to speak or teach in the name of Jesus. But Peter and John replied, 'We cannot help speaking about what we have seen and heard.' May the same Spirit empower us as we speak about the Lord Jesus Christ, this day and for evermore. Amen.

Helpful extras

Music and song ideas

Songs relevant to the themes of this service include: 'We shall stand'; 'I want to serve the purpose of God (what is on your heart?)'; 'May the words of my mouth'.

Notes and comments

The suggestion to tone down the gruesome details of John's execution in the **Bible reading** has a specific context. An increasing number of people, not just children, find references to blood and death distasteful. On the other hand, pre-teenage boys might love the blood and gore so would enjoy the classic art depicting this event. Do what is best for your congregation.

It is confusing to follow the Herodian dynasty, especially since individuals are referred to by different names in different sources. For your own confidence, rather than for inclusion in the service:

- King Herod (Mark 6) was Herod Antipas, the son of Herod the Great (Matthew 2).
- Philip, mentioned in Mark 6:17, is known as Herod Philip I, also a son of Herod the Great and a half-brother to Herod Antipas. He is called Herod II Boethus in some sources.
- Herodias was a granddaughter of Herod the Great, married first to Philip, and (after a divorce) to Antipas. Both men were, therefore, her half-uncle.

- According to Josephus (Jewish Antiquities XVIII, 5:4), the daughter's name was Salome, and she was the offspring of Philip not Herod.
- John's challenge to the marriage of Antipas and Herodias would have focused not just on their divorces (grounds for divorce was a keenly debated topic in first-century Israel), but the breaking of the incest law of Leviticus 18:16.

A different approach to the **Bible talk** makes use of the film *Amazing Grace*. Three scenes directly relate to the theme of this service:

- Wilberforce's ill health. Scenes from early in the film indicate that his health suffered as a result of trying to get the bill passed.
- The conversation with his butler and the inconvenience of God choosing Wilberforce and changing his life as a result.
- The dinner table scene with William Pitt's friends, including the former slave with the chains. The point is made that serving God and serving the country are one and the same when you campaign to change social ills.

Online resources

All suggested downloads are available at www.scriptureunion.org.uk/light. Visit www.lightlive.org for additional activities for children, young people and adults.

Proper 11

READINGS: **Jeremiah 23:1–6; Mark 6:30–34,53–56**
Psalm 23; Ephesians 2:11–22

Bible foundations

Aim: to explore God's leadership of his people, as a shepherd – a model for leadership

In biblical times a shepherd led his flock from the front, guarding and guiding his sheep and even protecting them with his own life. The shepherd was not merely a hired labourer, but his whole life was concerned with the sheep's welfare. In the Old Testament, God is presented as the ultimate shepherd (Psalm 23). Biblical kings were God's shepherds, given responsibility by him for his sheep, his people. Their whole life was to be committed to the welfare of God's people. In the New Testament, Jesus and leaders of the church are referred to as shepherds.

Jeremiah the prophet cries out against his nation's useless shepherds (Jeremiah 23:2) (see also 1 Kings 22:17; Ezekiel 34:5,6). This is echoed by Jesus (Mark 6:34), coming immediately after the story of the beheading of John the Baptist, thus condemning Herod as a bad shepherd. Jeremiah (23:3–5) foretells a future Davidic leader to lead as a wise, good and just shepherd king. Mark links this prophecy with Jesus, giving an insight into what shepherd leadership meant for Jesus and those who follow him.

The good, compassionate shepherd recognises the needs of his sheep. Jesus recognised that his disciples needed relaxation and refreshment (Mark 6:31). More than five thousand people came out to find nourishment in Jesus' teaching and guidance (v 34). This they received in abundance just as later that day they received food in abundance (vs 35–44). Later still (vs 53–56) Jesus ministered to those who came to him in need of healing and salvation.

Just as Jesus makes himself available, so those who follow him are to do the same. Following Jesus is not simply a matter of enjoying the wonderful things he says and does. It is to share those things, and to start doing them in his way, with his character and priorities (v 30). It is to be good shepherds in Jesus' name.

Beginning the service

With: actors and sheep masks; a prominently displayed visual to set the scene such as a green cloth and a blue one; foil placed on the cloth to represent a stream; rocks; 'prickly' bushes; soft toy sheep; a shepherd's crook; alternatively, combine with the Bible talk display

Someone dressed as a shepherd interrupts the welcome by calling his sheep by name (an 'unruly' group wearing sheep masks), looking for them, offering to lead them to fresh green grass and cool clear water, warning them to keep away from brambles and rocks and watch out for wolves. The sheep scamper all around the church, but gradually gather together behind the shepherd. The shepherd wipes his forehead with a big neckerchief and then leads the sheep to their seats, checking they are all there.

An alternative shepherd mime for **Beginning the service** is available as a download (YearB.Proper11_2).

Bible reading

Explain the background to Jeremiah 23:1–6. God's people living in Jerusalem were threatened by an invading army and the leaders were weak and listening to false prophets. They were like weak shepherds. It was into this situation that Jeremiah brought God's message.

The reading from Mark 6:30–34,53–56 is full of action. Someone gifted in mime could act out some of the obvious key actions.

The first two verses of Psalm 23 are available in a form suitable for younger children as a download (YearB.Proper11_3). You could put together a simple PowerPoint projection of pictures of sheep, with and without shepherds, interspersed with pictures of Jesus healing and teaching. Alternatively, a large visual display illustrating Psalm 23 could be in a prominent position.

Bible talk

With: large sheep shapes (roughly 15x20 cm); thick felt pens; sticky dots; a large background of fields, stream and 'dangerous places' attached to a board; two shepherd shapes (about 30x20 cm), one with 'Good shepherd', one with 'Bad shepherd' written on the head; two scribes (young people)

The needs of sheep
Invite members of the congregation to tell you what they think sheep need. Write the ideas on some of the sheep shapes stuck to the display board. If you know a shepherd, invite them to tell the congregation about their work. Ask for ideas on what makes for a good shepherd or a bad shepherd. Write the ideas on the relevant shepherd shape. Stick the shepherd shapes on the board.

Explain the difference between shepherds today who, with their dogs, herd sheep from behind and shepherds in the Bible who call and lead their sheep from the front so that the sheep follow. Wonder with the congregation which they think is the best way. Which way would they like best if they were a sheep?

Leaders are shepherds
Talk about how, in the Old Testament, God is

sometimes called a shepherd and the people of Israel are called God's sheep. The kings of Israel and the religious leaders are also sometimes called God's shepherds. Wonder with the congregation what sort of things people might need from their leaders. Write these on more sheep and stick them up – some things might be the same as what the sheep need.

The kings and religious leaders were supposed to care for God's people just like a good shepherd cares for his sheep. Unfortunately, lots of them did badly. In the Old Testament reading we heard Jeremiah tell the leaders that they were 'like shepherds that kill and scatter the sheep'. He also said that God would choose new leaders who care for his people like real shepherds. Even more importantly, Jeremiah said God was going to send a very special shepherd king 'who will be wise and rule with justice'.

Jesus is the shepherd

Remind everyone that Jesus said, 'I am the good shepherd.' In the New Testament reading, from Mark's Gospel, the crowd ran round the lake because they wanted to hear more of Jesus' teaching. Jesus thought they looked just like 'sheep without a shepherd'. He felt sorry for them. He knew they needed him to lead them and guide them, far more than they knew. So he taught them 'many things'. Towards the end of the day, they badly needed food and rest. Later loads more people flocked to see Jesus bringing the sick for him to heal. He must have been very tired, but he didn't send them away. Like a good shepherd, he put his own needs aside and gave the people what they needed.

We are sheep and shepherds

Jesus still is the Good Shepherd – he is the wise Shepherd King. He gives us what we need. And, just as Jeremiah said, he sends new leaders to care for his people like real shepherds – just like Jesus cares. Wonder with the congregation who these shepherds might be. Maybe the disciples? Maybe your church leaders? Maybe you? Remember how tired the disciples were at the beginning of the story? They had been very busy on a mission to teach and heal just like Jesus did. They were learning that to follow Jesus is not just about enjoying the wonderful things he says and does. As with the disciples, Jesus calls us to share those things, and to start doing them ourselves just like he would, and with as much love and care as he has.

Prayer activity

With: a ball of sheep's wool (or a ball of cotton wool); a pipe cleaner for each person; the sheep shape from the **Bible talk**; a copy of the prayer response

Pass around the ball of wool for people to break off a piece and take a pipe cleaner during a hymn or song, or give them out at the beginning of the service. Invite the congregation to make a shepherd's crook from the pipe cleaner. Explain the responses below, which are also available as a download (YearB.Proper11_1) to be projected or printed on service sheets. Do not rush the prayers. Speak slowly and give people enough time to think.

Ask the congregation to look at the sheep's wool and imagine the sheep it came from. Think about the things sheep need. Slowly read out some of the things written on the displayed sheep shape. Think about the things we need that God gives us (food, shelter, love, guidance). Now look at the shepherd's crook you have made. Think about the people who teach us about God and show God's care to us.

Leader: Thank you, God, for giving us what we need.
All: Thank you for being our Good Shepherd.
Leader: Thank you for leaders to care for us and teach us.
All: Thank you for being our Good Shepherd.

Think of some of the people who do not have what they need (food, shelter, justice, peace, love, security). Think how you could be a good shepherd to some of them. Think of people who are sick or sad or feel lost. Think how you could be a good shepherd to some of them. Now think of those people who do not know about God, people who do not know God loves them – it may be someone you know. Think how you could be a good shepherd to them.

Leader: Help us to be your caring shepherds.
All: Help us to be good shepherds.
Leader: Help us to be your loving shepherds.
All: Help us to be good shepherds.

People can take home their wool and shepherd's crook to remind them to thank God for caring for them like a good shepherd and to prompt them to be good shepherds themselves to other people.

Ending the service

With: cards on which are printed a sheep and a shepherd; pens

Give everyone a pen and the card and invite them to write their own name under the shepherd. On the back invite them to write or draw two ways in which Jesus would like them to be one of his good shepherds this week: a caring way (suggest examples) and a teaching way (for example, invite a friend or neighbour along to a church group, or a lonely person to Sunday lunch, or children could help a friend or invite a friend to come to their midweek club). Everyone holds up their card to think of the people Jesus wants them to care about this week.

Leader: Good Shepherd, help us share your story.
All: Amen.
Leader: Good Shepherd, help us share your love.
All: Amen.
Leader: Go in peace to love and serve our Shepherd King.
All: Amen.

Helpful extras

Music and song ideas
There are various hymn versions of Psalm 23; 'Be thou my guardian and my guide'; 'Christ who knows all his sheep'; 'Colours of day'; 'Faithful Shepherd, feed me'; 'Jesus' hands were kind hands'; 'Peace, perfect peace'; 'The King of love'; 'The Lord's my shepherd' (various tunes – some would be suitable for the choir to sing as an anthem); 'To be in your presence (My desire)'; 'We will lay our

burden down'; 'When I needed a neighbour'; 'Will you come and follow me?'

Music at the beginning and end of the service could include classical pastoral themes, played by a small ensemble of adults, children or a mixed group, or alternatively from a CD.

Notes and comments

This material would fit in well with a baptism, emphasising the call to all baptised Christians to share what they have received, from the youngest to the oldest. Explore how a small child can share God's love. It would also be appropriate for a service where certain members of the congregation are being commissioned for a particular role in leadership or a task over the summer holidays such as a holiday club. The newly commissioned are like the disciples, sent on a mission yet returning to the fold once more, to be fed with others to prepare them to be sent out again.

Although the feeding of the 5,000 is not included in the Mark reading, in a service of Communion the idea of being fed abundantly with Jesus' teaching naturally links with being fed abundantly with the food of Jesus' life. Leadership for Jesus also meant being the Good Shepherd who would lay down his life for the sheep. Holy Communion celebrates the fact that Jesus did just that – laid down his life for us.

Online resources

All suggested downloads are available at www.scriptureunion.org.uk/light. Visit www.lightlive.org for additional activities for children, young people and adults. For your convenience, the following activities are available as downloads: YearB.Proper11_2 Shepherd Mime; YearB.Proper11_3 Psalm 23 for younger children.

Proper 12

READINGS: **2 Kings 4:42–44; John 6:1–21**
Psalm 145:10–18; Ephesians 3:14–21

Bible foundations

Aim: to recognise the power of God at work in providing food for those in need

In Bible times, the possibility of hunger or starvation was a constant reminder of the importance of food for health and life. So, the writers of the Old Testament frequently acknowledge that food was the gracious provision of Israel's God, evidenced in creation (Genesis 1:29) and in God's ongoing care for human beings (Psalm 145:10–18). Ultimately we are all dependent on him for our daily existence. We should respond with gratitude.

Contained in 2 Kings 4 are four vivid miracle stories from the life of the prophet, Elisha. Each incident shows him bringing hope into a situation of deep human need which exceeds all human expectations. For example, the feeding miracle in verses 42–44 should be seen in the context of the famine in v 38. Elisha's compassion reflects his understanding of God's character (see Deuteronomy 10:18).

Jesus' feeding of the 5,000 (John 6:1–15) includes echoes of Elisha's 'feeding of the 100'. Jesus, motivated by compassion (vs 2, 5), demonstrates the transformative power of God that provides more than enough for all (v 13), in the face of apparently inadequate resources and unbelief (vs 7, 9). His action transcends that of Elisha, in terms of both scale and significance. This miracle points to Jesus not only as the sustainer of physical life, but also as the source of spiritual life (v 35).

These two incidents call upon us to celebrate God's goodness in providing 'our daily bread' (Luke 11:3). They also challenge us to respond to a needy, hungry world, not with a feeling of inadequacy and hopelessness, but with faith that the Living God can use even us to bring hope and comfort. After all, the unnamed boy of John 6:9 was probably as surprised as anyone at the impact his limited resources could have when God's power was at work!

Beginning the service

It is so easy to take things for granted. We assume we shall have food. Ask who got up this morning and wondered whether there was any food in the house! (Be aware that there may be some for whom this might be true.) Some families do struggle to support each other but this is not the case for most people. We assume love and care from our family. Today we are making sure we do not take God for granted. He gives us love and support. He gives us bread to eat.

Bread-making alternative beginnings and endings to the service are available as a download (YearB.Proper12_2).

Bible reading

The reading from 2 Kings 4:42–44 can be in three parts, a narrator, Elisha, and a servant.

The Gospel reading, John 6:1–21 lends itself to a dramatic reading with a narrator, Jesus, Philip, Andrew and people (all readers together). Props of a basket, five small loaves, two small fish (plastic or paper) and 12 full baskets (carried by children in a round-the-church walk) can be displayed to increase the force of the words. Using props necessitates a rehearsal to get the timings right. The narrator reads verses 16 to 21 except for verse 20b which is for Jesus.

A **Prayer of intercession** based on Psalm 145 is available as a download (YearB. Proper12_1).

Bible talk

With: an empty bowl or plate; coins or money notes; breads (see later in **Bible talk**); 12 baskets

Food shortages

Hold up the empty bowl. In many parts of the world people are short of food. This can be because of civil war and fighting within a country or because of drought or famine. Sometimes bribery and corruption make the situation worse.

Hold up the money or rattle some coins. Usually we do not experience food shortages because we have money and if our harvest fails we buy food from elsewhere. In fact we have so much food that it is reckoned that each British family throws away £420 worth of food a year. We buy more than we need, put more on our plates than we can eat, and expect the supermarket shelves to be constantly full of foods from all over the world. (One London restaurant has tried to discourage people from eating more than they need by letting them select the amount of food they want but fining them for any left on their plates. The money raised went to charity.)

Basic food supplies

Everyone relies on God the creator for basic food. In many parts of the world, bread is one of the most basic foods. Show a series of different breads (made from kneaded dough) asking people where they come from. It is important to stress the countries of origin because this makes the point that God provides for the needs of everyone.

Breads could include: baguettes from France; naan bread, a staple accompaniment to meals in Central and South Asia, including

Afghanistan, Iran, northern India, Pakistan; unleavened bread (Matzoth) from Israel; tortilla from Mexico; focaccia (with herbs and olive oil) from Italy. Add whatever might be appropriate to your congregation's international or regional background. It might be a currant loaf or a North Staffordshire oatcake! These breads could feature in the faith lunch or picnic – see **Notes and comments**.

God provides the grain: wheat, barley, oats or rye. He is always meeting our need for food. At times miracles draw our attention to God's provision of our needs. What is otherwise ordinary, daily and taken for granted is highlighted in the miracles of Elijah and Jesus.

Bread for all

In both Old and New Testament miracles it is barley bread which is used. This was the cheapest form of bread. (Bread made from wheat was more expensive and bought by well-off people.) Elijah used 20 loaves of barley bread to feed 100 people. God's powerful provision was such that there was bread left over.

Jesus did an even greater and more powerful miracle. The feeding of the 5,000 is the only miracle recorded in all four Gospels. It was seen by the Gospel writers as so very important. Jesus started with not just 20 loaves like Elijah, but with only five small ones. He fed not just 100 people but, as John reports, 5,000 men. The total number with women and children was probably far greater. Some have suggested it would be nearer 10,000. Once again there was more than enough, for 12 baskets of leftovers were

gathered. (Bring the 12 baskets to the front.) Perhaps these leftovers were distributed to the poor rather than thrown away in a bin.

So often we trust in what we call 'dough' – money. God provides us with our basic dough – for bread. In a family, one person is often identified as the breadwinner (who brings in the money to pay for food). God is the breadwinner.

Prayers of intercession

With: pictures of a cross, rucksack, group of people in the congregation and a Bible can be printed on the service sheet, on an overhead or on PowerPoint slides

This prayer is based on Ephesians 3:14–21, accompanied by actions. Draw attention to the objects as you pray.

God is the source of all good things. He is all-powerful.

We pray that he will strengthen us with power through his Spirit so we can face the challenges of our time.

We hand over to God those areas of difficulty in our own personal lives. Each of us has a rucksack of burdens. (*Look at the picture of a rucksack.*)

We pray that Christ will dwell in our hearts through faith so we are indeed never alone.

We pray that in our relationship with God our Father, we may grasp how wide and long and high and deep is the love of Christ. The cross points upwards and downwards, out to the east and out to the west. (*Look at the* picture of the cross.)

We pray that in our relationships with one another we may be rooted and established in love. (*Look at the picture of the group of people or around at other members of the congregation.*)

We pray that as we develop in knowledge and love of God we may be filled with the fullness of God.

Help us to understand your Word. (*Look at the picture of the Bible or at the Bibles which people have with them.*)

Lord, help us to grow to maturity of faith. Amen.

An alternative **Prayers of intercession**, based on Psalm 145:10–18 is available as a download (YearB.Proper12_1). The words in bold can be said by the congregation or by a second voice.

Prayer activity

With: breads from the **Bible talk**

Lord, you made the world and gave it to us to care for.
You gave us grains, oats and wheat, barley and rye, so we could have bread to eat. We pray for the farmers who grow our cereal crops. Help them to work in harmony with nature and for the common good.
We remember farmers in Asia (*hold up the naan*), in Mexico (*hold up the tortilla*), in Israel (*hold up the unleavened bread*), in Italy (*hold up the focaccia*) and in France (*hold up the baguette*). May they be fairly rewarded for their work. May we appreciate one another,

and one another's different lifestyles. In Jesus' name. Amen.

Then share out a piece of bread with everyone. This has obvious links to a Communion service. Be aware of those who may need gluten-free bread.

Ending the service

Praise God because day by day he gives us bread to nourish us.
Praise God because he can use such small things like five loaves to help others.
May we, as small as we are, give ourselves to God to be used by him.

(And/or the final blessing is taken from Ephesians 3:20,21)

Now to him who is able to do immeasurably more than all we ask or imagine, according to his power that is at work within us, to him be glory in the church and in Christ Jesus throughout all generations, for ever and ever! Amen.

Helpful extras

Music and song ideas
As you announce the songs, highlight their relevance to the service theme.

'We plough the fields and scatter' where the chorus may be used as a grace before a meal if you are going to have a church picnic; 'I, the Lord of sea and sky' – with the lines 'finest bread I will provide/till their hearts be satisfied'; 'For the fruits of his creation' reminds us of what God has made and what we enjoy, probably best sung to the tune 'All through the night'; 'The Lord's my shepherd' highlights God's personal provision and care ('Brother James' Air' is a lively setting or try Stuart Townend's version); 'Fairest Lord Jesus' celebrates God's goodness; 'Let us with a gladsome mind' celebrates the kindness and goodness of God; 'Thank you, Lord' can be sung to words suggested by the congregation, for example, Thank you, Lord, for juice to drink; Thank you, Lord, for bread to chew; Thank you, Lord, for pizza and chips!

Notes and comments

Note that last week's Bible passages surrounded Mark's account of feeding the crowd. You might want to draw attention to this.

This is the first in a series of four service outlines that are linked by the theme of bread, food and picnics. As it is summertime in the northern hemisphere, you could arrange for a picnic lunch as one response to the series.

Focus on the importance of thanking God for food by commenting on 'saying grace' or 'giving thanks', a challenge as to how often we give thanks for food.

A member of the congregation could talk about the various graces they use, serious and humorous. The traditional Jewish grace is, 'Blessed are you, Lord our God who brings forth bread from the earth'. Different graces may include practices (such as singing or holding hands or using a cuboid with a grace printed on every side) or memorable occasions when saying grace in a restaurant or out in the open. You could challenge people to research different graces. There are

many available on the Internet. These could be printed in the next parish magazine or people could be challenged to have a Grace Box of their own from which they select a grace for a meal.

If the service includes Holy Communion, comment that Jesus took bread and, when he had given thanks, he broke it. He was maintaining his practice of saying grace and giving thanks.

A farmer in the congregation could be invited to speak about the mystery of planting, growth and harvest and how it brings him closer to understanding the Lord. Alternatively, invite a volunteer to talk about home baking and to demonstrate kneading and shaping the dough, leaving it to prove.

Find out about a project that provides food along with the good news of Jesus to people in need. If you already support such a project, take the opportunity to give the congregation up-to-date information and to pray. The Peruvian Bible Society runs the 'Pan de vida' project in Lima, providing street children with breakfast. For more information in English see www.biblesociety.org.uk and search for 'Bread of life'.

Online resources

All suggested downloads are available at www.scriptureunion.org.uk/light. Visit www.lightlive.org for additional activities for children, young people and adults. For your convenience, the following activity is available as a download: YearB. Proper12_2 Making bread.

Proper 13

READINGS: **Exodus 16:2–4,9–15; John 6:24–35**
Psalm 78:23–29; Ephesians 4:1–16

Bible foundations

Aim: to explore the image of Jesus as the Bread of Life

The amazing event of the Exodus, when Israel was delivered from oppressive slavery to the Egyptians, was the pivotal moment in the history of God's people. Their journey from Egypt to Canaan was not without its problems, particularly when the hardness of life in the wilderness became a reality. When they were hungry and grumbling, God responded with the gift of 'bread' known as manna, which tasted like a wafer and was described by Moses as 'the bread the LORD has given you to eat' (Exodus 16:15). This miraculous provision was intended to point both them and us beyond mere physical sustenance to the basis of 'true' life – to a grateful and obedient dependence on the Living God (Exodus 16:4; Deuteronomy 8:1–3).

The New Testament often describes Jesus as 'greater than' an Old Testament character or incident (see Matthew 12:6,41,42) and all that has gone before. The miracle of the feeding of the 5,000 (John 6:1–15) clearly echoed Exodus 16, particularly given the closeness of the Passover Feast (v 4). Jesus' action was motivated by compassion for the hungry (v 5), but it was also a sign (v 14) pointing to the one even 'greater than' Moses (v 32).

In the first of his astounding 'I am' statements found in John's Gospel, Jesus uses the image of bread to speak of himself as God's supreme gift to the world (bread being the most basic means for survival), which far surpasses the manna provided in the wilderness (vs 32–35). Jesus, as 'the bread of life' (v 35) is the one who meets our greatest needs and satisfies our deepest spiritual hunger; for he is the source of 'eternal life' in which we share as God's people (v 27). This is a powerful message for those who worship God with you at this service!

Beginning the service

Introduce the theme by reminding people that last week you saw how God provides us with bread day by day. He satisfies our physical hunger. This week we think how God provides us with truth. He satisfies our spiritual hunger. Then talk about God's priorities. In Isaiah 55:2 God says, 'Why spend money on what is not bread, and your labour on what does not satisfy?' Particularly at Christmas-time people go to great lengths to buy original gifts. Ask for suggestions for useless gifts or show some images of such gifts that you have downloaded from the Internet. Repeat Isaiah 55:2.

Alternatively, talk about the commercial ventures that use the name 'manna' – a search engine will provide you with plenty of examples from restaurants to bakeries, Christian bookshops to charities, organic suppliers to cookery courses! Manna was originally sent by God from heaven to sustain the Israelites. Jesus is also God's manna, his truth from heaven to nourish and sustain us. Today we are thinking of the types of manna that God gives us from heaven.

Bible reading

Exodus 16:2–4,9–15 could be read with a picture of a desert as a backdrop on a PowerPoint slide. Parts of Psalm 78:23–29 could be interspersed into the Exodus 16 reading, as follows:

After Exodus 16:9–13a, Psalm 78:26–29 could be read from the back of the worship space.

After Exodus 16:13b–15, Psalm 78:23–25 can be read.

John 6:24–35 can be read with a narrator, disciples and Jesus.

Bible talk

With: two picnic hampers: one marked 'Israel' containing a plate on which is the word 'manna', and a plate with the word 'quail' and inside a card on which is written 'Health warning: eat on the same day as collected'; the second hamper, labelled 'The Word' containing a plate or New Testament book with the name 'Jesus' and inside a card on which is written 'Health promise: lasts for ever'

Health warning: eat on the same day as collected

The first part of this talk picks out the main points from the Old Testament reading. The Israelites had escaped from Egypt and were in the desert. They were hungry. God provided for them.

Take the hamper marked 'Israel' and ask everyone what God sent for them to eat in the morning. Take out the plate marked 'manna'. Recap the details of the story, and then ask someone to describe manna. The Israelites had never seen anything like this before. All they could say is 'What is it?' (v 15) or 'What's it called?' ('manna' in Hebrew) and so 'manna' became its name. They could only take enough manna for one day. This is explained in verse 20. Take out the 'Health warning' card. It only lasted for one day and then the food went off. So for 40 years the Israelites gathered manna as food.

But their diet was also varied because another type of food appeared at night.

Take out the plate marked 'quail'. These birds migrated through the desert. They were a luxury food item yet they were available for this group of escaped slaves.

Health promise: lasts for ever
Most of us have more than enough to eat. But there is still an inner hunger, a longing and a thirst. This is a hunger to know God; to feel valued, loved and special; to be forgiven by God; to be part of God's people. Take the hamper marked 'The Word'. Who is the Bread of Life from our reading from John?

Take out the plate/book marked 'Jesus'. Jesus came to teach us about God and so we feed on his truth and we grow in our experience of God. Take out the 'Health promise'. This food doesn't need the same kind of warning as the manna had. God's truth does not spoil and last for only a short time. It lasts for ever, into eternity.

In the desert God had hoped the Israelites would see that just as physically they depended on God-given manna to exist, so spiritually they should depend on God's truth for full life. Jesus spelled this out.

Optional: Significantly, the people with Jesus were still over-concerned with the physical. He had fed 5,000 people in one afternoon but the questions from the disciples in verse 31 show they were trying to force him to keep doing physical feedings. Hadn't Moses, they said, fed all the Israelites, not just 5,000 men? And hadn't he fed them for 40 years? They were challenging Jesus to do something similar and supposedly greater.

Jesus pointed out that it was God not Moses who had fed the people. And God wants us to feed on him. He said he was the Bread of Life. We do not live by physical bread alone. We can have overfed bodies but undernourished souls. We live by God's Word and truth as found in Jesus. It is that Word which enables us to grow spiritually. It satisfies our hunger for God. Jesus is bread that not only sustains us and keeps us going but bread that changes us into how God wants us.

Prayer activity

With: wafers broken into a piece that will require three nibbles to consume

Give out the wafers and insist that no one nibbles it until you say so. Be aware of any allergies. Explain that the manna was to help God's people to remember and be thankful to him for his care. Every time they ate, they should be thankful. In the same way today, you are going to eat the wafer and be thankful to God at the same time. Only on the third nibble can you finish off eating the wafer!

Ask everyone to close their eyes and think of one way in which God has kept them safe this week. After a suitable pause:

Leader: We eat this and are thankful to God. **Response: Thank you, God** (*and everyone takes a nibble*).

Ask everyone to think of some food they have enjoyed this week. After a suitable pause:

Leader: We eat this and are thankful to God. **Response: Thank you, God** (*and everyone takes a nibble*).

Ask everyone to focus on one story where Jesus came to help those who were in need, which might be feeding the large crowd from last week's service, or another one.

Leader: We eat this and are thankful to God. **Response: Thank you, God** (*and everyone takes a nibble*).

Conclude by saying, Jesus said: I am the bread of life. No one who comes to me will ever be hungry. No one who has faith in me will ever be thirsty. We feed on you, Lord, in our hearts, and we are thankful.

You could finish by saying the Lord's Prayer together. The expression 'Give us this day our daily bread' probably originates from the manna given daily in the wilderness; it refers to God's supply of our basic foods and it points to our dependence on Jesus each day.

Prayers of intercession

These are based on Ephesians 4:1–16 accompanied by pictures projected on a screen to provide a focus or show the actual objects. The emboldened words could be said by another voice or by the congregation. The words of response are also available as a download (YearB.Proper13_3).

We pray for the church, the body of Christ, nourished on his Word of truth. (*Show Scripture Union's* Daily Bread *notes or a Bible.*) **Lord, help us to study your Word. Help us to learn and may we appreciate those who teach us.**

Lord, feed us as members of your church in this place. (*Show a picture of a church or a group of church people or point to several*

people in church.) **Lord, help us to grow in knowledge of you and love for you and for one another. We pray especially for...**

Lord, plant in us a spirit of gentleness. Give each of us a spirit of humility. (*Show a real towel and basin or a picture of one.*) **May we seek to serve and may we seek to encourage.**

Help us to be patient and supportive. (*Show a heavy sack or a picture of people carrying burdens such as the drawing in the Good News Bible for Galatians 6:2.*) **May we support one another in love, and speak the truth in love.**

Help us to use the gifts you have given to each of us; some as prophets, some as evangelists, some teachers, some pastors, to prepare the whole church for service. (*Show a foot outline or a picture of footsteps.*) **May we grow into a mature understanding of our faith, as we grow into the likeness of Christ and walk in his ways.**

We remember that Paul wrote these words from prison. We pray for those who are in prison or anyone who feels trapped in any way. (*Hold your wrists as though handcuffed or show a picture of prison bars.*) Lord, help us to trust in you, in your presence and in your power.
So may each of us live a life worthy of our calling, growing up into Jesus Christ.
Amen.

Ending the service

There are some shops which bake bread and also sell it. Other shops sell the bread but do not bake it. These are bread supply centres. As a church we are a bread supply centre. God has given us Jesus 'the Bread of Life'. We make that bread, Jesus, available to all as we tell others about him.

Give everyone a piece of bread and ask them to take it out of the church building as a symbolic act of sharing Jesus with others.

Helpful extras

Music and song ideas

The hymns develop the idea that we hunger and thirst for God. He feeds us with Jesus and his truth. See **Music and song ideas** for last week, but also: 'Bread of heaven'; 'I hunger and I thirst' states that Jesus is our manna from heaven; 'The Lord's my shepherd' can be sung again but to a different tune from last time; 'As the deer' describes our thirst for God; 'I, the Lord of sea and sky' talks of the 'finest bread' God provides; 'Eat this bread' celebrates the manna in the wilderness; 'There is a longing in our hearts, O Lord' could be quietly sung by a small group as a meditation with the words on display – they highlight the idea of longing and hungering for God and his truth.

Notes and comments

If this is a Holy Communion service, the idea of feasting on Jesus and his truth is embodied in eating the bread.

'The Ballad of the Bread Man' by Charles Causley could be an additional reading for church or home group.

This is an opportunity to feature Scripture Union's Bible-reading notes *Daily Bread*. A PowerPoint presentation of this adult Bible-reading guide is available as a download (YearB.Proper13_1). Someone who uses this guide could introduce it as one way of feeding day by day on God's truth and could be invited to give a testimony. They could select examples from two or three days when the reading was especially helpful to them. The passages could be projected onto a screen.

The service could be followed by a faith lunch or picnic. 'Gather around for the table is spread' is a song which is particularly appropriate to be sung on such an occasion. Mention can be made of last week's focus on saying 'thank you/grace' before meals. The idea can be developed to include saying 'thank you' not just for physical food but also for the spiritual nourishment from Jesus.

Describe some recent examples from Tearfund's work or more local projects that care not just for the physical but also the spiritual needs of those who need help.

Online resources

All suggested downloads are available at www.scriptureunion.org.uk/light. Visit www.lightlive.org for additional activities for children, young people and adults. For your convenience, the following activities are available as downloads: YearB.Proper12_2 Making bread; YearB. Proper13_2 Rhyme for under-5s.

Proper 14

READINGS: **I Kings 19:4–8; John 6:35,41–51**
Psalm 34:1–8; Ephesians 4:25 – 5:2

Bible foundations

Aim: to understand more of the life that Jesus offers as the Bread of Life

Individual believers and local churches can swing between the extremes of faith and despair. This has been true for God's people down the ages. Note that in I Kings 19 Elijah stands in stark contrast to the Elijah in I Kings 18. Gone is the mighty prophet of God who has courageously confronted King Ahab and the false prophets of Baal. Faced with threats from Queen Jezebel (19:2), apostasy in Israel (v 10) and exhaustion, he flees into the Judean wilderness. In despair he prays that he might die (v 4). Yet God, the one who meets us in our needs, provides him with food, giving him strength as he travels to Horeb (v 8) for a fresh encounter with the Living God (vs 9–18) and a new sense of purpose. Like David (Psalm 34:1–8), Elijah experiences God as the source of salvation and life.

By declaring himself to be 'the bread of life' (John 6:35,48), Jesus is restating that he is essential for true life, not a luxury or an optional extra. To be 'fed' by God necessitates us coming to Jesus and believing on him (v 35). He alone mediates the message and presence of God. Jesus is the source of 'eternal' or 'everlasting' life. From John 17:3 the very essence of eternal life is knowing the Father and the Son (by the Spirit), thereby sharing in their life. This is both a present and future reality for God's people.

Right now, Jesus meets our deepest needs (v 35), providing a quality of life, meaning and contentment that this world cannot give. Such life goes on beyond death, for by believing, as we taste of this 'living bread' we experience resurrection life (vs 40,51). Jesus points forward to his sacrifice on the cross, proclaiming that he will give his life ('flesh') for the life of the world (v 51).

Beginning the service

The first verse of the old hymn 'Guide me, O thou great Redeemer' holds this service outline together. It is a classic Welsh male voice choir item! If possible, arrange for at least two men to sing it loudly in two-part harmony but interrupt them as they begin the second verse by asking them what they think the words mean. What does 'Bread of heaven' mean? This is what you will all find out this service. If people do not know these lines, make sure everyone does before you proceed.

Background information on this hymn is available as a download (YearB.Proper14_1).

Bible reading

To read 1 Kings 19:4−8 (NIV) as below, use three readers or actors: Elijah, the angel and a narrator. Explain briefly that Elijah has run away from King Ahab's wife, Jezebel, because he had killed the prophets of Baal that she put her trust in. The first book of Kings, in the Old Testament, tells what happened next.

> Narrator: Elijah went a day's journey into the wilderness. (*Elijah walks in slowly, showing he is exhausted.*) He came to a broom tree, sat down under it and prayed that he might die. (*Elijah sits down and prepares to pray.*)
> Elijah: I have had enough, LORD. Take my life; I am no better than my ancestors.
> Narrator: Then he lay down under the tree and fell asleep. (*Elijah lies down to sleep. Enter the angel.*)
> Narrator: All at once an angel touched him. (*Angel shakes Elijah gently.*)
> Angel: Get up and eat.

> Narrator: He looked around, and there by his head was a cake of bread baked over hot coals, and a jar of water. He ate and drank and then lay down again. (*Elijah wakes up and mimes finding the bread, eating it and drinking.*)
> Narrator: The angel of the LORD came back a second time and touched him. (*Angel shakes Elijah again.*)
> Angel: Get up and eat, for the journey is too much for you. (*Angel goes off.*)
> Narrator: So he got up and ate and drank. (*Elijah gets up, stretches, eats and drinks.*) Strengthened by that food, he travelled forty days and forty nights until he reached Horeb, the mountain of God. (*Elijah indicates he is feeling stronger and strides purposefully through the church.*)
> 1 Kings 19:4−8 (NIV)

To balance the dramatised reading of the Old Testament passage, read John 6:35,41−51 from the GNB or CEV.

Bible talk

Ask what people want to eat when they feel exhausted. Then ask what they want to eat when they have been unwell for a couple of days. Among the answers should be the words 'bread' or 'toast'. Bread is one of the most basic and comforting essentials of life.

God provided Elijah with real bread

Elijah was exhausted. Check that everyone knows the story and the background. He was running away from God and was afraid for his life. Where was God? He had only been doing the right thing and now look where he was! God sent an angel to bring him bread to provide strength for his journey. Perhaps Elijah was able to sing after he had eaten: Bread of heaven, bread of heaven, feed me now and evermore, feed me now and evermore. God provided him with real food, and he provided Elijah with encouragement too. Elijah was not alone. God was with him. Elijah must have been so surprised to find the bread and water right beside him when he woke up.

Jesus offers spiritual bread

Mention that in the second reading Jesus said, 'I am the bread of life. Whoever comes to me will never go hungry, and whoever believes in me will never be thirsty.' Remind everyone that Jesus offers us spiritual bread – food for our souls, the bread of heaven so that we need never feel lonely or worried again; but we have to pray for God to feed us. Elijah was surprised to find the food and water waiting for him. Ask if we would be surprised to find God making that sort of provision for us. Or perhaps we just don't notice. Explain that we can practise expecting God to feed us by singing Bread of heaven, bread of heaven, feed me now and evermore, feed me now and evermore. Question whether we expect God to feed us with the bread of heaven now, as well as evermore?

Bread from heaven

It would be appropriate to ask for someone to share what it means to them in practice to feed on the bread from heaven.

Point out that it is easy to remember to ask God to feed us with spiritual bread when we are gathered together in church, but we can forget to do that at home or at work during the week. Explain that here is a challenge to help everyone remember when they are not in church: Every time this week that you eat some bread, either out loud or inside your head, sing Bread of heaven, bread of heaven, feed me now and evermore, feed me now and evermore.

Prayers of intercession

Elijah had run away and felt far from God. He had to wait some time before God came to him in a remarkable way. These prayers are for those who feel far from God or have even rejected him and for those who long to meet with God and are searching.

Ask everyone to turn to face the back of church, with their backs to the cross. If there is a cross at the back, turn to a position in the building which is not facing a cross – symbolic of turning from God. Ask everyone to think of someone who has turned from God or is not interested in him, either by what they say or by how they behave.

Then pray: Father God, you have said that you will come close to anyone who comes close to you. We pray for all those we know who have not turned to you yet, and we pray that this day they will realise who you are and will turn to you.

Then ask everyone to sit down with their hands stretched out expectantly. Ask them to think of someone who is seeking God, either by what they say or by how they behave or if they are part of an Alpha course or a children's midweek club.

Then pray: Father God, we pray for all those who are seeking you, those who want to know you but have not yet found you, those who are waiting patiently to hear from you.

Come close to them, this day, we pray.

It would be appropriate to pray for any outreach activities you are holding or have held recently, especially any holiday club activities.

Prayer of confession

With: a small baguette

If the IT system has a '3-D visualiser', place the bread onto it so that it is projected up for everyone to watch. Otherwise hold the baguette high so people can see. Explain that a third of the food bought in this country gets thrown away uneaten; tear off a third of the loaf and throw it on the floor. Ask everyone to say sorry to God for the amount of food they waste.

Point out that people in this country usually have three meals a day and still complain about what they have to eat, but most people in the world only have one plain meal. Take a big handful of bread and explain that you are going to be greedy and eat it while everyone else says sorry for being greedy with food.

Finally hold up the remaining bread so that everyone can ask God for his forgiveness for being selfish or thoughtless with his gifts.

Ending the service

Explain that even if we go out for a meal at a restaurant, or share a meal with friends, we soon feel hungry again. We can often feel excited about loving God and trying to live like Jesus when we come to church, but we will soon feel hungry if we don't come regularly to hear God's Word, to meet with

his people and to pray with them. Challenge everyone to feed on the bread of heaven through the week by reading something every day in their Bible. Sing 'Bread of heaven' one last time.

If a bread-making machine was set up at the beginning, its rapid bake cycle should have finished so that everyone can have a fresh piece of bread to take home or to eat with their coffee. If last week people took bread with them out of the church, symbolic of wanting to share Jesus, ask how far that helped them to share Jesus with others.

Helpful extras

Music and song ideas
'Guide me, O thou great Redeemer' is the key hymn for this service. Learn the last two lines of the first verse, at **Beginning the service**, Bread of heaven, bread of heaven, feed me now and evermore, feed me now and evermore to sing at various points during the service; 'I am the Bread of Life' can be difficult for younger children to sing, but if everyone learns the chorus first then all can join in with enthusiasm; 'We plough the fields and scatter the good seed on the land' reminds everyone that all good gifts, especially food, come from God; the third verse of 'Alleluia, sing to Jesus' is a good choice for churches that enjoy singing traditional hymns – particularly if the service will include Holy Communion.

Notes and comments

The theme of today's service is very suitable to use with Holy Communion and provides an opportunity to teach the congregation more about this. It would be possible to sing the lines from 'Bread of heaven' at appropriate points in the prayer of consecration.

Elijah was fed with bread baked on hot stones and water. If you have a church kitchen with an oven, share Communion together using warm, fresh-baked bread and water instead of bread and wine, focusing on God's provision for Elijah and God's provision for us in the death of Jesus.

In churches where children are admitted to Communion, the day's theme would make it a good occasion to admit them for the first time.

If you have not already decided to focus on a world-in-need project from two weeks ago, you could choose to build on the theme of God providing bread for all his children by arranging a special collection for the work of Christian Aid, Tearfund or a similar aid organisation and having a display of information for everyone to see.

As this session falls in the middle of the summer, think about organising a picnic to follow the service. An outing to somewhere special could work, but picnics can be just as much fun in the churchyard or garden or even in the main building. Even if everyone brings their own food, provide drinks to be shared.

Online resources

All suggested downloads are available at www.scriptureunion.org.uk/light. Visit www.lightlive.org for additional activities for children, young people and adults. For your convenience, the following activity is available as a download: YearB. Proper12_2 Making bread.

Proper 15

READINGS: **Ephesians 5:15–20; John 6:51–58**
Proverbs 9:1–6; Psalm 34:9–14

Bible foundations

Aim: to explore the implications of putting our trust in Jesus, the bread of life

Jesus' announcement that people need to eat his flesh and drink his blood (John 6:51–58) startled his hearers, friends and foes alike (vs 52,60). Understandably, contemporary readers have also found these words puzzling. The verbal closeness between verses 40 and 54 demonstrates that 'eating and drinking' as a metaphor underlines the importance of placing our trust in Jesus. Such language conveys a sense of ongoing close dependence on Jesus (vs 56,57). It is this union between Jesus and God's people which gives true life. Many commentators have found echoes of the institution of the Lord's Supper (Mark 14:22–25) with Jesus' references to 'bread' (v 51) and 'eating and drinking' (v 54). The vivid language of this passage (also true of the drama of Holy Communion) points to Jesus' sacrifice, when he would give his life for the life of the world (v 51).

As believers, our present union with Christ affects the way we live, individually and corporately. To feed on the bread of life is to gain true wisdom so we can walk in the way of understanding (Proverbs 9:1–6). In Ephesians 5:15–20 this is expressed by way of three contrasts. First, we are to live 'not as unwise [people] but as wise' (v 15) making good use of the time God has given us (v 16). Secondly, we are not to be foolish but to understand God's will for our life (v 17) making wise choices in daily living, not just when confronted by major life-changing decisions. Thirdly, we are not to get drunk but be 'filled with the Spirit' (v 18). Believing in Jesus and possessing the Holy Spirit are seen as distinctive marks of the people of God (see Ephesians 1:13). It is by this selfsame Spirit that we are united with Christ and changed into his likeness. Such wise living transforms communal life for believers, creating a worshipping, thankful people (vs 19,20).

Beginning the service

With: on display: a trumpet, a glove puppet, a new rubbish sack, a kettle

Invite everyone to discuss in small groups what these items have in common.

Take some suggestions about possible connections, but don't worry if no one mentions that each item only fulfils its purpose if it is filled with something – trumpet (air), glove puppet (hand), rubbish sack (rubbish) and kettle (water) – this will be explained later in the Bible talk.

Bible reading

Read Ephesians 5:15–20 with two readers, one (in the TNIV) to read the sections in bold below (the positive instructions) and one to read the rest (the negative parts).

Be very careful, then, how you live – not as unwise **but as wise, making the most of every opportunity,** because the days are evil. Therefore do not be foolish, **but understand what the Lord's will is**. Do not get drunk on wine, which leads to debauchery. **Instead, be filled with the Spirit, speaking from the Spirit to one another with psalms, hymns and spiritual songs. Sing and make music from your heart to the Lord, always giving thanks to God the Father for everything, in the name of our Lord Jesus Christ.**

Make sure that whoever reads John 6:51–58 includes 'Jesus said' at the beginning of verse 51 so that everyone is clear that it is Jesus who makes this claim.

Bible talk

With: the props used in **Beginning the service**; the points from Ephesians 5 on a PowerPoint or displayed in some way, available as a download (YearB.Proper15_1).

Ask if anyone has yet worked out the connection between the objects, or remind them (if the connection was guessed at the beginning) that all these objects only fulfil their purpose if they are filled in some way.

Explain that as some people get older, they sometimes wonder why they are alive, or what the purpose of life is. 'Why are we here?' they sometimes ask. Mention that Christians believe that God created people to worship him and to be his friends – that is their purpose. But they can only fulfil their purpose if they have accepted God as their Creator, and Jesus as their Saviour. In the reading from John's Gospel, Jesus says, 'I am the living bread that came down from heaven. If anyone eats of this bread, he [or she] will live for ever.' Explain that it is necessary for everyone, whatever their age, to ask God to give them faith in him and faith to follow Jesus' teaching, so that they can find their purpose in life.

Point out that the kettle needs to be filled with water and the trumpet needs to be filled with air so they can be a useful kettle or a tuneful trumpet. The glove puppet might be nice to look at or cuddle, but it only comes 'alive' with a hand inside to make it move. The rubbish sack is not pretty and could seem like a waste of space in the cupboard, but it becomes extremely useful when there is rubbish to clear up. In the same way, everyone needs to follow the instructions in the reading from Ephesians if they are going to be loving, joyful, serving followers of Jesus. Remind them of those instructions and give personal examples to illustrate them (so that this is not just theory):

Be careful about how you live
We need to think through the consequences of our actions.

Be wise and make the most of every opportunity
This is because life is too precious to waste.

Understand what the Lord's will is
This can be done by reading the Bible regularly, by listening to God in prayer and by spending time with other Christians.

Be filled with the Spirit
Ask God to guide us through life and rely on him.

Speak to one another with psalms, hymns and spiritual songs
Everyone needs to learn the words of psalms, hymns and songs by heart so they can quote them and 'hide' them in their hearts, whether or not people are musical.

Sing and make music in your heart to the Lord
For example, playing Christian CDs in the car or at home, and singing along even if we don't feel like it. Praising God like this will lift us and honour him.

Always giving thanks to God the Father for everything
Remind everybody that everyone has so

much to give thanks for, even when it feels as if everything is going wrong. Saying thank you to God helps to keep things in perspective and develop a spirit of gratitude.

Make it clear that the more everyone remembers to do all these things, the more they will find that they become like Jesus and will be better equipped to serve him as they serve the people they meet each day.

Prayers of intercession

When the leader says, 'Jesus, the living bread', the response is '**Bring us to eternal life'.**

Pray that everyone in church today may follow the instructions they have heard to help them become loving, joyful followers of Christ.

Jesus, the living bread,
Bring us to eternal life.

Pray that all Christians may grow in faith so they are ready to serve God whenever he asks them to do so. Jesus, the living bread,
Bring us to eternal life.

Pray for people, both in the local area and in the wider world, who do not yet know Jesus as their Saviour, that they may hear and respond to his good news. Jesus, the living bread,
Bring us to eternal life.

Pray for people who are sad, ill, lonely, hungry or afraid, that they may be comforted.
Jesus, the living bread,
Bring us to eternal life.

Announce a short time of silence for people

to bring their own particular prayers before God. (Allow at least 30 seconds for this.) Jesus, the living bread,
Bring us to eternal life.

Close by inviting everyone to say the Lord's Prayer together.

Ending the service

If the service has included Holy Communion, challenge everyone to consider what difference it will make to the way they behave in the coming week knowing that they have eaten the 'living bread'.

Give everyone a copy of the main instructions for living the Christian life printed onto a postcard or similar (highlighted in the **Bible talk** and available as a download (YearB.Proper15_1). Include illustrations of a kettle, trumpet, glove puppet and rubbish sack to remind everyone of the day's introduction. Suggest they place the card onto the fridge door, kitchen pinboard or bathroom mirror where they will see it regularly and be reminded to put the instructions into practice. Challenge everyone to feed more on the 'living bread' of Jesus during the coming week.

Helpful extras

Music and song ideas
'Spirit of the living God, fall afresh on me' picks up the idea of people being filled so that they can fulfil their purpose in life; 'Breathe on me, breath of God' and 'Come down, O love divine';'Beautiful Lord (the Potter's Hand)' expresses the sense of God calling and equipping people to serve him and

invites a response; 'King of Kings, Majesty' is a reflective song to sing after the Prayers of intercession; the Taizé chant, 'Eat this bread' is simple enough to sing from memory if it is taught first, which enables poor or non-readers to join in – sing it quietly and repetitively as people receive Communion; 'I am the Bread of Life', suggested for the previous week, fits with the theme and could be repeated; provide a joyful close to the service with 'You shall go out with joy'.

Game
Play a version of 'Simon Says', but with 'Jesus Says' instead, as the trigger for doing the action. Demonstrate and practise some actions for some of the main instructions for Christian living before playing the game. Explaining and leading the game is a good way to involve a teenager or new leader in a presentation role.

Be careful about how you live (*wag a finger to instruct someone*)
Understand what the Lord's will is (*mime opening a Bible*)
Speak to one another with psalms, hymns and spiritual songs (*everyone says: This is the day that the Lord has made*)
Sing and make music in your heart to the Lord (*sing the first line of a song that everyone knows well, for example, 'Our God is a great big God'*)
Give thanks to God (*everyone shouts, 'Thank you, God.'*)

Introduce each of these with 'Jesus says' so everyone can do the action, but occasionally catch people out by including other commands such as 'scowl' or 'stand up' or 'pat your nose' or 'shout at someone' or 'stand on one leg'. Don't play it as a 'knock-out' game – keep everyone involved in the fun for a few minutes.

Notes and comments

Displaying a PowerPoint (or in some other format) of the instructions for Christian living from Ephesians 5 will help those who are visual learners to process the information.

Make sure that everyone can see the trumpet (or similar), glove puppet, kettle and rubbish sack during **Beginning the service** and **Bible talk**. Children will benefit from seeing the kettle filled with water and the trumpet blown at the appropriate moment. The visual connection will be effective – and if you can arrange for the kettle to be plugged in and come to the boil, the illustration will be even more effective. Young children will not readily understand the abstract concept of feeding on Jesus, the living Bread, so concrete illustrations such as these are important to help them understand today's theme.

The theme of this service provides an opportunity for a member of the congregation to share their testimony. For example, an older child or teenager who receives Communion could talk about what that means to them. An older person, perhaps someone facing particular difficulties, could talk about the way other people have encouraged them with words from psalms or hymns, or how they have a special hymn they sing by themselves to help them keep going.

Online resources

All suggested downloads are available at www.scriptureunion.org.uk/light. Visit www.lightlive.org for additional activities for children, young people and adults. For your convenience, the following activity is available as a download: YearB. Proper15_2 Further worship.

Proper 16

READINGS: **Joshua 24:1,2,14–18; John 6:56–58**
Psalm 34:15–22; Ephesians 6:10–20

Bible foundations

Aim: to consider the choice to follow God's way

At a number of key points in their history, people in the Old Testament were faced with a choice. The stakes were often very high. During the Exodus, Moses challenged the Israelites to choose between God – the way of 'life' – and idolatry – the way of 'death' (Deuteronomy 30:19,20). In Joshua 24, Joshua, Moses' successor, calls upon the Israelites to renew their 'covenant' (or commitment) with God as they begin to settle in the Promised Land. He highlights God's mighty acts in the past and present (vs 3–13) before calling for both a right attitude ('fear' or reverence) and right actions (faithful service) in verse 14. Joshua then spells out the alternatives (vs 14,15) – to choose between the gods associated with their ancestors (v 2), the new gods of Canaan or the God of the covenant. God, who continually demonstrated his goodness (vs 16–18) required (and requires) a clear-cut decision. He will not share allegiance with other 'gods'.

Similarly, in his person and teaching, Jesus confronted people with a stark choice. His hard teaching and the associated cost of discipleship proved to be too much for some (John 6:60,61,66). ('Disciples' is used here to describe those who associated with him but did not necessarily trust him.) The twelve may not have fully understood his teaching, but they recognised that here was 'the Holy One of God', the source of eternal life. They could affirm their allegiance to Jesus.

As the people of God, we face competing claims for our loyalty. Jesus makes it clear that the one true God can have no rivals, whatever form they take (Matthew 6:24; Luke 14:26). We too are called to choose God's way revealed to us in Christ, whatever the cost. Like the twelve, there is no real alternative to following Jesus; for to choose him is to choose true life (John 6:68,69).

Beginning the service

With: copies of a college or school prospectus or advertisements for holidays, luxury flats or new furniture, an invitation to a party – anything that requires a choice

Talk about all the choices we have to make, some insignificant, some life-changing. Show the objects above. How do you decide? If there is anyone who is about to start a new job or school or who has just come back from holiday or moved house, ask them how they made that choice. Explain that the theme of this service is making right choices which are God-focused ones.

Bible reading

The reading of Joshua 24:1,2,14–18 requires two readers with one other person facing the front between the two readers, having to make a choice. A question mark could be pinned to this person's back. Explain that God's people had been wandering around the desert for many years and were about to go into the land God has promised them. At the end the person at the front with the question mark turns to face everyone and asks, rhetorically, 'What shall I do?' Read as follows:

Reader 1: Joshua called the tribes of Israel together for a meeting at Shechem. He made the leaders, including the old men, the judges, and the officials, come up and stand near the sacred tent. Then Joshua told everyone to listen to this message from the LORD, the God of Israel:

Worship the LORD, obey him, and always be faithful. Get rid of the idols your

---

ancestors worshipped when they lived on the other side of the Euphrates river and in Egypt.

Reader 2: But if you don't want to worship the LORD, then choose right now! Will you worship the same idols your ancestors did? Or since you're living on land that once belonged to the Amorites, perhaps you'll worship their gods.

Reader 1: I won't. My family and I are going to worship and obey the LORD. Joshua 24:1,2,14–18 (CEV)

John 6:56–69 could be read with people reading as a narrator, Jesus and Simon Peter.

Bible talk

With: copies of old family photographs or old newspapers, either on show or displayed as a PowerPoint; copies of magazines; a cross or a symbol of Jesus

Explain how the people were about to come into the land that God had promised to Moses, and to their great ancestor, Abraham. A new start often calls for an assessment of what is important. This is what Joshua challenged the people to consider. They had three choices.

The choice based on the past

Show copies of old family photos or old newspapers, anything that represents a long time ago, and talk about why we keep these and what they say to us. Abraham had lived in the area around what we now know as Iraq. His relatives had worshipped some ancient gods but it was here that God spoke to him. God called Abraham to obey him, to leave his home and extended family and travel to a land that God would show him. Abraham did not know where this land was but God promised to be with him and to bless him. Abraham did not have to obey God but he chose to. He left behind so much, including the ancient gods.

Today some people still hang on to the past and refuse to move on. *(Give a personal example of how you have hung on to the past way of doing something which has proved to be the wrong thing to do.)* People find it hard to trust God to be with them in the present and the future. They may think that the old ways of doing church are the only ways and the old songs are the only ones worth singing. Expand on this theme as appropriate, not dismissing all that is old as useless but recognising the diversity of Christian worship today and the changes within the contemporary church. One can sometimes get the impression that the old ways of doing things have become the object of worship! But today God says, Choose to serve me!

The choice based on the present
As God's people moved into the land God had promised, they were going to encounter people who worshipped idols and false gods. This worship led people to do dreadful things. God's people were tempted to accept these gods. Show the contemporary magazines.

There is a real pull on people today to be so influenced by what is not of God that they make choices that displease God. Give some examples: maybe the way that people are not committed to church, the way they speak, the way they handle money and time. Recall last

Sunday's key points from Ephesians 5. See if anyone can recall any of these or if they have displayed the words in a prominent place. But today God says, Choose to serve me!

The choice with an eye on the future
Joshua challenged God's people to choose to serve God, both then and in the future. Reread John 6:66–69 and reflect on the fact that those associated with Jesus had a choice: were they going to leave him or not? Simon Peter made that powerful statement, 'We have faith in you, and we are sure that you are God's Holy One.' They may not have understood everything about Jesus (how could they, since Jesus had not died), but they knew he was true. Today God says, Choose to serve me!

Show the cross or other symbol of Jesus. For Jesus' followers it was a costly choice but it was the only sensible choice to make. What choice will you make?

It would be appropriate at this point for someone to share their choice to follow Jesus. Use the language of following Jesus, rather than choosing to become a Christian. It would also be appropriate to play or sing Brian Doerksen's song 'Today (As for me and my house)' which is a powerful musical presentation of Joshua's challenge. If you are playing a CD version, display the words. Follow this with the **Prayer activity**.

Prayer activity
With: at three points in the building, place a visible pile of things: a) from a previous era which might include old hymn books, old clothes, old furniture; b) symbols of

233

contemporary life; c) a symbol of Jesus

The response for those who want to join in is: **We are going to worship and obey the Lord.**

Invite everyone to turn to the pile of old things. Remind them how Abraham did what God had called him to do. He obeyed.

Lord God, we can cling to things from the past and refuse to trust you. (*Pause for people to reflect on what this means for them.*)

We are going to worship and obey the Lord.

Invite everyone to turn to the contemporary symbols. Remind them of how God's people were tempted to join in with what the people around them believed and did.

Lord God, we can be attracted by the values of people around us, people who do not want to love and serve you. We can speak in a way that does not please you (*pause*), we can use our money in a way that does not please you (*pause*), we can behave selfishly (*pause*), we can treat people in a way that damages them (*pause*). Please forgive us. You call us to follow you!

We are going to worship and obey the Lord.

Invite everyone to turn to the symbol of Jesus. Those who truly followed Jesus chose to stay with him and not to leave. Jesus calls us all to follow him, with everything we have, both for now and into the future.

Lord God, as we think about what we shall be doing and where we shall be in the next few weeks, you call us to choose to follow you. (*Pause to reflect on what that will mean.*)

We are going to worship and obey the Lord.

Prayers of intercession

Draw attention to the fact that Joshua addressed his challenge to the leaders of the community. It would therefore be appropriate to pray for all those who are in a position to influence the faith of others. Ask the following to stand: anyone in a position to influence the faith of others, whether parents or grandparents, anyone working in a school, people in leadership within the community or within the church, leaders of a Christian Union, etc. Those not standing should now stand to pray for these people, asking God to help them behave in a way that will help others to turn to God, and also that what they say will point others to Christ.

Conclude by praying for everyone present, that we might all point others to Jesus.

Ending the service

Give people a choice of how they are going to end the service. All of the choices are equally acceptable but point out that every decision has implications in that everyone will meet different people wherever they go and may get involved in some project or other. Every choice gives them an opportunity to serve the Lord in some way. Everyone, unless they are physically unable, needs to move from their seat. If possible, accommodate the less mobile.

- Go straight for refreshments (and they will be available for everyone, so the refreshments will not run out).
- Gather round the musicians to sing a closing song.
- Gather round a church leader who has something significant to show people (this should be kept secret) – a photograph of a newborn baby, wedding photos, plans for the harvest supper.
- Get together to pray for one another or for a specific need within the church.
- Construct a family door-hanger for their home on which they put the words: My family and I are going to worship and obey the Lord! A template of a door-hanger is available as a download (YearB.Proper16_2).

Helpful extras

Music and song ideas

Choose songs which are both old and new, if possible singing two versions of the same song. Because of the choice element of this service, in advance you could ask some people to choose the music. Brian Doerksen's song 'Today (As for me and my house)' is especially suitable and can be purchased on iTunes; 'Choose you this day whom you will serve' is an old CSSM chorus available as a download (YearB.Proper16_3); 'I want to serve the purpose of God'; 'Let me have my way among you'; 'Come, now is the time to worship'; 'Let it be to me' (Graham Kendrick's statement of Mary's choice) and songs that express a corporate decision to serve God.

Game

A multiple choice quiz would be appropriate. Emphasise that this quiz is an example of having to make choices. Alternatively, recognising that the people of Israel were leaving the desert, a true and false desert PowerPoint picture quiz is available as a download (YearB.Proper16_1).

Notes and comments

Children do not have a strong sense of time – past, present and future – after all, they have not lived very long. Make sure that your examples of past, present and future are ones they can understand. For example, in the past refer to a fear of computers or mobile phones which some people are still apprehensive about, but most people would admit that they have enhanced life.

If this is a Holy Communion service, emphasise that God invites us to participate but we have the choice to accept the invitation.

Make sure there are booklets available for anyone who signals that they want to make a personal choice to follow Jesus. The six-session online course to help Christian parents nurture the faith of their children, called *Survival skills for Christian parents* based on the book *Families with faith* is available from www.scriptureunion.org.uk/families (follow the links). For details of all these go to page 240.

Online resources

All suggested downloads are available at www.scriptureunion.org.uk/light. Visit www.lightlive.org for additional activities for children, young people and adults.

Proper 17

READINGS: **James 1:17–27; Mark 7:1–8,14,15,21–23**
Deuteronomy 4:1,2,6–9; Psalm 15

Bible foundations

Aim: to honour Jesus in our thoughts, words and actions

The services for the next few weeks focus on the book of James. A number of different 'James' are referred to in the New Testament, but it seems most likely that this letter was written by James, half-brother of Jesus and leader of the church in Jerusalem. Martin Luther referred to this book as 'an epistle of straw' which is perhaps a little harsh since it is packed with very practical advice on living out the Christian faith and growing in maturity as individuals and as church communities.

In Mark 7 Jesus, speaking to the Pharisees, clearly indicates that it's not enough to be clean on the outside. We also need to be transformed on the inside – in fact what's on the inside will be demonstrated by how we conduct our lives on the outside.

James develops this same idea, challenging his readers to clear out the rubbish from their lives and live by God's Word. He uses two powerful illustrations. If we see our dirty face in a mirror but do nothing about it, there is no value in having looked at all. We need to look carefully and then respond to what we have seen. In the same way we can allow God's Word to be like a mirror to our lives and change in the light of it. The second illustration is that if we claim to be religious but cannot control our tongue then our religion is worthless. (James will return to this in chapter 3.) Our tongues indicate the state of our hearts. James says we must not simply listen to or read God's Word but put it into action. Deuteronomy 4 encourages the people of Israel to keep God's laws and David, in Psalm 15, reminds people that God looks for those who are pure in heart and lifestyle.

Beginning the service

Ask everyone to think about the perfect gift. If they could give anything they wanted to anyone they wanted, what would they give and to whom? Then ask them to share their answers in small groups. After a few minutes either invite a few people to come to the front to talk about their perfect gift or go round the congregation with a roving microphone collecting answers. Read James 1:17 to briefly brainstorm the good and perfect gifts God has given us. Offer a prayer of thanksgiving followed by a hymn of thankfulness such as 'Now thank we all our God' or a song like 'Thank you, Lord'.

Bible reading

Most of James 1:17–27 is clear whichever version you choose. However the difficult images in verses 17 and 18 are probably clearest in the CEV. You could ask children to listen out for what James says about a mirror then check that they have understood. Introduce the reading by explaining who James was (see **Bible foundations**) and saying that you will be looking at the letter he wrote in the next few services.

Mark 7:1–8,14,15,21–23 may be read by three people: a narrator, Pharisees and Jesus. You may wish to read the whole passage from verses 1 to 23 rather than the three separate sections.

Bible talk

With: images of the following signs: Wet paint, No swimming, One way, No parking, which are available as a download (YearB.

Proper17_1); a Bible; a flipchart and pens or the 5 C's PowerPoint (YearB.Proper17_2); two cups or mugs, one dirty on the outside but clean inside the other clean on the outside but dirty inside

Without any explanation, someone comes to speak to you during the song before the Bible talk. Make sure they are clearly visible. Remain in apparent conversation for two or three minutes while you perform at least two distinct actions. At the start of this talk ask what people noticed. Can they describe the person or your actions? Point out how difficult it can be to remember what we've seen or what someone looked like or did. But what if we couldn't remember what we ourselves looked like?

It would be very strange if we looked in the mirror and saw a stranger looking out at us. James says that the person who reads the Bible (or looks at the perfect law) and doesn't do what it says is just like someone who looks in the mirror and then forgets what they look like.

One at a time, display the pictures as a PowerPoint display or as hard copy. In each case ask what happens if you ignore what you read. Someone may suggest that the paint may have already dried or a traffic warden might not catch you; in other words, you might get away with ignoring the warning. If not, suggest this yourself. Point out that this is true but if you keep ignoring the warning, sooner or later you will have to face the consequences.

Hold up a Bible. Ask what happens if you ignore what the Bible says. The consequences are not just that one day we have to face God in judgement but that here and now we don't get the best out of life because we are ignoring all that God has shown us about himself and the way he wants us to live which we find in the pages of this book.

Write on a flip chart a large letter C or use the 5 C's PowerPoint. Talk about some of the practical instructions James gives and write them down.

- C urb our tempers (vs 19,20)
- C lean up our minds (v 21)
- C ontrol our tongues (v 26)
- C are for others (v 27)
- C ommit our lives to Jesus (v 21)

Either give simple examples of each, such as: arguments, not getting our own way, books, magazines, TV, pop music, Internet in which we read or see what does not please God; gossip, lies, bad language and jokes; helping people who are new or lonely at school or work, or neighbours in need, the sick or homeless; either a biblical example (Peter, Paul) or your own testimony of being committed to Jesus.

Or, in advance, ask up to five people to briefly tell a personal story about each of the instructions. Rehearse them so they keep to time.

Conclude by showing two cups or mugs. One should be very dirty while the other is apparently spotlessly clean. Ask which of the two anyone would want to drink from. Then show that the dirty one is clean on the inside while the clean one is dirty inside. Explain that when we just try harder to 'be good' it's

like cleaning the outside but leaving the inside dirty. When we commit our lives to Jesus we are changed inside and given the power to really and practically change the way we live. If appropriate give some opportunity at this point or later in the service for those who would like to talk or pray about commitment to Christ.

Prayer activity

With: a Post-it note and pen for each person; a board to stick the Post-it notes on

Talk briefly about how some people write a 'to do' list to help them tackle jobs they have to do, ticking off the jobs as they are done. But what about the jobs which don't get ticked off because we forget or because we can't be bothered or are too busy? How does that affect other people? (Of course, some tasks may not have needed doing in the first place or were not important.) Ask everyone (adults can help young children) to think of things they should have done recently and haven't, which have affected others. Write or draw these on the Post-it notes. People can stick their note on the board. When this is done, in your own words, ask God for forgiveness for the sins of omission, or use the following prayer:

Lord, sometimes we do wrong things and let people down. But often we do wrong by simply not doing the things we should have done. Please forgive us. Where we can put right the things we have written about, help us to do this. And for the future, give us energy and enthusiasm to do the things we know we should do. Amen.

Ending the service

Use the following prayer to end the service, also available as a download (YearB. Proper17_3).

Leader: Lord, in this coming week,
Response: **Help us to listen to you.**
Help us to speak about you.
Help us to live for you. Amen.

If you would like this to be more focused, before using the prayer ask people to think quietly about one important thing that they think is likely to happen in the coming week (at home, at school, at work, at church). Then give a short time for everyone to tell someone else what their 'important thing' is. Alternatively, ask them to think of one thing they ought to do and have not done but which they could do this week. Conclude with the prayer above.

Helpful extras

Music and song ideas
For **Beginning the service**, 'Now thank we all our God'; 'Praise God from whom all blessings flow'; 'All things bright and beautiful'; 'Thank you, Lord, for this fine day' can be easily adapted to include anything mentioned by the congregation as a gift from God – (thank you, Lord, for mums and dads; for fish and chips, etc)

Traditional hymns in which we promise to do what God calls us to do include: 'O Jesus, I have promised'; 'Take my life'; 'Be thou my vision'.

Other songs include 'Jesus, be the centre'; 'I want to serve the purpose of God'; 'Lord, I

come to you'; a children's song on the theme of obedience (which adults can sing without embarrassment) is 'Don't build your house on the sandy land'.

Game
With: the following words or phrases jumbled up on ten separate large pieces of card as shown below and hidden around the building: Curb/our tempers, Clean up/our minds, Control/our tongues, Care for/others, Commit/our lives to Jesus

This needs to take place after the **Bible talk**. Children find the ten pieces of card and then put them together. Comment on odd pairings such as 'Clean up our tongues' or 'Care for our tempers'. You may need to show the PowerPoint or display if they have forgotten what the correct phrases are.

Notes and comments

The passages in James, both this week and next week, lend themselves to a practical response. Brainstorm ideas for something practical to help others that the church could do over the next few weeks. Two or three people (arranged beforehand) could take the ideas away and report back next week on what activity you're going to do and what needs to be done.

You could develop **Beginning the service** by showing an image of a sundial (download from Google images). Ask for explanations about how it works. Point out that the shadow moves round the dial as time passes. Everything in life changes as time passes. But God never changes (James 1:17). Alternatively make the same point using images of the stars at night or the phases of the moon.

Fascinating facts about the tongue can be found on www.kidshealth.org/kid/htbw/tongue.html. To demonstrate the importance of the tongue, ask everyone to press their tongues firmly against their teeth and then without moving their tongues sing together a simple song.

The **Prayer activity** could be adapted to be just a **Prayer of confession** since we rarely focus just upon the sins of omission – the things we have left undone.

Online resources

All suggested downloads are available at www.scriptureunion.org.uk/light. Visit www.lightlive.org for additional activities for children, young people and adults.

Families with faith
978 1 84427 247 1

Families are under threat. How can Christian parents create strong, loving family experiences that nurture faith in Jesus? Parents, counsellors and church leaders will welcome this readable and affirming guide that is strong on common sense and inspirational in its aim to put God at the centre of family life.

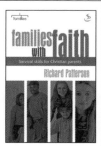

Survival skills for Christian parents

This six session course is based on the book Families with faith. It is interactive, discussion-based, to be run weekly, monthly or once a term! It is easy to use and flexible enough to suit any group, including being used with parents in a school setting who want to explore the values they pass onto their children.

This is available as an online resource with free downloads.

For more details, visit www.scriptureunion.org.uk

Harvest (Common Worship)

READINGS: **Psalm 126; Matthew 6:25–33**
Joel 2:21–27; I Timothy 2:1–7

Bible foundations

Aim: to trust God in our futures, including trusting him as the harvest-provider

Those things that we catch ourselves thinking or worrying about in an unguarded moment are a good indication of our priorities. For example, it is easy to be preoccupied about the physical necessities of life, particularly when we are faced with difficult financial circumstances.

The Sermon on the Mount is a call to the followers of Jesus Christ to be distinctive, reflecting the priorities of God's kingdom, or 'reign'. In Matthew 6:25–33, Jesus explains that one crucial area where Christians should be different is their attitude towards material needs, pictured here in terms of food, drink and clothes. (Note: the 'pagans run after ... But seek first' contrast with verses 32,33). Jesus is not advocating a 'happy-go-lucky' approach to life, nor is he saying it is wrong to make responsible provision for the future, for instance by planting seeds for a future crop, nor is he arguing that we should deny or despise our basic needs. Our Father knows we need such things (v 32). But, Jesus is saying that as God's children we should not be preoccupied by such matters or worry about what the future holds in store. The basis of our confidence is in a heavenly Father who cares for us; the Creator and Sustainer of life (even of birds and flowers), whose goodness is demonstrated in the imagery and reality of the annual harvest (Joel 2:21–27). To worry about the future reflects both a distrust of God (v 30) and a placing of 'these things' above God's priorities (v 33). It is also pointless (v 27).

Like the Israelites whose joyful return from exile was followed by hardship and tears (Psalm 126), we, as the contemporary people of God, are not exempt from troubles. At such times we, like them (Psalm 126:4–6), can be confident that our future will clearly reveal God's faithfulness. This year's harvest celebration is a token of such faithfulness.

Beginning the service

Welcome everyone and explain that this harvest service is a celebration of God's goodness to us. It is a time to look back at God's love for us and to look forward too. We all have a future where we will be protected under God's care. Therefore, we need not worry or fear anything. God is inviting us to trust him simply because he can be trusted.

If you are having a traditional harvest display, invite people to bring their contributions to the front as you sing the first hymn.

Bible reading

If possible, Psalm 126 is best read from the NIV by an older person, someone with experience of the ups and downs of life, who can read it slowly and with feeling.

To contrast with this, a child or younger person could read Matthew 6:25–33 from the CEV or GNB. Three pictures are available as a download (YearB.Harvest_1) which could be displayed while the Matthew passage is read. These illustrate three questions in verse 31:

What shall we eat?
What shall we drink?
What shall we wear?

Contrast the different occasions these questions might be asked and challenge people to think about their own concerns and priorities. To give extra emphasis, you might choose to have the Gospel passage read twice – once without the pictures and once with them. The second time it could be read from *The Message*, as this will give people a different perspective.

Bible talk

The tone of this talk needs to be gentle, but celebratory. The readings from both the Old and New Testament link together to show how we can trust God because he cares so much for his creation. He's an understanding heavenly Father who doesn't want his children to fret about anything. Often in the Bible, the Old Testament points forward to events that eventually take place in the New Testament. However, for this talk it is better to swap things around. Matthew 6:25–33 tells us that we can trust God, and Psalm 126 gives us an example of what happens when we do trust him. The fact that God will lead and deliver us through hard times to an abundant life is the main theme of this psalm. This needs to be highlighted in your talk.

Jesus says: Do not worry

The passage in Matthew tells us not to worry – and these words are from Jesus, after all – but it is easier said than done. Explain to the congregation that Jesus doesn't mean this flippantly. He's not saying 'get over it' or 'pull yourself together'. He means it genuinely. He says do not worry because he loves us and doesn't want us to be anxious about anything (vs 26,30).

Explain also that we do not need to worry because we have a God we can trust in (v 33). If we put our faith in him, then we can stand firm no matter what the circumstances. Emphasise to the congregation that putting our trust in God doesn't mean that problems won't come our way. However, we can be certain that God will come through for us.

God comes to the rescue

This is the point to bring out of Psalm 126. The people of Jerusalem have been attacked by King Sennacherib of Assyria, but God comes to the rescue and Sennacherib is defeated. At last they can come back and resume normal life! Ask if anyone can think of a time when they had been away from home for a long time. This could be someone in the Armed Forces, or a student, or someone in hospital for a long time. For young children with no sense of the passing of time, just being away on holiday may seem ages and ages. It would be appropriate to ask any who have been away in the past few weeks what it was that they did when they first got home. If no one nominates themselves to talk about this (or you have not been able to prepare someone in advance), you could talk about what a soldier involved in warfare far from home would miss. What would their family miss? What would be the first things they might do when they got home? If appropriate show some images that have been in the news recently.

Now imagine what it was like for God's people on their return. Driven out of their homeland and city they have now come back. Normality was symbolised by planting seeds in preparation for a harvest. This is a joyous psalm that tells of triumph over adversity (v 1). Even though it may not come as quickly as we want it to, God will come to our rescue. It may or may not happen in this life, but it will certainly happen in the next. Tears will turn to joy (v 5) and misfortunes will be reversed (v 6). Emphasise that, at the end of this psalm, the situation that the people find themselves in is far better than at any other time. It is far better than they could have imagined.

Conclude with the fact that the people of Jerusalem were looked after by God during their time of affliction, and had their fortunes reversed. In Psalm 126, they are living a life of freedom, a life of joy. It is an abundant life. The same is true for us today. We do not need to worry, for we have a God who loves us, wants the best for us and will deliver us from hard times. We should therefore put our trust in him, wait upon him and expect blessings to come.

Prayer activity

If you have the space to do so, lay out a large sheet or long roll of paper at the front of the church, along with plenty of colouring pens and crayons. Invite people to write or draw on the paper something they are worried about, that they want to trust God to deal with. This could be something personal, or a concern for the world. Encourage people of all ages to take part. If you have a large congregation, you may need to invite people forward in rows or in age groups.

After people have offered their concerns to God, invite them to collect a flower (either a real or plastic/paper one) from a designated person or place at the front. Explain that this symbolises that they have handed over their worry to God, and want to place their trust in him from now on.

During this time play some quiet music, either on CD or by your music group. The song 'Seek ye first' would be particularly appropriate.

Ending the service

Ask your congregation to think about the week ahead, to think about the trials, temptations and tests that it may bring – known and unknown. Ask them to hold any worries that they may have in their mind, and then lead them in bringing those things to God through this prayer which is also available as a download (YearB.Harvest_2).

Leader: Lord, we place the things that lie ahead of us this week at your feet.
All: Lord, we give our future to you.

Leader: Lord, we bring our worries to you for the next week. Thank you that you care about them and want to help us through them. All we need to do is ask.
All: Lord, we give our worries to you. Please take them from us, and let your peace dwell in our hearts, minds and souls.

Leader: Lord, we commit our families and friends to your care.
All: Lord, we give those we love to you. Keep them under your wings of shelter. Thank you that you care for them even more than we do.

Leader: Lord, we offer ourselves to you. Help us to have faith that will move mountains.
All: Lord, we give you our lives. Help us to trust you as you lead us through this week and beyond.

Leader: Lord, thank you that you love us.
All: Thank you, Lord. Amen.

Helpful extras

Music and song ideas

You may choose traditional harvest hymns such as 'We plough the fields and scatter', but there are also various songs you could sing on the theme of God's faithfulness and provision, such as: 'Trust and obey'; 'What a friend we have in Jesus'; 'Faithful One'; 'He's got the whole world in his hands' (either the traditional hymn or the Tim Hughes version); 'Seek ye first'.

If you have a lot of young children present, include 'My God shall supply all my needs' or 'Who put the colours in the rainbow?'.

For something a little different, you could play 'Why Worry' by Dire Straits during a time of quiet reflection or prayer – perhaps just after the **Bible talk**.

Game

At the start of the service, or as people arrive, give each person or family a sheet of paper divided into four quarters – 'A', 'B', 'C' and 'D'. Explain that this is their answer card for the game 'Worry or trust?' They can either tear the paper into four pieces or fold it so that each letter can be displayed separately.

Ask the questions in the Worry Questionnaire available as a download (YearB.Harvest_6), and encourage each person or family to decide on an answer and to hold up the corresponding letter. They should keep track of their own answers. Encourage people to answer honestly!

Conclude the game by asking people to consider the answers they gave. Are they more likely to worry or trust?

Notes and comments

The themes explored in this service would fit well with a Eucharist service – we can trust God to provide for our needs because he has already provided us with eternal life through his Son, who is the bread of life.

If a baptism is included in your service, talk about the provision of new life, and link with the theme of trusting God for our future.

People who are not regular churchgoers sometimes come to a harvest service, so it is important to make everyone feel welcome and included. Make sure the language you use is understandable to an outsider, and that they know what they should be doing, saying or singing throughout the service. This may also be a good opportunity to invite people to other church events, such as Alpha groups or children's clubs.

Personal testimony would fit in well with the themes of this service, and could be a very powerful encouragement to others. Ask one or two people to share a specific example of times where they have trusted God for their future and he has provided for them.

A harvest service is always a good opportunity to remind people about the plight of farmers around the world and to pray for them. If your church has any links with organisations such as Tearfund, Christian Aid or World Vision, you could ask them to provide a display on these issues for people to look at after the service. This might be the concluding Sunday for the programme that you set up in July/August.

Online resources

All suggested downloads are available at www.scriptureunion.org.uk/light. Visit www.lightlive.org for additional activities for children, young people and adults. For your convenience the following activities are available as downloads: YearB.Harvest_3 Future game for 5 to 11s; YearB.Harvest_4 Reflective prayer for all ages; YearB.Harvest_5 Going deeper discussion points.

Proper 18

READINGS: **James 2:1–10,14–17; Mark 7:24–37**
Isaiah 35:4–7a; Psalm 146

Bible foundations

Aim: to understand how we are to love others

In Mark 7 we read about two encounters that Jesus had with people who would have been considered outsiders or rejects in his culture, the Syro-Phoenician woman and a deaf and mute boy. Jesus demonstrates here his unconditional love for people and reaches out to them in their need. These are characteristics that we consistently see in God's concern for the poor and needy reflected in Psalm 146 and Isaiah 35.

James challenges the church to express this same kind of unconditional love and to show no favouritism in the way that they treat different people. He gives them a practical example: imagine two people come into your meeting, one dressed in designer clothes and the other in shabby clothes; how would you treat them? He challenges them that if they discriminate on the basis of appearance or wealth they are passing judgement on another person and not expressing the character of God.

He says that we need to have God's perspective on the poor – God has chosen the poor to be rich in faith and inherit the kingdom. He challenges them against insulting the poor when in fact it's the rich who are exploiting them, dragging them into court and slandering Christ. He brings us back to first principles; we are to love our neighbour as ourselves. There is no room for favouritism, for discrimination on any basis is a breaking of the law of Christ who calls us to love one another as we have been loved by him.

In the rest of chapter 2, James reiterates the importance of what he's said in chapter 1, that faith must work itself out in action. If someone is cold and hungry and we only offer platitudes it is worthless – we must do something. He is as blunt as to say that faith without deeds is useless and dead.

Beginning the service

Start the service wearing a football shirt or showing a football shirt or scarf. Take a quick survey of the congregation as to who supports which team. How do we choose which team we support (favour)? Local? Successful? Have players we like? Ask if God has a favourite football team! Wouldn't it be terrible if the results were always rigged because one team had God 'on their side'? Explain that sometimes countries have believed that God was on their side – loved them more than anyone else – usually with disastrous results.

Read Acts 10:34 and then sing a song or hymn reflecting God's rule over and care for the whole earth, for example 'This earth belongs to God' or 'There's a wideness in God's mercy'. See **Music and song ideas** below.

Bible reading

Use two completely contrasting people to read James 2:1–10,14–17. Voice one reads verses 1–4 and 8–10; voice two reads verses 5–7,14–17. One should be dressed very casually (T-shirt, jeans), the other formally (suit or dress).

Mark 7:24–37 should be read after **Bible retelling**. Introduce the reading with the words, 'My story uses a certain amount of imagination. Here's how the Bible records it.'

Psalm 146 to be used for **Ending the service** is available as a download (YearB. Proper_18_1).

Bible Retelling

Mark 7:24–30 to be told by a woman.
As soon as I heard he was coming up our way I knew I had to go. You see, I'd heard the stories – the stories about him healing people and the way he especially cared for children. Of course I knew he was Jewish and I know all about the Jews being stand-offish. They think the rest of us are 'unclean'. Let me explain – I was born in Phoenicia – I'm not Jewish. And some Jews are funny about women – won't have anything to do with them. I'd heard this man was different.

There was a story our people tell, of how hundreds of years ago a Jewish prophet by the name of Elijah came to our land. He lived with a widow and worked amazing miracles for her. Maybe this man had come to do the same thing. I was really interested. But most of all I went because I was desperate. My little girl had been ill for so long. Something took hold of her and threw her about and made her hurt herself. None of our doctors or priests or holy men had been able to do anything to help. So I had to take a chance on this Jewish miracle-worker – Jesus.

It was easy enough to find him. As soon as I got near him I threw myself at his feet and begged him to heal my little girl. I must have looked so stupid! I looked up into his face to see what he would do. He turned to me and said, 'My food is for the children of the family – we can't just take it and throw it to the dogs.' I knew what he was saying. His miracles were for the Jews, not for us Gentiles (some Jews call us 'Gentile dogs', you know).

Saying something like this could have been crushing – except that there was something about the way he looked at me as he said it. The words were hard but the look was full of love. So I dared to say, and to this day I don't know where the words came from 'Lord, even dogs are allowed to eat the scraps.' He smiled at me. I think it was the sort of answer he was looking for. He simply said, 'Go home, your daughter is cured.' And it was true. Although he hadn't even seen her, he had healed her.

It makes you think, doesn't it? Maybe God doesn't have favourites after all… maybe, if you're prepared to trust him, whoever you are he will help you.

Bible talk

With: a box of chocolates; *The Sunday Times* Rich List (check www.timesonline.co.uk/richlist to obtain the necessary information)

Ask, who is the richest person in the world and how much money do they have? After some guesses give the answer. Disclose the fortunes of any people whose name might be recognised (eg football club owners). What would we do if someone from the top ten richest people joined the church? Would we give them a special seat? Would we pay more attention to the things they say?

Before anyone can answer these questions pick up a box of chocolates and ask for a volunteer to come to the front. Give the person a chocolate. Ask their name and find out a little about them. Give them a chair to sit on and then ask for another volunteer. To this person say, 'Stand over there and wait.' Do not give them a chocolate. Ask for more volunteers and randomly ignore them or give them chocolate and pay attention to them. After you've made the point, ask the congregation what they think of the way you've behaved. Ask the volunteers how they feel. (Maybe even some of the favoured ones will think it was unfair.) Ask how things could be put right. Give chocolates to those who haven't had them and introduce them to the congregation in the same way you did the favoured ones.

After all the volunteers have returned to their seats point out that this is what we do when we only talk to certain people or won't sit beside some people. At this point you might like to retell (or have retold) the story from Mark 7:24–30 followed by the **Bible reading**.

The story ends with the woman wondering about whether God accepts anyone who puts their trust in him. There is an opportunity to make an evangelistic application and invite people to place their trust in Jesus. But the main challenge of the teaching today is for us to mirror the behaviour of Jesus and not show favouritism but treat everyone with love.

Put people into groups, asking them to think of a simple practical thing they could do in the next week to befriend/care for/help someone who might otherwise feel left out. Each group in turn should mime their scenario while the rest of the congregation tries to guess what is being shown. (If this seems too ambitious, prime some people to prepare the mimes beforehand and use them instead of dividing into groups.)

Point out that James' teaching is for all of us. Being told not to murder, or steal or commit adultery might only apply to some of us. But all of us meet people every day, so every one of us has dozens of opportunities to treat people fairly and kindly and love them as God does, without favouritism.

Prayer activity

With: a selection of newspapers

Divide the congregation into groups and give each group a newspaper. Ask each group to tear out stories about those who are poor, those who are exploited or those who are discriminated against. Each group should choose one story and write a prayer for the people involved. One person from each group reads their prayers.

Ending the service

Use Psalm 146 to end the service. (CEV is a good clear translation for all ages.) First explain that the psalmist is warning us against thinking we'll get ahead by favouring and flattering the rich, powerful and influential. As God's people we must put our trust in God entirely. God loves and cares for all people, rich and poor, weak and powerful but especially redresses the balance by caring for those that no one else cares for.

In reading Psalm 146 together we can commit ourselves to treat others the way God does. It can be read by the whole congregation together or in two groups (A and B) with a leader (L), and read as follows (from the CEV) with verse 10 read by all. In some versions the last phrase of verse 8

needs to be read with verse 9. This is also available as a download (YearB.Proper18_1).

A	Shout praises to the LORD! With all that I am, I will shout his praises.
B	I will sing and praise the LORD God for as long as I live.
L	You can't depend on anyone, not even a great leader. Once they die and are buried, that will be the end of all their plans.
A	The LORD God of Jacob blesses everyone who trusts him and depends on him.
B	God made heaven and earth; he created the sea and everything else. God always keeps his word.
A	He gives justice to the poor and food to the hungry. The LORD sets prisoners free
B	and heals blind eyes. He gives a helping hand to everyone who falls. The LORD loves good people
A	and looks after strangers. He defends the rights of orphans and widows, but destroys the wicked.
All	The LORD God of Zion will rule forever! Shout praises to the Lord!

Psalm 146 (CEV)

Helpful extras

Music and song ideas

Songs reflecting God's rule over and care for the whole world include: 'This earth belongs to God'; 'Over all the world'; 'There's a wideness in God's mercy'; 'God is love: let heaven adore him'; songs about the love of

God include: 'O Father of the fatherless'; 'O, the deep, deep love of Jesus'; 'God's love is deeper than the deepest ocean'; songs of commitment/challenge to love one another include: 'Brother, sister, let me serve you'; 'Make me a channel of your peace'; 'God loves you and I love you'; 'I love you with the love of the Lord'.

Statement of faith

A statement of faith, made up of various scriptures from TNIV, is available as a download (YearB.Proper18_2). References are given for information but should not be read as part of the statement.

Notes and comments

If you identified a practical project last week, take time to follow up on it this week. If you didn't start anything last week you could follow up the fairness/favouritism theme by looking at Fairtrade. (A search engine produces lots of information.) Introduce the idea by referring back to the chocolates you used in the **Bible talk**. Show the box to demonstrate that they are Fairtrade and ask people what they understand by that.

To set people's minds working before the **Bible talk**, play (audio or video) 'My favourite things' from *The Sound of Music*. In groups or all together share what your favourite things are and move onto who our favourite people are and why.

One of the most common examples of unfair treatment is bullying. You may know people in your congregation who could share stories about being bullied and the effect it had (is having) on them, and what things can be done to stop bullying and help those being bullied. At the start of the academic year in the UK, you could pray for those starting a new school term in the light of this.

As an alternative **Ending the service** in groups everyone stands up in turn and says: 'I am (name), I am x years old and I (something particular about them – support Man U, work in retail) and God, who has no favourites, loves me.'

Proper 19

READINGS: **James 3:1–12; Mark 8:27–38**
Isaiah 50:4–9a; Psalm 116:1–9

Bible foundations

Aim: to consider how best to watch what we say

James doesn't mince his words here as he gives challenging instruction of how to use a very small yet powerful muscle – the tongue. He has a particular warning for those who aspire to be teachers for they will be more severely judged. But he acknowledges that we all stumble at times and no one is perfect in every respect!

To make his points more clear he uses illustrations of two small things with the power to control: bits in the mouth to make horses obey the rider; rudders to steer ships even in strong winds. Likewise, the tongue is a small part of the body, but capable of amazingly powerful outbursts. James likens it to a small spark that sets a forest on fire – a reminder of the potentially destructive influence of the use of wrong words. He reinforces the power of the tongue by comparing our responsibility for it with trying to tame an animal – surprisingly, while we are able to tame all sorts of animals, no one can tame the tongue.

Peter's encounter with Jesus, recorded in Mark 8:27–38, is an example of how easy it is to switch between speaking the truth with our tongue (Peter confesses that Jesus is the Messiah) and speaking in error (Peter tries to dissuade Jesus from travelling to Jerusalem to fulfil God's purpose). James 3:9–12 picks this up, acknowledging that with our tongues we are able to praise God and curse others. He goes on to give two illustrations of why this is not a logical position – fresh water and salt water cannot come from the same spring, nor can olives come from a fig tree or figs come from vines. James' challenge is to keep our hearts pure so that, as Jesus put it, our tongues will be the positive overflow of our hearts.

Beginning the service

With: audio collage – available as a download (YearB.Proper19_1)

Establish the theme as people enter in the following ways: Play an audio collage of people's voices – speaking, whispering, shouting, crowds at a football match, people at a party, family conversation, voices after church, children in a school playground. Create your own, finding examples which fit with the character of your congregation, or use the downloadable audio track. Turn the volume up as more people arrive. If you have music playing, make sure the audio track is audible above this.

When you are ready to begin your service, gradually turn down the audio track volume and let the musicians play more softly – until there is silence.

Briefly welcome people, then immediately lead into a short time of silent prayer/reflection, using words such as: 'Now, let's be silent for a few moments and get ready to listen to what God wants to say to us today.' Aim for a complete contrast with the noise of the first moments of your time together. After a minute's silence, introduce the theme of the service, thinking about the power of the words we speak and how best we can watch what we say.

Bible reading

With: PowerPoint slide show with images and James 3:1–12, available as a download (YearB.Proper19_2), or the following pictures to display that accompany the reading: a horse and rider, boat, forest fire, fresh water, dirty water

James 3:1–12 should be read from the CEV by a good, well-rehearsed reader. Accompany the reading with the pictures above, controlling this so that the pictures fit the words. Alternatively, show the PowerPoint and ask people to read it for themselves, or read out loud if there are non-readers in the congregation. This could take place in the **Bible talk**.

Mark 8:27–38 is read during the **Bible talk**, where indicated. Ask two or three volunteers to prepare this, reading alternate paragraphs or taking on the voices of narrator, the disciples and Jesus.

Bible talk

With: drama sketch, available as a download (YearB.Proper19_3); PowerPoint slides used with **Bible reading**; delicious-looking piece of cake; tired-looking piece of fruit

What's the problem?
Begin with the sketch which needs to be rehearsed. Keep it light-hearted. Make sure that it can't be misinterpreted as depicting actual individuals in your congregation!

Alternatively, give an example where people in a church service have been listening to God saying one thing, but have promptly said negative things about someone else.

Continue by helping the congregation identify examples in their own lives when their words haven't matched up to being followers of Christ. Be aware of the different age groups present. Point out that controlling what we say can be a problem. The **Bible**

reading from James 3:1–12 using the PowerPoint slides could take place here or, if you have already had the reading, just show the images again as a reminder.

Slide 2 (horse-rider), slide 3 (boat)
Although our tongues are small, words can be powerful for good – or for evil. Give some examples for both scenarios that may be familiar in your situation.

Slide 5 (forest fire)
Just as a forest fire begins with a small spark, so casual gossip can spread and cause great damage. Give some examples.

Slide 8 (fresh water)
Read James 3:9–11: 'My dear friends, with our tongues we speak both praises and curses. We praise our Lord and Father, and we curse people who were created to be like God, and this isn't right. Can clean water and dirty water both flow from the same spring?' (CEV)

Comment that we know what we're like and know that we often say things that aren't right as people who claim to be God's children. So, what can we do?

How can we watch our words?
Self-control (James 3:1,2)

Do this two-minute exercise. Ask people to talk to each other in pairs for exactly two minutes. They can talk about anything they like, but they mustn't say 'I'. Ask each pair to keep a note of how many times they do say 'I'. At the end of the time, the pair with the lowest 'score' is the winner!

Just for fun you could invite the pair that

wins to the front to receive their 'prizes'. Bring out the 'prizes' (previously hidden). One is a delicious-looking piece of cake (chocolate, cream, etc); the other is a tired-looking piece of fruit. Which one will they choose?

Comment that in this exercise, and in the choice of prizes, self-control was needed. After all, they couldn't both have the delicious piece of cake! James makes the point that the way to get our words right is self-control. Getting our talk right leads to right actions and right living.

Getting our hearts right (James 3:9–12)
Bring out the challenge of these verses. Reinforce this with Jesus' words in Mark 7:14–23 where the link is made between words, thoughts and deeds – and the state of our hearts.

Focus on Jesus (Mark 8:27–38)
Read: Mark 8:27–38, as described in **Bible reading**.

Highlight the following points from these verses:

- Recognise who Jesus is and believe in him (vs 27–30).
- Deliberately live your life for Jesus – in action (vs 34–37) and words (v 38).
- Follow Jesus' example – forget about looking after your own interests (vs 31,34,35).

Close with a challenge about our commitment to Jesus and how that is key in controlling what we say. If we say we are God's people, our words should demonstrate that.

Prayer activity

With: long strips of paper, felt tip pens/markers

Words can heal or words can wound. Ask people in groups to write words and phrases of kindness on a long strip of paper as if on a graffiti wall. These could be phrases about people, things that have happened or specific things people want to thank God for. Then pray together in thanks to God. Display the 'graffiti' at the end of the service.

Prayer of confession

With: PowerPoint slide show with photos of people in a variety of everyday situations, for example, families, holiday photos, church, work, driving a car, playing sport, eating a meal, being at school – available as a download (YearB.Proper19_4)

Read: James 3:8–10

Invite people to join in a time of quiet reflection and private confession. Ask them to think back over the past week and things they have said. Prompt thoughts with pictures (run as a 'loop') showing everyday situations. Encourage everyone to bring things to God that they have said that they know were wrong and ask his forgiveness.

Ending the service

With: small cards/thick paper cut-outs of the pictures used earlier in the **Bible reading** (YearB.Proper19_2) of horse, boat, fire, fresh water (but not dirty water) – enough for everyone in the congregation; PowerPoint slide of words of Psalm 19:14

(NIV), available as a download (YearB. Proper19_5)

Pass baskets with the pictures around the congregation and ask everyone to choose and take one picture. Encourage people to take this home and stick it up somewhere they will see it often in the coming week as a reminder to watch their words.

Close with the words of Psalm 19:14. Encourage people to say or sing these words together as your closing prayer for one another.

Helpful extras

Music and song ideas

'O for a thousand tongues'; 'Let everything that has breath'; 'May the words of my mouth and the meditation of my heart'; 'Many are the words we speak (Now to live the life)'; 'Let my words be few (You are God in heaven)'; 'Be still for the presence of the Lord'; 'Dear Lord and Father of mankind'.

You may find video clips of some of the songs above on YouTube which may be suitable for use in your service, for example 'Let my words be few'. A song with words and images might be appropriate for a time of meditation instead of singing together.

Game

Use this as a light-hearted 'starter' for thinking about watching our words.

Ask for four volunteers to play two or three rounds of the Radio 4 game *Just a Minute*. Include topics such as: my family, my friends, people at work, people at church, people at school/college, my worst Christmas. Rules are as for the radio programme (to speak for 60 seconds with no repetition, hesitation or deviation) plus an extra rule: no negative words about other people.

One person is the chairperson and can make the final judgements for points, but they can also ask for audience involvement in deciding controversial points. Appoint a time-keeper who will also keep the 'score'.

Congratulate and applaud the winner.

Notes and comments

The aim of the service is to focus on the words we speak. The challenge is how to control these so that what we say reflects the life of Jesus. The service outline aims to create an awareness of our words and their power and the challenge of the Bible teaching – from the beginning to the end of your time together.

You will need to do some preparation. Make sure that you have downloaded the PowerPoint slides referred to in the outline if at all possible, or you could prepare your own. You'll need to rehearse your use of some of these, for example, the pictures which accompany the reading from James 3:1–12. You will also need to copy and cut

out the picture 'cards' referred to in **Ending the service**.

Well-rehearsed volunteers will be needed for some parts of the service. You'll need three or four readers and four people (two adult females and two teenage boys) for the sketch – if numbers are limited, use the same people for the readings and the sketch. For the **Game**, participants can be selected on the day, but do so with care, thinking about individuals' confidence and audibility. You'll also need someone to keep time and the score.

And, of course, as you prepare for this service, pray that God will take and bless all the words that will be spoken during your time together – for his glory!

If this is a service of Holy Communion, comment on the words that you say as you administer the sacraments.

Online resources

All suggested downloads are available at www.scriptureunion.org.uk/light. Visit www.lightlive.org for additional activities for children, young people and adults.

Proper 20

READINGS: **James 3:13 – 4:3,7,8; Mark 9:30–37**
Jeremiah 11:18–20; Psalm 54

Bible foundations

Aim: to learn the wisdom of being a servant

In Mark 9:30–37 Jesus, journeying with his disciples, discusses his imminent death and resurrection with them. They haven't grasped that the way to greatness is in taking the place of a servant. They are not really listening to Jesus but arguing among themselves about who is the greatest. Jesus draws a child into the circle to show them that the values of the kingdom of heaven are often the opposite of the values of the world. Whoever wishes to be the greatest must be the least, like a child.

James 3:13 – 4:3,7,8 reflects this view. The opposite of wisdom is envy and selfish ambition which demonstrates itself in quarrelling and strife. Wisdom, on the other hand, demonstrates itself in humility. Reflect on James 3:17 and 18. The kind of wise attitude that James speaks of has the power to transform communities from being divided by quarrels and selfishness to being empowered by the grace of God.

Wisdom is not just a theoretical concept to be confused with intelligence. It is a way to live life, reflecting the attitude and practice of Jesus. His followers should be like him. Even before Jesus came, those who sought to live by God's law often learned the wisdom of humility and the place of a servant. Jeremiah 11 tells us that, as one of God's chosen prophets, he could describe himself as a 'gentle lamb led to the slaughter'; he was plotted against and victimised as he sought to serve God.

David in Psalm 54 describes a very similar experience as he hid from King Saul, who was trying to kill him. According to the Bible, more often than not the way up is down. This is not a popular message for today, but is the path Jesus walked.

Beginning the service

With: stickers which say either 'Servant' or 'Wise person', enough for one each per person at the service; pictures, as below, of ten people, to show via PowerPoint – also available as a download (YearB.Proper20_1); paper and pens

As people arrive, give out the stickers and ask people to wear these throughout the service. As far as possible, aim to have roughly half the congregation as 'servants' and half as 'wise people'. Make sure that stickers are spread evenly through age groups.

At the beginning of the service, comment on the stickers people have been given and should now be wearing. Say that you want everyone, throughout your time together, to act and speak deliberately according to the description on their badges.

Say that you're going to see some pictures of well-known people or situations. In twos or threes you'd like them to decide on a 'label' for each one, either 'servant', 'wise person' or 'don't know'. Take paper and pen (supplies spread throughout congregation), write down numbers 1–10, and decide together how each one should be labelled. Pictures might include:

1 The prime minister
2 Teacher in front of class (might be one of your congregation)
3 President of the US
4 Mother Teresa
5 Mother with child (might be one of your congregation)
6 The Archbishop of Canterbury
7 Nurse, doctor or dentist (might be one of your congregation)
8 *University Challenge*, or students graduating/getting exam results (may be in the congregation)
9 A judge in his wig and gown
10 A small child (may be in the congregation).

Briefly, talk through people's ideas for each example. Point out that being wise and being a servant often don't seem that different. Introduce the theme of the service by saying that in the Bible the kind of wisdom talked about – it might seen surprising to us – means putting others first and serving others.

Bible reading

With: copies of the verses from James 3:13 – 4:3,7,8 printed in large, clear type, each verse on an A3 sheet of paper without verse numbers. The verses from the CEV are available as a download (YearB.Proper20_2)

Say that you're going to do your Bible reading together as a challenge.

Around your meeting area there are different tables with the Bible reading verses laid out, but the verses are jumbled up. In groups of four to six people, try to put the verses in the correct order.

After a few minutes, ask everyone to listen carefully to the reading, to check whether their team got it right. Check who got their puzzle correctly worked out and congratulate teams that succeeded.

After everyone is settled, introduce Mark 9:30–37. Ask a family with children to read these verses. Different family members can read different verses, with the youngest child or children reading verses 36 and 37.

Bible talk

With: drama sketch (rehearsed in advance); camcorder; camera with flash; microphone; three or four volunteers (Mr X needs to be confident); props for Mr Wise/Mr Foolish (Mr F turns around to become Mr W); a sandwich board with blank sheets of flip chart on both sides; Mr F's props such as hat, shoes; Mr W's props such as hat, shoes, glasses, beard; board markers; PowerPoint slide or display of James 3:13 – 4:3,7,8 available as a download (YearB. Proper20_3)

Begin with no introduction
Fifteen Minutes of Fame
A two or three-man 'TV crew' enter (as realistically as possible), looking for 'Mr X'. Members of the congregation will probably point him out. If possible, organise some kind of spotlight to focus on him. 'Cameraman' constantly circles to get good angles. TV presenter encourages Mr X (who appears very bashful) out of his seat into the aisle or leads him to the front. TV presenter encourages applause/cheers throughout.

TV presenter: OK everyone… sorry to interrupt… but we've come to celebrate with you one very special member of your church. As you all know this is Mr X, currently one of the stars on the all-time record-breaking show everyone is talking about, *FIFTEEN MINUTES OF FAME!*

TV presenter: Mr X… in recent weeks we have seen your amazing skill at *[something*

everyday and mundane, eg making a cheese sandwich]. Could you tell us how you got into this in the first place?

Mr X: *[Improvise, according to the 'skill', prepared in advance.]*

TV presenter: And what made you enter *Fifteen Minutes of Fame?*

Mr X: *[Improvise, according to the 'skill', prepared in advance. End with:]*… and I've always wanted to be famous and I thought 'I can win this'.

TV presenter: And what are you hoping for now?

Mr X: To win! I'm going to be the best. It's my picture that's going to be in the papers and on TV. The others are good – but I'm better!

TV presenter: Thank you, people of St Y's *[Your church's name.].* Don't forget to support Mr X and watch to see how he gets on in next week's final of *Fifteen Minutes of Fame!*

(Encourage applause/cheers. TV crew exit. Mr X returns to his seat.)

After everyone has settled down, read Mark 9:33–35. Comment that human beings haven't changed that much. The disciples see success as getting the top place (v 34), a bit like people today wanting to be in the spotlight of fame. Jesus had a different view of greatness (v 35).

James looks at these ideas in his continuing discussion of what makes for true wisdom. Refer to last week's service in which you thought about self-control of our words being the key to wisdom. In today's reading from James he continues his discussion of wisdom as he contrasts the kind of behaviour which results from 'wisdom that doesn't come from above' with that resulting from 'wisdom that does come from above'. So what does 'wisdom' and 'not-wisdom' look like from God's point of view? Introduce Mr Foolish (not-wisdom).

Display the James 3:13 – 4:3,7,8 sheet. Ask: So what does wisdom that doesn't come from above look like? Then invite everyone to look at the passage and come up with answers from the verses. For example: jealousy; selfishness; lying; covering up the truth; causing trouble; doing cruel things; fighting; arguing; killing. As people make suggestions, encourage them to come and write up the words with verse references on the sandwich board with the sheet of flip chart paper stuck on Mr Foolish. You may wish to comment on each, giving some everyday examples.

Ask: So what does true wisdom, wisdom that comes from above, or, from God, look like? Mr Foolish turns around to become Mr Wise, quickly adding different props, as appropriate. Again, invite the congregation to look at the passage and come up with answers from the verses. For example: right living; being humble; pure; friendly; gentle; sensible; kind; helpful; genuine; sincere; a peacemaker; behaviour resulting in justice; surrendering to God; resisting the devil.

Again, as people make suggestions, encourage them to write up the words with verse references, this time on Mr Wise. You may wish to comment on each, giving some everyday examples.

This is wisdom, in other words, always putting others before your own interests, being a servant. Read: Mark 9:30–32. Ultimately this wisdom is explained in Jesus who gave up his place in heaven to come to earth to give his life for us so that we could have eternal life.

Prayers of intercession

With: PowerPoint images of three or four current news stories

Begin with the words of James 3:18. Then display the images one at a time, pausing on each for a few moments. Invite the congregation, aloud or in silence, to offer prayers of intercession for these different situations.

If your church building has Wi-Fi you could go to a news website, eg www.bbc.co.uk or www.guardian.co.uk and look together at featured news stories.

Close with a prayer for the 'peacemakers' in these situations and for yourselves that you will 'plant seeds of peace' as opportunities arise.

Prayer of confession

Begin with the words of James 4:8.

Invite Mr Foolish to the front. Point out that all of us have been guilty of some of these things written on the sandwich board. Invite everyone to think through the list, highlighting some, and then ask them to think back over the past week to when they might have behaved like this. Leave a few moments of silence for quiet reflection and prayer, then say:

Leader: In your mercy…
All: … forgive us, Lord.

Close by saying James 4:7 and 8: 'Surrender to God! Resist the devil, and he will run from you. Come near to God, and he will come near to you.'

Ending the service

Refer to the fact that at **Beginning the service** everyone was given a sticker/badge which labels them as a 'wise person' or a 'servant'. Ask everyone to find someone with a different badge and swap it.

Comment that, unlike what is often said in our society, true wisdom is about being a servant. In fact, whether your label says 'wise man' or 'servant', in God's eyes it means the same thing. The perfect example is Jesus. Challenge everyone, as you leave church or share coffee together or during the week ahead, to show this kind of wisdom, to put others first and ultimately, to put Jesus first.

Helpful extras

Music and song ideas
'From heaven you came' (The Servant King); 'You chose the cross'; 'A new commandment I give unto you'; 'Here is love'; 'Make me a channel of your peace'; 'Love divine all loves excelling'.

Notes and comments

The overall aim of this outline is to explore the themes of the service in every element.

The focus is on the Bible passages and every age group should be helped to engage with the scriptures in some way. Encourage everyone to participate.

In **Beginning the service** use the suggested pictures and display on a screen or find your own similar examples. Alternate pictures of people who will be recognised as 'important' with people in 'ordinary' or 'everyday' roles and jobs. To encourage the congregation's engagement, use photos of people who are known, such as a mother and child, teacher with class, doctor or nurse with patient.

These suggested activities can be as complex as the expertise within the congregation allows. Use your imagination! For example, the *Fifteen Minutes of Fame* sketch could be done with simple props, or you could actually film this as it happens to play back during coffee time.

The actors need to rehearse the sketch. Before the service check through the outline to see what you'll need and have everything prepared. Potentially there are lots of materials and props needed.

Online resources

All suggested downloads are available at www.scriptureunion.org.uk/light. Visit www.lightlive.org for additional activities for children, young people and adults.

Proper 21

READINGS: **Numbers 11:4–6,10–16,24–29; James 5:13–20**
Psalm 19:7–14; Mark 9:38–50

Bible foundations

Aim: to recognise that God's people need each other

We are tempted to live in isolation and independence but that's not God's way.
He has put us into communities and created us to be relational (we're made in his
image). This allows us to be helped and formed through relationships. Sometimes
we find community a joy but sometimes it's a source of stress!

Numbers 11 reminds us of the time when Moses' experience of leading the people
of Israel became almost too much for him. He was overwhelmed by the magnitude
of the task, especially when people started complaining. He prayed for God's
intervention. The way God intervened was to use others. Moses was to share out
the pressure and responsibility. The Spirit anointed all the leaders, to the confusion
of Joshua, who clearly presumed only specially selected people could receive God's
anointing – a foretaste of what was to come when God would pour out his Spirit
on all people.

Sometimes God seems to use people in ways we don't immediately understand.
Jesus faced similar confusion and questions from his disciples in Mark 9 when
they witnessed other people driving out demons in Jesus' name. Jesus didn't seem
concerned but to the disciples these were people outside Jesus' specially selected
group, people they viewed with suspicion.

Martin Luther, the Reformer, highlighted from Scripture the doctrine of the
priesthood of all believers. We are familiar with teaching on the value of every
part of the body of Christ in 1 Corinthians 12–14. James 5 demonstrates this in
practice, acknowledging the function of leadership but also individual and corporate
responsibility. He writes about the value of praying for the sick, confessing our sins
to each other so that we might find help and forgiveness, praying for one another,
correcting each other – all appropriate expressions for the community of those
who follow Jesus.

Beginning the service

With: dark glasses made out of cardboard that are completely impossible to see through; the words 'share', 'care' and 'prayer' on a screen or a flip chart

Invite a volunteer to the front to try on your new sunglasses. Explain you are going to test their effectiveness. Show the volunteer a number of objects and invite them to identify them, firstly by sight (which should be impossible) and then by touch. Having established that they can't see a thing, ask them to identify your facial expressions – happy, sad, angry or confused. Again, this is completely impossible. Ask them to remove their glasses and try again.

Point out that it is difficult for us to care for each other as people unless we know a bit about one another. We need to share needs before we know what to pray for. We need to know why someone is happy before we can rejoice with them.

Display the words 'share', 'care' and 'prayer'. The church is a community of people, called to follow Christ. God wants us to grow in peace and wholeness. The purpose of the church is to provide a community within which this can happen. As we share with each other, we begin to care for each other and this leads us into prayer. This may be an appropriate time to share news and pray for each other.

Bible reading

A dramatised version of Numbers 11:4–6, 10–16, 24–29 is available as a download (YearB.Proper21_1). This illustrates the way that God pours out the Spirit upon the elders of Israel so that Moses will not have to bear all the responsibility by himself.

The reading from James 5:13–20 is shorter but contains a few important words of advice for church members. Invite the congregation to pick out some practical instructions for living as they listen to the reading. You could read this a second time and hold up cards, or display words and pictures on a screen when each piece of advice is mentioned.

Bible talk

With: very simple jigsaws borrowed from church families, put in separate bags or boxes but mixed up – keep one piece from each jigsaw for yourself

Give the jigsaws to volunteers and ask them to do them on their own. While this is happening, talk about how Moses was a lonely leader who had to bear all the complaints of the people all by himself. Many people today have to carry burdens or responsibilities on their own. Others feel lonely or lost because there is no one to care for them.

By this point your volunteers should have discovered that they can't complete their jigsaws on their own because they don't have all the pieces that they need. Invite them to work together and see if they can finish them as a group. While they do this, talk about the way we need each other. The Bible encourages us to bear each other's burdens and look after one another. Paul talks about the different gifts that God gives to each believer. James tells us to pray for one another, confess our sins and help each other to follow Christ.

At this point your volunteers should have sorted out their pieces and almost finished their puzzles, but they will have discovered that they still don't hold all the pieces. Being a Christian is easier if we have the help of our brothers and sisters but even this is not enough. Remind people of the story about Moses and the elders. Moses needed the elders to work with him, but it was only when God poured out the Spirit upon them that they were able to share his responsibility. They all needed God's help.

James told believers to help each other by praying for help, confessing their sins and bringing people back to the way of truth. The emphasis in all of these actions is on God. They are all actions which help people to receive God's grace. Looking after each other is good, but without God there is something missing. Your volunteers had a better chance of finishing the jigsaws together but they will never be successful without all the pieces.

Give your volunteers the missing pieces for them to finish their jigsaws. Remind everyone that the church is made up of individuals who support each other as a community, but that this community is only effective when God's grace is at work within it.

Prayer activity

With: one or two strips of paper for each person; pens

Give each person a strip of paper and ask them to hold it with one of their neighbours.

This should create a complex network or web linking everyone present. Remind people that this is how God wants his people to live, depending on one another as brothers and sisters. Unfortunately, however, we often prefer to ignore one another or find ourselves in situations where we become lonely or isolated.

Ask everyone to tear or break the strips that link them with one another. This symbolises the brokenness we often experience in our homes, workplaces, schools or churches.

Moses felt isolated and alone. There are people all over the world who need the help and support of others but who are unable or unwilling to ask for it. Invite people to write names of isolated people they know on their torn piece of paper or just allow it to represent someone who is lonely, isolated or in need of help. Give them a moment of quiet to pray for these people.

To symbolise the way we help one another, ask people to send their strips of paper forward by passing them from person to person. Gather the strips at the front and symbolically offer them to God in prayer.

Prayer of confession

James tells us to confess our sins to each other. He also says that bringing a person back to God can 'save them from death and cover over a multitude of sins'. We need to encourage one another to stay on the way of Jesus and also bring each other back when we get lost. It is easy to forget this calling because society sees faith, spirituality and morality as an individual matter. The

Prayer of confession reminds us of our responsibility to others and asks God to forgive us for neglecting each other.

Ask the congregation to put their hands on their eyes when you say the word 'eyes' or 'see', put their hands on their ears when you say 'ears' or 'hear' and their hands on their heart when you say 'love'. Ask them to join hands with their neighbours when you say 'join'. Practise this before using it as a prayer.

Lord, we are sorry for closing our **eyes** so that we cannot **see** what causes others to be happy or sad.
We are sorry for closing our **ears** so that we cannot **hear** what they have to say.
Open our **eyes** and open our **ears** and help us to **love** others.
May you **join** us with one another in a community of peace so that we all find forgiveness and wholeness in you. Amen.

Ending the service

With: the dark glasses used at **Beginning the service**; a number of cards with positive statements on them, such as: God loves you; You are forgiven; The Spirit is with you; You are a beautiful person

Ask a volunteer to wear the glasses, and then show the cards to them and to the congregation. Ask the volunteer how they feel, and then ask the congregation to explain why the cards are important and what they mean – without using the phrases in question!

It is not enough to receive help from others. It is really important to receive help from God and to see ourselves from his point of view. Talk about God's love for us and his commitment to us. We may find it difficult to receive his love because we close our eyes and ears to him. We may find it hard to believe he loves us because we feel unworthy or think that we need to earn his approval. It can be helpful for others to speak God's words to us to help us believe and accept the truth of God's Word for ourselves.

Show the cards to the congregation one at a time. Ask them to read the words to each other as a way of encouraging and supporting each other on their Christian journey. You may conclude with: Go in peace to love and serve the Lord – in the name of Christ. Amen.

Helpful extras

Music and song ideas
At some point in the service, you could play a popular song about loneliness or isolation such as 'I am a rock' (Simon and Garfunkel) or 'Eleanor Rigby' (The Beatles).

Songs about Christian community or the role of the Holy Spirit include 'A new commandment'; 'All over the world the Spirit is moving'; 'An army of ordinary people'; 'As we are gathered'; 'Bind us together'; 'For I'm building a people of power'; 'Jesus stand among us at the meeting of our lives'; 'Let there be love shared among us'.

More challenging songs about welcoming others include 'Here in this place'; 'Let us build a house where love can dwell'; 'For everyone born, a place at the table'.

Game

This requires some preparation, but can help people get to know each other better.

Compile a list of statements that may be true about particular individuals in the congregation. For example, 'I used to drive a train', 'I have been to Belgium on holiday' or 'I go to the same school as my brother'. Photocopy these lists and give them out to all members of the congregation. The task is to find out how many people could honestly agree with each statement. The winner is the person with the most names on their sheet – and it is, of course, possible for more than one individual to agree with each statement so this number could be quite high!

This is a good game to play before the service as people arrive, or during refreshments after the service which might persuade people to stay longer to take part in community time.

Notes and comments

It is important to be sensitive about the way we use biblical language about sight or hearing. There is often a lot to gain when deaf, blind or partially-sighted people are able to help others understand what it is like to experience the world as they do. If you have the opportunity, ask someone to do this as part of **Beginning the service**.

The language of community, confession and wholeness are particularly appropriate for a Communion service. There is a lot of liturgical material that draws attention to these themes. If you don't often celebrate Communion, this may be an appropriate occasion to do so.

James writes about prayer in James 5. His words could be read to suggest that healing follows automatically from confession, intercession and anointing – particularly if the person praying is 'righteous'. This raises questions about the purpose and effectiveness of prayer which would be worth exploring in a small group or in a more reflective service. Some people may value the opportunity to think about these issues in more depth. One recent book that many people have found helpful in thinking about apparently unanswered prayer is *God on mute* by Pete Greig published by Survivor (Kingsway Communications Ltd).

Both **Bible readings** mention elders. Take this opportunity to celebrate the ministry of your elders and church leaders (who may be the same!) and to think about their role.

Online resources

All suggested downloads are available at www.scriptureunion.org.uk/light. Visit www.lightlive.org for additional activities for children, young people and adults.

Dedication/Anniversary

READINGS: **Genesis 28:11–18; 1 Peter 2:1–10**
Psalm 122; John 10:22–29

Bible foundations

Aim: to recognise how good it is to be God's people and to know that he is always with us

From the very beginning, God wanted to be in relationship with human beings and for them to love and obey him as they loved and served others as his people. He chose individuals and their families to demonstrate his love and purposes for them. One of those individuals was Jacob. In Genesis 28 Jacob flees from his family; he has cheated his older brother Esau out of his birthright and firstborn's blessing, and now is escaping to his Uncle Laban's home, 800 km away. This change of location gives the opportunity for character change as he encounters God. God promises that he will be with him and has a purpose for Jacob's life. Jacob recognises God's intervention in this most unlikely place at this most unlikely time and vows that if God remains with him and provides for him he will serve him.

From the descendants of these patriarchs, God chooses a people to love who will be a demonstration of his grace and purpose to the world. Psalm 122 is a song about how God's people loved to meet together in the Temple to worship and to pray for the peace of their community.

In the New Testament the people of God are no longer one nation but a community formed around Jesus. 1 Peter 2 describes what this means. Peter challenges the community to purity and maturity. He reminds them that they are like living stones being built into a spiritual house. He draws from the Old Testament, applying the idea of priesthood to the whole church. This church community is built upon the foundation of Jesus. Peter introduces four powerful pictures to describe church: chosen people, royal priesthood, holy nation and people belonging to God. He makes it clear that the purpose of the church is to declare God's praise for what God has done, applying to worship and mission.

Beginning the service

Today's service is about offering praise to God because he has chosen us and invited us to be his special people. Begin with a suitable hymn or song of praise. Encourage everyone to take part and to imagine that they are literally lifting praise up to God. Make a joyful noise!

Read five short statements concerning the history of your church or congregation, none of which should be immediately obvious or verifiable. For example, if the name of the architect is well known, one statement could be 'The name of the architect's mother was Mabel'. Using dates or numbers with no obvious relevance will catch out even the most historically minded, for example, 'The third minister performed his first baptism on 4 April 1964'. One statement should be untrue. Vote by a show of hands which is the false statement. Use these (mostly irrelevant) introductory statements as a brief reminder of the important points concerning how and when your church was founded.

Bible reading

Mime Genesis 28:11–18 as a narrator reads it as follows: Jacob takes a 'stone' to lie down to sleep; a group walks majestically up and down whatever steps you have in the church (or improvise a set of steps); use a drum roll or similar majestic sound to announce the presence of God; a second reader should read the Lord's words in verses 13–15; Jacob wakes up and shows a suitable expression of awe; he pours oil from a small container over the stone. An NIV version is available as a download (YearB.Dedication_1). Mime to the words in italics.

Enact a symbolic mime during the reading of 1 Peter 2:1–10. Put Jacob's stone from the Old Testament reading in a central position (v 4). Invite members of the congregation to come forward one at a time and reverently add a smaller (probably real) stone to form a small cairn. Each person should remain by the cairn and, towards the end of the reading, link hands and raise them.

Bible talk

With: these key words from the Bible passages on the overhead display or on large pieces of card: Dream, Promise, Blessing, Chosen, Dedication, Living stones. As you introduce each one, keep the previous ones on view.

Introduction

Why do we celebrate anniversaries? Why do we like to remember special events in our personal lives such as birthdays or weddings, in families such as moving house, or in the local community such as the opening of a new sports centre? Not only are these events memorable markers of time, but every time we remember, we think again about something good that happened and feel thankful. Some people say they can't remember the last time anything good happened. We should remind them of an anniversary. Today is the anniversary of the dedication/opening of our church (substitute whatever it is you are celebrating) and we want this to be a happy occasion for all of us, whether or not you were actually there at the beginning. We are all part of the body of Christ which worships in (name of church) today.

Talk about the following six key words from Genesis 28 and 1 Peter 2.

Dream

The main purpose of Jacob's dream was to reveal God to him. (Make sure that everyone knows the story about Jacob.) He had not been aware that God was there. Before this church/building/congregation was here, God was here. Jacob's response is one of awe. He calls the stony, deserted place where he had lain down to sleep 'the house of God, the gate of heaven'. God's presence with us transforms these ordinary bricks, plaster, wood, lights and fabric into 'the gate of heaven'. We may not all dream such dreams. But someone, in the history of our church (name the person or persons if known) also dreamed of turning a bare piece of earth into a house of God.

Promise

God's promise to Jacob is one of the most thrilling in the Bible. 'I am with you and will watch over you wherever you go, and I will... not leave you'. What promises has God given to us in this congregation? People of all times and races have felt an urge to raise monuments, temples and shrines to what they understand to be divine. It is the God of Abraham, Jacob and Isaac, our God, who responds in a tangible, personal way with the promise of his presence. The same applies to our church.

Blessing

By worshipping God in this place, Jacob and his descendants were to 'spread out to the west and to the east, to the north and to the south. All peoples on earth will be blessed through you and your offspring'. Can we claim God's promise to be with us as we reach out west, east, north and south of this building? What does it mean to be a blessing to the people around us? (Mention some of the outreach or charitable activities of the past year in the local community.)

Chosen

The chosen people of God in the Old Testament, Jacob's family and descendants, are mirrored in the New Testament by those who belong to God. That includes us. Peter twice stresses that Jesus Christ was chosen by God and precious to him. As Christ's followers, we are chosen and precious too. We have received mercy and been brought into the wonderful light.

Dedication

Jacob could not have simply rubbed his eyes in the morning and been on his way. He wanted to dedicate the site of God's wonderful revelation, promise and blessing. He called it Bethel, which means 'house of God'.

Choose as appropriate:

- We worship in a building which is hundreds of years old. It was dedicated to (...) and today is the anniversary of that dedication/St X's Day. Why was it important to the people then? (Find the answer to this question from parish research and tell the congregation.)
- The saint to whom this church is dedicated was ... (give a brief account, then choose one or two good reasons/ qualities/characteristics for people today to remember them).
- Our church is named after the place where it is (eg street name, town, locality).

Our name tells us not only that we belong here, but it reminds us that God wants us to be active here, blessing those around us.

- We thought long and hard about what name to give our congregation. (If your church uses a Greek or Hebrew word in its name, such as 'Ichthus', 'Maranatha' or 'Bethany', remind the congregation of the meaning, and its significance.)

Living stones

Some church buildings are beautiful; some are rather ugly. The older they get, the more repairs they need. While we celebrate our church's anniversary, let's not forget what the church really is – the body of Christ, or as Peter puts it, living stones built into a spiritual house. This is invisible and those who were living stones in it on earth and have moved on to be with God in eternity are still part of it. It is a most incredible structure and can never fall down. It never needs repairing. Its purpose is to declare the praises of God. We are just a small part of something greater than we can imagine.

As appropriate, ask people to share a relevant personal testimony.

Prayer activity

Use Psalm 122. Reword it to fit your congregation. For example:

I rejoiced with those who said to me, 'Let us go to (St Mary's)'.
Our feet are standing in your house.
This is where people come to praise the name of the Lord.
Let us pray for the peace of this congregation.
May those who belong in it be secure.
May there be peace and security within its walls.
For the sake of the house of the Lord, let us say to one another, 'Peace be with you'.

Prayers of intercession

Pray for the church worldwide, as appropriate. Incorporate some of the following key phrases from today's readings: All peoples on earth will be blessed; I am with you and will watch over you wherever you go; Surely the Lord is in this place; Offer spiritual sacrifices acceptable to God through Jesus Christ.

Ending the service

Blessing: But you are a chosen people, a royal priesthood, a holy nation, a people belonging to God, that you may declare the praises of him who called you out of darkness into his wonderful light. May God bless us, keep us, and be always with us, watching over us wherever we go. Amen.

Helpful extras

Music and song ideas

'Angel voices ever singing'; 'Let saints on earth in concert sing'; 'As we are gathered'; 'For I'm building a people of power'; 'Lord, for the years'.

Game

Bible dreams quiz

Depending on the composition of the congregation, create two all-age teams (one preschooler, one primary schoolchild, one secondary schoolchild and one adult – or two families with a comparable mixed age-range) or else ask members of the congregation to put their hands up if they know the answer. The quiz could be a warm-up to the **Bible talk**.

1. Who dreamed that his girlfriend was pregnant? (Joseph, Matthew 1)
2. Who dreamed that the sun, moon and stars bowed down to him? (Joseph, Genesis 37)
3. Who had dreams about cows? (Pharaoh, Genesis 41)
4. Who was told in a dream he could ask for whatever he wanted? (Solomon, 1 Kings 3)
5. Who wanted his advisers to explain his dream to them without telling them what it was? (Nebuchadnezzar, Daniel 2)
6. Who were warned to change their plans in a dream? (The wise men, Matthew 2)
7. Who had a really bad night dreaming about a person who was on trial? (Pilate's wife, Matthew 27)
8. Which people did the prophet Joel say would particularly dream dreams? (Old men, Joel 2)

For ideas on scoring for a quiz, look at *Ultimate Quizzes* by Richard and Mary Chewter available from Scripture Union Mail Order (01908 856006) or at your local Christian bookshop.

Statement of faith
Say together the usual creed or choose one of the following available through an Internet search: St Patrick's *Confessio* or The Korean Creed (Methodist).

Notes and comments

This service is suitable for celebrating a church anniversary or dedication of any type.

As part of the **Prayer activity** encourage everyone to greet each other with the words of the Peace. If you are celebrating the Eucharist, use this suggestion as an alternative at the appropriate point in the service.

If this service is celebrating the anniversary of the church leader, make sure that there is a time of praise for their ministry as well as looking to the future. You could also thank God for all those who have led the church in the past. Make sure that this is not just a trip down memory lane, but engages people of all ages and those who have recently joined the church.

Online resources

All suggested downloads are available at www.scriptureunion.org.uk/light. Visit www.lightlive.org for additional activities for children, young people and adults. For your convenience the following activities are available as downloads: YearB.Dedication_2 Talk about Jacob's dream with 5 to 11s; YearB.Dedication_3 Craft activity for 5 to 11s.

Proper 22

READINGS: **Genesis 2:18–24; Psalm 8**
Mark 10:2–16; Hebrews 1:1–4; 2:5–12

Bible foundations

Aim: to celebrate marriage and relationship building as part of God's creation

God cares for humanity. That's the bottom line, and the story of creation in Genesis amply demonstrates that. Although human beings persistently ignore and disobey him, God has given us great dignity and continues to offer guidance with faithfulness and love, based upon relationships. Psalm 8 celebrates these 'givens' of creation, observing that while the angels may be glorious and mighty, humanity is 'crowned… with glory and honour' (v 5) and has a special responsibility of trust for the rest of God's creation (vs 6–8). The psalmist is amazed at this honour, considering the magnificence of the rest of God's creation.

But all relationships are flawed, the most stark example of this damage being the broken bond of relationship between man and woman (Genesis 3). In Mark 10, we find Jesus being challenged by the Pharisees to arbitrate over the acceptable grounds for divorce to cope with this damage. Jesus goes right back to God's intentions in creation. Moses (he tells them in v 5) had to engage in compromise in the way that we, in real life, often have to. Marriages do break down and guidelines must be provided to limit the damage (Deuteronomy 24:1–4). But Jesus stresses God's desire to see men and women united for ever in responsible and durable unions in this most fundamental of relationships. Breaking that bond is against God's original intentions. Was Jesus forbidding divorce under any circumstances? Not necessarily. What he refuses is the terms of the discussion begun by the Pharisees – what can we get away with? Divorce is always a tragedy.

In Matthew 19:9, a fuller account of this teaching, Jesus allows for divorce under certain circumstances, but Mark's account concentrates on the terms of what God ideally requires of marriage. Interestingly enough, this teaching is followed by his warm and countercultural reception of children who were brought to him (vs 13–16).

Beginning the service

With: the music of Jack Johnson's 'Better together', playing as people arrive

Explain that you are going to celebrate marriage and relationships, as part of God's creation. Recognise that for those who have had a positive experience of marriage this will be easier than for those who have not. But whatever experience, the fact that marriage is part of God's good creation is still true!

Read Ecclesiastes 3:1–8 to remind people that there is a time to be sad and a time to rejoice. Begin with a song of celebration for all that God gives us – see **Music and song ideas**.

Bible reading

With: large pictures of animals and birds (use the most splendid examples) attached to sticks/canes; volunteers to be a man/boy, a woman/girl and others for the animals and birds

Ask someone to read Genesis 2:18–24, involving volunteers as follows:

The man/boy walks alone up to the front and as verse 18 is read the girl stands at the other side of the building at the front. As the reading continues give the pictures on the canes to other volunteers who walk towards the man/boy for him to correctly name them out loud. (Allow for extemporisation – with help from the congregation.) With all the animals and birds around him the boy falls into a sleep. Verse 22 is read and the girl joins him as he awakes!

Remind everyone that even with all these animals and birds around him, God knew the man still needed more and created the woman. His plan was for them to be joined in what we understand as marriage.

Alternate verses of Psalm 8 can be read by two people or by the whole church with everyone saying verses 1 and 9 together. This is available as a download (YearB. Proper22_1).

Bible talk

With: a hard copy relationship pyramid for everyone and/or a large pyramid, available as a download (YearB.Proper22_2) (a pyramid with five levels: from the bottom – people we see around but don't know the names of; people we sometimes do things with, eg in our class; our friends; people close to us; an empty level filled with the words 'marriage partner' at the appropriate time); pens and pencils; play dough – a small piece for everyone

Our Creator God knows everything about us and how we work best. This includes his care over our relationships. He created us to be in relationships. Genesis 2:18 clearly says it is not good for a man to be alone. Ask how people feel when they are alone. Emphasise the negative feelings and suggest that there is an alternative – being with others – but that this is not always easy to find. God provided a relationship for the man in the Genesis story.

Variety in relationships
Show the friendship pyramid and ask people in small groups to talk about the people they

know. Who fits into which group? Give each person a copy of an empty pyramid for them to write or draw people who fit each level except the top one. Encourage feedback or show an example of what your own pyramid looks like. Comment on the fact that there are fewer and fewer people as you go up the pyramid. Close family and friends are towards the top.

The man was lonely. Ask why the birds and animals were not the right partner for him. This could be done humorously thinking about the conversation the man might have with a lizard or if he tried to hug a parrot or go running with a tortoise.

The marriage relationship
He was still lonely. So God had to make a partner who would be perfect for him. When the man saw this partner, he knew straight away that she was just right! Point out the empty level. The relationship that we have that has the most effect on us is the marriage relationship, someone who is different but who complements us, someone who adds variety. In the pyramid, either write in or click the 'marriage partner' phrase in the top triangle.

Comment that this partnership fits into the triangle and there is no room for anyone else. So these two people have to leave out all other partnerships and friendships, as much as they might love and like the people lower down the pyramid. Read out Genesis 2:24. God did not intend that even close family members could fit into that triangle.

Point out that the man gave the woman her name and they became as one person,

sharing life together. Not even their families were that close to them. Briefly comment on some of the features of building a marriage relationship, as appropriate – such as couples affirming each other, speaking positively about one another, spending time together, booking time together in the diary which cannot be pushed out of the way by other more 'urgent' items, working at resolving conflict.

Comment too on the importance of respecting the marriage relationship of others.

Above all, remember what Jesus says in Mark 10:9. Where God has joined people together we should all be in the business of building that up.

Growing relationships
But of course, not everyone is in a marriage relationship. Talk about the wonderful things about family life. Acknowledge that relationships can go wrong and when a marriage or family relationship goes wrong, it is really awful for everyone involved, including the children, because of where it is in the pyramid.

All relationships, at any level of the pyramid, need working at if they are to develop. Ask for specific suggestions of how someone from the bottom level could engage with someone on the next level, such as discovering someone's name, talking with them, doing things with them. Then think about the fourth level. Ask what people are doing to get to know people in this level.

Emphasise how important it is to develop

close relationships with those who can share our hopes and fears. Challenge married people to think about whom in the next levels down they should be supporting in some way. Challenge everyone to think who they could get to know who will not be in the top of their pyramid but the next level down or who they might support in a marriage. Ask the children to think about their friendships, but being aware of child protection, make a comment about ensuring we are comfortable with friendships.

Family relationships

Remind everyone that families and relationships were God's great idea. He didn't want Adam to be alone. He recognised the variety of different personalities. Everyone who has ever been born is quite unique, which means that every relationship is quite unique. God creates families to be different and diverse too, so that our lives may enrich each other's.

God shaped the man from the soil. Give each person a piece of play dough and ask them to shape something that says how important relationships are to them. Suggest ideas such as two hands held together, a favourite toy or food that is shared, a ring or a special gift from someone who loves them. Encourage people to show their creation to those around them.

It would be appropriate to ask for some personal testimonies about how families can have fun times together but can also have special family celebrations that include others and are also acts of gratitude to God.

Prayers of confession

This is available as a PowerPoint download (YearB.Proper22_4).

Prayers of intercession

Ask two or more married couples to prepare prayers along the following lines:

- for marriages in your community, even naming couples who have been married in your church this year
- for Christian marriages, particularly all the marriages in your church family, that they will be protected and remain strong and that couples will look to God for strength, being wise in the use of their time
- for marriages and families where members do not all love God, that God's love will flow through those who do know him to those who do not yet
- that Christian marriage in your community would be a powerful model/example to other couples and that the joy of marriage would be evident
- for families where relationships are breaking down, that there will be those who offer support and do all that they can to strengthen the partnership and care for those who are hurting.

Ending the service

With: something to write with; a card with the following points, also available as a download (YearB.Proper22_3)

This week I need to work at my relationship with: (name)…
I will do this by…

My prayer is…

Encourage everyone to identify one relationship that they need to work on this week, at home, at school, at work.

Prepare a card for each person to complete and then pray a concluding prayer.

Alternatively, hold up the play dough models to thank God for what is precious in family life or relationships. End on a note of praise.

Helpful extras

Music and song ideas

Play Jack Johnson's 'Better together' as background music at **Beginning the service** or at the end or during the small group time in the **Bible talk**. In Beginning the service, 'Come on and celebrate'; 'Wake every heart and every tongue'; 'My heart will sing to you'.

Songs of gratitude to God, 'My heart will sing to you because of your great love' (Robin Mark); 'Say the name of love, Jesus, Jesus' (Graham Kendrick).

In the **Prayer of confession**, 'Turn our hearts' (Graham Kendrick).

Other background music to sing or play during a group or a reflective time at the end: 'You' (Tim Hughes); 'Giver of life'; 'When the tears fall' – helpful for those struggling with not being part of a family; 'You pour out grace' (Gareth Robinson).

Notes and comments

The theme of this service is marriage and, more widely, relationships in general. The marriage theme will probably be a sensitive issue for some in your fellowship and yet it cannot be ignored because it is so important. Be aware of anyone who is hurting because of broken relationships, their own or perhaps their children's, or those who would love to be married and are not, or those for whom marriage is a no-go subject. Your congregation may also include those who are living with a partner and have no intention of marrying.

Communicate something of God's best for us in creation, and at the same time the sadness that many experience as a result of the brokenness of the world, sin or personal disobedience. We have all made selfish decisions at some time or other – for some the implications and consequences of these decisions are much greater. Whatever the outcome, however bad things seem, nothing is beyond God's redeeming love (as we are reminded in John 1:1–13 and 1 John 1:9).

It would be appropriate to promote any families ministry or marriage courses you provide. For details of Scripture Union's *Survival skills for Christian parents* six-session online course, visit www.scriptureunion. org.uk/familieswithfaith. See also *Top Tips on Growing faith with families* (SU).

Online resources

All suggested downloads are available at www.scriptureunion.org.uk/light. Visit www.lightlive.org for additional activities for children, young people and adults.

Proper 23

READINGS: **Amos 5:6,7,10–15; Mark 10:17–31**
Psalm 90:12–17; Hebrews 4:12–16

Bible foundations

Aim: to appreciate the cost and benefit of following Jesus

The man in Mark 10 is like many Jewish people of his day. He respects Jesus and genuinely wants to know his opinion on religious matters, considering him to be a holy man and a teacher, despite his lack of formal qualifications. He is eager and respectful (v 17). Jesus suggests the expected categories of the Law (v 19) though ones which focus upon actions rather than attitudes of the heart (see the Ten Commandments in Exodus 20:1–17). The man passes the test, but when it comes to real devotion and sacrificial lifestyle, putting God before absolutely anything else, he is dismayed (v 22). Other things in life are apparently more important. Jesus' challenge is clearly too much for him and others like him, though not for the disciples (v 28). But they, like us, cannot get away from just how hard it is. God's people at the time of Amos demonstrate what a challenge it is to turn back to God and be just.

This leads to Hebrews 3 and 4 where the writer demonstrates that the word of God in the wilderness proved far too demanding for that generation of Israelites. It is a word which, as the citation of Psalm 95 demonstrates, is eternally relevant for God's people. God's Word is hugely penetrative (vs 12,13) and would lead to total despair were it not for God's provision of a great high priest who understands what it is like to struggle with weaknesses and sinfulness. This high priest has experienced that exposure to human life with all of its challenges. Not that he succumbed. But he understands with compassion.

The man in Mark 10 approaches Jesus with confidence in himself, only to be taught a real lesson concerning what is in his heart. The Christian approaches God's throne with much greater confidence because of what Jesus, the great high priest, has done – all a question of where such confidence is placed.

Beginning the service

With: small wrapped sweets (or chocolate) or larger sweets (or snack-size bars)

Arrange for those on the welcoming team to give a small sweet to everyone as they come in. Give no explanation or direction – simply smile. When you are ready to begin, ask who still has an uneaten sweet. Invite volunteers to show their evidence for this. In advance arrange for one or two others to step forward to say that they were not given one. See if any volunteers will give them theirs. (A few may!) Thank everyone and send them to sit down. Announce the first hymn/song and, just as the music starts, stop it and then present a large sweet or chocolate bar to any generous volunteers who gave their sweets away. Ask for a round of applause. If no one was generous, decide how you will proceed. Continue with the song, leaving this unexplained.

Bible reading

Amos 5:6,7,10−15 could be read with an urging voice or tone for verses 6 and 7, irritable voice for verses 10−13, and a weighty voice for verses 14 and 15.

Hebrews 4:12−16 forms the **Prayer of confession**.

Mark 10:17−31 can be read as a dramatised reading, as below from the CEV. This is also available as a download (YearB.Proper23_1).

Mark: As Jesus was walking down a road, a man ran up to him. He knelt down, and asked:

Rich man: Good teacher, what can I do to have eternal life?
Mark: Jesus replied:
Jesus: Why do you call me good? Only God is good. You know the commandments. 'Do not murder. Be faithful in marriage. Do not steal. Do not tell lies about others. Do not cheat. Respect your father and mother.'
Mark: The man answered:
Rich man: Teacher, I have obeyed all these commandments since I was a young man.
Mark: Jesus looked closely at the man. He liked him and said:
Jesus: There's one thing you still need to do. Go sell everything you own. Give the money to the poor, and you will have riches in heaven. Then come with me.
Mark: When the man heard Jesus say this, he went away gloomy and sad because he was very rich. Jesus looked around and said to his disciples:
Jesus: It's hard for rich people to get into God's kingdom!
Mark: The disciples were shocked to hear this. So Jesus told them again:
Jesus: It's terribly hard to get into God's kingdom! In fact, it's easier for a camel to go through the eye of a needle than for a rich person to get into God's kingdom.
Mark: Jesus' disciples were even more amazed. They asked each other:
Disciples: How can anyone ever be saved?
Mark: Jesus looked at them and said:
Jesus: There are some things that people cannot do, but God can do anything.
Mark: Peter replied:
Peter: Remember, we left everything to be your followers!
Mark: Jesus told him:
Jesus: You can be sure that anyone who gives up home or brothers or sisters or mother or father or children or land

for me and for the good news will be rewarded. In this world they will be given a hundred times as many houses and brothers and sisters and mothers and children and pieces of land, though they will also be mistreated. And in the world to come, they will have eternal life. But many who are now first will be last, and many who are now last will be first.

Mark 10:17–31 (CEV)

Bible talk

With: sweet jar with a narrow top (research and trial an appropriate-sized jar as a visual aid for the talk); small sweets or nuts; paper and pens

The tale of the monkey with the clenched fist

Use the following story of the greedy monkey to demonstrate the main point – the cost and the benefit of following Jesus. Freely embellish the story as you tell it. (Alternatively, you could show a film clip from the film *Winnie the Pooh* as he gets stuck in the rabbit hole. Those who have read the story will know that Pooh has to lose weight before being extricated from the hole – losing something to gain something else.)

The story is told of the monkey who was out one day looking for food and came across a dried up riverbed. As he walked along he saw there was a deep pit. He jumped down into it to investigate. In the side of the pit he spotted a small hole. He peered inside and could see something that looked good to eat. Perhaps they were nuts!

He slid his hand into the hole and grabbed

hold of what he had seen. It was nuts. Mmm! These were going to taste good. He held onto them tightly in his fist. Just then he heard the sound of rain and running water.

Oh dear! the monkey thought. *The river is starting to fill up again. I'd better be off!* But he had just got time to eat those nuts. He tried to pull his hand out, but it was stuck. That's strange – he'd put it inside easily enough! But now that the nuts were tightly grasped in his tight little fist he couldn't get his hand out.

Oh no! The water started to trickle down beside him into the deep pit! Well, he'd just pull his hand out and eat up those nuts and he'd be gone. He pulled and he pulled and he pulled. He even had his feet up on the wall pulling as hard as he could. The water was rising in the pit. Soon it would be up to his waist. What was he going to do?

Open up a discussion to speculate on the options. At the end clarify that the only safe option was to leave the nuts in the hole, release his hand and escape from the rising water. Use a narrow-necked jar with sweets or nuts inside and invite a volunteer to demonstrate the point of the story. You will probably need to pour the sweets out to give them as a reward once the point has been made!

Jesus' story of the rich man with the clenched fist

This story sheds light on the Bible reading, Mark 10:17–31. Explain that the rich man found it hard to give up his great wealth to gain eternal life. Jesus said it was terribly hard to get into God's kingdom; in fact he said it was easier for a camel to go through the eye of a needle than for a rich man to get into God's kingdom.

Remind everyone of the sweets they received as they came into church. Have an interactive conversation with your congregation, and remark upon the generosity of those who gave their sweets to those who had none and subsequently were rewarded. Refer back to what Jesus instructed the rich man to do in Mark 10:21b – 'Go, sell everything you have and give to the poor and you will have treasure in heaven. Then come, follow me.'

Refer to the Bible reading from Amos 5:6,7,10–15. The people of Judah were challenged to live as God's holy people by being honest and fair, choosing good not evil. That was the way to really live. It was the same sort of challenge!

Unclenching our fists for God

Ask for comments on how we can respond to this in our lives, to suggest ways of being generous and showing willingness to share. Expect differing responses from differing age groups. Then ask the congregation to remember the rest of what Jesus asked the rich man to do – 'Then come with me' – to walk with God, to follow Jesus. What might that mean to us?

Ask someone to share their own experience of giving something up to please God but discovering they received far more in return – not that this is always measured in material possessions. Invite everyone to quietly consider how they may turn these thoughts and suggestions into reality this week.

Prayer activity

With: pens and paper; a copy of the suggested words of response below, also available as a download (YearB.Proper23_2)

It would be appropriate in the light of the story of Jesus' conversation with the rich man to pray for those who live in poverty. Throughout the Bible God encourages his people to care for the poor and to act justly (for example, Deuteronomy 15:7–11; Psalm 140:12, Amos 5). Discuss different types of poverty we see around the world such as those who are jobless, earn very little, are homeless, are in debt, lack medical care, lack emotional care, are without hope, don't know Jesus' love.

Divide into small groups, giving each a subject to focus on from the list above. Provide each group with some visual images or headlines to inspire comments and insights. Allow four or five minutes for them to compose a short prayer completing the following two lines:

Father God, we pray...................................
....
Help them...
....

Each group nominates a person to read out their prayer or the group could speak together. Conclude with the following response:

Leader: Lord God, through the prophet Amos, you told your people how much you hated the way they abused the poor and cheated honest people. You challenged them to stop doing wrong.

All: Lord God, help us to stop doing wrong and start doing right.
May we see that justice is done!

Prayer of confession

Read Hebrews 4:12,13 followed by the congregational response:
Forgive us our sins.

Mighty God, nothing is hidden from you. We pause to acknowledge that we have thought and done many things which have displeased you. *(Pause)*
Forgive us our sins.

Mighty God, we have left undone many things we should have done and in particular we have held onto the material possessions that matter so much to us that we cannot let go of them. We have often not been generous to those in need. *(Pause)*
Forgive us our sins.

Read Hebrews 4:14–16
Mighty God, you understand our weaknesses. In our need for forgiveness we come to you and say:
Forgive us our sins. Amen.

Ending the service

Lord Jesus, you call us to follow you with all that we have and all that we are.
May we generously give out of our riches to those in need.
May we not hold onto what we think might bring us wealth or happiness.
May we trust you to provide us with all that we need.
Amen.

Helpful extras

Music and song ideas:
'Take my life'; 'Light of the world'; 'Into your hands, I commit again' (Reuben Morgan); 'All I once held dear'; 'Filled with compassion'; 'Jesus, all for Jesus'; 'Show me the way of the cross once again'; 'When I survey'.

The track 'Cold water' from Damien Rice's album *O* could be played either on its own or with some projected images of different types of poverty to link up the **Prayer activity** as inspiration before the writing of a group prayer.

Notes and comments

To make sure **Beginning the service** runs as planned, you should arrange for a 'plant' to give away their sweet.

Photographs and images to fit the 'Cold water' track can be downloaded from an Internet search from sites such as Make Poverty History, War on Want, World Vision, Christian Aid and Global Issues.

The **Prayer of confession** could be used to lead into a service of Holy Communion. The hymn 'When I survey' will also suit the reading and the celebration of Jesus' death and resurrection.

Online resources

All suggested downloads are available at www.scriptureunion.org.uk/light. Visit www.lightlive.org for additional activities for children, young people and adults. For your convenience the following activities are available as downloads: YearB.Proper23_3 Bible story for 5s and under; YearB.Proper23_4 Adult sermon.

Proper 24

READINGS: **Hebrews 5:1–10; Mark 10:35–45**
Isaiah 53:4–12; Psalm 91:9–16

Bible foundations

Aim: to learn to serve with Jesus, following his example

The request of James and John is preposterous (Mark 10:35,37). Had they simply not been listening (vs 32–34)? Had they learnt nothing from what Jesus had said or how he had lived? Very patiently Jesus asks them, almost ironically, what he could do for them. Even when they reflect on whether they could really keep pace with his standards, they exhibit a brainless sort of confidence nurtured by self-help purveyors of a good self-image (vs 38,39)!

Of course, as Jesus says later, they will follow him in his suffering as must all true disciples to a greater or lesser degree. No wonder the rest of the disciples, possibly out of jealousy, get annoyed with them (v 41). Jesus' leadership contrasts starkly with the way that the 'real' world (the Gentiles in this instance) operates – through bullying and being distant. Service is the hallmark of any leadership which deserves to be called 'like Jesus' or 'Christian'.

The writer to the Hebrews portrays Jesus as a great high priest. The normal pattern or expectation in the Old Testament is that the priest, as a fallible human being, should be able to adequately represent broken humanity to God. He had to sacrifice for his own sins before he could do anything about the sins of others (vs 1–5). He was specially appointed, as Christ was too, not as a fallible and sinful high priest, but as one who had shared human experience without succumbing to the sinfulness of human experience. Jesus experienced everything else and his 'perfection' is to be found in this. Throughout his life he chose obedience to the Father (vs 6–10) which included the ultimate challenge of facing death. Many consider verses 7 and 8 as a description of Gethsemane where Jesus passed the ultimate test, submitting to the will of his Father. This is the ultimate test of genuine Jesus-shaped leadership and status.

Beginning the service

With: two helpers who are members of the same family

As you welcome people, two helpers should disrupt proceedings by arguing very loudly over who should do a household task such as washing the car or tidying the kitchen. A range of reasons for not doing the job can be given, such as being too tired, being the eldest in the family or not being to blame for the mess. This needs to be rehearsed so that the argument does not run out of steam but remains very heated.

Interrupt the argument and invite the helpers to join the service because of the relevance of the topic. Explain to everyone that you're going to learn about being servants by following Jesus' example.

Bible reading

Use either the CEV or NIV translations for these readings.

With Mark 10:35–45 everyone can do simple actions that reflect the contrast between a desire for glory and power with a life of service. For verses 35–37 people stand proudly, for verses 38–40 they kneel and bow their heads, for verses 41–43 they stand proudly and for verses 43–45 kneel once more. Encourage those with limited mobility to raise their heads proudly and lower them humbly. Practise the moves before the reading, with someone at the front to demonstrate the actions.

Accompany Hebrews 5:1–10 with a simple mime with background music; see **Music**

and song ideas. This focuses on the role of the high priest and the sacrifice, for Jesus took on both roles.

(During verses 1 to 4 someone representing the high priest moves to the front holding a box or a plate to represent a sacrifice offering. He kneels with his back to the congregation and lifts the sacrifice above his head.)
Verses 1–4: Every high priest is appointed to help others by offering gifts and sacrifices to God because of their sins. A high priest has weaknesses of his own, and he feels sorry for foolish and sinful people. That is why he must offer sacrifices for his own sins and for the sins of others. But no one can have the honour of being a high priest simply by wanting to be one. Only God can choose a priest, and God is the one who chose Aaron.

(During verses 5 and 6 someone, representing Jesus, takes the place of the high priest. He kneels with his back to the congregation, empty-handed.)
Verses 5,6: That is how it was with Christ. He became a high priest, but not just because he wanted the honour of being one. It was God who told him, 'You are my Son, because today I have become your Father!'

In another place, God says, 'You are a priest forever just like Melchizedek.' God had the power to save Jesus from death.

(During verses 7 to 9, the figure of Jesus slowly stands with his back to the congregation and holds out his arms in the shape of a cross.)
Verses 7–9: And while Jesus was on earth, he begged God with loud crying and tears to save him. He truly worshipped God, and God listened to his prayers. Jesus is God's

own Son, but still he had to suffer before he could learn what it really means to obey God. Suffering made Jesus perfect, and now he can save for ever all who obey him. This is because God chose him to be a high priest like Melchizedek.

Bible talk

With: strips of cloth for everyone, approximately 70 cm long to be tied around people's heads (a cleaning cloth would be ideal, cut lengthways into four strips)

A servant not a celebrity
Distribute a strip of cloth to everyone. Ask them to tie it around their heads to represent a crown. It is very appealing to want to be seen as someone important, like a king or a celebrity, with everyone making a fuss of you.

Refer to the **Bible reading** from Mark 10. James and John wanted to have lots of glory and fuss and the best position in heaven, sitting next to Jesus. Later, Jesus pointed out that the local politicians and officials acted very arrogantly. A desire for fame, power and glory is nothing new. There is plenty of pressure in our society to want these things. The media nurtures this desire for celebrity by making it appear within the reach of ordinary people.

A servant gets dirty
Ask everyone to take off their crowns and use the cloth to do some cleaning and dusting. Jesus told his friends they had to live a different way. Quote Mark 10:43–45. Instead of being a celebrity, Jesus' followers should make it their goal to be servants or

slaves. He could tell his friends to do this, because that was what he also did. Refer to Mark 10:45. If anyone had the right to be a celebrity, the Son of Man did. Instead, he chose to be a servant. Emphasise that this command is still true for Jesus' friends today. Give some examples of being a servant which are pertinent to the congregation.

A servant suffers
Ask people to use the cloth to wipe away imaginary tears and to wipe sweat from their foreheads. Refer to the comments of the servants in the **Game** if you used this. Being a servant is not an easy thing to do. Hebrews 5:8 states that Jesus suffered as he lived as a human being and obeyed what the Father wanted him to do. He got sore feet and dirty hands, he was laughed at, criticised and threatened. Ultimately he was killed. This suffering had a purpose; it made him perfect for the job of saving all human beings. So we should not be surprised that when we put ourselves last and become a servant we might also suffer. The examples you give here will depend on previous examples but could include: going somewhere your little brother wants to go, letting someone else get all the praise, giving up a career or being overlooked for promotion, getting very dirty, feeling very bored. Or it might be something much more serious. Our suffering has a purpose although we may not understand it, but it does mirror God's love to people and shows them what God is really like.

A servant looks out for others
Conclude by asking people to tie the cloth around their wrists to remind them that to be servants they need to help each other. In

Mark 10:38, Jesus' response to James' and John's request for the best seat in the house was to ask if they were able to be suffering servants like he was. Encourage people to ask this simple question when they see the cloth on their wrist: Am I willing to be a servant like Jesus? James and John said 'Yes' without knowing what it would involve. Ask if people are also willing to say 'Yes', whatever that involves – and maybe we have a better idea than James and John did!

Prayer activity

With: a variety of prayer stations set around the church, each displaying pictures, words and symbols to help people focus on the theme of the service

Show relevant groups of people who serve; church leaders, carers, volunteers, parents, world leaders, teachers and the military. Include a station labelled 'People who help me'. At each station place a bowl, large teardrop shapes and something to write with.

Hebrews 5 reminds us that Jesus prayed with tears. This prayer activity uses the symbol of a teardrop to encourage people to pray for things that concern them. Allow time and space for people to visit the prayer stations that interest them most, either as individuals or as family groups. They can write the name of a person, a sentence or a full prayer, or simply draw a picture on a teardrop to place in the bowl at the prayer station.

Draw the activity together by bringing the bowls of teardrops to the front and laying them on the altar or at another suitable point. Say a simple prayer such as, 'Thank you,

Father, that you hear all our prayers. Amen.'

Prayer of confession

With: a copy of the prayer below, also available as a download (YearB.Proper24_1) projected onto a screen or printed in the service sheet; a small group of people of mixed ages and backgrounds to read out the group statement

Group: For the times we want to be the centre of attention –
All: We are sorry, Father God, when we don't act like servants.
Group: For the times we only think about ourselves –
All: We are sorry, Father God, when we don't act like servants.
Group: For the times we complain about helping others –
All: We are sorry, Father God, when we don't act like servants.
Group: For the times we can't be bothered to help others –
All: We are sorry, Father God, when we don't act like servants.
Group: Thank you that you can forgive us, because as a servant, you died on the cross.
All: Amen.

Ending the service

With: the two helpers from **Beginning the service**; a list of jobs that need doing projected on a screen

Remind the two helpers about their previous argument. Ask if they've learnt anything useful from today's service. They should give a brief summary of the message of the service:

Jesus acted like a servant, even though it wasn't easy. He did it because he loved us. If we want to follow Jesus, we should also be willing to be servants too. They should then show willing to do the job(s) they were arguing about.

Show the possible list of jobs so that everyone in the congregation can do an act of service for someone else as the church service concludes. You could include: getting someone a drink, helping to tidy away music equipment, collecting books, offering a lift home, distributing flowers, offering to do something later in the week. Specific requests for help could be incorporated into this time. To make this feel part of the service, play music in the background (see **Music and song ideas**).

Helpful extras

Music and song ideas
There are several opportunities for background music to enhance the environment: gentle music for the **Bible reading** from Hebrews 5 and **Prayer activity**, clowning music such as 'The Entertainer' for the **Game** and an upbeat tune played over the sound system for **Ending the service**.

Songs to express gratitude for Christ's servanthood and sacrifice, and expressing a commitment to following his example of servanthood: 'From heaven you came (Servant King)'; 'You laid aside your majesty'; 'Be thou my vision'; 'I will be a living sacrifice'; 'I will offer up my life'.

Game
A light-hearted game providing insights into the challenges of serving others is available as a download (YearB.Proper24_2).

Notes and comments

If this is part of a Eucharist service, consider distributing the bread and wine so that people serve their neighbour. Display a simple blessing on the screen so that people can say it if their neighbour is not taking Communion.

Before the service, find out from younger members of the congregation who are the current top celebrities and which reality television shows they are watching. Use these in the **Bible talk**.

Use personal testimony for examples of people who have benefited from another person's service. The emphasis needs to be on the fruits of the service and how it pointed the person to God. Alternatively mention the testimony of Adrian Plass who writes of how he remembers his mother going out every evening at 9.30 to push their elderly neighbour up the stairs to bed because she had bad knees. She did this physically demanding and awkward task year after year, and it shouted to him of God's compassion and humility (*Jesus – Safe, Tender, Extreme* by Adrian Plass, p153).

Online resources
All suggested downloads are available at www.scriptureunion.org.uk/light. Visit www.lightlive.org for additional activities for children, young people and adults.

Proper 25

READINGS: **Hebrews 7:23–28; Mark 10:46–52**
Jeremiah 31:7–9; Psalm 126

Bible foundations

Aim: to celebrate that Jesus is the ideal person to save us

Signs point to something – perhaps the path you must follow to get where you
need to be, or to a person or place you're unsure about. In the Bible, miracles are
spoken of as signs. (Indeed that is what the Gospel of John calls them throughout.)
Bartimaeus is a kind of double sign. Despite his blindness he is able to identify
Jesus as the Son of David (Mark 10:47) and though others had previously failed
properly to understand who Jesus was, they rebuke him and try to put him back in
his place (v 48). Bartimaeus, however, points to the true identity of Jesus and knows
exactly what Jesus, and only Jesus, can do for him (v 51). A blind man points the way
forward. Bartimaeus is also a sign in that he shows symbolically how Jesus' true
identity is being progressively defined and made clear as the story evolves. Blindness
gives way to sight.

The book of Hebrews opens up similar windows of understanding, casting light
upon how Jesus is far greater than angels (ch 1), how he fulfils all the expectations
of Israel (chs 3,4), is the high priest (ch 5), fulfils the covenant (ch 8) and the
demands of the sacrificial system (chs 9,10), and so on. In chapter 7 the writer
elucidates how even the mysterious priesthood of Melchizedek (see Genesis 14)
points to certain features of Jesus' identity and ministry. The death of Melchizedek
is never recorded and Jesus, in a somewhat similar way, lives now for ever (v 24)
and performs the duties of a priesthood which will never pass away (vs 25–27).
The permanence includes salvation and intercession. His qualities match and
exceed those of Melchizedek in purity, offering and essential status. In a strange way
the mysterious Melchizedek, to whom even Abraham paid respect, acts as a sign
pointing to his greater successor.

Beginning the service

With: materials to make a flag (straws and rectangles of card, sticky tape, colour pencils); ready-made flags for latecomers

Lay out the flag-making materials on tables. As people arrive, invite them to make a flag for use throughout the service. When the service begins, explain that at points in the service everyone will need to wave their flags. The service is a celebration because Jesus is able to help us. Therefore ask everyone to wave their flags and cheer. Sing a simple and lively praise song such as 'Clap your hands' (see **Music and song ideas**).

Bible reading

Read Mark 10:46–52 and ask people to wave their flags and shout 'Help!' after appropriate verses (47, 48, 51), so they can engage with Bartimaeus' desire to be helped by Jesus. Someone can stand at the front to indicate when everyone should join in. A version of the reading with appropriate directions is available as a download (YearB.Proper25_1).

Bible retelling

With: approximately six actors (only two of whom have speaking roles); chairs and clipboards for each angel (scripts can be attached to the clipboards, reducing the need to memorise lines)

The drama *The new way* clarifies the message of Hebrews 7:23–28 by giving the congregation a chance to eavesdrop on an imaginary meeting of angels held on Easter Day. The script is also available as a download (YearB.Proper25_2).

The new way
(General air of excitement as angels bring on their chairs and clipboards. They wait for the Chief Angel, chatting to each other.)

Chief Angel: Good morning, angels. Thank you for coming along to this special briefing.
Minor Angel: *(Raises a hand.)* Is it true, Chief Angel?
Chief Angel: Yes, it is true! Jesus did indeed die. But now he is very much alive and was last spotted strolling around the garden. *(Big cheer.)* So this means we're entering a new stage in the plan called 'The new way'. It's all on the briefing sheet. I want to focus on the main points. *(Everyone looks down to study their sheets of paper.)* People continue to mess up and hurt God. *(Everyone shakes their heads.)* 'The old way' to say sorry was for the high priest to offer sacrifices on behalf of the people. *(Everyone nods.)* But that had its problems, didn't it? *(Everyone nods.)* So high priests and animal sacrifices are out. *(Everyone pauses.)* Jesus is in! *(Angels look confused.)*
Minor Angel: *(Raises a hand.)* I don't understand.
Chief Angel: Jesus is 'The new way'. He became a human and lived a perfect life. Did nothing wrong at all. Nothing! Not an insy-winsy, teeny-weeny, itsy-bitsy thing wrong. *(Angels nod.)* He agreed to be killed even though he did not deserve it. *(Angels nod.)* So, that makes him a perfect sacrifice.
Minor Angel: *(Raises a hand and interrupts.)* … And so when people want to say sorry for what they've done, there's no need to find a high priest and kill an animal. Jesus has done the job already.
Chief Angel: Exactly! And if you check your

notes you'll see there's more. *(Everyone looks at their notes.)* Jesus is now acting as these people's representative.

Minor Angel: *(Raises a hand.)* I don't understand.

Chief Angel: When people want to talk to God, Jesus will speak up on their behalf. He'll remind the Father about his sacrifice and ask him to help them.

Minor Angel: *(Raises a hand.)* God must really love these guys!

Chief Angel: He does!

Bible talk

With: a large wall made out of cardboard boxes; two large marker pens; a bowl of sweet-smelling flowers (or something that speaks of beauty, freshness and hope) hidden behind the wall; two helpers to write on the wall and reassemble it when it is knocked down

The wall that separates

Ask everyone to try to lick their elbow. It's impossible! Some things people can do for themselves, but some things are just impossible. One of those things is to break the barrier that exists between us and God. Hebrews 7 explains how Jesus does that for us.

Point to the large wall and explain that people build a wall between them and God by what they say, do and think. Hebrews 7 calls these things 'sin'. Ask people of all ages to give examples of sins which the helpers can write on the wall. This wall is a barrier to experiencing God's love and blessing. His blessings are currently out of sight!

The wall that gets rebuilt

Appoint one child to be a high priest to try to knock down the wall. Once one box is knocked off, the two helpers immediately put it back again. Refer to Hebrews 7 and explain that the job of the high priest was to offer sacrifices for his and other people's sins. This was a way of saying sorry and it helped knock down the wall. However, because these people were not perfect and because people continued to sin, they had to keep on offering sacrifices day after day. Nothing they could do kept the wall down permanently. Nowadays we might try to break down the wall by doing good things, giving away money, spending time supporting the church community, making a sacrifice for someone. But just like the high priest, we cannot break down the wall; we're not perfect and the wall will be built up again. We cannot earn God's acceptance.

The wall that is permanently destroyed

Only Jesus is able to destroy the wall for ever. Invite another member of the congregation to knock down the wall. Explain that this person represents Jesus. They break the wall down without being impeded and then stand in the space where the wall was. This time the wall should not be rebuilt. Jesus was able to break down the wall completely and permanently because of who he was and what he did. Ask people to look through Hebrews 7:23–28 to find out what it tells us about Jesus. You could put it on the screen if that will help more people engage with the verses. This is available as a download (YearB.Proper25_3). Answers include: he lives forever (v 24), people come to God through him (v 25), he speaks on our behalf (v 25), he is holy, perfect and set apart (v 26), he offered himself as a sacrifice (v 27), and he was appointed to do the job (v 28). This means that although we cannot save ourselves, Jesus is able to do that.

People could cheer and wave their flags at this point.
Instead of trying to break down the wall and earn God's acceptance we need to do what Bartimaeus did. Refer to Mark 10:47 and 48 when Bartimaeus cried out, 'Have pity on me!' He knew he did not deserve Jesus' help, but he really needed it and so he asked for it. Rather than trying to force God to help us, it is better to simply tell him what we need and trust that Jesus is making sure the message gets through. This is faith.

Passing through the wall
Ask if anyone would like to go through the wall to see what is on the other side. (Hopefully at least one person will put their hand up.) Invite the person representing Jesus to get a few of the volunteers to lead through to the other side of the wall. Hebrews 7:25 states that we approach God through Jesus.

A bowl of fresh flowers should be waiting on the other side to represent God's blessings. You might find you get more volunteers to come through the wall once they realise there is a gift waiting for them.

Conclude by reiterating that Jesus was the only person who could save us; neither the high priest nor our own selves can do it. That's what we are celebrating this service. 'Jesus, we celebrate your victory' would be a good song to flow from the **Bible talk**.

Prayer activity
With: a copy of the concluding prayer projected on screen or as hard copy, also available as a download (YearB.Proper25_4)

Remind people that when we pray to God, Jesus speaks on our behalf. So we don't need to worry about saying the right words or perfect sentences to impress God.

Invite everyone to simultaneously shout out a word or phrase that reflects what they want to say to God on the following four topics. These topics, inspired by today's Bible verses, reflect the truth that God is able to help in matters big and small: someone who is ill, a church leader, a place in the world where people need help, something we need help with. Allow time for people to decide what they want to say on each topic. Give children all the support they need. Ensure everyone shouts simultaneously by counting to three, then make a gesture to show when to shout and when to end.

Conclude by saying together the following prayer of thanks:
Thank you, God, that you hear our prayers.
Thank you, God, that you can help us.
Thank you, God, that you love us. Amen.

Ending the service
With: the flags made at **Beginning the service**

As the theme of the service is celebration, choose a familiar song of praise to sing with joy. Encourage the waving of flags and the use of instruments (see **Music and song ideas**).

Conclude with a prayer from your regular liturgy or read Psalm 126:3 aloud. As a final act of celebration, give three cheers for Jesus. Encourage everyone to wave their flags as they do this.

Helpful extras

Music and song ideas

Julia Plaut's song 'Clap your hands' involves simple actions and the repetition of the phrase 'God is good'. It is accessible for all ages for **Beginning the service**. Consider processing around the church as you sing it. The track is available on the CD *Thank You God for Snails*, with both a backing track and a full version.

The use of various percussion instruments during singing and at other points in the service will create a celebratory upbeat atmosphere. During the **Bible talk**, add some sound effects when the wall is being destroyed, such as cymbals clashing. During the **Statement of faith**, set the pace with an egg shaker, cow bell or bass drum.

Celebratory hymns and songs include: 'Thank you for saving me'; 'O happy day'; 'I will sing the wondrous story'; 'In Christ alone'; 'Thank you, Jesus, thank you, Jesus'; 'Jesus, we celebrate your victory'. These can be played with a fast, swinging tempo. Consider distributing kazoos, whistles and other 'party' instruments for use during one or two of the songs to enhance the celebratory feel.

Statement of faith

Use percussion instruments and the words displayed on a screen or printed in the service sheet, available as a download (Year B. Proper 25_5). The upbeat chant is based on

Hebrews 7. The instruments set the rhythm and pace of the response, and encourage a confident shout. Repeat it a few times, or process around the church shouting it.

Notes and comments

This theme lends itself to the use of personal testimony. Ask someone to explain the difference it has made to them, knowing that the barrier between them and God has been destroyed. If this is a baptism service it might be appropriate for this testimony to be given by the person being baptised or one of their supporters.

If the service involves the Eucharist, serve the bread and wine in such a position that people can see the collapsed wall. Invite them to focus on the image as they receive Communion or the blessing. Remind people as the bread is broken and the wine is offered that Jesus is both the high priest and the sacrifice.

If your church uses large flags or ribbons as part of worship, incorporate these at the flag-waving and processional opportunities.

This Sunday is often celebrated as Bible Sunday, see the following service outline. For additional resources visit www.biblesociety.org.uk or www.scriptureunion.org.uk.

Online resources

All suggested downloads are available at www.scriptureunion.org.uk/light. Visit www.lightlive.org for additional activities for children, young people and adults.

Bible Sunday

READINGS: **2 Timothy 3:14 – 4:5; John 5:36b–47**
                 Isaiah 55:1–11; Psalm 19:7–14

Bible foundations

Aim: to discover God speaks to his people, longing for them to respond

The Bible is God's book, his Word written for us – and Jesus is that word made flesh (John 1:14). God reveals himself in amazing and varied ways. Yet, despite all that, we sometimes doubt that God wants to speak with us.

It is far more frequent for teaching on prayer to be about speaking to God, rather than listening to him, as though the conversation is a one-way flow of information, requests, praise and pleas. These Bible passages show that God's book was not written for that reason. He expects us to meet him through it and for that encounter to change us. He expects obedience that flows from love and relationship, not empty legalism. We need to consider the biblical models of meditating on the Word, learning from a 'pre-literate' age when people memorised Scripture because they could not read it.

Psalm 19 reveals the joy and delight that come from knowing and obeying the law. Paul urged Timothy to keep on living by God's message, as seen in the Scriptures, and sharing it, although the costs may be high. Isaiah declared God's overflowing generous invitation to the thirsty.

Lest we grow complacent, however, Jesus himself gave a warning. He spoke in John 5 to the Jews who opposed his work (v 16) as they considered him a law breaker. These same Jews tried their hardest to follow the minutiae of the Law, believing that the very study of the Law would bring them life. They had lost sight of the big picture. Concentration on the content of the Law meant they forgot the purpose of the Law. So when God in the flesh was in front of them, fulfilling prophecies and doing 'the work' of God (which the Greek makes obvious), they just did not see it. On this Bible Sunday, may we all keep our eyes and ears open to receive God's invitation, in familiar and unfamiliar ways, and respond to his message.

Beginning the service

With: people of all ages primed to interrupt the service leader; a letter; a mobile phone; a 'protest' style banner

The service leader attempts to welcome people (following the usual practice) and introduces the theme. However, in rapid succession, the leader is interrupted by members of the congregation, such as a teenager using their mobile phone with the ring tone set to 'loud' which is then allowed to ring long enough for everyone to hear, followed by a loud one-way conversation; a child bringing a letter or note to the leader; an adult marching to the front with a protest banner saying: I want to talk to you. Eventually the leader finishes explaining that today's theme is finding out just how much God wants to communicate with us and longs for us to respond.

Bible reading

Isaiah 55:1–11 is a dramatic passage and would benefit from being read by at least two people, who pause after each phrase to let it sink in. For maximum effect this should be practised, exploring what amplification to use and whether to have roving microphones or not.

2 Timothy 3:14 – 4:5 can be read interactively with 'Paul', sitting at a table writing the letter, and 'Timothy' commenting on what Paul has written. A script is below. You could show Paul's letter on a screen – available as a download (YearB.BibleSun_1).

> Paul: Keep on being faithful to what you were taught and to what you believed.

After all, you know who taught you these things.

Tim: Yes, dear old Gran and Mum too. I suppose Paul just explained how it all tied in with Jesus… how he brought things to completion.

Paul: Since childhood, you have known the Holy Scriptures that are able to make you wise enough to have faith in Christ Jesus and be saved.

Tim: Umm. It would have taken longer to believe in Jesus if I hadn't known all those prophecies about the Messiah.

Paul: Everything in the Scriptures is God's Word. All of it is useful for teaching and helping people and for correcting them and showing them how to live.

Tim: Just because it shows us, it doesn't always make it easy!

Paul: The Scriptures train God's servants to do all kinds of good deeds.

Tim: Exactly my point! We have to train hard to do what Scripture says, especially when it comes to loving people who hate us.

Paul: When Christ Jesus comes as king, he will be the judge of everyone, whether they are living or dead.

Tim: That's going to come as a shock for some of them, I expect.

Paul: So with God and Christ as witnesses, I command you to preach God's message. Do it willingly, even if it isn't the popular thing to do. You must correct people and point out their sins. But also cheer them up, and when you instruct them, always be patient.

Tim: That's easier said than done – no one likes being put right, but I guess if it saves them from punishment, it's worth being a bit unpopular. Hopefully, though, if I cheer them up too they might like me…

Paul: The time is coming when people

won't listen to good teaching. Instead, they will look for teachers who will please them by telling them only what they are itching to hear.

Tim: Surely no one would turn down God's free offer just so they can carry on choosing bad things?

Paul: They will turn from the truth and eagerly listen to senseless stories.

Tim: But that is a ridiculous choice!

Paul: But you must stay calm and be willing to suffer. You must work hard to tell the good news and to do your job well.

Tim: Be willing to suffer, that doesn't sound fun… but maybe that's how it will be if I carry on following Jesus…

(2 Timothy 3:14 – 4:5 CEV, with comments from Timothy)

Bible talk

With: the mobile phone, letter and banner from **Beginning the service**; pictures of angels, Moses and the burning bush, a finger writing on a wall (Belshazzar), a donkey (Balaam), a person asleep (such as Jacob or Joseph), available as a PowerPoint download (YearB.BibleSun_2); a radio with a manual tuner detuned from any stations

Ask how people communicate with each other – prompt with objects from **Beginning the service** if needed. Explain that we communicate with each other in many ways, tailoring the method we use to both the audience and the contents – a love-struck man might hire an acrobatic plane to sky-write 'Will you marry me?' for his girlfriend but will probably use a different means of telling the plumber, 'My drain is blocked!'

How and what God communicated

God tailors his means of communication to the receiver and the message. Think who God spoke to in the following ways – show the pictures and ask people to identify who 'heard' God that way (angelic messengers, Moses, Belshazzar, Balaam, numerous people in dreams). This could be done as a mini-quiz before the **Bible talk**. God chooses to use means that individuals will recognise.

In Isaiah 55:1–11, Isaiah tells us of the wideness of God's call, inviting all who are thirsty. Remind people of some of the great statements of invitation in those verses, such as coming close to drink from him; to come to him to live; to turn to him and to find him; to come close to him; to be forgiven. You could ask people to look up these verses in the Bibles in the pews and contribute their observations.

Responding to God's communication

But not all people hear the invitation. At this point you could play or refer to the **Game**, seeing how messages can be misheard. Some people are 'tuned in' to the wrong channel. Turn on the radio and ask how it can become a proper 'receiver'. Invite someone from the congregation to come and tune it in.

In 2 Timothy 3:14 – 4:5 Paul encourages Timothy to correct people when they are detuned – or listening to the wrong station! Jesus warns that some people are so busy analysing the signal they miss the message – and miss the invitation.

Hearing a message clearly is like accepting an invitation to a party and putting it in your diary. But once an invitation has been accepted, you have to prepare for the party. Talk about the fun of getting changed for a party, buying a present and so on. It is not enough to read the invitation, which is what the Jews did in the Gospel reading when they stuck rigidly to the rules and regulations which they had studied so carefully. Receiving an invitation must lead to a change in behaviour. God wants us to respond to him.

Communicating the communication

Finally it is not even enough to hear clearly and act upon the invitation to come to God. God's people also need to pass on the invitation, which is what Paul urges Timothy to do, to preach God's message, doing it willingly, even if it isn't the popular thing to do (4:2). God is keener to communicate with us than we are to hear from him. It is important that we pay attention to his words.

So are you listening?
Are you responding?
Who can you share God's message with this week?

Prayer activity

With: writing implements, small pieces of card (two each)

Invite people to think about whom they could share God's invitation with this week – in words, by offering to pray, by getting to know them better. Ask them to choose one person and write their name, or draw it, on both pieces of card. One card should go in their pocket or in a place that will remind them of what they plan to do. The other should be collected (in the same or separate collection as any offerings) and brought

to the front. As this happens, each person should ask God to already be at work, talking to that person, so they are ready to hear what he is saying.

Prayer of confession

Mighty God,
You delight in making yourself known.
We don't always delight in your invitation.
Sometimes we don't read your Word or think about you for days or weeks at a time.
We are sorry, and want to take delight in you as the Bible writers did.
We are thirsty and you invite us to drink your living water.
Forgive us our forgetfulness.
Forgive us for the times when we are not listening.
Forgive us for the times when we mishear you.
Help us to hear your voice and respond.
Amen.

Assure people that God will forgive them.

Ending the service

With: pictures from the **Bible talk**

Scroll through the pictures and remind everyone just what lengths God has always gone to in order to get his message across. This is because he loves us so much he doesn't want anyone to miss his invitation to come to him, to find him near. Suggest that we have a role to play in getting that message across to some people and will only be able to do that if we delight in God's Word.

Close with a traditional blessing from your liturgy book or the Bible, thanking God that he communicates with us, wanting us to listen and respond.

Helpful extras

Music and song ideas
Traditional songs or hymns might include 'Thou whose almighty word'; 'Tell me the stories of Jesus'; 'Thy hand O God has guided'; 'I heard the voice of Jesus say'. More modern songs might include 'Call to me'; 'Thy word is a lamp unto my feet'.

As people think about those with whom they might share God's invitation during the week, play some quiet instrumental music – worship music or a classical piece.

Game
Devise a game whereby people try to communicate a message but it gets misheard or distorted, for example with background noise, or ask people to act out a message but their lower bodies are covered up by a long sheet so those watching will have difficulty understanding it.

Statement of faith
This is available as a download (YearB. BibleSun_3).

Notes and comments

Bible Sunday is a good time to explore how God uses many ways to speak to people and offers a perfect opportunity for asking people to share their experience of hearing God's voice and responding to his invitation – through the Bible, conscience, dreams, a sense of peace, circumstances, a friend. Visit the Scripture Union website for more information on Bible Sunday.

For parade services, it might be appropriate to interview the leader or some members of the organisations to ask if they have special means of communicating (for example, throughout the Girl Guides an open hand raised into the air means stop talking, stand still and listen). If there are deaf or blind church members, ask them about Sign Language or Braille and how they access the Bible message.

In both a baptism and Communion service, remind the congregation that God uses signs and symbols to speak to us; this includes the rainbow as a sign of his promise, bread and wine as symbols or signs of Jesus' sacrifice for us and our union with Jesus in both death and new life in baptism. In churches where liturgical colours are used, this may be an appropriate time to remind everyone of the symbolism of the colours.

For churches with an emphasis on the use of spiritual gifts corporately or individually, you could identify gifts that help us discern the voice of God and how these fit with the message we receive from the Bible (which is our primary means for testing all the other messages we believe to come from God).

Online resources
All suggested downloads are available at www.scriptureunion.org.uk/light. Visit www.lightlive.org for additional activities for children, young people and adults. For your convenience the following activity is available as a download: YearB. BibleSun_4 Song for 5s and under.

All Saints' Day

READINGS: **Revelation 21:1–6a; John 11:32–44**
Isaiah 25:6–9; Psalm 24:1–6

Bible foundations

Aim: to celebrate the new life that Jesus gives

The Bible always presents God as the gracious, generous, loving Creator and sustainer of the entire universe. He is the Giver of Life in every understanding of the word. He created all life in the first place, and Psalm 24 clearly expects those who acknowledge God as the giver of all life to keep their hands clean and their hearts pure if they truly want to worship. The prophets were very conscious of the sin of God's people and other nations, often living life without much reference to the life that God gives. They looked forward to the day when God would reveal himself fully (remove the veil, as Isaiah puts it) and the whole order of creation be put right again.

We live in a time where the kingdom of God is breaking into the physical world, shown manifestly by the raising of Lazarus from death. Jesus, who had restricted himself to the first century, and suffered its limitations, engaged fully as a man of his time. But remarkably, the God who made time then brought new life to a very human family situation. There was no more crying with sadness in Bethany on that day. Jesus used this incident to point to the bigger picture – he is the one who offers people life into eternity. We still look forward to the time when God's reign is complete. John and Isaiah both talk about 'the wiping of tears from people's eyes'. We will only experience a truly full life with God when we are physically with him all the time, which will be when both the heavens and earth are restored. In the meantime, we can live the 'life to the full' that Jesus came to give us if we closely follow him.

Moving between past, present and future during this service will give people of all ages some insights into the meaning of All Saints' Day.

Beginning the service

Interview a family with a baby, or a child who has got a puppy or kitten. Where available, show suitable images of babies, puppies or kittens. Follow this up by interviewing someone who has come to faith or become a Christian recently.

Choose your questions carefully! They may include things like; what signs were there that new life was coming? What planning did you have to do? What difference does having a 'xxx' make? How did you feel when you first saw the 'xxx'? Ask the 'new believer' what drew them to Christianity. What preparation did they have to do? How did they feel after they had made a profession of faith?

Bible reading

John 11:32–44 lends itself to an interactive telling as below, including using sound effects such as wailing and a drum roll as Lazarus emerges. This is also available as a download (YearB.AllSaints_1). You will need to tell the story leading up to verse 32 in your own words.

Narrator: Mary went to where Jesus was. Then as soon as she saw him, she knelt at his feet and said:
Mary: Lord, if you had been here, my brother would not have died.
Narrator: When Jesus saw that Mary and the people with her were crying, he was terribly upset and asked:
Jesus: Where have you put his body?
Crowd: Lord, come and you will see.
Narrator: Jesus started crying, and the people said:
Crowd: See how much he loved Lazarus.

Narrator: Some of the crowd said:
Crowd: He gives sight to the blind. Why couldn't he have kept Lazarus from dying?
Narrator: Jesus was still terribly upset. So he went to the tomb, which was a cave with a stone rolled against the entrance. Then he told the people to roll the stone away. But Martha said:
Martha: Lord, you know that Lazarus has been dead four days, and there will be a bad smell.
Jesus: Didn't I tell you that if you had faith, you would see the glory of God?
Narrator: After the stone had been rolled aside, Jesus looked up toward heaven and prayed:
Jesus: Father, I thank you for answering my prayer. I know that you always answer my prayers. But I said this, so that the people here would believe that you sent me.
Narrator: When Jesus had finished praying, he shouted:
Jesus: Lazarus, come out!
Narrator: The man who had been dead came out. His hands and feet were wrapped with strips of burial cloth, and a cloth covered his face. Jesus then told the people:
Jesus: Untie him and let him go.

John 11:32–44 (CEV)

Revelation 21:1–6a is very dramatic. Verses 3 and 4 can be effectively presented using hand or body signs, devised by all ages. This aids memory and comprehension. This will take up to five minutes, but is worth doing and can be referred to in the **Bible talk** and **Ending the service**. (One child presented God making his home with his people by taking off outdoor shoes and putting on slippers!)

Bible talk

With: a giant timeline marked PAST, PRESENT and FUTURE with space above to write; marker pens; song words of an old hymn/song

Past

Ask several people, of all ages, about their earliest memories. You may need to prime them in advance. Write their memories above the PAST part of the timeline. Comment that we all had a beginning, nine months (more or less) before we were born, after the point when we were 'made'. God, the Creator, watched over our development and has been watching over us ever since.

Read Psalm 24:1 and 2 and comment that God has created a wonderful world and it all belongs to him, including the people. Down through the ages people have rejoiced in the fact that they belong to God who blesses them. This has led them to worship him. Psalm 24 is a song of worship which people sang as they went to the Temple to worship God.

At this point, pause to sing an old song, one which people have sung in the past, either a psalm or a song from a past century. Acknowledge that people as saints have been worshipping God for years and years and we can join with them.

Present

Turn to the timeline and ask what features of life we would think are typical of our present day. This could include contemporary issues in the news, current trends or technological developments. Write these above PRESENT on the timeline. Comment that Jesus, who was around at the beginning of time, came as God into this world. He limited himself to the first century. Ask what features there would have been in the world he lived in – for example (and stress the first two) slow transport, limited medicine, the Roman authorities, strong family identity. Write these above PRESENT. This was the background to his world when he heard the news about the sickness of his friend Lazarus in the **Bible reading**.

Ask the following questions to ensure that people know the story in John 11. You may need to ask people to look up in the Bible the details in the verses outside of the actual reading.

What did Jesus say when he heard about Lazarus' sickness? (vs 3–7 – it might not have been a disease which would kill people these days)
How long had Lazarus been dead by the time Jesus arrived? (v 17 – evidence of slow transport)
How did Jesus show that he had ordinary relationships with people?
What evidence is there, from what Jesus said and did, that he had come as God into the present?

He brought new physical life to Lazarus. But Jesus had also brought newness to the quality of life for those alive who knew and loved him then. He healed the sick, he forgave those who recognised they were sinners and he brought hope to those without hope. He changed people's lives for ever.

But Lazarus and his sisters were eventually to

die and they became part of the past. Jesus of course also died but he came alive again. He is part of the past, the present and the future – the alpha and the omega, the beginning and the end. He is alive for us now in the present but he will also be there in the future.

Future
Ask what you should write above FUTURE on the timeline and then record the suggestions. Much of this will be speculative since we do not really know much for certain. John, who was a prisoner on the island of Patmos, had a vision of what heaven would be like, a mixture of a fabulous city and a splendid wedding. If you created the signs for Revelation 21:3 and 4 in the **Bible reading**, go over these again. Read verses 5 and 6a. We cannot really imagine what heaven will be like, but we do know that God will make his home with his people. Everyone who has ever loved God, the saints, will be there – past, present and future.

But right now, we have to live in the present, experiencing the new life that Jesus brings, knowing that the best is yet to come. The **Prayer of confession** naturally follows on from this.

Prayer of confession

With: a mini-timeline for each person, with PAST, PRESENT and FUTURE marked on the line, and written above FUTURE, 'God has made his home with us'; pens and pencils

Give out the mini-timelines and ask each person to think of something in the past where they have not lived to please God, not reflecting the new life God has given to

his people. They can write or draw it above PAST.

Above PRESENT, everyone writes or draws something in which they want to see more of God's new life.

In silence, allow people to speak to God and then declare that God forgives those who ask him to, and comes to live with them in a new way. End with the final phrase: Come and make your home with us, everlasting God, the beginning and the end.

Prayers of intercession

With: people of different ages leading each section with the following congregational response: Bring them new life, we pray.

L: Lord, we remember everyone who is sad because a friend or relative has died. Comfort them and give them strength.
C: Bring them new life we pray.
L: Jesus, we remember people we know who are ill or sick. Bring them healing and wholeness.
C: Bring them new life, we pray.
L: Father, we think about people who do not have enough to live on; those without food, clothes or shelter. Give them hope and provide for their needs.
C: Bring them new life, we pray.
L: Spirit, we remember anyone who is stressed or worried. Calm their hearts and minds, bring them your peace.
C: Bring them new life, we pray.
L: Creator of all, we think about people who do not know that you love them. Show yourself to them and draw them close.
C: Bring them new life, we pray.

Ending the service

With: a box of tissues

Remind everyone that we already see evidence of new life in us as we follow God and allow him to change us. However, we are still in a world where horrible things happen, so we still need tissues to mop up our tears.

Remind everyone of Revelation 21. Throw the box in the bin. God will wipe every tear from our eyes and once they are gone, we will never have cause to weep again. That promise is true and trustworthy and we can already start to celebrate what God is doing in and through us.

May God make his home with us this week.
May we rejoice that we are his people.
May our lives be filled with hope as God goes with us into the future.

Helpful extras

Music and song ideas

'I am a new creation'; 'There must be more than this'; 'Restore, O Lord'; 'Forth in thy name, O Lord I go'; 'Come down, O love divine'.

If the congregation is struggling with a difficult situation or collective bereavement, it might be helpful and appropriate to have a reflective time listening to 'Kindle the flame' by Jill Sutheran, recorded by the Northumbria Community on the *Waymarks* CD.

Statement of faith

This is available as a download (YearB. AllSaints_2).

Notes and comments

In preparation, reflect on what people think of when they hear the word 'saints'. This service is an opportunity to present saints not as dusty figures from the past or those who are so holy they are unreachable. We are all saints, living in the present, with an eye on the future. This is not to decry those whose lives inspire us, both those from Bible times and since then.

If a baptism is taking place, the family (if it is an infant baptism) or the candidate (if it is an adult baptism) will be obvious people to interview at **Beginning the service**.

If Communion is taking place, explain how the sacrifice of Jesus within the new covenant brings us new life, acknowledging that we celebrate the Eucharist only until Jesus returns – we have an eye to the future.

Many churches provide alternative events to recognise Halloween, such as Light parties. Check out for ideas from http://www. eauk.org/resources/info/listings/halloween-resources.cfm.

Online resources

All suggested downloads are available at www.scriptureunion.org.uk/light. Visit www.lightlive.org for additional activities for children, young people and adults. For your convenience the following activity is available as a download: YearB. AllSaints_3 Bible story with story slider for 5 to 8s.

Fourth Sunday before Advent

READINGS: **Deuteronomy 6:1–9; Mark 12:28–34**
Psalm 119:1–8; Hebrews 9:11–14

Bible foundations

Aim: to explore how we can talk about God as we carry out the routines of daily living

The Shema, Deuteronomy 6:4 and 5, is the statement which embraces the heart of the Jewish faith. Jesus expanded upon it when speaking with one of the teachers of the Law of Moses in Mark 12, to include 'the mind' in our love of God (which is simply to state the all-embracing extent of our response to God) as well as a love for our neighbours. Whereas Jesus was urging an individual to be wholehearted in his response to God, the statements in the Old Testament have much more of a community flavour.

As the people of Israel were preparing to cross over the River Jordan into the Promised Land, it was essential that they remained faithful to God, and their unique commitment to him would be tested many times. What could be seen as a mission statement was vital to keep them focused, although as time would tell, unless the commitment was of the heart, simply the existence of such a statement was not adequate. Psalm 119 is full of love and commitment to God's law which is transforming in its power. Today's verses (1–8) are an appropriate summary. Christ himself fulfilled all the demands of the law, becoming the great high priest (Hebrews 9:11).

The central belief was to be passed on from one generation to another, from adult to child, and talked about as families went about their everyday business. (Some sections of the Jewish community even today take this very literally.) The spirit of these commands to pass on the truths of God is straightforward – just talk about the uniqueness of God and go on loving him wholeheartedly whatever you do and wherever you find yourself. Many in the church today would long to see families and the wider Christian faith community 'gossiping' the good news of Jesus, children with adults, adults with young people, on the way to school or work, preparing to go to bed, eating together and so on. It is a challenge to leaders of all-age services, to enable faith to be passed on across the generations. Look for ways to make this possible during the course of this service.

Beginning the service

Ask how many people came to church with someone else. This should probably include every child in the building. Then ask if anyone can remember at least one thing that they talked about as they came, whether walking or coming by car or some other form of transport. If appropriate, make a note of the topics. Comment that walking with someone or travelling together often provides a good opportunity to chat together, including talking about the things that matter to you. You could describe an incident of this in your own life. Introduce the theme of this service.

Bible reading

Mark 12:28–34 could be read with a narrator and someone taking the parts of Jesus and the teacher of the Law of Moses.

Psalm 119:1–8 could be read with two halves of the congregation reading alternate verses using the church Bibles.

Bible retelling

With: two adults sitting down at the end of the day, children in bed – two friends or parents – amend as appropriate

This is a contemporary presentation of Deuteronomy 6:1–9.

A: Talk about being cross-questioned. X never stops asking questions. He wants to know how the central heating system works, why we get bruises, what we are having for tea tomorrow and all about the next school trip. He was still asking questions as I walked out of the door.

I think he's asleep now.

B: Was he satisfied with all your answers?

A: Oh no, I gave him one answer which immediately led to another question. He wasn't listening to the answers.

B: Did you ask *him* any questions or just talk about what *you* had done or thought over the day?

A: (*Pause*). Actually, I just got frustrated. I suppose I should have asked him about how he felt about things and then told him about my day.

B: I don't want to make you feel bad, but did you say anything about God and what you had said to him over the day? Did you chat together about what Jesus might have meant to either of you today?

A: Ahhh! Well, you know how it is.

B: Only too well. But I was thinking about that as we walked to school this morning. X was talking about how two girls in his class had a big fight in the playground yesterday. One of them had a new pink bag and the other girl, who is a bit of a bully, was jealous. And then we talked about what God thought about that. It was such a natural way to bring God into the conversation. And we talked about it again over our evening meal. And this evening we chatted to God about it and X talked about how Joseph had been bullied by his brothers – he heard that story in his Sunday group last week.

A: I don't often think about that.

B: God's people were told something about this when they crossed over the River Jordan into the Promised Land. Let me read it to you (*looks around to find a Bible and then reads Deuteronomy 6:4–8*).

A: I guess I need to look for natural

opportunities to chat about God with the children.

B: That's right (*pause*) and you may find that they start talking about him long before you do!

Bible talk

With: four large placards labelled 'Home', 'Out', 'Night', 'Day'; a collection of objects that you use when you are either at home, going out, asleep or wide awake

Places we find ourselves over 24 hours
Show the objects above and together sort them into one of the four categories, putting them underneath one of the four placards: Home, Out, Night, Day. Some of the objects might fit into more than one category – a favoured teddy bear may go to many places, someone working on a night-time shift has a different body clock! Make it clear that we find ourselves in lots of different places over 24 hours.

Then identify the people who are with us as we get ready to go to these four places. What sort of things do we talk about as we get up in the morning, get ready to go out, come home from work or get ready for bed?

What is true about God over 24 hours
Explain that the people of Israel were given a brief statement about God and their response to it, which would be true wherever they found themselves. At this point it is important to introduce Deuteronomy 6:4 and 5 or Mark 12:29–31 and to learn it. You can either do this by simply reciting it (in the spirit of Deuteronomy) or by singing it, for example

using the *Learn and remember* verse 'Love the Lord' – see **Music and songs ideas**. God's people were never to forget this. They were to keep it locked in their minds to help them to always go on loving God wholeheartedly. You could also do the wordsearch in the **Game** at this point to reinforce the message of Deuteronomy 6.

Talking about God over 24 hours
But this was not just something to do on your own. God knows that we need others to help us to grow in our faith. We need others to urge us to go on loving God and to remain focused. That is why we belong to church. We need each other. God's people were instructed to pass their faith onto the next generation and to do that in all sorts of places and throughout the whole day.

Return to the four placards again. How might you talk about God as you get ready to go out to school or work in the morning? (Refer to the **Bible retelling** if you used that.) Or what about when you are at work or school or busy over the weekend or on holiday? What about when you are pottering around at home? Finally, how can you talk about God as you get ready for bed? Although this is an opportunity to talk about how adults can pray and read the Bible with their children at the start of the day and as they go to bed, it is equally relevant for adults whether or not they have children.

Invite four people to talk about how they talk about God with others when they are in each of the four places identified by the placards. They should be honest and also inspirational; many parents need encouraging to share their faith with their children, as well as being given some practical ideas. If you do not use the clock idea in the **Prayer activity**, give each family some sort of challenge to take away with them from the service.

Conclude by saying the *Learn and remember* verse again. If you are planning on making the banner to put across the doorpost of the church in **Ending the service**, you could talk about how God's people were not only to recite the words about God, they were to write them down and put them over the entrance to their home. (You could do the preparation of the banner at this point in the service before moving onto the **Prayer activity**.)

Prayer activity

Create a card clock for each person which is at least 7 cm in diameter with the numbers 1–12 as a clock face. It is divided into four equal sections, 'Night' is dark blue in colour, 'Day' is yellow, 'Home' has a front door in one corner, while 'Out' has a flowing scarf around the edge – available as a black and white download (YearB.4SunB4Advent_1).

Give each person their clock. Then in turn ask them to think where they are when they are in each of the clock segments or getting ready to move into a segment. God is with them. How do they know that? What can they say to God in each of these places? Give some suggestions in terms of asking for safety, courage, wisdom, fun, sleep or thanking God for time spent when sleeping, out and about or at home.

Conclude by saying together:

We will love the Lord our God wherever we are – with all our heart, with all our soul, with all our mind and with all our strength.

Prayer of confession

Father God,
We have not always loved you with all our heart and soul. (Pause)
We have not always loved you with all of our mind and strength. (Pause)
We have not loved our neighbours as we have loved ourselves. (Pause)
Father, forgive us.
Amen.

Prayers of intercession

These prayers should be led by people from different generations, in two parts.

Thank God for those who have passed on the faith to us: parents, grandparents, godparents, Sunday group leaders, church leaders and others known to us.

Pray for those who lead groups within the church which exist to nurture faith, whether these are home/growth groups or children's or youth groups. Also pray for parents and grandparents as they pass on their faith to the next generation.

Ending the service

With: a large sheet of paper/wallpaper which fits over the main exit of the building; felt tips, if needed; sheets of paper and glue

What important truths about God would you want to pass onto others – so important that you would stick them over the doorposts of your home? Give some examples, which could simply be a rephrasing of Deuteronomy 6:4 and 5 or Mark 12:29–31 or a phrase such as 'God loves this world' or 'Jesus died for us'. Either in small groups on a small sheet of paper (which can be stuck on the large sheet of paper) or altogether on the one large sheet of paper, write or draw what you would want to be reminded of every time you entered or left the church building.

When the large sheet has been stuck above the doorpost, everyone should pass under it, singing the *Learn and remember* verse (Deuteronomy 6:5) or saying their own particular important phrase about God.

Helpful extras

Music and song ideas
The *Learn and remember* verse (Deuteronomy 6:5) is available as the song 'Love the Lord' from *Bitesize Bible Songs* CD (SU); 'All the time' from *Reach Up!* CD (SU); 'All my days'; 'A new commandment I give unto you'; 'Tell out my soul'; 'I will worship … with all of my heart'; 'May God's blessing be upon you now' (*Spring Harvest Kids' Praise Party 3*).

Statement of faith
The Shema could be described as a statement of faith. You could recite Deuteronomy 6:4 and 5 in place of your usual creed.

Game
Show the wordsearch on the screen, available as a download (YearB.4SunB4Advent_2), with 11 words that appear in the **Bible talk** – heart, soul, might, love, children, mind, home, out, doorpost, night, day. The leftover letters spell 'talk'. As someone identifies one of the words, click the first letter and the line should change colour. Note that some of the letters appear in more than one word. Talk about why the leftover letters spell 'talk' to review the importance of talking about God.

Notes and comments

Two books to recommend that encourage the nurture of faith are: *Families with faith – Survival skills for Christian parents* (SU) by Richard Patterson and *Parenting children for a life of faith – Helping children meet and know God* (BRF) by Rachel Turner. For more ideas on tools to help people of all ages read the Bible and pray, visit www.scriptureunion.org. uk/You/BibleReading.

As you prepare for this service, reflect on ways in which you can support parents as they seek to nurture the faith of their children/ grandchildren/godchildren as well as helping leaders of children's groups to play their part.

Online resources
All suggested downloads are available at www.scriptureunion.org.uk/light. Visit www.lightlive.org for additional activities for children, young people and adults.

Third Sunday before Advent/ Remembrance Sunday

READINGS: **Hebrews 9:24–28; Mark 1:14–20**
Jonah 3:1–5; Psalm 62:5–12 [RCL: 1 Kings 17:8–16; Psalm 146]

Bible foundations

Aim: to understand the image of Jesus as priest and sacrifice

The background and imagery of the passage from Hebrews for this week and next is the ritual for the Day of Atonement, described in Leviticus 16. This was the one day in the year when the high priest went into the holiest part of the Temple (and before the Temple was built, in the tent in the wilderness). This inner sanctuary was hidden from view by a curtain. Inside was the 'mercy seat' where the presence of God rested (Leviticus 16:2). Only on this day did God make it possible for the high priest to enter this holy space and live. God did this so that once a year all the people could be cleansed from their sins. He gave Moses instructions about how Aaron, the first high priest, should carry out the cleansing sacrifices correctly. It was to be 'an everlasting statute' (Leviticus 16:34), to be repeated year after year.

Without this background we can't fully understand the message of Hebrews. Hebrews 9:24–28 is the culmination of the whole chapter. The writer draws a contrast between the work of the priests under the first covenant and what Jesus does as the one who brings about the new covenant. Heaven is the true place of worship. The earthly Temple is like a shadow of this, and the sacrifices cannot effect any real change. By contrast, through his own willing death, Jesus entered heaven itself causing the relationship between human beings and God to be fundamentally changed in a way that could never happen through animal sacrifice. Jonah 3 is an example of how God responded to human action (and this on the part of foreigners) but the message of Hebrews would indicate that this is neither enough nor lasting. Only Christ can bring lasting reconciliation – as John proclaimed: God's kingdom will soon be here. Turn back to God (Mark 1:15).

Beginning the service

Today's service looks at how God takes the initiative in making a right relationship with us, first through the sacrificial system and then through Jesus. Verses from Psalm 62 focus on God in stillness at the start of the service, and acknowledge our dependency on him. They could be used before or after an opening hymn or song of praise. A version of this from the CEV is available as a PowerPoint download (YearB.3SunB4Advent_1). The suggested **Game** could also be used at this point.

Bible reading

The following version of Hebrews 9:24–28 is adapted for two voices, to highlight the contrast the writer makes between Jesus and what went before.

> Voice 1: This is why Christ did not go into a tent that had been made by humans and was only a copy of the real one.
> Voice 2: Instead, he went into heaven and is now there with God to help us.
> Voice 1: Christ did not have to offer himself many times. He wasn't like a high priest who goes into the most holy place each year to offer the blood of an animal. If he had offered himself every year, he would have suffered many times since the creation of the world.
> Voice 2: But instead, near the end of time he offered himself once and for all, so that he could be a sacrifice that does away with sin.
> Voice 1: We die only once, and then we are judged.
> Voice 2: So Christ died only once to take away the sins of many people.

> Voice 1: But when he comes again, it will not be to take away sin.
> Voice 2: He will come to save everyone who is waiting for him.
> Hebrews 9:24–28 (CEV)

Bible talk

With: a remembrance poppy (a large one if available); a curtain (on a pole if possible); optional – about twelve cardboard boxes; cloth to be a linen tunic and turban; cuddly toys/cardboard cut-outs to represent a bull, sheep and goat

This **Bible talk** aims to see how the writer of Hebrews uses pictures familiar to his readers to help them understand Jesus' death and resurrection.

On Remembrance Sunday, the poppy offers a useful example of a picture that 'speaks volumes'. It has become a symbol of what happened on the battlefields of the First World War. It is used in this way because after the war thousands of poppies grew there on the soil churned up by fighting. Being red, it reminds us of blood, but there is no inherent connection between the poppy itself and the fighting. It also offers an example of how we understand sacrifice. (If Remembrance Sunday is being acknowledged in a separate service, you could simply omit this section of the talk.)

Pictures help us understand important things. Think about two pictures that help us with the idea of Jesus as priest and sacrifice.

Picture 1: the poppy

Hold up your poppy, and use a simple process of question and answer to tease out its significance:

Why do people wear poppies today? *(It's the Sunday nearest to 11 November, Armistice Day, when the First World War ended.)*
What are we remembering? *(The end of the First World War, the people who fought, were killed or were wounded.)*
Why is it a little poppy that reminds us of such a huge and significant event? *(Because when the soil settled after the fighting, thousands of poppies grew on the battlefields; because it is red like blood.)*
'Sacrifice' is a word often used on Remembrance Sunday. What do we mean when we use it? *(Soldiers went to fight to save the country even though they knew they might die – the 'bigger picture' was more important.)*

Not everyone's sacrifice meant dying. For some it meant giving things up, doing something they didn't like to help others, changing the way they lived. Women weren't allowed to fight, but many took on challenging jobs to help the country. (This could be an appropriate moment for an act of remembrance.)

Picture 2: the Temple

The reading from Hebrews talks about a sanctuary made by human hands. Explain that at the beginning, the holy place where people met God was simply a tent in the wilderness. But when God's people were settled in Jerusalem and Solomon was king, the first Temple was built. It had a big space for worship, and a much smaller place at one end called 'the holy of holies'.

If you are using cardboard boxes (you could refer back to the outline from Proper 25), ask some volunteers to build two walls, each at least three boxes high, across which you can rest the curtain pole and curtain. Alternatively, ask for two volunteers to just hold the curtain pole. During this building process, talk briefly about what happened on the Day of Atonement. Invite someone to be the high priest, putting on a tunic and turban to represent the 'holy vestments' (Leviticus 16:4), and give them the representations of the animals which they need to take into the 'holy of holies' for the cleansing sacrifices. Invite them to go behind the curtain, then ask everyone else what they can see – nothing. The high priest went into the presence of God on this one day in the year, but to everyone else this transaction or conversation with God was unseen.

The writer of Hebrews says that this way of worshipping on earth was a picture or copy of the holiest place of worship – heaven itself. But the high priest couldn't go into heaven, only to the most holy part of the Temple. Through Jesus, God changed some things for ever:

Jesus was like the high priest, but he didn't go behind the actual curtain in the Temple – he went into heaven itself. Like the high priest Jesus was obedient to the will of God. In the past, people had been cleansed by animal sacrifice, in which the animals had no choice. Jesus gave his own life in obedience to God's will, so that the relationship between human beings and God could be recreated. Animal sacrifice couldn't change anything, so it had to be repeated every year. Because Jesus' sacrifice was a willing self-offering, it only had to happen once.

Invite the high priest to come from behind the curtain. One by one take away the things that are no longer needed: animals, clothes to wear in the holy place, the priest himself, and finally the curtain. Jesus, as priest and sacrifice, transformed the way we approach God.

The bigger picture enabled people to give their lives in the war and the tiny poppy reminds us of this. The writer of Hebrews reminds us that the Temple worship was a pointer to the bigger picture – the worship of heaven. Jesus' willing self-offering was so that everyone could have an open relationship with God. As followers of Jesus, what is our bigger picture, and how does it show in the way we live our lives?

Prayer of confession

Ask people to repeat the emboldened response after you.

Lord God, in the red petal of the poppy
we are reminded of lives lost,
of blood shed,
of human greed,
and lives marked by grief and pain.
For spoiling your creation,
Lord, in your mercy, forgive us.

In the green leaf of the poppy
we are reminded of the possibility of new life.
Remembering the past,
help us to act in the present
to bring an end to fighting and bloodshed.
We pray that the desire for peace and not for domination
will thrive in the soil of human hearts.

Lord, in your mercy, hear us and help us. Amen.

Prayers of intercession

With: pens; five outline drawings, one per A6 sheet of paper: hand, foot, mouth, head and heart – everyone needs one copy of each shape

This activity can be done in a variety of different ways. With a small congregation, each shape could be located in a different part of the building and everyone visits each place following the leader and in turn prays about a different aspect of life. End at a central point.
Alternatively ask younger children to hand out the outlines and pens during a song, then adults and children work together. Otherwise complete these individually, gather them up and pin them on a display board.

If there is an offering in the service, the prayers could be gathered in a large basket and placed at the front as a sign of our self-offering. This might be particularly appropriate if it is a Communion service.

Ending the service

The following prayer picks up the themes of the service followed by a suitable celebratory hymn or song.

Lord God,
we give you thanks for the love you bear for your world, broken and beautiful.
We give you thanks for showing your love in Jesus, priest and sacrifice.
As he offered himself, so we offer our lives to you.

Here are our hands and feet, our minds and mouths and hearts, to be yours for your work in the world.
Amen.

Helpful extras

Music and song ideas

Using the imagery used in Hebrews: 'Alleluia, sing to Jesus'; 'Jesus is King and I will extol him'; 'Within the veil'; 'I am a new creation' celebrates the freedom we have in Christ; 'You shall go out with joy' would be an obvious ending. On the theme of self-offering: 'Take my life and let it be'; 'Just as I am without one plea'; 'Jesus, take me as I am'.

Game

Write the letters of the words 'Jesus', 'priest' and 'sacrifice' on pieces of coloured card, choosing a different colour for each word. Hide these in the place of worship and invite children to find them, sort them and see if they can make them into the three words. Explain that they all have something to do with us, and something to do with God, and that's what the service is about.

Notes and comments

No one picture can fully explain what God did through Jesus on the cross. 'Priest' and 'sacrifice' are two out of several that the New Testament offers us. It is important not to get hung up on the question of how sacrifice actually worked, but to let the picture speak!

Although the focus is mostly on Hebrews and Remembrance, there are obvious links with the other readings: Jonah's reluctant but eventual self-giving brings about God's work in Nineveh; the fishermen respond to Jesus' calling and give up much in following him. In the RCL, both 1 Kings 17 and Psalm 146 are examples of what it means to trust God enough to live sacrificially under difficult circumstances.

If it is a Holy Communion service, point out the importance of remembering and of sacrifice in the words.

Second Sunday before Advent

READINGS: **Hebrews 10:11–14 (15–18),19–25; Mark 13:1–8**
Daniel 12:1–3; Psalm 16

Bible foundations

Aim: to discover our identity in Christ, which lasts for ever

Hebrews 10:11–25 seems to begin with a repetition of last week. However, the focus constantly shifts between detail and the larger vision. We have our attention drawn again to the role of the priest in the Temple (v 11), but the wider context is clear from verse 25 (and what follows). At this time there was a well-established belief in 'the day of the Lord', when God would act decisively for the salvation and judgement of his people. The statement in verse 12 of Christ's heavenly enthronement is an indication of decisive action, although it is clear from verse 13 that the judgement has yet to be completed. The once-for-all nature of what God has done in Jesus is rooted in the promise God made through the prophet Jeremiah (vs 15–17). In looking both back and forward, there is a strong sense of seeing humanity from God's perspective.

It is in this light that we are to live out what we know to be true, and act on the new relationship we have with God. The transforming work of God in Christ should enable us to act with the assurance of people who know they are loved, forgiven and accepted. This will have an effect on our relationships with other Christians. This is our true identity.

The 'day of the Lord' and the question of assurance are also to be found in Mark 13:1–8. When one of the disciples marvels at the grandeur of the Temple buildings, Jesus responds with a prediction of their destruction. The very thing that was a focus of religious identity will be destroyed. This unnerves his followers. Not surprisingly, they want more information, but Jesus warns of uncertainty and insecurity. Significantly, he uses the image of birth pangs to describe what lies ahead. Birth pangs, although painful, are of course not about destruction but about new life.

Beginning the service

A strong hymn of praise, such as 'All for Jesus!' is a really good start to set the theme of our hope in Jesus for now and the future. You could read Hebrews 10:19–22 as an invitation to worship.

Bible reading

For Mark 13:1–8, it would be easy to arrange for different readers to be the narrator, the disciples and Jesus.

Hebrews 10:11–14,(15–18),19–25 doesn't obviously lend itself to interactive reading, but the Bible retelling option may be helpful.

Bible retelling

Hebrews 10:11–14,(15–18),19–25 is densely packed with images and ideas that flow seamlessly into one another. The script for an entertaining interrupted reading, based on the Good News Bible which offers explanation as it goes along is available as a download (YearB.2SunB4Advent_1). Voice 1 is a childlike character, and voice 2 that of an adult who explains what is going on. If the expertise is available, it would work with a ventriloquist and dummy, or similarly with a hand puppet being Voice 1. The presentation needs to be at a reasonable pace. The section between the asterisks relates to the verses which could be omitted.

Bible talk

The main point of this is that our identity is rooted in God's love for us as his children.

With: five really large badges (chest-size, with a cardboard base, safety pin at the back and laminated or covered with acetate); a water-based marker and permanent marker; a damp cloth; a naked baby doll

What best describes you?
Ask five people to think about the most important thing in their life that, in one phrase, best describes their identity such as their job, role in the family or community, football club supporter, significant event that made them famous, etc. You will probably want them to think about this beforehand. Give them each a badge and ask them, using the water-based marker, to write the phrase on their badge. They then stick the badge on their chest and stand at the front.

Talk about the other things that mark out our identity. But just suppose this identity was taken away or changed beyond recognition – someone loses their job, their family grows up, or their team goes down a league. This sort of identity, however important it is, is not guaranteed to last. Rub out the phrases with the damp cloth. These people have lost their identity.

What best described the disciples?
Point out that it was a bit like this for the disciples whose identity was tied up with them being Jews. In the **Bible reading** in Mark 13, when Jesus said the Temple buildings would be destroyed, this was a core part of their religious identity. It was as though part of their identity was being rubbed out. People could suggest how the disciples might have felt – insecure, anxious, wanting information. Knowing times and dates would have made preparation easier, as it would offer a chance to be in control.

How does Jesus describe you?

The priests used to make daily sacrifices but they were never effective long-term. They could not take away sin. What was needed was an identity that would last. Jesus gave himself as a sacrifice so that sin could be taken away for ever – not like the sacrifices of the priests. Write on the five badges, with the permanent marker, the word 'Forgiven'. Try to rub it off. It won't come off.

These people have a new identity, a forgiven person because of what Jesus has done. And this can never be taken away.

Hold up the baby doll. Suggest that having our identity taken away might make us feel a bit like the baby: naked. Cradle the baby in your arms and ask whether a baby minds being naked. The answer should be no: the baby is being cuddled, whether or not it has clothes on. As long as the baby knows it is loved, it will feel secure and happy.

Make the point that we are a bit like that baby:
What matters is that God loves us, accepts us and has forgiven us.
We may worry about whether or not he likes us, or about things we have done wrong. The writer of Hebrews keeps reminding us that in Jesus the sins that separate us from God have been dealt with – once and for all. If we know we are loved, we feel confident about who we are and what we can do. We have a new identity.

Go back to the disciples. Jesus does not hide from them that there is hardship ahead. They could not know about his coming death, or his resurrection. Jesus doesn't give them the details they want. They must have felt very insecure. Perhaps the most important thing is that he describes the coming disruption as 'birth pangs'. Birth is positive – there's no way of avoiding pain and discomfort, but the point of it is new life. After the resurrection, these four disciples were among those who built up the church community, based on their experience of Jesus.

If there is someone in the congregation whose experience of God is one of stripping away and discovering something newer and deeper, see if they would be willing to give their testimony.

Remind people of the lost bits of identity that have been rubbed out from the badges. But what will last is our identity as forgiven people who have a place in heaven through Jesus. It is building up this community that matters.

To be faced with the reality of our ultimate security lying only in Jesus, whatever happens, is a challenge to most of us. We are not always aware of how much trust we place in earthly things until these things are shaken in some way. If appropriate, after the Bible talk, allow individuals to think about their own situation. Play some music if silence is difficult. It might be appropriate to offer someone to pray with anyone who wishes it, either now or at the end of the service. Suggest as an alternative that people think about what identifying phrase they would like Jesus to write on their badge.

Prayers of intercession

From the reading there are two broad areas

for prayer:
those in situations of violence and disruption
the church community, local and more widely.

Ask two people to prepare appropriate
prayers. Verses 1 and 2 and 11 of Psalm 16
could be used as a framework for prayer, or
as a response.

For example, verses 1 and 2 might be used
with the first area for prayer:
Keep me safe, my God, for in you I take
refuge.
I say to the LORD, 'You are my Lord;
Apart from you I have no good thing.'

And verse 11 might be used with the second:
You make known to me the path of life,
You will fill me with joy in your presence;
with eternal pleasures at your right hand.

Alternatively, given the emphasis on the
church community, have a time of prayer for
your own church. Invite people to identify
the strengths and weaknesses of the church
and how the life of the church might develop.
These could be shared in small groups who
pray together, or the ideas could be jotted
down on pieces of paper or even mini-
badges. Key phrases could be copied onto
the five large badges to be displayed by the
church entrance as a symbol of how you
would describe the expression of God's
community that you are.

Ending the service

End with an outward focus, since you
are people in the world whose identity
is rooted in Christ. The following verse
from Hebrews 10:23 could be used as an

affirmation or word of encouragement said
to one another. It is available as a download
(YearB.2SunB4Advent_2).

Let us hold fast the confession of our hope
without wavering, for He who promised is
faithful. (NKJV)

Helpful extras

Music and song ideas
'All for Jesus! All for Jesus!'; 'All my hope
on God is founded'; 'All I once held dear';
'Blessed assurance, Jesus is mine!'; 'Be Thou
my vision'; 'In Christ alone'. On building
community: 'Bind us together'; 'Jesus, stand
among us'. To end: 'Great is thy faithfulness';
'Forth in the peace of Christ we go'.

Taizé music might be particularly appropriate
for a time of quiet reflection.

Statement of faith
This is also available as a download
(YearB.2SunB4Advent_3).

We believe in God:
Creator, Saviour and Judge of all.
We believe in Jesus,
**who has opened up the way to heaven
and cleansed us of our sin.**
We believe in the Holy Spirit,
who gives life to the church.
We believe in God,
Creator, Saviour and Judge of all.

Notes and comments

In the early church, candidates for baptism
usually changed their clothes after being
baptised. New clothes were a sign of the
new identity – the new life given in Christ. It

is still common for babies to be dressed in white or ivory-coloured dresses for baptism, and for older people to wear special clothes for the occasion. This could be mentioned in the **Bible talk** in relation to the nakedness of the baby. It would obviously be particularly appropriate if there is a baptism in the service!

If it is a Communion service, point out how that anchors our identity: we are a community brought into being by Jesus' self-giving on the cross.

If you make use of the time of quiet after the **Bible talk**, you could display either or both of the following quotations, simply as an aid to reflection.

'He is no fool who gives what he cannot keep to gain that which he cannot lose.' *Jim Elliot*

'The faithful God often lets his friends fall sick and lets every prop on which they lean be knocked out from under them... their pious works are supports, stays, or footings to them. Our Lord wants to take these things all away, for he would like to be their only stay. He does this because of his simple goodness and mercy... He will not be influenced in the least to give or do by any act of ours. Our Lord wants his friend to be rid of all such notions. That is why he removes every prop, so that he alone may support them.' *Meister Eckhart*

Online resources

All suggested downloads are available at www.scriptureunion.org.uk/light. Visit www.lightlive.org for additional activities for children, young people and adults.

Christmas Wrapped Up!
978 1 85999 795 6
- All-age Advent, Christmas Day and Nativity services
- Assembly outlines
- Christmas quizzes and dramas
- Songs, rap and rhymes

Everything you need to get the most out of Christmas!

Christmas Bible Comic
9781 84427 543 4
Delight children aged 8 to11 with this comic-strip retelling of the Christmas story. Through the high-quality illustration and text, children will encounter the true story of Christmas, together with quizzes, puzzles, facts and information to help them engage with the story more fully.

For more details, visit www.scriptureunion.org.uk

Sunday next before Advent, Christ the King

READINGS: **Revelation 1:4b–8; John 18:33–37**
Daniel 7:9,10,13,14; Psalm 93

Bible foundations

Aim: to celebrate Christ as king

The book of Revelation begins in a traditional form, stating the sender and the recipient, followed by a greeting. Sometimes ancient letters might continue with a thanksgiving to the relevant god and prayers for the recipient. John follows this pattern as he writes to a group of seven churches in the Roman province of Asia. The first song resonates with statements about Jesus Christ, the king, the one who is going to fulfil the prophetic expectation of Daniel 7, as quoted in verse 7. Psalm 93 also acknowledges God as king and creator, described in powerful terms. No human king in Israel would ever expect such praise.

In John 18:33–37, Pilate interrogated Jesus. Was he genuinely interested, threatened, or puzzled? Who was this king of the Jews whom the Jewish authorities obviously didn't want to recognise? The man standing before him did not look like a Caesar-figure. He had no power and no powerful supporters. Somehow Pilate must have understood that the chief priests wanted to get rid of Jesus because he claimed to be the Messiah (Hebrew for 'Christ'), seen in Jewish expectation to be a type of Davidic king. If this man claimed to be king, he had to realise that there could be no other king in Israel.

Jesus pointed out that his kingdom wasn't typical. The word he used for 'kingdom' has a primary meaning of 'reign' rather than a specific place. Jesus had no argument against the Romans. He hasn't come to overthrow their governance of the territory. But he had come to reveal the truth, to reveal God. The suggestion of the chief priests that he would usurp Roman rule was false. As Don Carson writes in *The Gospel According to John*, 'Disclosing the truth of God, of salvation and of judgement, was the principal way of making subjects, of exercising his saving kingship.'

Beginning the service

With: silhouettes of royal items which are available as a download (YearB. SunB4Advent_1)

Welcome everyone to the service. Explain that you're going to have a quiz to reveal the theme of the service. One at a time, display the royal silhouettes (such as a crown, throne, carriage and sceptre). Some should be harder to guess than others. Then ask what the common theme is. Explain that the service is about a king, Christ the king, and that Christ (Messiah) means God's chosen or appointed one.

Bible reading

Revelation 1:4b–8 contains many statements about Jesus, the king. Each of the statements from verse 5b onwards could be read by individuals scattered around the church.

John 18:33–37 lends itself to being read as a drama script as laid out below from the NIV, with a narrator, Jesus and Pilate. It would be good to practise beforehand.

Narrator: Pilate then went back inside the palace, summoned Jesus and asked him:
Pilate: Are you the king of the Jews?
Narrator: Jesus said:
Jesus: Is that your own idea or did others talk to you about me?
Pilate: Am I a Jew? It was your people and your chief priests who handed you over to me. What is it you have done?
Jesus: My kingdom is not of this world. If it were, my servants would fight to prevent my arrest by the Jews. But now my kingdom is from another place.
Pilate: You are a king, then!
Jesus: You are right in saying I am a king. In fact, for this reason I was born, and for this I came into the world, to testify to the truth. Everyone on the side of truth listens to me.

Bible talk

With: four simple outline images of kings – a Roman emperor with a laurel crown, a sword to represent a warrior messiah, a man with rope binding his wrists (Jesus on trial) and the outline of Jesus with a bright light behind him facing a globe with his arms stretched out – available as a download (YearB.SunB4Advent_2); a copy of Revelation 1:4b–8; someone to bring Revelation 1:5b,7 to the front in an envelope addressed to your church

A king needs subjects

Ask the congregation what makes a king. What does a king do who is a king in exile? You could find, download and show an image of deposed King Kigeli V of Rwanda or King Constantine II of Greece. You need to make the point that a king has little power unless he has subjects to rule.

Explain that in the **Bible reading** from John 18, Jesus had been arrested and put on trial before Pilate, the Roman governor in charge of Palestine at that time. A few days before his arrest, Jesus had ridden into Jerusalem and been treated just like a king by the cheering crowd. They had waved branches like flags and shouted out praises to him. This was how victorious military leaders returned home after battle. This could have been interpreted as a blatant challenge to the Roman and Jewish authorities. The crowd certainly was filled with hope at the sight of Jesus, a conqueror! Could he be the expected Messianic King?

A king has earthly power

Explain that there were three distinct views of a king represented at Jesus' trial. What sort of a king did Pilate expect? Show the laurel leaves of the emperor. The Roman emperor was all-powerful, dominant and to be obeyed. Jesus was nothing like this.

A king leads his army

What sort of a king did the Jewish authorities expect? Show the sword image. Explain that at the time of Jesus, there were various expectations in relation to the Messiah, the one sent from God. He might be a prophet like Moses or he might be a king who delivered God's people from the Romans. Jesus was nothing like this.

Jesus, the humble king, declared the truth of God

Jesus stood before Pilate like this. Show the image of a prisoner. What sort of a king was this? Jesus boldly declared that the people he ruled, his kingdom, were not of this world. He had come to bring God's truth to this world. Pilate, along with the Jewish authorities and the crowd, rejected this sort of king.

At this point, your messenger delivers the envelope to the front, containing Revelation 1:5b and 7. Open the envelope and read the verses. Explain that this letter was originally sent to seven churches after the events of Jesus' trial. It was written by someone called John who had several dreams or visions from God. Ask whether it sounded as though

John was celebrating that Jesus was king? You could reread the verses, or put them up on the screen.

Jesus the king will come in power

Make the point that we are the church today and these words are as true to us as they were when John first wrote and sent them. We can celebrate Jesus, or Christ, as king. At the end of time, Jesus will come as king over all the world and everyone will see him as such. He is not acknowledged as king by all, yet, but nonetheless his power is over all. We are his subjects and acknowledge him and put our trust in his power and goodness.

Prayers of intercession

In the Middle Ages a king's subjects could bring their petitions to the king and his parliament, asking for justice or some form of royal intervention. This was called petitioning – not that many people had direct access to the monarch but there were people appointed to act in his place. Most ordinary people could only ever hope to make a petition to the next person up the chain of command, and never to the king himself. When someone came into the presence of a more senior person to make their request they would bow their head at the very least – some would even go on their knees.

But Jesus, as our king, is totally different. He is available for everyone to talk to and to receive our petitions, which is what we do when we pray. We don't need to give him gifts to buy his favour, we don't have to dress up in a special way and we don't need to go to a special place or even make an appointment. We can bring to Jesus anything that bothers us.

Ask everyone to identify one thing they want to ask Jesus to do. Then as you bring your petitions to Jesus, the king, suggest that, if physically possible, everyone goes down on their knees. They could come out to the front or into an aisle to do this or just where they sit. Pray this prayer as follows and then allow time for silent petitions to be made to Jesus.

Dear Lord Jesus,
We thank you that you are a king.
We thank you that we can make our requests to you at any time and in any place.
We thank you that we do not have to give you a gift to force you to listen to us.
We ask now that you would hear our requests and meet our needs.
May we go on trusting you as our king until you return in all your glory. Amen.

Ending the service

With: large sheets of card; paints; a selection of sticks and handles to make banners to use during a march

When a king or queen is crowned, they usually parade through the streets as part of the coronation ceremony while the crowds, or subjects, shout their praises. Jesus is our king, chosen by God, and called Christ. We can celebrate this in the way we live and by praising him. Remind people that Jesus was quite clear that his power and rule were very different from any earthly ruler, lest those who are opposed to the monarchy are offended.

Allow everyone to have access to the card, sticks, handles and art equipment if they so wish. They create a banner (a piece of card attached to a stick or handle) to wave in praise of Christ the king. Younger children will need help. Everyone can copy down their own phrase of worship, or one from Revelation 1 such as 'I am Alpha and Omega', 'the one who is and was and is coming' or 'I am God All-Powerful'.

Once the banners have been completed, either wave them as you sing a song of praise or, if appropriate, march around the church waving the banners and shouting out praise to Christ the king. Conclude by explaining that we shouldn't just celebrate Christ as king during a church service, but in every moment of our lives. Encourage everyone to remember to praise and celebrate that Jesus is our king throughout the week.

Helpful extras

Music and song ideas
'Hail to the King'; ' Majesty, worship his majesty'; 'King of kings, majesty'; 'Come on and Celebrate'; 'Praise God from whom all blessings flow'; 'To God be the glory'; 'Crown him with many crowns'; 'Come, see the Lord in his breathtaking splendour' by Martin Leckebusch (Carol Praise) is a gloriously new and clear statement about what makes Jesus the king. (It would be especially good to sing more powerful and lively songs at the end of the service when you are celebrating Christ as king.)

Statement of faith
Ask the congregation what sort of occasion prompts people to cheer, such as sports

matches, an inspiring speech, when someone is really happy. Focus on when people cheer in agreement. Then explain that you are now going to read a Statement of faith based on Revelation 1 from the CEV, explaining what we believe and why we should celebrate Christ as king. After each statement everyone joins in a loud cheer of celebration, if they agree with what has just been said. The words for display are available as a download (YearB.SunB4Advent_3).

Jesus, you were the first to conquer death and this we celebrate *(cheer)*.
Jesus you are the ruler of all earthly kings, and this we celebrate *(cheer)*.
Jesus Christ, you love us, and this we celebrate *(cheer)*.
Jesus, you set us free from our sins, and this we celebrate *(cheer)*.
Jesus, you will return, coming with the clouds, and this we celebrate *(cheer)*.
Everyone will see you, and this we celebrate *(cheer)*.
Yes, it will happen! And this we celebrate *(cheer)*.
Amen. And this we celebrate *(cheer)*.

Notes and comments

Some people will not support the idea of monarchy. Kingship is a biblical concept and Jesus' kingship was so very different from any human model, but do bear this in mind.

Revelation 1 and John 18 both contain elements that could be explored with a more mature congregation. Accepting Jesus as king should have a profound effect on each person. As each person accepts Christ's kingship in their life, the flipside is that they become a subject and subject to him. To truly celebrate Christ as king is to live in the truth, with Christ reigning in our lives. By entering the kingdom of God we are free from judgement, and salvation is ours. Christ's kingship is a revolution of truth, a change from human understanding into the truth of God.

The background story of Jesus' trial makes obvious connections in the Eucharist.

Online resources

All suggested downloads are available at www.scriptureunion.org.uk/light. Visit www.lightlive.org for additional activities for children, young people and adults.